T0305366

FX Options and Structured Products

For other titles in the Wiley Finance Series
please see www.wiley.com/finance

FX Options and Structured Products

Uwe Wystup

John Wiley & Sons, Ltd

Other Wiley Editorial Offices

John Wiley & Sons Inc., 111 River Street, Hoboken, NJ 07030, USA

Jossey-Bass, 989 Market Street, San Francisco, CA 94103-1741, USA

Wiley-VCH Verlag GmbH, Boschstr. 12, D-69469 Weinheim, Germany

John Wiley & Sons Australia Ltd, 42 McDougall Street, Milton, Queensland 4064, Australia

John Wiley & Sons (Asia) Pte Ltd, 2 Clementi Loop #02-01, Jin Xing Distripark, Singapore 129809

John Wiley & Sons Canada Ltd, 6045 Freemont Blvd, Mississauga, Ontario, L5R 4J3, Canada

Wiley also publishes its books in a variety of electronic formats. Some content that appears
in print may not be available in electronic books.

Library of Congress Cataloging-in-Publication Data

Wystup, Uwe.
   FX options and structured products / Uwe Wystup.
      p.   cm.
   Includes bibliographical references.
   ISBN-13: 978-0-470-01145-4
   ISBN-10: 0-470-01145-9
   1. Foreign exchange options.   2. Structured notes (Securities)   3. Derivative securities.   I. Title.
HG3853. W88 2006
332.4′5—dc22   2006020352

British Library Cataloguing in Publication Data

A catalogue record for this book is available from the British Library

ISBN: 978-0-470-01145-4 (H/B)

Typeset in 10/12pt Times by TechBooks, New Delhi, India

To Ansua

Contents

NOTE TO READER: Please note the CD has been converted to URL.
Go to the following website www.wiley.com/go/wystupfxoptions

Preface

SCOPE OF THIS BOOK

Treasury management of international corporates involves dealing with cash flows in different currencies. Therefore the natural service of an investment bank consists of a variety of money market and foreign exchange products. This book explains the most popular products and strategies with a focus on everything beyond vanilla options.

The book explains all the FX options, common structures and tailor-made solutions in examples with a special focus on their application with views from traders and sales as well as from a corporate client perspective.

The book contains actual traded deals with corresponding motivations explaining why the structures have been traded. This way the reader gets a feel for how to build new structures to suit clients' needs.

Several sections deal with the quantitative aspect of FX options, such as quanto adjustment, deferred delivery, traders' rule of thumb and settlement issues.

One entire chapter is devoted to hedge accounting, after which the foundations of a typical structured FX forward are examined in a case study.

The exercises are meant as practice. Several of them are actually difficult to solve and can serve as incentives to further research and testing. Solutions to the exercises are not part of this book. They will, however, be published on the web page for the book, fxoptions.mathfinance.com.

THE READERSHIP

A prerequisite is some basic knowledge of FX markets, for example taken from *Foreign Exchange Primer* by Shami Shamah, John Wiley & Sons, Ltd, 2003, see [1]. For the quantitative sections some knowledge of Stochastic Calculus as in Steven E. Shreve's volumes on *Stochastic Calculus for Finance* [2] is useful. The target readers are

- Graduate students and Faculty of Financial Engineering Programs, who can use this book as a textbook for a course named *structured products* or *exotic currency options*.
- Traders, Trainee Structurers, Product Developers, Sales and Quants with an interest in the FX product line. For them it can serve as a source of ideas and as well as a reference guide.
- Treasurers of corporates interested in managing their books. With this book at hand they can structure their solutions themselves.

The readers more interested in the quantitative and modeling aspects are recommended to read *Foreign Exchange Risk* by J. Hakala and U. Wystup, Risk Publications, London, 2002, see [50]. This book explains several exotic FX options with a special focus on the underlying models and mathematics, but does not contain any structures or corporate clients' or investors' view.

ABOUT THE AUTHOR

Uwe Wystup, Professor of Quantitative Finance at HfB Business School of Finance and Management in Frankfurt, Germany

Uwe Wystup is also CEO of MathFinance AG, a global network of quants specializing in Quantitative Finance, Exotic Options advisory and Front Office Software Production. Previously he was a Financial Engineer and Structurer in the FX Options Trading Team at Commerzbank. Before that he worked for Deutsche Bank, Citibank, UBS and Sal. Oppenheim jr. & Cie. He is founder and manager of the web site MathFinance.de and the MathFinance Newsletter. Uwe holds a PhD in mathematical finance from Carnegie Mellon University. He also lectures on mathematical finance for Goethe University Frankfurt, organizes the *Frankfurt MathFinance Colloquium* and is founding director of the *Frankfurt MathFinance Institute*. He has given several seminars on exotic options, computational finance and volatility modeling. His areas of specialization are the quantitative aspects and the design of structured products of foreign exchange markets. He published a book on *Foreign Exchange Risk* and articles in *Finance and Stochastics* and the *Journal of Derivatives*. Uwe has given many presentations at both universities and banks around the world. Further information on his curriculum vitae and a detailed publication list is available at www.mathfinance.com/wystup/.

ACKNOWLEDGMENTS

I would like to thank *HfB-Business School of Finance and Management* in Frankfurt for supporting this book project by allocating the necessary time.

I would like to thank my former colleagues on the trading floor, most of all Michael Braun, Jürgen Hakala, Tamás Korchmáros, Behnouch Mostachfi, Bereshad Nonas, Gustave Rieunier, Tino Senge, Ingo Schneider, Jan Schrader, Noel Speake, Roman Stauss, Andreas Weber, and all my colleagues and co-authors, specially Christoph Becker, Susanne Griebsch, Christoph Kühn, Sebastian Krug, Marion Linck, Wolfgang Schmidt and Robert Tompkins.

I would like to thank Steve Shreve for his training in stochastic calculus and continuously supporting my academic activities.

Chris Swain, Rachael Wilkie and many others of Wiley publications deserve respect for dealing with my tardiness in completing this book.

Nicole van de Locht and Choon Peng Toh deserve a medal for their detailed proof reading.

1

Foreign Exchange Options

FX Structured Products are tailor-made linear combinations of FX Options including both vanilla and exotic options. We recommend the book by Shamah [1] as a source to learn about FX Markets with a focus on market conventions, spot, forward and swap contracts and vanilla options. For pricing and modeling of exotic FX options we suggest Hakala and Wystup [3] or Lipton [4] as useful companions to this book.

The market for structured products is restricted to the market of the necessary ingredients. Hence, typically there are mostly structured products traded in the currency pairs that can be formed between USD, JPY, EUR, CHF, GBP, CAD and AUD. In this chapter we start with a brief history of options, followed by a technical section on vanilla options and volatility, and deal with commonly used linear combinations of vanilla options. Then we will illustrate the most important ingredients for FX structured products: the first and second generation exotics.

1.1 A JOURNEY THROUGH THE HISTORY OF OPTIONS

The very first options and futures were traded in ancient Greece, when olives were sold before they had reached ripeness. Thereafter the market evolved in the following way:

16th century Ever since the 15th century tulips, which were popular because of their exotic appearance, were grown in Turkey. The head of the royal medical gardens in Vienna, Austria, was the first to cultivate Turkish tulips successfully in Europe. When he fled to Holland because of religious persecution, he took the bulbs along. As the new head of the botanical gardens of Leiden, Netherlands, he cultivated several new strains. It was from these gardens that avaricious traders stole the bulbs in order to commercialize them, because tulips were a great status symbol.

17th century The first futures on tulips were traded in 1630. From 1634, people could buy special tulip strains according to the weight of their bulbs, the same value was chosen for the bulbs as for gold. Along with regular trading, speculators entered the market and prices skyrocketed. A bulb of the strain "Semper Octavian" was worth two wagonloads of wheat, four loads of rye, four fat oxen, eight fat swine, twelve fat sheep, two hogsheads of wine, four barrels of beer, two barrels of butter, 1,000 pounds of cheese, one marriage bed with linen and one sizable wagon. People left their families, sold all their belongings, and even borrowed money to become tulip traders. When in 1637, this supposedly risk-free market crashed, traders as well as private individuals went bankrupt. The government prohibited speculative trading; this period became famous as Tulipmania.

18th century In 1728, the Royal West-Indian and Guinea Company, the monopolist in trading with the Caribbean Islands and the African coast issued the first stock options. These were options on the purchase of the French Island of Ste. Croix, on which sugar plantings were planned. The project was realized in 1733 and paper stocks were issued in 1734. Along with the stock, people purchased a relative share of the island and the possessions, as well as the privileges and the rights of the company.

19th century   In 1848, 82 businessmen founded the Chicago Board of Trade (CBOT). Today it is the biggest and oldest futures market in the entire world. Most written documents were lost in the great fire of 1871, however, it is commonly believed that the first standardized futures were traded in 1860. CBOT now trades several futures and forwards, not only T-bonds and treasury bonds, but also options and gold.

In 1870, the New York Cotton Exchange was founded. In 1880, the gold standard was introduced.

20th century

- In 1914, the gold standard was abandoned because of the war.
- In 1919, the Chicago Produce Exchange, in charge of trading agricultural products was renamed to Chicago Mercantile Exchange. Today it is the most important futures market for Eurodollar, foreign exchange, and livestock.
- In 1944, the Bretton Woods System was implemented in an attempt to stabilize the currency system.
- In 1970, the Bretton Woods System was abandoned for several reasons.
- In 1971, the Smithsonian Agreement on fixed exchange rates was introduced.
- In 1972, the International Monetary Market (IMM) traded futures on coins, currencies and precious metal.
- In 1973, the CBOE (Chicago Board of Exchange) first traded call options; and four years later also put options. The Smithsonian Agreement was abandoned; the currencies followed managed floating.
- In 1975, the CBOT sold the first interest rate future, the first future with no "real" underlying asset.
- In 1978, the Dutch stock market traded the first standardized financial derivatives.
- In 1979, the European Currency System was implemented, and the European Currency Unit (ECU) was introduced.
- In 1991, the Maastricht Treaty on a common currency and economic policy in Europe was signed.
- In 1999, the Euro was introduced, but the countries still used their old currencies, while the exchange rates were kept fixed.

21st century   In 2002, the Euro was introduced as new money in the form of cash.

1.2   TECHNICAL ISSUES FOR VANILLA OPTIONS

We consider the model *geometric Brownian motion*

$$dS_t = (r_d - r_f)S_t \, dt + \sigma S_t \, dW_t \tag{1.1}$$

for the underlying exchange rate quoted in FOR-DOM (foreign-domestic), which means that one unit of the foreign currency costs FOR-DOM units of the domestic currency. In the case of EUR-USD with a spot of 1.2000, this means that the price of one EUR is 1.2000 USD. The notion of *foreign* and *domestic* does not refer to the location of the trading entity, but only

exchange rate development   probability density

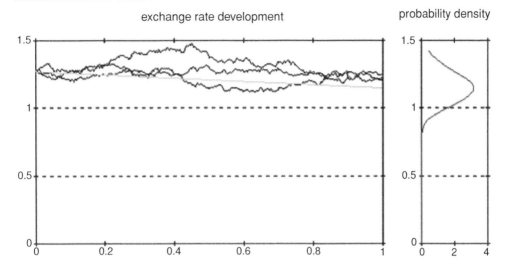

Figure 1.1   Simulated paths of a geometric Brownian motion. The distribution of the spot S_T at time T is log-normal. The light gray line reflects the average spot movement.

to this quotation convention. We denote the (continuous) foreign interest rate by r_f and the (continuous) domestic interest rate by r_d. In an equity scenario, r_f would represent a continuous dividend rate. The volatility is denoted by σ, and W_t is a standard Brownian motion. The sample paths are displayed in Figure 1.1.[1] We consider this standard model, not because it reflects the statistical properties of the exchange rate (in fact, it doesn't), but because it is widely used in practice and front office systems and mainly serves as a tool to communicate prices in FX options. These prices are generally quoted in terms of volatility in the sense of this model.

Applying Itô's rule to $\ln S_t$ yields the following solution for the process S_t

$$S_t = S_0 \exp\left\{ \left(r_d - r_f - \frac{1}{2}\sigma^2 \right) t + \sigma W_t \right\}, \tag{1.2}$$

which shows that S_t is log-normally distributed, more precisely, $\ln S_t$ is normal with mean $\ln S_0 + (r_d - r_f - \frac{1}{2}\sigma^2)t$ and variance $\sigma^2 t$. Further model assumptions are

1. There is no arbitrage
2. Trading is frictionless, no transaction costs
3. Any position can be taken at any time, short, long, arbitrary fraction, no liquidity constraints

The payoff for a vanilla option (European put or call) is given by

$$F = [\phi(S_T - K)]^+, \tag{1.3}$$

where the contractual parameters are the strike K, the expiration time T and the type ϕ, a binary variable which takes the value $+1$ in the case of a call and -1 in the case of a put. The symbol x^+ denotes the positive part of x, i.e., $x^+ \stackrel{\Delta}{=} \max(0, x) \stackrel{\Delta}{=} 0 \vee x$. We generally use the symbol $\stackrel{\Delta}{=}$ to *define* a quantity. Most commonly, vanilla options on foreign exchange are of *European style*, i.e. the holder can only exercise the option at time T. *American style options*,

---

[1] Generated with Tino Kluge's shape price simulator at www.mathfinance.com/TinoKluge/tools/sharesim/black-scholes.php

where the holder can exercise any time, or *Bermudian style options*, where the holder can exercise at selected times, are not used very often except for time options, see Section 2.1.18.

1.2.1   Value

In the Black-Scholes model the value of the payoff F at time t if the spot is at x is denoted by $v(t, x)$ and can be computed either as the solution of the *Black-Scholes partial differential equation* (see [5])

$$v_t - r_d v + (r_d - r_f) x v_x + \frac{1}{2}\sigma^2 x^2 v_{xx} = 0, \tag{1.4}$$

$$v(T, x) = F. \tag{1.5}$$

or equivalently (*Feynman-Kac-Theorem*) as the discounted expected value of the payoff-function,

$$v(x, K, T, t, \sigma, r_d, r_f, \phi) = e^{-r_d \tau} I\!E[F]. \tag{1.6}$$

This is the reason why basic financial engineering is mostly concerned with solving partial differential equations or computing expectations (numerical integration). The result is the *Black-Scholes formula*

$$v(x, K, T, t, \sigma, r_d, r_f, \phi) = \phi e^{-r_d \tau} [f \mathcal{N}(\phi d_+) - K \mathcal{N}(\phi d_-)]. \tag{1.7}$$

We abbreviate

- x: current price of the underlying
- $\tau \stackrel{\Delta}{=} T - t$: time to maturity
- $f \stackrel{\Delta}{=} I\!E[S_T | S_t = x] = x e^{(r_d - r_f)\tau}$: forward price of the underlying
- $\theta_\pm \stackrel{\Delta}{=} \frac{r_d - r_f}{\sigma} \pm \frac{\sigma}{2}$
- $d_\pm \stackrel{\Delta}{=} \frac{\ln \frac{x}{K} + \sigma \theta_\pm \tau}{\sigma \sqrt{\tau}} = \frac{\ln \frac{x}{K} \pm \frac{\sigma^2}{2}\tau}{\sigma \sqrt{\tau}}$
- $n(t) \stackrel{\Delta}{=} \frac{1}{\sqrt{2\pi}} e^{-\frac{1}{2}t^2} = n(-t)$
- $\mathcal{N}(x) \stackrel{\Delta}{=} \int_{-\infty}^{x} n(t)\, dt = 1 - \mathcal{N}(-x)$

The Black-Scholes formula can be derived using the integral representation of Equation (1.6)

$$v = e^{-r_d \tau} I\!E[F]$$

$$= e^{-r_d \tau} I\!E[[\phi(S_T - K)]^+]$$

$$= e^{-r_d \tau} \int_{-\infty}^{+\infty} \left[\phi \left(x e^{(r_d - r_f - \frac{1}{2}\sigma^2)\tau + \sigma \sqrt{\tau} y} - K \right) \right]^+ n(y)\, dy. \tag{1.8}$$

Next one has to deal with the positive part and then complete the square to get the Black-Scholes formula. A derivation based on the partial differential equation can be done using results about the well-studied *heat-equation*.

1.2.2   A note on the forward

The *forward price* f is the strike which makes the time zero value of the *forward contract*

$$F = S_T - f \tag{1.9}$$

equal to zero. It follows that $f = I\!E[S_T] = xe^{(r_d-r_f)T}$, i.e. the forward price is the expected price of the underlying at time T in a risk-neutral setup (drift of the geometric Brownian motion is equal to cost of carry $r_d - r_f$). The situation $r_d > r_f$ is called *contango*, and the situation $r_d < r_f$ is called *backwardation*. Note that in the Black-Scholes model the class of forward price curves is quite restricted. For example, no seasonal effects can be included. Note that the value of the forward contract after time zero is usually different from zero, and since one of the counterparties is always short, there may be risk of default of the short party. A *futures contract* prevents this dangerous affair: it is basically a forward contract, but the counterparties have to maintain a *margin account* to ensure the amount of cash or commodity owed does not exceed a specified limit.

1.2.3 Greeks

Greeks are derivatives of the value function with respect to model and contract parameters. They are an important information for traders and have become standard information provided by front-office systems. More details on Greeks and the relations among Greeks are presented in Hakala and Wystup [3] or Reiss and Wystup [6]. For vanilla options we list some of them now.

(Spot) delta

$$\frac{\partial v}{\partial x} = \phi e^{-r_f \tau} \mathcal{N}(\phi d_+)$$
(1.10)

Forward delta

$$\frac{\partial v}{\partial f} = \phi e^{-r_d \tau} \mathcal{N}(\phi d_+)$$
(1.11)

Driftless delta

$$\phi \mathcal{N}(\phi d_+)$$
(1.12)

Gamma

$$\frac{\partial^2 v}{\partial x^2} = e^{-r_f \tau} \frac{n(d_+)}{x\sigma\sqrt{\tau}}$$
(1.13)

Speed

$$\frac{\partial^3 v}{\partial x^3} = -e^{-r_f \tau} \frac{n(d_+)}{x^2\sigma\sqrt{\tau}} \left(\frac{d_+}{\sigma\sqrt{\tau}} + 1\right)$$
(1.14)

Theta

$$\frac{\partial v}{\partial t} = -e^{-r_f \tau} \frac{n(d_+)x\sigma}{2\sqrt{\tau}}$$
$$+ \phi[r_f x e^{-r_f \tau} \mathcal{N}(\phi d_+) - r_d K e^{-r_d \tau} \mathcal{N}(\phi d_-)]$$
(1.15)

Charm

$$\frac{\partial^2 v}{\partial x \partial \tau} = -\phi r_f e^{-r_f \tau} \mathcal{N}(\phi d_+) + \phi e^{-r_f \tau} n(d_+) \frac{2(r_d - r_f)\tau - d_-\sigma\sqrt{\tau}}{2\tau\sigma\sqrt{\tau}}$$
(1.16)

Color

$$\frac{\partial^3 v}{\partial x^2 \partial \tau} = -e^{-r_f \tau} \frac{n(d_+)}{2x\tau\sigma\sqrt{\tau}} \left[2r_f \tau + 1 + \frac{2(r_d - r_f)\tau - d_-\sigma\sqrt{\tau}}{2\tau\sigma\sqrt{\tau}} d_+ \right] \qquad (1.17)$$

Vega

$$\frac{\partial v}{\partial \sigma} = xe^{-r_f \tau}\sqrt{\tau}n(d_+) \qquad (1.18)$$

Volga

$$\frac{\partial^2 v}{\partial \sigma^2} = xe^{-r_f \tau}\sqrt{\tau}n(d_+)\frac{d_+ d_-}{\sigma} \qquad (1.19)$$

Volga is also sometimes called *vomma* or *volgamma*.

Vanna

$$\frac{\partial^2 v}{\partial \sigma \partial x} = -e^{-r_f \tau}n(d_+)\frac{d_-}{\sigma} \qquad (1.20)$$

Rho

$$\frac{\partial v}{\partial r_d} = \phi K \tau e^{-r_d \tau} \mathcal{N}(\phi d_-) \qquad (1.21)$$

$$\frac{\partial v}{\partial r_f} = -\phi x\tau e^{-r_f \tau} \mathcal{N}(\phi d_+) \qquad (1.22)$$

Dual delta

$$\frac{\partial v}{\partial K} = -\phi e^{-r_d \tau} \mathcal{N}(\phi d_-) \qquad (1.23)$$

Dual gamma

$$\frac{\partial^2 v}{\partial K^2} = e^{-r_d \tau}\frac{n(d_-)}{K\sigma\sqrt{\tau}} \qquad (1.24)$$

Dual theta

$$\frac{\partial v}{\partial T} = -v_t \qquad (1.25)$$

1.2.4   Identities

$$\frac{\partial d_\pm}{\partial \sigma} = -\frac{d_\mp}{\sigma} \qquad (1.26)$$

$$\frac{\partial d_\pm}{\partial r_d} = \frac{\sqrt{\tau}}{\sigma} \qquad (1.27)$$

$$\frac{\partial d_\pm}{\partial r_f} = -\frac{\sqrt{\tau}}{\sigma} \qquad (1.28)$$

$$xe^{-r_f \tau}n(d_+) = Ke^{-r_d \tau}n(d_-). \qquad (1.29)$$

$$\mathcal{N}(\phi d_-) = I\!P[\phi S_T \geq \phi K] \qquad (1.30)$$

$$\mathcal{N}(\phi d_+) = I\!P\left[\phi S_T \leq \phi\frac{f^2}{K}\right] \qquad (1.31)$$

The *put-call-parity* is the relationship

$$v(x, K, T, t, \sigma, r_d, r_f, +1) - v(x, K, T, t, \sigma, r_d, r_f, -1) = xe^{-r_f\tau} - Ke^{-r_d\tau}, \qquad (1.32)$$

which is just a more complicated way to write the trivial equation $x = x^+ - x^-$. The *put-call delta parity* is

$$\frac{\partial v(x, K, T, t, \sigma, r_d, r_f, +1)}{\partial x} - \frac{\partial v(x, K, T, t, \sigma, r_d, r_f, -1)}{\partial x} = e^{-r_f\tau}. \qquad (1.33)$$

In particular, we learn that the absolute value of a put delta and a call delta are not exactly adding up to one, but only to a positive number $e^{-r_f\tau}$. They add up to one approximately if either the time to expiration τ is short or if the foreign interest rate r_f is close to zero.

Whereas the choice $K = f$ produces identical values for call and put, we seek the *delta-symmetric strike* $\check{K}$ which produces absolutely identical deltas (spot, forward or driftless). This condition implies $d_+ = 0$ and thus

$$\check{K} = fe^{\frac{\sigma^2}{2}T}, \qquad (1.34)$$

in which case the absolute delta is $e^{-r_f\tau}/2$. In particular, we learn, that always $\check{K} > f$, i.e., there can't be a put and a call with identical values *and* deltas. Note that the strike $\check{K}$ is usually chosen as the middle strike when trading a straddle or a butterfly. Similarly the dual-delta-symmetric strike $\hat{K} = fe^{-\frac{\sigma^2}{2}T}$ can be derived from the condition $d_- = 0$.

1.2.5 Homogeneity based relationships

We may wish to measure the value of the underlying in a different unit. This will obviously effect the option pricing formula as follows.

$$av(x, K, T, t, \sigma, r_d, r_f, \phi) = v(ax, aK, T, t, \sigma, r_d, r_f, \phi) \text{ for all } a > 0. \qquad (1.35)$$

Differentiating both sides with respect to a and then setting $a = 1$ yields

$$v = xv_x + Kv_K. \qquad (1.36)$$

Comparing the coefficients of x and K in Equations (1.7) and (1.36) leads to suggestive results for the delta v_x and dual delta v_K. This *space-homogeneity* is the reason behind the simplicity of the delta formulas, whose tedious computation can be saved this way.

We can perform a similar computation for the time-affected parameters and obtain the obvious equation

$$v(x, K, T, t, \sigma, r_d, r_f, \phi) = v\left(x, K, \frac{T}{a}, \frac{t}{a}, \sqrt{a}\sigma, ar_d, ar_f, \phi\right) \text{ for all } a > 0. \qquad (1.37)$$

Differentiating both sides with respect to a and then setting $a = 1$ yields

$$0 = \tau v_t + \frac{1}{2}\sigma v_\sigma + r_d v_{r_d} + r_f v_{r_f}. \qquad (1.38)$$

Of course, this can also be verified by direct computation. The overall use of such equations is to generate double checking benchmarks when computing Greeks. These homogeneity methods can easily be extended to other more complex options.

By *put-call symmetry* we understand the relationship (see [7], [8],[9] and [10])

$$v(x, K, T, t, \sigma, r_d, r_f, +1) = \frac{K}{f}v\left(x, \frac{f^2}{K}, T, t, \sigma, r_d, r_f, -1\right). \qquad (1.39)$$

The strike of the put and the strike of the call result in a geometric mean equal to the forward f. The forward can be interpreted as a *geometric mirror* reflecting a call into a certain number of puts. Note that for at-the-money options $(K = f)$ the put-call symmetry coincides with the special case of the put-call parity where the call and the put have the same value.

Direct computation shows that the *rates symmetry*

$$\frac{\partial v}{\partial r_d} + \frac{\partial v}{\partial r_f} = -\tau v \tag{1.40}$$

holds for vanilla options. This relationship, in fact, holds for all European options and a wide class of path-dependent options as shown in [6].

One can directly verify the relationship the *foreign-domestic symmetry*

$$\frac{1}{x} v(x, K, T, t, \sigma, r_d, r_f, \phi) = K v \left(\frac{1}{x}, \frac{1}{K}, T, t, \sigma, r_f, r_d, -\phi \right). \tag{1.41}$$

This equality can be viewed as one of the faces of put-call symmetry. The reason is that the value of an option can be computed both in a domestic as well as in a foreign scenario. We consider the example of S_t modeling the exchange rate of EUR/USD. In New York, the call option $(S_T - K)^+$ costs $v(x, K, T, t, \sigma, r_{usd}, r_{eur}, 1)$ USD and hence $v(x, K, T, t, \sigma, r_{usd}, r_{eur}, 1)/x$ EUR. This EUR-call option can also be viewed as a USD-put option with payoff $K(\frac{1}{K} - \frac{1}{S_T})^+$. This option costs $K v(\frac{1}{x}, \frac{1}{K}, T, t, \sigma, r_{eur}, r_{usd}, -1)$ EUR in Frankfurt, because S_t and $\frac{1}{S_t}$ have the same volatility. Of course, the New York value and the Frankfurt value must agree, which leads to (1.41). We will also learn later, that this symmetry is just one possible result based on *change of numeraire*.

1.2.6 Quotation

Quotation of the underlying exchange rate

Equation (1.1) is a model for the exchange rate. The quotation is a constantly confusing issue, so let us clarify this here. The exchange rate means how much of the *domestic* currency is needed to buy one unit of *foreign* currency. For example, if we take EUR/USD as an exchange rate, then the default quotation is EUR-USD, where USD is the domestic currency and EUR is the foreign currency. The term *domestic* is in no way related to the location of the trader or any country. It merely means the *numeraire* currency. The terms *domestic*, *numeraire* or *base currency* are synonyms as are *foreign* and *underlying*. Throughout this book we denote with the slash (/) the currency pair and with a dash (−) the quotation. The slash (/) does *not* mean a division. For instance, EUR/USD can also be quoted in either EUR-USD, which then means how many USD are needed to buy one EUR, or in USD-EUR, which then means how many EUR are needed to buy one USD. There are certain market standard quotations listed in Table 1.1.

Trading floor language

We call one million a *buck*, one billion a *yard*. This is because a billion is called 'milliarde' in French, German and other languages. For the British Pound one million is also often called a *quid*.

Certain currency pairs have names. For instance, GBP/USD is called *cable*, because the exchange rate information used to be sent through a cable in the Atlantic ocean between

Table 1.1 Standard market quotation of major currency pairs
with sample spot prices

Currency pair	Default quotation	Sample quote
GBP/USD	GPB-USD	1.8000
GBP/CHF	GBP-CHF	2.2500
EUR/USD	EUR-USD	1.2000
EUR/GBP	EUR-GBP	0.6900
EUR/JPY	EUR-JPY	135.00
EUR/CHF	EUR-CHF	1.5500
USD/JPY	USD-JPY	108.00
USD/CHF	USD-CHF	1.2800

America and England. EUR/JPY is called the *cross*, because it is the cross rate of the more liquidly traded USD/JPY and EUR/USD.

Certain currencies also have names, e.g. the New Zealand Dollar NZD is called a *kiwi*, the Australian Dollar AUD is called *Aussie*, the Scandinavian currencies DKR, NOK and SEK are called *Scandies*.

Exchange rates are generally quoted up to five relevant figures, e.g. in EUR-USD we could observe a quote of 1.2375. The last digit '5' is called the *pip*, the middle digit '3' is called the *big figure*, as exchange rates are often displayed in trading floors and the big figure, which is displayed in bigger size, is the most relevant information. The digits left to the big figure are known anyway, the pips right of the big figure are often negligible. To make it clear, a rise of USD-JPY 108.25 by 20 pips will be 108.45 and a rise by 2 big figures will be 110.25.

Quotation of option prices

Values and prices of vanilla options may be quoted in the six ways explained in Table 1.2.

The Black-Scholes formula quotes **d pips**. The others can be computed using the following instruction.

$$\textbf{d pips} \xrightarrow{\times \frac{1}{S_0}} \textbf{\%f} \xrightarrow{\times \frac{S_0}{K}} \textbf{\%d} \xrightarrow{\times \frac{1}{S_0}} \textbf{f pips} \xrightarrow{\times S_0 K} \textbf{d pips} \tag{1.42}$$

Table 1.2 Standard market quotation types for option values

Name	Symbol	Value in units of	Example
domestic cash	d	DOM	29,148 USD
foreign cash	f	FOR	24,290 EUR
% domestic	% d	DOM per unit of DOM	2.3318 % USD
% foreign	% f	FOR per unit of FOR	2.4290 % EUR
domestic pips	d pips	DOM per unit of FOR	291.48 USD pips per EUR
foreign pips	f pips	FOR per unit of DOM	194.32 EUR pips per USD

In this example we take FOR = EUR, DOM = USD, $S_0 = 1.2000, r_d = 3.0\%, r_f = 2.5\%, \sigma = 10\%, K = 1.2500$, $T = 1$ year, $\phi = +1$ (call), notional = 1,000,000 EUR = 1,250,000 USD. For the pips, the quotation 291.48 USD pips per EUR is also sometimes stated as 2.9148 % USD per 1 EUR. Similarly, the 194.32 EUR pips per USD can also be quoted as 1.9432 % EUR per 1 USD.

Delta and premium convention

The spot delta of a European option without premium is well known. It will be called *raw spot delta* δ_{raw} now. It can be quoted in either of the two currencies involved. The relationship is

$$\delta_{raw}^{reverse} = -\delta_{raw} \frac{S}{K}. \tag{1.43}$$

The delta is used to buy or sell spot in the corresponding amount in order to hedge the option up to first order.

For consistency the premium needs to be incorporated into the delta hedge, since a premium in foreign currency will already hedge part of the option's delta risk. To make this clear, let us consider EUR-USD. In the standard arbitrage theory, $v(x)$ denotes the value or premium in USD of an option with 1 EUR notional, if the spot is at x, and the raw delta v_x denotes the number of EUR to buy for the delta hedge. Therefore, $x v_x$ is the number of USD to sell. If now the premium is paid in EUR rather than in USD, then we already have $\frac{v}{x}$ EUR, and the number of EUR to buy has to be reduced by this amount, i.e. if EUR is the premium currency, we need to buy $v_x - \frac{v}{x}$ EUR for the delta hedge or equivalently sell $x v_x - v$ USD.

The entire FX quotation story becomes generally a mess, because we need to first sort out which currency is domestic, which is foreign, what is the notional currency of the option, and what is the premium currency. Unfortunately this is not symmetrial, since the counterpart might have another notion of domestic currency for a given currency pair. Hence in the professional inter bank market there is one notion of delta per currency pair. Normally it is the left hand side delta of the *Fenics* screen if the option is traded in left hand side premium, which is normally the standard and right hand side delta if it is traded with right hand side premium, e.g. EUR/USD lhs, USD/JPY lhs, EUR/JPY lhs, AUD/USD rhs, etc... Since OTM options are traded most of time the difference is not huge and hence does not create a huge spot risk.

Additionally the standard delta per currency pair [left hand side delta in *Fenics* for most cases] is used to quote options in volatility. This has to be specified by currency.

This standard inter bank notion must be adapted to the real delta-risk of the bank for an automated trading system. For currencies where the risk–free currency of the bank is the base currency of the currency it is clear that the delta is the raw delta of the option and for risky premium this premium must be included. In the opposite case the risky premium and the market value must be taken into account for the base currency premium, so that these offset each other. And for premium in underlying currency of the contract the market-value needs to be taken into account. In that way the delta hedge is invariant with respect to the risky currency notion of the bank, e.g. the delta is the same for a USD-based bank and a EUR-based bank.

Examples
We consider two examples in Tables 1.3 and 1.4 to compare the various versions of deltas that are used in practice.

1.2.7   Strike in terms of delta

Since $v_x = \Delta = \phi e^{-r_f \tau} \mathcal{N}(\phi d_+)$ we can retrieve the strike as

$$K = x \exp\left\{-\phi \mathcal{N}^{-1}(\phi \Delta e^{r_f \tau})\sigma \sqrt{\tau} + \sigma \theta_+ \tau\right\}. \tag{1.44}$$

Table 1.3 1y EUR call USD put strike $K = 0.9090$ for a EUR-based bank

Delta ccy	Prem ccy	Fenics	Formula	Delta
% EUR	EUR	lhs	$\delta_{raw} - P$	44.72
% EUR	USD	rhs	δ_{raw}	49.15
% USD	EUR	rhs [flip F4]	$-(\delta_{raw} - P)S/K$	−44.72
% USD	USD	lhs [flip F4]	$-(\delta_{raw})S/K$	−49.15

Market data: spot $S = 0.9090$, volatility $\sigma = 12\,\%$, EUR rate $r_f = 3.96\,\%$, USD rate $r_d = 3.57\,\%$. The raw delta is 49.15 % EUR and the value is 4.427 % EUR.

Table 1.4 1y call EUR call USD put strike $K = 0.7000$ for a EUR-based bank

Delta ccy	Prem ccy	Fenics	Formula	Delta
% EUR	EUR	lhs	$\delta_{raw} - P$	72.94
% EUR	USD	rhs	δ_{raw}	94.82
% USD	EUR	rhs [flip F4]	$-(\delta_{raw} - P)S/K$	−94.72
% USD	USD	lhs [flip F4]	$-\delta_{raw}S/K$	−123.13

Market data: spot $S = 0.9090$, volatility $\sigma = 12\,\%$, EUR rate $r_f = 3.96\,\%$, USD rate $r_d = 3.57\,\%$. The raw delta is 94.82 % EUR and the value is 21.88 % EUR.

1.2.8 Volatility in terms of delta

The mapping $\sigma \mapsto \Delta = \phi e^{-r_f \tau} \mathcal{N}(\phi d_+)$ is not one-to-one. The two solutions are given by

$$\sigma_\pm = \frac{1}{\sqrt{\tau}} \left\{ \phi \mathcal{N}^{-1}(\phi \Delta e^{r_f \tau}) \pm \sqrt{(\mathcal{N}^{-1}(\phi \Delta e^{r_f \tau}))^2 - \sigma \sqrt{\tau}(d_+ + d_-)} \right\}. \tag{1.45}$$

Thus using just the delta to retrieve the volatility of an option is not advisable.

1.2.9 Volatility and delta for a given strike

The determination of the volatility and the delta for a given strike is an iterative process involving the determination of the delta for the option using at-the-money volatilities in a first step and then using the determined volatility to re–determine the delta and to continuously iterate the delta and volatility until the volatility does not change more than $\epsilon = 0.001\,\%$ between iterations. More precisely, one can perform the following algorithm. Let the given strike be K.

1. Choose $\sigma_0 =$ at-the-money volatility from the volatility matrix.
2. Calculate $\Delta_{n+1} = \Delta(\text{Call}(K, \sigma_n))$.
3. Take $\sigma_{n+1} = \sigma(\Delta_{n+1})$ from the volatility matrix, possibly via a suitable interpolation.
4. If $|\sigma_{n+1} - \sigma_n| < \epsilon$, then quit, otherwise continue with step 2.

In order to prove the convergence of this algorithm we need to establish convergence of the recursion

$$\Delta_{n+1} = e^{-r_f \tau} \mathcal{N}(d_+(\Delta_n))$$

$$= e^{-r_f \tau} \mathcal{N} \left(\frac{\ln(S/K) + (r_d - r_f + \frac{1}{2}\sigma^2(\Delta_n))\tau}{\sigma(\Delta_n)\sqrt{\tau}} \right) \qquad (1.46)$$

for sufficiently large $\sigma(\Delta_n)$ and a sufficiently smooth volatility smile surface. We must show that the sequence of these Δ_n converges to a fixed point $\Delta^* \in [0, 1]$ with a fixed volatility $\sigma^* = \sigma(\Delta^*)$.

This proof has been carried out in [11] and works like this. We consider the derivative

$$\frac{\partial \Delta_{n+1}}{\partial \Delta_n} = -e^{-r_f \tau} n(d_+(\Delta_n)) \frac{d_-(\Delta_n)}{\sigma(\Delta_n)} \cdot \frac{\partial}{\partial \Delta_n} \sigma(\Delta_n). \qquad (1.47)$$

The term

$$-e^{-r_f \tau} n(d_+(\Delta_n)) \frac{d_-(\Delta_n)}{\sigma(\Delta_n)}$$

converges rapidly to zero for very small and very large spots, being an argument of the standard normal density n. For sufficiently large $\sigma(\Delta_n)$ and a sufficiently smooth volatility surface in the sense that $\frac{\partial}{\partial \Delta_n} \sigma(\Delta_n)$ is sufficiently small, we obtain

$$\left| \frac{\partial}{\partial \Delta_n} \sigma(\Delta_n) \right| \overset{\Delta}{=} q < 1. \qquad (1.48)$$

Thus for any two values $\Delta_{n+1}^{(1)}, \Delta_{n+1}^{(2)}$, a continuously differentiable smile surface we obtain

$$|\Delta_{n+1}^{(1)} - \Delta_{n+1}^{(2)}| < q|\Delta_n^{(1)} - \Delta_n^{(2)}|, \qquad (1.49)$$

due to the mean value theorem. Hence the sequence Δ_n is a contraction in the sense of the fixed point theorem of Banach. This implies that the sequence converges to a unique fixed point in $[0, 1]$, which is given by $\sigma^* = \sigma(\Delta^*)$.

1.2.10 Greeks in terms of deltas

In Foreign Exchange markets the moneyness of vanilla options is always expressed in terms of deltas and prices are quoted in terms of volatility. This makes a ten-delta call a financial object as such independent of spot and strike. This method and the quotation in volatility makes objects and prices transparent in a very intelligent and user-friendly way. At this point we list the Greeks in terms of deltas instead of spot and strike. Let us introduce the quantities

$$\Delta_+ \overset{\Delta}{=} \phi e^{-r_f \tau} \mathcal{N}(\phi d_+) \text{ spot delta,} \qquad (1.50)$$

$$\Delta_- \overset{\Delta}{=} -\phi e^{-r_d \tau} \mathcal{N}(\phi d_-) \text{ dual delta,} \qquad (1.51)$$

which we assume to be given. From these we can retrieve

$$d_+ = \phi \mathcal{N}^{-1}(\phi e^{r_f \tau} \Delta_+), \qquad (1.52)$$

$$d_- = \phi \mathcal{N}^{-1}(-\phi e^{r_d \tau} \Delta_-). \qquad (1.53)$$

Interpretation of dual delta

The dual delta introduced in (1.23) as the sensitivity with respect to strike has another – more practical – interpretation in a foreign exchange setup. We have seen in Section 1.2.5 that the domestic value

$$v(x, K, \tau, \sigma, r_d, r_f, \phi) \tag{1.54}$$

corresponds to a foreign value

$$v\left(\frac{1}{x}, \frac{1}{K}, \tau, \sigma, r_f, r_d, -\phi\right) \tag{1.55}$$

up to an adjustment of the nominal amount by the factor xK. From a foreign viewpoint the delta is thus given by

$$
\begin{aligned}
&-\phi e^{-r_d \tau} \mathcal{N}\left(-\phi \frac{\ln(\frac{K}{x}) + (r_f - r_d + \frac{1}{2}\sigma^2\tau)}{\sigma\sqrt{\tau}}\right) \\
&= -\phi e^{-r_d \tau} \mathcal{N}\left(\phi \frac{\ln(\frac{x}{K}) + (r_d - r_f - \frac{1}{2}\sigma^2\tau)}{\sigma\sqrt{\tau}}\right) \\
&= \Delta_-,
\end{aligned}
\tag{1.56}
$$

which means the dual delta is the delta from the foreign viewpoint. We will see below that foreign rho, vega and gamma do not require to know the dual delta. We will now state the Greeks in terms of $x, \Delta_+, \Delta_-, r_d, r_f, \tau, \phi$.

Value

$$v(x, \Delta_+, \Delta_-, r_d, r_f, \tau, \phi) = x\Delta_+ + x\Delta_- \frac{e^{-r_f \tau} n(d_+)}{e^{-r_d \tau} n(d_-)} \tag{1.57}$$

(Spot) delta

$$\frac{\partial v}{\partial x} = \Delta_+ \tag{1.58}$$

Forward delta

$$\frac{\partial v}{\partial f} = e^{(r_f - r_d)\tau} \Delta_+ \tag{1.59}$$

Gamma

$$\frac{\partial^2 v}{\partial x^2} = e^{-r_f \tau} \frac{n(d_+)}{x(d_+ - d_-)} \tag{1.60}$$

Taking a trader's gamma (change of delta if spot moves by 1 %) additionally removes the spot dependence, because

$$\Gamma_{trader} = \frac{x}{100} \frac{\partial^2 v}{\partial x^2} = e^{-r_f \tau} \frac{n(d_+)}{100(d_+ - d_-)} \tag{1.61}$$

Speed

$$\frac{\partial^3 v}{\partial x^3} = -e^{-r_f \tau} \frac{n(d_+)}{x^2(d_+ - d_-)^2} (2d_+ - d_-) \tag{1.62}$$

Theta

$$\frac{1}{x}\frac{\partial v}{\partial t} = -e^{-r_f\tau}\frac{n(d_+)(d_+ - d_-)}{2\tau}$$
$$+ \left[r_f\Delta_+ + r_d\Delta_-\frac{e^{-r_f\tau}n(d_+)}{e^{-r_d\tau}n(d_-)}\right] \tag{1.63}$$

Charm

$$\frac{\partial^2 v}{\partial x\partial\tau} = -\phi r_f e^{-r_f\tau}\mathcal{N}(\phi d_+) + \phi e^{-r_f\tau}n(d_+)\frac{2(r_d - r_f)\tau - d_-(d_+ - d_-)}{2\tau(d_+ - d_-)} \tag{1.64}$$

Color

$$\frac{\partial^3 v}{\partial x^2\partial\tau} = -\frac{e^{-r_f\tau}n(d_+)}{2x\tau(d_+ - d_-)}\left[2r_f\tau + 1 + \frac{2(r_d - r_f)\tau - d_-(d_+ - d_-)}{2\tau(d_+ - d_-)}d_+\right] \tag{1.65}$$

Vega

$$\frac{\partial v}{\partial\sigma} = xe^{-r_f\tau}\sqrt{\tau}n(d_+) \tag{1.66}$$

Volga

$$\frac{\partial^2 v}{\partial\sigma^2} = xe^{-r_f\tau}\tau n(d_+)\frac{d_+ d_-}{d_+ - d_-} \tag{1.67}$$

Vanna

$$\frac{\partial^2 v}{\partial\sigma\partial x} = -e^{-r_f\tau}n(d_+)\frac{\sqrt{\tau}d_-}{d_+ - d_-} \tag{1.68}$$

Rho

$$\frac{\partial v}{\partial r_d} = -x\tau\Delta_-\frac{e^{-r_f\tau}n(d_+)}{e^{-r_d\tau}n(d_-)} \tag{1.69}$$

$$\frac{\partial v}{\partial r_f} = -x\tau\Delta_+ \tag{1.70}$$

Dual delta

$$\frac{\partial v}{\partial K} = \Delta_- \tag{1.71}$$

Dual gamma

$$K^2\frac{\partial^2 v}{\partial K^2} = x^2\frac{\partial^2 v}{\partial x^2} \tag{1.72}$$

Dual theta

$$\frac{\partial v}{\partial T} = -v_t \tag{1.73}$$

As an important example we consider vega.

Table 1.5   Vega in terms of Delta for the standard maturity labels and various deltas

Mat/Δ	50%	45%	40%	35%	30%	25%	20%	15%	10%	5%
1D	2	2	2	2	2	2	1	1	1	1
1W	6	5	5	5	5	4	4	3	2	1
1W	8	8	8	7	7	6	5	5	3	2
1M	11	11	11	11	10	9	8	7	5	3
2M	16	16	16	15	14	13	11	9	7	4
3M	20	20	19	18	17	16	14	12	9	5
6M	28	28	27	26	24	22	20	16	12	7
9M	34	34	33	32	30	27	24	20	15	9
1Y	39	39	38	36	34	31	28	23	17	10
2Y	53	53	52	50	48	44	39	32	24	14
3Y	63	63	62	60	57	53	47	39	30	18

It shows that one can vega hedge a long 9M 35 delta call with 4 short 1M 20 delta puts.

Vega in terms of delta

The mapping $\Delta \mapsto v_\sigma = xe^{-r_f \tau}\sqrt{\tau}n(\mathcal{N}^{-1}(e^{r_f \tau}\Delta))$ is important for trading vanilla options. Observe that this function does not depend on r_d or σ, just on r_f. Quoting vega in % foreign will additionally remove the spot dependence. This means that for a moderately stable foreign term structure curve, traders will be able to use a moderately stable vega matrix. For $r_f = 3\%$ the vega matrix is presented in Table 1.5.

1.3   VOLATILITY

Volatility is the *annualized standard deviation of the log-returns*. It is *the* crucial input parameter to determine the value of an option. Hence, the crucial question is where to derive the volatility from. If no active option market is present, the only source of information is estimating the historic volatility. This would give some clue about the *past*. In liquid currency pairs volatility is often a traded quantity on its own, which is quoted by traders, brokers and real-time data pages. These quotes reflect views of market participants about the *future*.

Since volatility normally does not stay constant, option traders are highly concerned with hedging their volatility exposure. Hedging vanilla options' vega is comparatively easy, because vanilla options have convex payoffs, whence the vega is always positive, i.e. the higher the volatility, the higher the price. Let us take for example a EUR-USD market with spot 1.2000, USD- and EUR rate at 2.5%. A 3-month at-the-money call with 1 million EUR notional would cost 29,000 USD at a volatility of 12%. If the volatility now drops to a value of 8%, then the value of the call would be only 19,000 USD. This monotone dependence is not guaranteed for non-convex payoffs as we illustrate in Figure 1.2.

1.3.1   Historic volatility

We briefly describe how to compute the historic volatility of a time series

$$S_0, S_1, \ldots, S_N \tag{1.74}$$

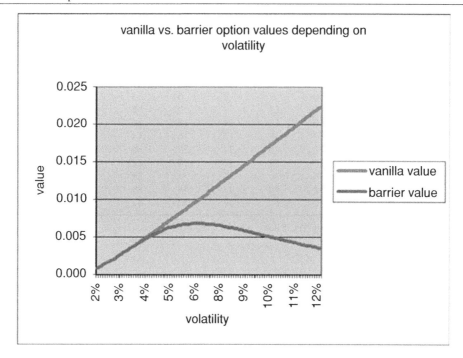

Figure 1.2   Dependence of a vanilla call and a reverse knock-out call on volatility
The vanilla value is monotone in the volatility, whereas the barrier value is not. The reason is that as the spot gets closer to the upper knock-out barrier, an increasing volatility would increase the chance of knock-out and hence decrease the value.

of daily data. First, we create the sequence of log-returns

$$r_i = \ln \frac{S_i}{S_{i-1}}, \quad i = 1, \ldots, N. \tag{1.75}$$

Then, we compute the average log-return

$$\bar{r} = \frac{1}{N} \sum_{i=1}^{N} r_i, \tag{1.76}$$

their variance

$$\hat{\sigma}^2 = \frac{1}{N-1} \sum_{i=1}^{N} (r_i - \bar{r})^2, \tag{1.77}$$

and their standard deviation

$$\hat{\sigma} = \sqrt{\frac{1}{N-1} \sum_{i=1}^{N} (r_i - \bar{r})^2}. \tag{1.78}$$

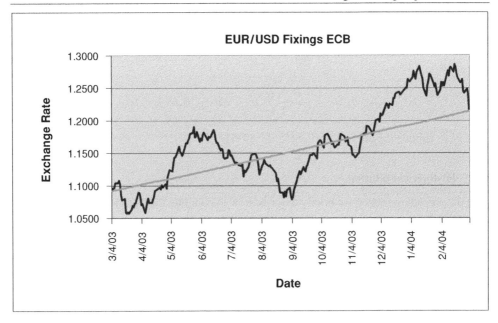

Figure 1.3 ECB-fixings of EUR-USD from 4 March 2003 to 3 March 2004 and the line of average growth

The annualized standard deviation, which is the volatility, is then given by

$$\hat{\sigma}_a = \sqrt{\frac{B}{N-1} \sum_{i=1}^{N} (r_i - \bar{r})^2}, \qquad (1.79)$$

where the *annualization factor* B is given by

$$B = \frac{N}{k} d, \qquad (1.80)$$

and k denotes the number of calendar days within the time series and d denotes the number of calendar days per year.

Assuming normally distributed log-returns, we know that $\hat{\sigma}^2$ is χ^2-distributed. Therefore, given a confidence level of p and a corresponding error probability $\alpha = 1 - p$, the p-confidence interval is given by

$$\left[\hat{\sigma}_a \sqrt{\frac{N-1}{\chi^2_{N-1;1-\frac{\alpha}{2}}}}, \hat{\sigma}_a \sqrt{\frac{N-1}{\chi^2_{N-1;\frac{\alpha}{2}}}} \right], \qquad (1.81)$$

where $\chi^2_{n;p}$ denotes the p-quantile of a χ^2-distribution[2] with n degrees of freedom.

As an example let us take the 256 ECB-fixings of EUR-USD from 4 March 2003 to 3 March 2004 displayed in Figure 1.3. We get $N = 255$ log-returns. Taking $k = d = 365$,

---

[2] values and quantiles of the χ^2-distribution and other distributions can be computed on the internet, e.g. at http://eswf.uni-koeln.de/allg/surfstat/tables.htm.

we obtain

$$\bar{r} = \frac{1}{N} \sum_{i=1}^{N} r_i = 0.0004166,$$

$$\hat{\sigma}_a = \sqrt{\frac{B}{N-1} \sum_{i=1}^{N} (r_i - \bar{r})^2} = 10.85\,\%,$$

and a 95 % confidence interval of $[9.99\,\%, 11.89\,\%]$.

1.3.2 Historic correlation

As in the preceding section we briefly describe how to compute the historic correlation of two time series

$$x_0, x_1, \ldots, x_N,$$

$$y_0, y_1, \ldots, y_N,$$

of daily data. First, we create the sequences of log-returns

$$X_i = \ln \frac{x_i}{x_{i-1}}, \quad i = 1, \ldots, N,$$

$$Y_i = \ln \frac{y_i}{y_{i-1}}, \quad i = 1, \ldots, N. \tag{1.82}$$

Then, we compute the average log-returns

$$\bar{X} = \frac{1}{N} \sum_{i=1}^{N} X_i,$$

$$\bar{Y} = \frac{1}{N} \sum_{i=1}^{N} Y_i, \tag{1.83}$$

their variances and covariance

$$\hat{\sigma}_X^2 = \frac{1}{N-1} \sum_{i=1}^{N} (X_i - \bar{X})^2, \tag{1.84}$$

$$\hat{\sigma}_Y^2 = \frac{1}{N-1} \sum_{i=1}^{N} (Y_i - \bar{Y})^2, \tag{1.85}$$

$$\hat{\sigma}_{XY} = \frac{1}{N-1} \sum_{i=1}^{N} (X_i - \bar{X})(Y_i - \bar{Y}), \tag{1.86}$$

and their standard deviations

$$\hat{\sigma}_X = \sqrt{\frac{1}{N-1} \sum_{i=1}^{N} (X_i - \bar{X})^2}, \tag{1.87}$$

$$\hat{\sigma}_Y = \sqrt{\frac{1}{N-1} \sum_{i=1}^{N} (Y_i - \bar{Y})^2}. \tag{1.88}$$

The estimate for the correlation of the log-returns is given by

$$\hat{\rho} = \frac{\hat{\sigma}_{XY}}{\hat{\sigma}_X \hat{\sigma}_Y}. \tag{1.89}$$

This correlation estimate is often not very stable, but on the other hand, often the only available information. More recent work by Jaekel [12] treats robust estimation of correlation. We will revisit FX correlation risk in Section 1.6.7.

1.3.3 Volatility smile

The Black-Scholes model assumes a constant volatility throughout. However, market prices of traded options imply different volatilities for different maturities and different deltas. We start with some technical issues how to imply the volatility from vanilla options.

Retrieving the volatility from vanilla options

Given the value of an option. Recall the Black-Scholes formula in Equation (1.7). We now look at the function $v(\sigma)$, whose derivative (vega) is

$$v'(\sigma) = x e^{-r_f T} \sqrt{T} n(d_+). \tag{1.90}$$

The function $\sigma \mapsto v(\sigma)$ is

1. strictly increasing,
2. concave up for $\sigma \in [0, \sqrt{2|\ln F - \ln K|/T})$,
3. concave down for $\sigma \in (\sqrt{2|\ln F - \ln K|/T}, \infty)$

and also satisfies

$$v(0) = [\phi(x e^{-r_f T} - K e^{-r_d T})]^+, \tag{1.91}$$

$$v(\infty, \phi = 1) = x e^{-r_f T}, \tag{1.92}$$

$$v(\sigma = \infty, \phi = -1) = K e^{-r_d T}, \tag{1.93}$$

$$v'(0) = x e^{-r_f T} \sqrt{T} / \sqrt{2\pi} \, 1\!1_{\{F=K\}}, \tag{1.94}$$

In particular the mapping $\sigma \mapsto v(\sigma)$ is invertible. However, the starting guess for employing Newton's method should be chosen with care, because the mapping $\sigma \mapsto v(\sigma)$ has a saddle point at

$$\left(\sqrt{\frac{2}{T} |\ln \frac{F}{K}|}, \phi e^{-r_d T} \left\{ F \mathcal{N} \left(\phi \sqrt{2T [\ln \frac{F}{K}]^+} \right) - K \mathcal{N} \left(\phi \sqrt{2T [\ln \frac{K}{F}]^+} \right) \right\} \right), \tag{1.95}$$

as illustrated in Figure 1.4.

To ensure convergence of Newton's method, we are advised to use initial guesses for σ on the same side of the saddle point as the desired implied volatility. The danger is that a large initial guess could lead to a negative successive guess for σ. Therefore one should start with small initial guesses at or below the saddle point. For at-the-money options, the saddle point is degenerate for a zero volatility and small volatilities serve as good initial guesses.

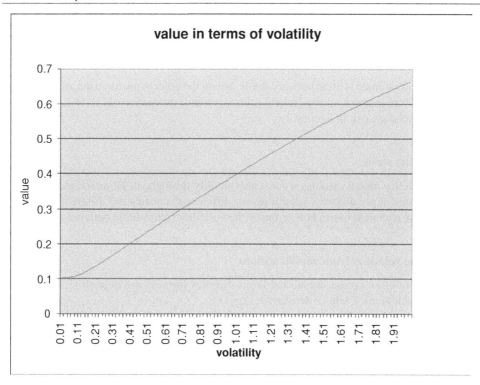

Figure 1.4   Value of a European call in terms of volatility with parameters $x = 1$, $K = 0.9$, $T = 1$, $r_d = 6\%$, $r_f = 5\%$. The saddle point is at $\sigma = 48\%$

Visual basic source code

```
Function VanillaVolRetriever(spot As Double, rd As Double, _
rf As Double, strike As Double, T As Double, _
type As Integer, GivenValue As Double) As Double
Dim func As Double
Dim dfunc As Double
Dim maxit As Integer 'maximum number of iterations
Dim j As Integer
Dim s As Double
'first check if a volatility exists, otherwise set result to zero
If GivenValue < Application.Max _
   (0, type * (spot * Exp(-rf * T) - strike * Exp(-rd * T))) Or _
   (type = 1 And GivenValue > spot * Exp(-rf * T)) Or _
   (type = -1 And GivenValue > strike * Exp(-rd * T)) Then
   VanillaVolRetriever = 0
Else
   ' there exists a volatility yielding the given value,
   ' now use Newton's method:
   ' the mapping vol to value has a saddle point.
   ' First compute this saddle point:
```

```
saddle = Sqr(2 / T * Abs(Log(spot / strike) + (rd - rf) * T))
If saddle > 0 Then
    VanillaVolRetriever = saddle * 0.9
Else
    VanillaVolRetriever = 0.1
End If
maxit = 100
For j = 1 To maxit Step 1
    func = Vanilla(spot, strike, VanillaVolRetriever, _
    rd, rf, T, type, value) - GivenValue
    dfunc = Vanilla(spot, strike, VanillaVolRetriever, _
    rd, rf, T, type, vega)
    VanillaVolRetriever = VanillaVolRetriever - func / dfunc
    If VanillaVolRetriever <= 0 Then VanillaVolRetriever = 0.01
    If Abs(func / dfunc) <= 0.0000001 Then j = maxit
Next j
End If
End Function
```

Market data

Now that we know how to imply the volatility from a given value, we can take a look at the market. We take EUR/GBP at the beginning of April 2005. The at-the-money volatilities for various maturities are listed in Table 1.6. We observe that implied volatilities are not constant, but depend on the time to maturity of the option as well as on the current time. This shows that the Black-Scholes assumption of a constant volatility is not fully justified looking at market data. We have a *term structure of volatility* as well as a stochastic nature of the term structure curve as time passes.

Besides the dependence on the time to maturity (term structure) we also observe different implied volatilities for different degrees of moneyness. This effect is called the *volatility smile*. The term structure and smile together are called a *volatility matrix* or *volatility surface*, if it is graphically displayed. Various possible reasons for this empirical phenomenon are discussed among others by Bates, e.g. in [8].

In Foreign Exchange Options markets implied volatilities are generally quoted and plotted against the deltas of out-of-the-money call and put options. This allows market participants to

Table 1.6   EUR/GBP implied volatilities in % for at-the-money vanilla options

Date	Spot	1 Week	1 Month	3 Month	6 Month	1 Year	2 Years
1-Apr-05	0.6864	4.69	4.83	5.42	5.79	6.02	6.09
4-Apr-05	0.6851	4.51	4.88	5.34	5.72	5.99	6.07
5-Apr-05	0.6840	4.66	4.95	5.34	5.70	5.97	6.03
6-Apr-05	0.6847	4.65	4.91	5.39	5.79	6.05	6.12
7-Apr-05	0.6875	4.78	4.97	5.39	5.79	6.01	6.10
8-Apr-05	0.6858	4.76	5.00	5.41	5.78	6.00	6.09

Source: BBA (British Bankers Association), http://www.bba.org.uk.

ask various partners for quotes on a 25-Delta call, which is spot independent. The actual strike will be set depending on the spot if the trade is close to being finalized. The at-the-money option is taken to be the one that has a strike equal to the forward, which is equivalent to the value of the call and the put being equal. Other types of *at-the-money* are discussed in Section 1.3.6. Their delta is

$$\frac{\partial v}{\partial x} = \phi e^{-r_f \tau} \mathcal{N}\left(\phi \frac{1}{2}\sigma \sqrt{\tau}\right), \tag{1.96}$$

for a small volatility σ and short time to maturity τ, a number near $\phi 50\%$. This is no more true for long-term vanilla options. Further market information consists of the implied volatilities for puts and calls with a delta of $\phi 25\%$. Other or additional implied volatilities for other deltas such as $\phi 10\%$ and $\phi 35\%$ are also quoted. Volatility matrices for more delta pillars are usually interpolated.

Symmetric decomposition

Generally in Foreign Exchange, volatilities are decomposed into a *symmetric* part of the smile reflecting the *convexity* and a *skew-symmetric* part of the smile reflecting the *skew*. The way this works is that the market quotes *risk reversals (RR)* and *butterflies (BF)* or strangles, see Sections 1.4.2 and 1.4.5 for the description of the *products* and Figure 1.5 for the payoffs. Here we are talking about the respective *volatilities* to use to price the products. Sample quotes are listed in Tables 1.7 and 1.8. The relationship between risk reversal and strangle/butterfly quotes and the volatility smile are explained graphically in Figure 1.6.

The relationship between risk reversal quoted in terms of volatility (RR) and butter-fly/strangle (BF) quoted in terms of volatility and the volatilities of 25-delta calls and puts

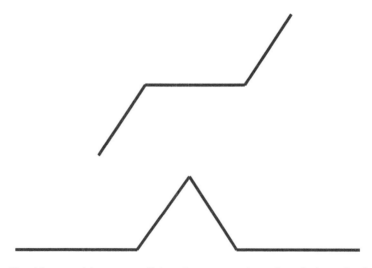

Figure 1.5   The risk reversal (upper payoff) is a skew symmetric product, the butterfly (lower payoff) a symmetric product

Table 1.7 EUR/GBP 25 Delta Risk Reversal in %

Date	Spot	1 Month	3 Month	1 Year
1-Apr-05	0.6864	0.18	0.23	0.30
4-Apr-05	0.6851	0.15	0.20	0.29
5-Apr-05	0.6840	0.11	0.19	0.28
6-Apr-05	0.6847	0.08	0.19	0.28
7-Apr-05	0.6875	0.13	0.19	0.28
8-Apr-05	0.6858	0.13	0.19	0.28

Source: BBA (British Bankers Association). This means that for example on 4 April 2005, the 1-month 25-delta EUR call was priced with a volatility of 0.15 % higher than the EUR put. At that moment the market apparently favored calls indicating a belief in an upward movement.

Table 1.8 EUR/GBP 25 Delta Strangle in %

Date	Spot	1 Month	3 Month	1 Year
1-Apr-05	0.6864	0.15	0.16	0.16
4-Apr-05	0.6851	0.15	0.16	0.16
5-Apr-05	0.6840	0.15	0.16	0.16
6-Apr-05	0.6847	0.15	0.16	0.16
7-Apr-05	0.6875	0.15	0.16	0.16
8-Apr-05	0.6858	0.15	0.16	0.16

Source: BBA (British Bankers Association). This means that for example on 4 April 2005, the 1-month 25-delta EUR call and the 1-month 25-delta EUR put are on average quoted with a volatility of 0.15 % higher than the 1-month at-the-money calls and puts. The result is that the 1-month EUR call is quoted with a volatility of 4.88 % + 0.075 % and the 1-month EUR put is quoted with a volatility of 4.88 % − 0.075 %.

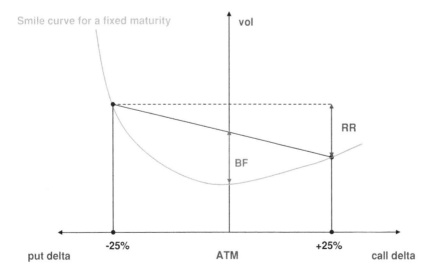

Figure 1.6 Risk reversal and butterfly in terms of volatility for a given FX vanilla option smile

Table 1.9   EUR/GBP implied volatilities in % of 1 April 2005

Maturity	25 delta put	At-the-money	25 delta call
1M	4.890	4.830	5.070
3M	5.465	5.420	5.695
1Y	6.030	6.020	6.330

Source: BBA (British Bankers Association). They are computed based on the market data displayed in Tables 1.6, 1.7 and 1.8 using Equations (1.97) and (1.98).

are given by

$$\sigma_+ = \text{ATM} + BF + \frac{1}{2}RR, \tag{1.97}$$

$$\sigma_- = \text{ATM} + BF - \frac{1}{2}RR, \tag{1.98}$$

$$RR = \sigma_+ - \sigma_-, \tag{1.99}$$

$$BF = \frac{\sigma_+ + \sigma_-}{2} - \sigma_0, \tag{1.100}$$

where σ_0 denotes the at-the-money volatility of both put and call, σ_+ the volatility of an out-of-the-money call (usually 25-Δ) and σ_- the volatility of an out-of-the-money put (usually 25-Δ). Our sample market data is given in terms of RR and BF. Translated into implied volatilities of vanillas we obtain the data listed in Table 1.9 and Figure 1.7.

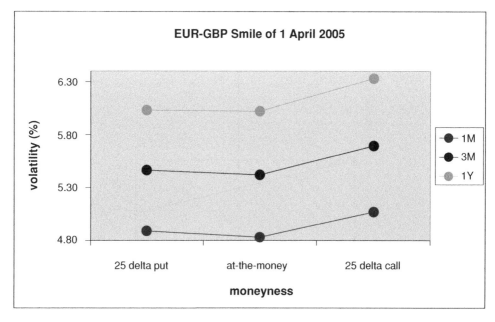

Figure 1.7   Implied volatilities for EUR-GBP vanilla options as of 1 April 2005
Source: BBA (British Bankers Association).

1.3.4   At-the-money volatility interpolation

The interpolation takes into account the effect of reduced volatility on weekends and on days closed in the global main trading centers London or New York and the local market, e.g. Tokyo for JPY-trades. The change is done for the one-day forward volatility. There is a reduction in the one-day forward variance of 25 % for each London and New York closed day. For local market holidays there is a reduction of 25 %, where local holidays for EUR are ignored. Weekends are accounted by a reduction to 15 % variance. The variance on trading days is adjusted to match the volatility on the pillars of the ATM-volatility curve exactly.

The procedure starts from the two pillars t_1, t_2 surrounding the date t_r in question. The ATM forward volatility for the period is calculated based on the consistency condition

$$\sigma^2(t_1)(t_1 - t_0) + \sigma_f^2(t_1, t_2)(t_2 - t_1) = \sigma^2(t_2)(t_2 - t_0), \tag{1.101}$$

whence

$$\sigma_f(t_1, t_2) = \sqrt{\frac{\sigma^2(t_2)(t_2 - t_0) - \sigma^2(t_1)(t_1 - t_0))}{t_2 - t_1}}. \tag{1.102}$$

For each day the factor is determined and from the constraint that the sum of one-day forward variances matches exactly the total variance the factor for the enlarged one day business variances $\alpha(t)$ with t business day is determined.

$$\sigma^2(t_1, t_2)(t_2 - t_1) = \sum_{t=t_1}^{t_r} \alpha(t)\sigma_f^2(t, t+1) \tag{1.103}$$

The variance for the period is the sum of variances to the start and sum of variances to the required date.

$$\sigma^2(t_r) = \sqrt{\frac{\sigma^2(t_1)(t_1 - t_0) + \sum_{t=t_1}^{t_r} \alpha(t)\sigma_f^2(t, t+1)}{t_r - t_0}} \tag{1.104}$$

1.3.5   Volatility smile conventions

The volatility smile is quoted in terms of delta and one at-the-money pillar. We recall that there are several notions of delta

- spot delta $e^{-r_f \tau} N(d_+)$,
- forward delta $e^{-r_d \tau} N(d_+)$,
- driftless delta $N(d_+)$,

and there is the premium which might be included in the delta. It is important to specify the notion that is used to quote the smile. There are three different deltas concerning plain vanilla options.

1.3.6   At-the-money definition

There is one specific at-the-money pillar in the middle. There are at least three notions for the meaning of *at-the-money (ATM)*.

Delta parity: delta call $= -$ delta put

Value parity: call value $=$ put value

Fifty delta: call delta $= 50\,\%$ and put delta $= 50\,\%$

Moreover, these notions use different versions of delta, namely either spot, forward, or driftless and premium included or excluded.

The standard for all currencies one can stick to is spot delta parity with premium included [left hand side *Fenics* delta for call and put is the same] or excluded [right hand side *Fenics* delta] is used.

1.3.7   Interpolation of the volatility on maturity pillars

To determine the spread to at-the-money we can take a kernel interpolation in one dimension to compute the volatility on the delta pillars. Given N points $(X_n, y_n), n = 1, \ldots, N$, where $X = (x^1, x^2) \in \mathbb{R}^2$ and $y \in \mathbb{R}$, a "smooth" interpolation of these points is given by a "smooth" function $g : \mathbb{R}^2 \to \mathbb{R}$ which suffices

$$g(X_n) = y_n \quad (n = 1, \ldots, N).\tag{1.105}$$

The kernel approach is

$$g(X) = g_{[\lambda, \alpha_1, \ldots, \alpha_N]}(X) \overset{\Delta}{=} \frac{1}{\Gamma_\lambda(X)} \sum_{n=1}^{N} \alpha_n K_\lambda(\|X - X_n\|),\tag{1.106}$$

where

$$\Gamma_\lambda(x) \overset{\Delta}{=} \sum_{n=1}^{N} K_\lambda(\|X - X_n\|)\tag{1.107}$$

and $\|.\|$ denotes the Euclidean norm. The required smoothness may be achieved by using analytic kernels K_λ, for instance $K_\lambda(u) \overset{\Delta}{=} e^{-\frac{u^2}{2\lambda^2}}$.

The idea behind this approach is as follows. The parameters which solve the interpolation conditions (1.105) are $\alpha_1, \ldots, \alpha_n$. The parameter λ determines the "smoothness" of the resulting interpolation g and should be fixed according to the nature of the points (X_n, y_n). If these points yield a smooth surface, a "large" λ might yield a good fit, whereas in the opposite case when for neighboring points X_k, X_n the appropriate values y_k, y_n vary significantly, only a small λ, that means $\lambda \ll \min_{n,k} \|X_k - X_n\|$, can provide the needed flexibility.

For the set of delta pillars of $10\,\%, 25\,\%, ATM, -25\,\%, -10\,\%$ one can use $\lambda = 25\,\%$ for a smooth interpolation.

1.3.8   Interpolation of the volatility spread between maturity pillars

The interpolation of the volatility spread to ATM uses the interpolation of the spread on the two surrounding maturity pillars for the initial Black–Scholes delta of the option. The spread is interpolated using square root of time where $\tilde{\sigma}$ is the volatility spread,

$$\tilde{\sigma}(t) = \tilde{\sigma}_1 + \frac{\sqrt{t} - \sqrt{t_1}}{\sqrt{t_2} - \sqrt{t_1}}(\tilde{\sigma}_2 - \tilde{\sigma}_1). \tag{1.108}$$

The spread is added to the interpolated ATM volatility as calculated above.

1.3.9 Volatility sources

1. BBA, the *British Bankers Association*, provides historic smile data for all major currency pairs in spread sheet format at http://www.bba.org.uk.
2. Olsen Associates (http://www.olsen.ch) can provide tic data of historic spot rates, from which the historic volatilities can be computed.
3. Bloomberg, not really the traditional FX data source, contains both implied volatilities and historic volatilities.
4. Reuters pages such as FXMOX, SGFXVOL01, and others are commonly used and contain mostly implied volatilities. JYSKEOPT is a common reference for volatilities of Scandinavia (scandie-vols). NMRC has some implied volatilities for precious metals.
5. Telerate pages such as 4720, see Figure 1.8, delivers implied volatilies.
6. Cantorspeed 90 also provides implied volatilities.

1.3.10 Volatility cones

Volatility cones visualize whether current at-the-money volatility levels for various maturities are high or low compared to a recent history of these implied volatilities. This indicates to a

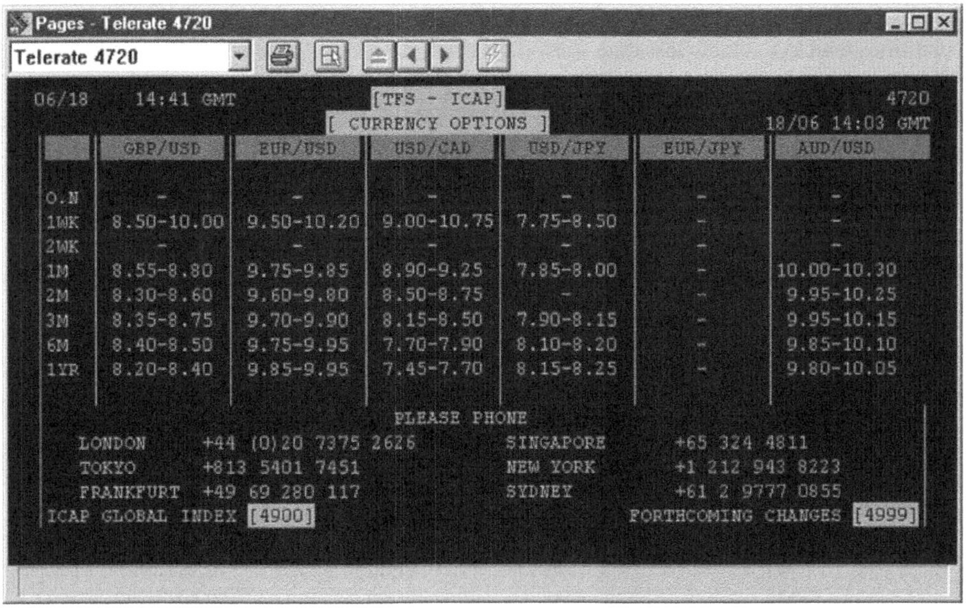
Pages - Telerate 4720

Telerate 4720

06/18 14:41 GMT [TFS - ICAP] 4720

[CURRENCY OPTIONS] 18/06 14:03 GMT

	GBP/USD	EUR/USD	USD/CAD	USD/JPY	EUR/JPY	AUD/USD
O.N	-	-	-	-	-	-
1WK	8.50-10.00	9.50-10.20	9.00-10.75	7.75-8.50	-	-
2WK	-	-	-	-	-	-
1M	8.55-8.80	9.75-9.85	8.90-9.25	7.85-8.00	-	10.00-10.30
2M	8.30-8.60	9.60-9.80	8.50-8.75	-	-	9.95-10.25
3M	8.35-8.75	9.70-9.90	8.15-8.50	7.90-8.15	-	9.95-10.15
6M	8.40-8.50	9.75-9.95	7.70-7.90	8.10-8.20	-	9.85-10.10
1YR	8.20-8.40	9.85-9.95	7.45-7.70	8.15-8.25	-	9.80-10.05

PLEASE PHONE

LONDON +44 (0)20 7375 2626 SINGAPORE +65 324 4811

TOKYO +813 5401 7451 NEW YORK +1 212 943 8223

FRANKFURT +49 69 280 117 SYDNEY +61 2 9777 0855

ICAP GLOBAL INDEX [4900] FORTHCOMING CHANGES [4999]

Figure 1.8 Telerate page 4720 quoting currency option volatilities

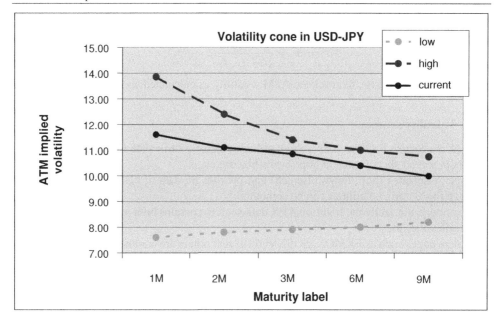

Figure 1.9 Example of a volatility cone in USD-JPY for a 9 months time horizon from 6 Sept 2003 to 24 Feb 2005

trader or risk taker whether it is currently advisable to buy volatility or sell volatility, i.e. to buy vanilla options or to sell vanilla options. We fix a time horizon of historic observations of mid market at-the-money implied volatility and look at the maximum, the minimum that traded over this time horizon and compare this with the current volatility level. Since long term volatilities tend to fluctuate less than short term volatility levels, the chart of the minimum and the maximum typically looks like a part of a cone. We illustrate this in Figure 1.9 based on the data provided in Table 1.10.

1.3.11 Stochastic volatility

Stochastic volatility models are very popular in FX Options, whereas *jump diffusion models* can be considered as the cherry on the cake. The most prominent reason for the popularity is very simple: FX volatility *is* stochastic as is shown for instance in Figure 1.10. Treating stochastic

Table 1.10 Sample data of a volatility cone in USD-JPY for a 9 months time horizon from 6 Sept 2003 to 24 Feb 2005

Maturity	Low	High	Current
1M	7.60	13.85	11.60
2M	7.80	12.40	11.10
3M	7.90	11.40	10.85
6M	8.00	11.00	10.40
12M	8.20	10.75	10.00

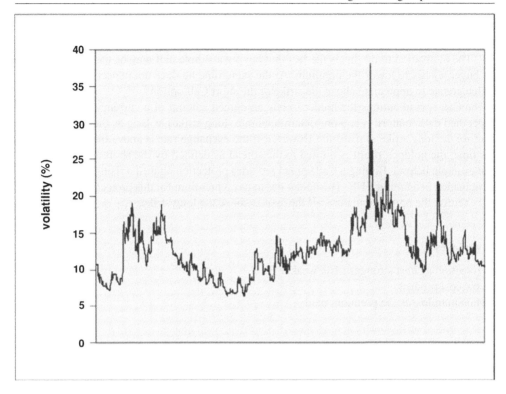

Figure 1.10 Implied volatilities for USD-JPY 1-month vanilla at-the-money options for the period of 1994 to 2000

volatility in detail here is way beyond the scope of this book. A more recent overview can be found in the article *The Heston Model and the Smile* by Weron and Wystup in [13].

1.3.12 Exercises

1. For the market data in Tables 1.6, 1.7 and 1.8 determine a smile matrix for at-the-money and the 25-deltas. Also compute the corresponding strikes for the three pillars or moneyness.
2. Taking the smile of the previous exercise, implement the functions for interpolation to generate a suitable implied volatility for any given time to maturity and any strike or delta.
3. Using the historic data, generate a volatility cone for USD-JPY.
4. It is often believed that an at-the-money (in the sense that the strike is set equal to the forward) vanilla call has a delta near 50 %. What can you say about the delta of a 15 year at-the-money USD-JPY call if USD rates are at 5 %, JPY rates are at 1 % and the volatility is at 11 %?

1.4   BASIC STRATEGIES CONTAINING VANILLA OPTIONS

Linear Combinations of vanillas are quite well known and have been explained in several text books including the one by Spies [14]. Therefore, we will restrict our attention in this section to the most basic strategies.

1.4.1   Call and put spread

A Call spread is a combination of a long and a short Call option. It is also called *capped call*. The motivation to do this is the fact that buying a simple call may be too expensive and the buyer wishes to lower the premium. At the same time he does not expect the underlying exchange rate to appreciate above the strike of the short Call option.

The Call spread entitles the holder to buy an agreed amount of a currency (say EUR) on a specified date (maturity) at a pre-determined rate (long strike) as long as the exchange rate is above the long strike at maturity. However, if the exchange rate is above the short strike at this time, the holder's profit is limited to the spread as defined by the short and long strikes (see example below). Buying a Call spread provides protection against a rising EUR with full participation in a falling EUR. The holder has to pay a premium for this protection. The holder will exercise the option at maturity if the spot is above the long strike.

Advantages

- Protection against stronger EUR/weaker USD
- Low cost product
- Maximum loss is the premium paid

Disadvantages

- Protection is limited when the exchange rate is above the long strike at maturity

The buyer has the chance of full participation in a weaker EUR/stronger USD. However, in case of very high EUR at maturity the protection works only up to the higher strike.

For example, a company wants to buy 1 Million EUR. At maturity:

1. If $S_T < K_1$, it will not exercise the option. The overall loss will be the option's premium. But instead the company can buy EUR at a lower spot in the market.
2. If $K_1 < S_T < K_2$, it will exercise the option and buy EUR at strike K_1.
3. If $S_T > K_2$, it will buy the 1 Million EUR at a rate $K_2 - K_1$ below S_T.

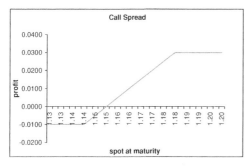 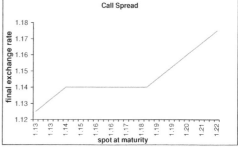

Figure 1.11   Payoff and Final Exchange Rate of a Call spread

Table 1.11   Example of a Call spread

Spot reference	1.1500 EUR-USD
Company buys	EUR call USD put with lower strike
Company sells	EUR call USD put with higher strike
Maturity	1 year
Notional of both the Call option	EUR 1,000,000
Strike of the long Call option	1.1400 EUR-USD
Strike of the short Call option	1.1800 EUR-USD
Premium	EUR 14,500.00
Premium of the long EUR call only	EUR 40,000.00

Example

A company wants to hedge receivables from an export transaction in USD due in 12 months time. It expects a stronger EUR/weaker USD. The company wishes to be able to buy EUR at a lower spot rate if the EUR weakens on the one hand, but on the other be protected against a stronger EUR. The Vanilla Call is too expensive, but the company does not expect a large upward movement of the EUR.

In this case a possible form of protection that the company can use is to buy a Call spread as, for example, listed in Table 1.11.

If the company's market expectation is correct, it can buy EUR at maturity at the strike of 1.1400.

If the EUR-USD exchange rate is below the strike at maturity the option expires worthless. However, the company would benefit from a lower spot when buying EUR.

If the EUR-USD exchange rate is above the short strike of 1.1800 at maturity, the company can buy the EUR amount 400 pips below the spot. Its risk is that the spot at maturity is very high.

The EUR seller can buy a EUR Put spread in a similar fashion.

1.4.2   Risk reversal

Very often corporates seek so-called zero-cost products to hedge their international cash-flows. Since buying a call requires a premium, the buyer can sell another option to finance the purchase of the call. A popular liquid product in FX markets is the Risk Reversal or collar. A Risk Reversal is a combination of a long call and a short put. It entitles the holder to buy an agreed amount of a currency (say EUR) on a specified date (maturity) at a pre-determined rate (long strike) assuming the exchange rate is above the long strike at maturity. However, if the exchange rate is below the strike of the short put at maturity, the holder is obliged to buy the amount of EUR determined by the short strike. Therefore, buying a Risk Reversal provides full protection against rising EUR. The holder will exercise the option only if the spot is above the long strike at maturity. The risk on the upside is financed by a risk on the downside. Since the risk is reversed, the product is named Risk Reversal.

Advantages

- Full protection against stronger EUR/weaker USD
- Zero cost product

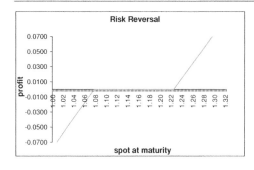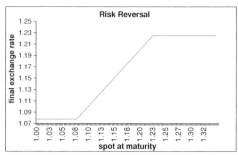

Figure 1.12   Payoff and Final Exchange Rate of a Risk Reversal

Disadvantages

• Participation in weaker EUR/stronger USD is limited to the strike of the sold put

For example, a company wants to sell 1 Million USD. At maturity T:

1. If $S_T < K_1$, it will be obliged to sell USD at K_1. Compared to the market spot the loss can be large. However, compared to the outright forward rate at inception of the trade, K_1 is usually only marginally worse.
2. If $K_1 < S_T < K_2$, it will not exercise the call option. The company can trade at the prevailing spot level.
3. If $S_T > K_2$, it will exercise the option and sell USD at strike K_2.

Example
A company wants to hedge receivables from an export transaction in USD due in 12 months time. It expects a stronger EUR/weaker USD. The company wishes to be fully protected against a stronger EUR. But it finds that the corresponding plain vanilla EUR call is too expensive and would prefer a zero cost strategy by financing the call with the sale of a put. In this case a possible form of protection that the company can use is to buy a Risk Reversal as for example indicated in Table 1.12.

If the company's market expectation is correct, it can buy EUR at maturity at the strike of 1.2250.

The risk is when EUR-USD exchange rate is below the strike of 1.0775 at maturity, the company is obliged to buy 1 Mio EUR at the rate of 1.0775. K_2 is the guaranteed worst case, which can be used as a budget rate.

Table 1.12   Example of a Risk Reversal

Spot reference	1.1500 EUR-USD
Company buys	EUR call USD put with higher strike
Company sells	EUR put USD call with lower strike
Maturity	1 year
Notional of both the Call option	EUR 1,000,000
Strike of the long Call option	1.2250 EUR-USD
Strike of the short Put option	1.0775 EUR-USD
Premium	EUR 0.00

1.4.3 Risk reversal flip

As a variation of the standard risk reversal, we consider the following trade on EUR/USD spot reference 1.2400 with a tenor of two months.

1. Long 1.2500/1.1900 risk reversal (long 1.2500 EUR call, short 1.1900 EUR put).
2. If 1.3000 trades before expiry, it flips into a 1.2900/1.3100 risk reversal (long 1.2900 EUR put, short 1.3100 EUR call).
3. Zero premium.

The corresponding view is that EUR/USD looks bullish and may break on the upside of a recent trading range. However, a runaway higher EUR/USD setting new all-time high within 2 months looks unlikely. However, if EUR/USD overshoots to 1.30, then it will likely retrace afterwards.

The main thrust is to long EUR/USD for zero cost, with a safe cap at 1.30. So the initial risk is EUR/USD below 1.19. If 1.30 is breached, then all accrued profit from the 1.25/1.19 risk reversal is lost, and the maximum risk becomes levels above 1.31. Therefore, this trade is not suitable for EUR bulls who feel there is scope above 1.30 within 2 months. On the other hand, this trade is suitable for those who feel that if spot overshoots to 1.30, then it will retrace down quickly. For early profit taking: with two weeks to go and spot at 1.2800, this trade should be worth approximately 0.84 % EUR. Maximum profit occurs at the trade's maturity.

Composition

This risk reversal flip is rather a proprietary trading strategy than a corporate hedging structure, but may work for corporates as well if the treasurer takes the above view.

The composition is presented in Table 1.13. The options used are standard barrier options, see Section 1.5.1.

1.4.4 Straddle

A straddle is a combination of a put and a call option with the same strike. It entitles the holder to buy an agreed amount of a currency (say EUR) on a specified date (maturity) at a pre-determined rate (strike) if the exchange rate is above the strike at maturity. Alternatively, if the exchange rate is below the strike at maturity, the holder is entitled to sell the amount at this strike. Buying a straddle provides participation in both and upward and a downward movement where the direction of the rate is unclear. The holder has to pay a premium for this product.

Advantages

- Full protection against market movement or increasing volatility
- Maximum loss is the premium paid

Table 1.13 Example of a Risk Reversal Flip

client buys	1.2500 EUR call up-and-out at 1.3000
client sells	1.1900 EUR put up-and-out at 1.3000
client buys	1.2900 EUR put up-and-in at 1.3000
client sells	1.3100 EUR call up-and-in at 1.3000

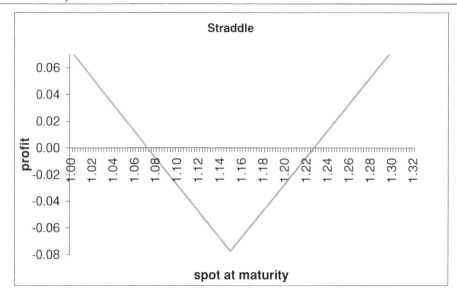

Figure 1.13   Profit of a long straddle

Disadvantages

- Expensive product
- Not suitable for hedge-accounting as it should be clear if the client wants to sell or buy EUR.

Potential profits of a long straddle arise from movements in the spot and also from increases in implied volatility. If the spot moves, the call or the put can be sold before maturity with profit. Conversely, if a quiet market phase persists the option is unlikely to generate much revenue.

Figure 1.13 shows the payoff of a long straddle. The payoff of a short straddle looks like the straddle below a seesaw on a children's playground, which is where the name straddle originated.

For example, a company has bought a straddle with a nominal of 1 Million EUR. At maturity T:

1. If $S_T < K$, it would sell 1 Mio EUR at strike K.
2. If $S_T > K$, it would buy 1 Mio EUR at strike K.

Example
A company wants to benefit from believing that the EUR-USD exchange rate will move far from a specified strike (straddle's strike). In this case a possible product to use is a straddle as, for example, listed in Table 1.14.

If the spot rate is above the strike at maturity, the company can buy 1 Mio EUR at the strike of 1.1500.

If the spot rate is below the strike at maturity, the company can sell 1 Mio EUR at the strike of 1.1500.

The break even points are 1.0726 for the put and 1.2274 for the call. If the spot is between the break even points at maturity, then the company will make an overall loss.

Table 1.14   Example of a straddle

Spot reference	1.1500 EUR-USD
Company buys	EUR call USD put
Company buys	EUR put USD call
Maturity	1 year
Notional of both the options	EUR 1,000,000
Strike of both options	1.1500 EUR-USD
Premium	EUR 77,500.00

1.4.5   Strangle

A strangle is a combination of an out-of-the-money put and call option with two different strikes. It entitles the holder to buy an agreed amount of currency (say EUR) on a specified date (maturity) at a pre-determined rate (call strike), if the exchange rate is above the call strike at maturity. Alternatively, if the exchange rate is below the put strike at maturity, the holder is entitled to sell the amount at this strike. Buying a strangle provides full participation in a strongly moving market, where the direction is not clear. The holder has to pay a premium for this product.

Advantages

- Full protection against a highly volatile exchange rate or increasing volatility
- Maximum loss is the premium paid
- Cheaper than the straddle

Disadvantages

- Expensive product
- Not suitable for hedge-accounting as it should be clear if the client wants to sell or buy EUR.

As in the straddle the chance of the strangle lies in spot movements. If the spot moves significantly, the call or the put can be sold before maturity with profit. Conversely, if a quiet market phase persists the option is unlikely to generate much revenue.

Figure 1.14 shows the profit diagram of a long strangle.

For example, a company has bought a strangle with a nominal of 1 Million EUR. At maturity T:

1. If $S_T < K_1$, it would sell 1 Mio EUR at strike K_1.
2. If $K_1 < S_T < K_2$, it would not exercise either of the two options. The overall loss will be the option's premium.
3. If $S_T > K_2$, it would buy 1 Mio EUR at strike K_2.

Example
A company wants to benefit from believing that the EUR-USD exchange rate will move far from two specified strikes (Strangle's strikes). In this case a possible product to use is a strangle as, for example, listed in Table 1.15.

If the spot rate is above the call strike at maturity, the company can buy 1 Mio EUR at the strike of 1.2000.

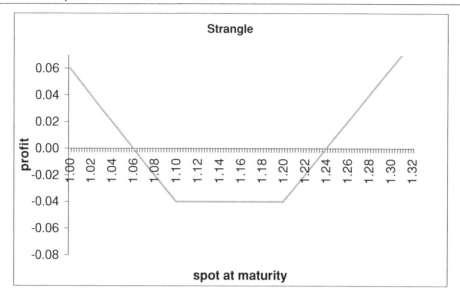

Figure 1.14   Profit of a strangle

If the spot rate is below the put strike at maturity, the company can sell 1 Mio EUR at the strike of 1.1000.

However, the risk is that, if the spot rate is between the put strike and the call strike at maturity, the option expires worthless.

The break even points are 1.0600 for the put and 1.2400 for the call. If the spot is between these points at maturity, then the company makes an overall loss.

1.4.6   Butterfly

A long Butterfly is a combination of a long strangle and a short straddle. Buying a long Butterfly provides participation where a highly volatile exchange rate condition exists. The holder has to pay a premium for this product.

Advantages

- Limited protection against market movement or increasing volatility
- Maximum loss is the premium paid
- Cheaper than the straddle

Table 1.15   Example of a strangle

Spot reference	1.1500 EUR-USD
Company buys	EUR call USD put
Company buys	EUR put USD call
Maturity	1 year
Notional of both the options	EUR 1,000,000
Put Strike	1.1000 EUR-USD
Call Strike	1.2000 EUR-USD
Premium	EUR 40,000.00

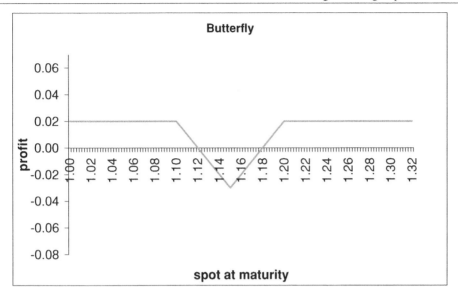

Figure 1.15 Profit of a Butterfly

Disadvantages

• Limited profit
• Not suitable for hedge-accounting as it should be clear if the client wants to sell or buy EUR

If the spot will remain volatile, the call or the put can be sold before maturity with profit. Conversely, if a quiet market phase persists the option is unlikely to be exercised.

Figure 1.15 shows the profit diagram of a long Butterfly.

For example, a company has bought a long Butterfly with a nominal of 1 Million EUR and strikes $K_1 < K_2 < K_3$. At maturity T:

1. If $S_T < K_1$, it would sell 1 Mio EUR at a rate $K_2 - K_1$ higher than the market.
2. If $K_1 < S_T < K_2$, it would sell 1 Mio EUR at strike K_2.
3. If $K_2 < S_T < K_3$, it would buy 1 Mio EUR at strike K_2.
4. If $S_T > K_3$, it would buy 1 Mio EUR at a rate $K_3 - K_2$ less than the market.

Example
A company wants to benefit from believing that the EUR-USD exchange rate will remain volatile from a specified strike (the middle strike K_2).

In this case a possible product to use is a long Butterfly as for example listed in Table 1.16.

If the spot rate is between the lower and the middle strike at maturity, the company can sell 1 Mio EUR at the strike of 1.1500.

If the spot rate is between the middle and the higher strike at maturity, the company can buy 1 Mio EUR at the strike of 1.1500.

If the spot rate is above the higher strike at maturity, the company will buy EUR 100 points below the spot.

If the spot rate is below the lower strike at maturity, the company will sell EUR 100 points above the spot.

Table 1.16   Example of a Butterfly

Spot reference	1.1500 EUR-USD
Maturity	1 year
Notional of both the options	EUR 1,000,000
Lower strike K_1	1.1400 EUR-USD
Middle strike K_2	1.1500 EUR-USD
Upper strike K_3	1.1600 EUR-USD
Premium	EUR 30,000.00

1.4.7   Seagull

A long Seagull Call strategy is a combination of a long call, a short call and a short put. It is similar to a Risk Reversal. So it entitles its holder to purchase an agreed amount of a currency (say EUR) on a specified date (maturity) at a pre-determined long call strike if the exchange rate at maturity is between the long call strike and the short call strike (see below for more information). If the exchange rate is below the short put strike at maturity, the holder must buy this amount in EUR at the short put strike. Buying a Seagull Call strategy provides good protection against a rising EUR.

Advantages

- Good protection against stronger EUR/weaker USD
- Better strikes than in a risk reversal
- Zero cost product

Disadvantages

- Maximum loss depending on spot rate at maturity and can be arbitrarily large

The protection against a rising EUR is limited to the interval from the long call strike and the short call strike. The biggest risk is a large upward movement of EUR.

Figure 1.16 shows the payoff and final exchange rate diagram of a Seagull. Rotating the payoff clockwise by about 45 degrees shows the shape of a flying seagull.

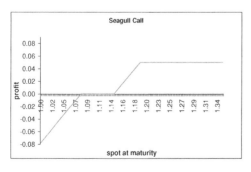
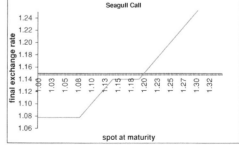

Figure 1.16   Payoff and Final Exchange Rate of a Seagull Call

Table 1.17 Example of a Seagull Call

Spot reference	1.1500 EUR-USD
Maturity	1 year
Notional	USD 1,000,000
Company buys	EUR call USD put strike 1.1400
Company sells	EUR call USD put strike 1.1900
Company sells	EUR put USD call strike 1.0775
Premium	USD 0.00

For example, a company wants to sell 1 Million USD and buy EUR. At maturity T:

1. If $S_T < K_1$, the company must sell 1 Mio USD at rate K_1.
2. If $K_1 < S_T < K_2$, all involved options expire worthless and the company can sell USD in the spot market.
3. If $K_2 < S_T < K_3$, the company would buy EUR at strike K_2.
4. If $S_T > K_3$, the company would sell 1 Mio USD at a rate $K_2 - K_1$ less than the market.

Example
A company wants to hedge receivables from an export transaction in USD due in 12 months time. It expects a stronger EUR/weaker USD but not a large upward movement of the EUR. The company wishes to be protected against a stronger EUR and finds that the corresponding plain vanilla is too expensive and would prefer a zero cost strategy and is willing to limit protection on the upside.

In this case a possible form of protection that the company can use is to buy a Seagull Call as for example presented in Table 1.17.

If the company's market expectation is correct, it can buy EUR at maturity at the strike of 1.1400.

If the EUR-USD exchange rate will be above the short call strike of 1.1900 at maturity, the company will sell USD at 500 points less than the spot.

However the risk is that, if the EUR-USD exchange rate is below the strike of 1.0775 at maturity, it will have to sell 1 Mio USD at the strike of 1.0775.

1.4.8 Exercises

1. For EUR/GBP spot ref 0.7000, volatility 8 %, EUR rate 2.5 %, GBP rate 4 % and flat smile find the strike of the short EUR put for a 6 months zero cost seagull put, where the strike of the long EUR put is 0.7150, the strike of the short call is 0.7300 and the desired sales margin is 0.1 % of the GBP notional. What is the value of the seagull put after three months if the spot is at 0.6900 and the volatility is at 7.8 %?

1.5   FIRST GENERATION EXOTICS

We consider EUR/USD – the most liquidly traded currency pair in the foreign exchange market. Internationally active market participants are always subject to changing foreign exchange rates. To hedge this exposure an immense variety of options are traded worldwide. Besides vanilla (European style put and call) options, the so-called first generation exotics have become

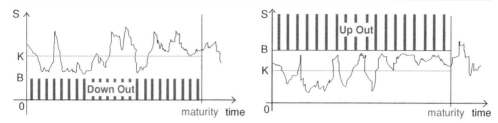

Figure 1.17 *Down-and-out* American barrier

If the exchange rate is never at or below B between the trade date and maturity, the option can be exercised. *Up-and-out* American barrier: If the exchange rate is never at or above B between the trade date and maturity, the option can be exercised.

standard derivative instruments. These are (a) vanilla options that knock in or out if the underlying hits a barrier (or one of two barriers) and (b) all kind of touch options: a one-touch [no-touch] pays a fixed amount of either USD or EUR if the spot ever [never] trades at or beyond the touch-level and zero otherwise. Double one-touch and no-touch options work the same way but have two barriers.

1.5.1   Barrier options

Knock Out Call option (American style barrier)

A Knock-Out Call option entitles the holder to purchase an agreed amount of a currency (say EUR) on a specified expiration date at a pre-determined rate called the strike K provided the exchange rate never hits or crosses a pre-determined barrier level B. However, there is no obligation to do so. Buying a EUR Knock-Out Call provides protection against a rising EUR if no Knock-Out event occurs between the trade date and expiration date whilst enabling full participation in a falling EUR. The holder has to pay a premium for this protection. The holder will exercise the option only if at expiration time the spot is above the strike and if the spot has failed to touch the barrier between the trade date and expiration date (American style barrier) of if the spot at expiration does not touch or cross the barrier (European style barrier), see Figure 1.17. We display the profit and the final exchange rate of an up-and-out call in Figure 1.18.

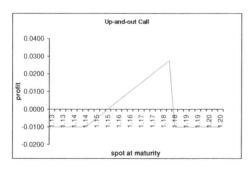
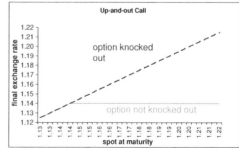

Figure 1.18 *Down-and-out* American barrier

If the exchange rate is never at or below B between the trade date and maturity, the option can be exercised. *Up-and-out* American barrier: If the exchange rate is never at or above B between the trade date and maturity, the option can be exercised.

Advantages

- Cheaper than a plain vanilla
- Conditional protection against stronger EUR/weaker USD
- Full participation in a weaker EUR/stronger USD

Disadvantages

- Option may knock out
- Premium has to be paid

For example the company wants to sell 1 MIO USD. If as usual S_t denotes the exchange rate at time t then at maturity

1. if $S_T < K$, the company would not exercise the option,
2. if $S_T > K$ and if S has respected the conditions pre-determined by the barrier, the company would exercise the option and sell 1 MIO USD at strike K.

Example

A company wants to hedge receivables from an export transaction in USD due in 12 months time. It expects a stronger EUR/weaker USD. The company wishes to be able to buy EUR at a lower spot rate if the EUR becomes weaker on the one hand, but on the other hand be protected against a stronger EUR, and finds that the corresponding vanilla call is too expensive and is prepared to take more risk.

In this case a possible form of protection that the company can use is to buy a EUR Knock-Out Call option as for example listed in Table 1.18.

If the company's market expectation is correct, then it can buy EUR at maturity at the strike of 1.1500.

If the EUR–USD exchange rate touches the barrier at least once between the trade date and maturity the option will expire worthless.

Types of barrier options

Generally the payoff of a standard knock-out option can be stated as

$$[\phi(S_T - K)]^+ I\!I_{\{\eta S_t > \eta B, \, 0 \le t \le T\}}, \qquad (1.109)$$

where $\phi \in \{+1, -1\}$ is the usual put/call indicator and $\eta \in \{+1, -1\}$ takes the value $+1$ for a lower barrier (down-and-out) or -1 for an upper barrier (up-and-out). The corresponding

Table 1.18 Example of an up-and-out call

Spot reference	1.1500 EUR-USD
Maturity	1 year
Notional	EUR 1,000,000
Company buys	EUR call USD put
Strike	1.1500 EUR-USD
Up-and-out American barrier	1.3000 EUR-USD
Premium	EUR 12,553.00

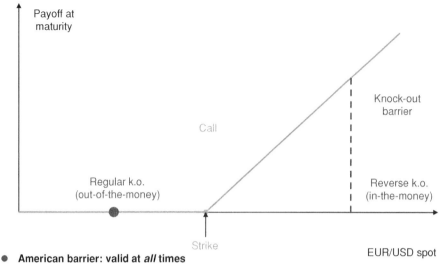

Figure 1.19   Barrier option terminology: regular barriers are out of the money, reverse barriers are in the money

knock-in options only become alive, if the spot ever trades at or beyond the barrier between trade date and expiration date. Naturally,

$$\text{knock-out} + \text{knock-in} = \text{vanilla}. \tag{1.110}$$

Furthermore, we distinguish (see Figure 1.19)

Regular knock out: the barrier is out of the money.

Reverse knock out: the barrier is in the money.

Strike out: the barrier is at the strike.

Losing a reverse barrier option due to the spot hitting the barrier is more painful since the owner already has accumulated a positive intrinsic value.

This means that there are in total 16 different types of barrier options, call or put, in or out, up or down, regular or reverse.

Theoretical value of barrier options

For the standard type of FX barriers options a detailed derivation of values and Greeks can be found in [3].

Barrier option terminology

This paragraph is based on Hakala and Wystup [15]

American vs. European – Traditionally barrier options are of American style, which means that the barrier level is active during the entire duration of the option: at any time between today and maturity the spot hits the barrier, the option becomes worthless. If the barrier level is only active at maturity the barrier option is of European style and can in fact be replicated by a vertical spread and a digital option.

Single, double and outside barriers – Instead of taking just a lower or an upper barrier one could have both if one feels sure about the spot to remain in a range for a while. In this case besides vanillas, constant payoffs at maturity are popular, they are called range binaries. If the barrier and strike are in different exchange rates, the contract is called an outside barrier option or double asset barrier option. Such options traded a few years ago with the strike in USD/DEM and the barrier in USD/FRF taking advantage of the misbalance between implied and historic correlation between the two currency pairs.

Rebates – For knock-in options an amount R is paid at expiration by the seller of the option to the holder of the option if the option failed to kick in during its lifetime. For knock-out options an amount R is paid by the seller of the option to the holder of the option, if the option knocks out. The payment of the rebate is either at maturity or at the first time the barrier is hit. Including such rebate features makes hedging easier for reverse barrier options and serves as a consolation for the holder's disappointment. The rebate part of a barrier option can be completely separated from the barrier contract and can in fact be traded separately, in which case it is called a one-touch (digital) option or hit option (in the knock-out case) and no-touch option (in the knock-in case). We treat the touch options in detail in Section 1.5.2.

Determination of knock-out event – We discuss how breaching the barrier is determined in the beginning of Section 1.5.2.

**How the barrier is monitored (Continuous vs. Discrete)
and how this influences the value**

How often and when exactly do you check whether an option has knocked out or kicked in? This question is not trivial and should be clearly stated in the deal. The intensity of monitoring can create any price between a standard barrier and a vanilla contract. The standard for barrier options is continuous monitoring. Any time the exchange rate hits the barrier the option is knocked out. An alternative is to consider just daily/weekly/monthly fixings which makes the knock-out option more expensive because chances of knocking out are smaller (see Figure 1.20). A detailed discussion of the valuation of discrete barriers can be found in [16].

The popularity of barrier options

• They are less expensive than vanilla contracts: in fact, the closer the spot is to the barrier, the cheaper the knock-out option. Any price between zero and the vanilla premium can be obtained by taking an appropriate barrier level, as we see in Figure 1.21. One must be aware however, that too cheap barrier options are very likely to knock out.
• They allow one to design foreign exchange risk exposure to the special needs of customers. Instead of lowering the premium one can increase the nominal coverage of the vanilla contract by admitting a barrier. Some customers feel sure about exchange rate levels not being hit

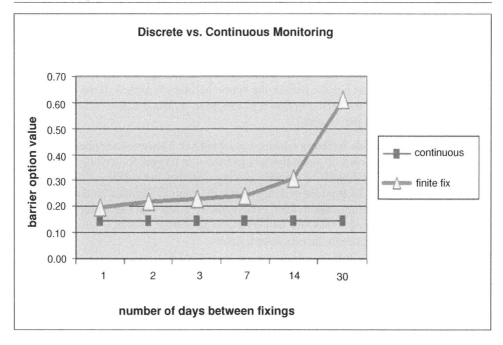

Figure 1.20 Comparison of a discretely and a continuously monitored knock-out barrier option

during the next month which could be exploited to lower the premium. Others really only want to cover their exchange rate exposure if the market moves drastically which would require a knock-in option.

• The savings can be used for another hedge of foreign exchange risk exposure if the first barrier option happened to knock out.
• The contract is easy to understand if one knows about vanillas.
• Many pricing and trading systems include barrier option calculations in their standard.
• Pricing and hedging barriers in the Black-Scholes model is well-understood and most premium calculations use closed-form solutions which allow fast and stable implementation.
• Barrier options are standard ingredients in structured FX forwards, see, for example, the *shark forward* in Section 2.1.5.

Barrier option crisis in 1994–96

In the currency market barrier options became popular in 1994. The exchange rate between USD and DEM was then between 1.50 and 1.70. Since the all time low before 1995 was 1.3870 at September 2 1992 there were a lot of down and out barrier contracts written with a lower knock-out barrier of 1.3800. The sudden fall of the US Dollar in the beginning of 1995 was unexpected and the 1.3800 barrier was hit at 10:30 am on March 29 1995 and fell even more to its all time low of 1.3500 at 9:30 am on April 19 1995. Numerous barrier option holders were shocked to learn that losing the entire option was something that could really happen (see

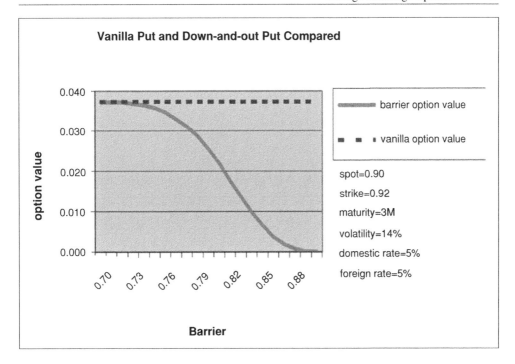

Figure 1.21   Comparison of a vanilla put and a down-and-out put
As the barrier moves far away from the current spot, the barrier option behaves like a vanilla options. As the barrier moves close to the current spot, the barrier option becomes worthless.

Figure 1.22). The shock lasted for more than a year and barrier options were unpopular for a while until many market participants had forgotten that it had happened. Events like this often raise the question about using exotics. Complicated products can in fact lead to unpleasant surprises. However, in order to cover foreign exchange risk in an individual design at minimal cost requires exotic options. Often they appear as an integral part of an investment portfolio. The number of market participants understanding the advantages and pitfalls is growing steadily.

Hedging methods

Several authors claim that barrier options can be hedged statically with a portfolio of vanilla options. These approaches are problematic if the hedging portfolio has to be unwound at hitting time, since volatilities for the vanillas may have changed between the time the hedge is composed and the time the barrier is hit. Moreover, the occasionally high nominals and low deltas can cause a high price for the hedge. The approach by Maruhn and Sachs in [17] appears most promising. For regular barriers a delta and vega hedge is more advisable. A vega hedge can be done almost statically using two vanilla options. In the example we consider a 3-month up-and-out put with strike 1.0100 and barrier 0.9800. The vega minimizing hedge consists of 0.9 short 3-month 50 delta calls and 0.8 long 2-month 25 delta calls. Spot reference for EUR/USD is 0.9400 with rates 3.05 % and 6.50 % and volatility 11.9 %, see Figure 1.23.

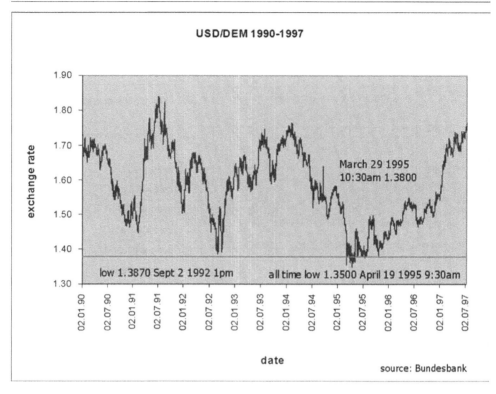

USD/DEM 1990-1997

Figure 1.22   Barrier had lost popularity in 1994–96, when USD-DEM had dropped below its historic low

One can also think of statically hedging regular barriers with a risk reversal as indicated in Figure 1.24. The problem is of course, that the value of the risk reversal at knock-out time need not be zero, in fact, considering hedging a down-and-out call with a spot approaching the barrier, the calls will tend to be cheaper than the puts, so to unwind the hedge one would get little for the call one could sell and pay more than expected for the put to be bought back. Therefore, many traders and researchers like to think of stochastic skew models taking exactly this effect into account.

Reverse barrier options have extremely high values for delta, gamma and theta when the spot is near the barrier and the time is close to expiry, see for example the delta in Figure 1.25. This is because the intrinsic value of the option jumps from a positive value to zero when the barrier is hit. In such a situation a simple delta hedge is impractical. However, there are ways to tackle this undesirable state of affairs by moving the barrier or more systematically apply valuation subject to portfolio constraints such as limited leverage, see Schmock, Shreve and Wystup in [18].

How large barrier contracts affect the market

Let's take the example of a reverse up-and-out call in EUR/USD with strike 1.2000 and barrier 1.3000. An investment bank delta-hedging a short position with nominal 10 Million has to

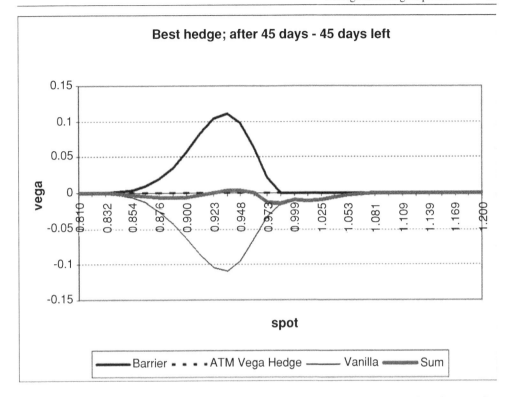

Figure 1.23 Vega depending on spot of an up-and-out put and a vega hedge consisting of two vanilla options

buy 10 Million times delta EUR, which is negative in this example. As the spot goes up to the barrier, delta becomes smaller and smaller requiring the hedging institution to sell more and more EUR. This can influence the market since steadily offering EUR slows down the spot movement towards the barrier and can in extreme cases prevent the spot from crossing the barrier. This is illustrated in Figure 1.26.

On the other hand, if the hedger runs out of breath or the upward market movement can't be stopped by the delta-hedging institution, then the option knocks out and the hedge is unwound.

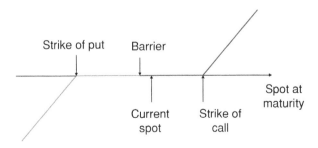

Figure 1.24 Hedging the regular knock-out with a risk reversal
A short down-and-out call is hedged by a long call with the same strike and a short put with a strike chosen in such a way that the value of the call and put portfolio is zero if the spot is at the barrier.

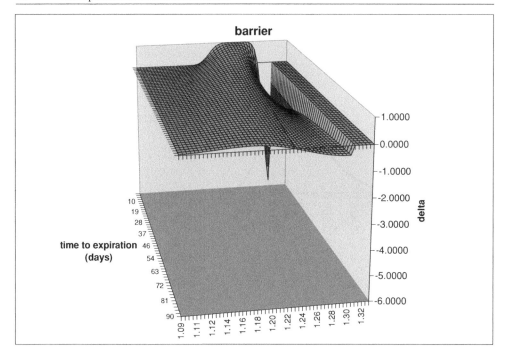

Figure 1.25   Delta of a reverse knock-out call in EUR-USD with strike 1.2000, barrier 1.3000

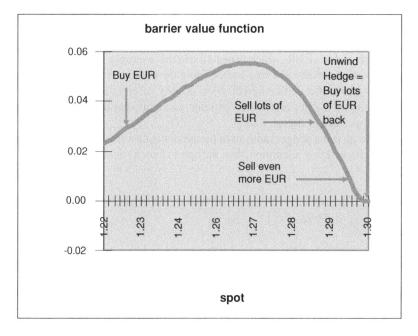

Figure 1.26   Delta hedging a short reverse knock-out call

Then suddenly more EUR are asked whence the upward movement of an exchange rate can be accelerated once a large barrier contract in the market has knocked out. Situations like this have happened to the USD-DEM spot in the early 90s (see again Figure 1.22), where many reverse knock-out puts have been written by banks, as traders are telling.

The reverse situation occurs when the bank hedges a long position, in which case EUR has to be bought when the spot approaches the barrier. This can cause an accelerated movement of the exchange rate towards the barrier and a sudden halt once the barrier is breached.

1.5.2   Digital options, touch options and rebates

Now we take a more detailed look at the pricing of one-touch options – often called (American style) binary or digital options, hit options or rebate options. They trade as listed and over-the-counter products.

The touch-time is the first time the underlying trades at or beyond the touch-level. The barrier determination agent, who is specified in the contract, determines the touch-event. The *Foreign Exchange Committee* recommends to the foreign exchange community a set of best practices for the barrier options market. In the next stage of this project, the Committee is planning on publishing a revision of the *International Currency Options Master Agreement (ICOM) User Guide* to reflect the new recommendations.[3] Some key features are:

- Determination whether the spot has breached the barrier must be due to actual transactions in the foreign exchange markets.
- Transactions must occur between 5:00 a.m. Sydney time on Monday and 5:00 p.m. New York time on Friday.
- Transactions must be of commercial size. In liquid markets, dealers generally accept that commercial size transactions are a minimum of 3 million USD.
- The barrier options determination agent may use cross-currency rates to determine whether a barrier has been breached in respect of a currency pair that is not commonly quoted.

The barrier or touch-level is usually monitored continuously over time. A further contractual issue to specify is the time of the payment of the one-touch. Typically, the notional is paid at the delivery date, which is two business days after the maturity. Another common practice is 2 business days after the touch event. In FX markets the former is the default.

Applications of one-touch options

Market participants of a rather speculative nature like to use one-touch options as bets on a rising or falling exchange rate.[4] Hedging oriented clients often buy one-touch options as a rebate, so they receive a payment as a consolation if the strategy they believe in does not work. One-touch options also often serve as parts of structured products designed to enhance a forward rate or an interest rate.

---

[3] For details see http://www.ny.frb.org/fxc/fxann000217.html.
[4] Individuals can trade them over the internet, for example at http://www.boxoption.com/.

Theoretical value of a one-touch option

In the standard Black-Scholes model for the underlying exchange rate of EUR/USD,

$$dS_t = S_t[(r_d - r_f)dt + \sigma dW_t], \tag{1.111}$$

where t denotes the running time in years, r_d the USD interest rate, r_f the EUR interest rate, σ the volatility, W_t a standard Brownian motion under the risk-neutral measure, the payoff is given by

$$R1\!\!1_{\{\tau_B \leq T\}}, \tag{1.112}$$

$$\tau_B \overset{\Delta}{=} \inf\{t \geq 0 : \eta S_t \leq \eta B\}. \tag{1.113}$$

This type of option pays a domestic cash amount R USD if a barrier B is hit any time before the expiration time. We use the binary variable η to describe whether B is a lower barrier ($\eta = 1$) or an upper barrier ($\eta = -1$). The stopping time τ_B is called the first hitting time. The option can be either viewed as the rebate portion of a knock-out barrier option or as an American cash-or-nothing digital option. In FX markets it is usually called a *one-touch (option)*, *one-touch-digital* or *hit option*. The modified payoff of a *no-touch (option)*, $R1\!\!1_{\{\tau_B \geq T\}}$ describes a rebate which is being paid if a knock-in-option has not knocked in by the time it expires and can be valued similarly simply by exploiting the identity

$$R1\!\!1_{\{\tau_B \leq T\}} + R1\!\!1_{\{\tau_B > T\}} = R. \tag{1.114}$$

We will further distinguish the cases

$\omega = 0$, rebate paid at hit,

$\omega = 1$, rebate paid at end.

It is important to mention that the payoff is one unit of the base currency. For a payment in the underlying currency EUR, one needs to exchange r_d and r_f, replace S and B by their reciprocal values and change the sign of η.

For the one-touch we will use the abbreviations:

- T: expiration time (in years)
- t: running time (in years)
- $\tau \overset{\Delta}{=} T - t$: time to expiration (in years)
- $\theta_\pm \overset{\Delta}{=} \frac{r_d - r_f}{\sigma} \pm \frac{\sigma}{2}$
- $S_t = S_0 e^{\sigma W_t + \sigma \theta_- t}$: price of the underlying at time t
- $n(t) \overset{\Delta}{=} \frac{1}{\sqrt{2\pi}} e^{-\frac{1}{2}t^2}$
- $\mathcal{N}(x) \overset{\Delta}{=} \int_{-\infty}^{x} n(t)\,dt$
- $\vartheta_- \overset{\Delta}{=} \sqrt{\theta_-^2 + 2(1-\omega)r_d}$
- $e_\pm \overset{\Delta}{=} \frac{\pm \ln \frac{x}{B} - \sigma \vartheta_- \tau}{\sigma \sqrt{\tau}}$

We can describe the value function of the one-touch as a solution to a partial differential equation setup. Let $v(t, x)$ denote the value of the option at time t when the underlying is at x.

Then $v(t, x)$ is the solution of

$$v_t + (r_d - r_f)xv_x + \frac{1}{2}\sigma^2 x^2 v_{xx} - r_d v = 0, \ t \in [0, T], \ \eta x \geq \eta B, \tag{1.115}$$

$$v(T, x) = 0, \ \eta x \geq \eta B, \tag{1.116}$$

$$v(t, B) = R e^{-\omega r_d \tau}, \ t \in [0, T]. \tag{1.117}$$

The theoretical value of the one-touch turns out to be

$$v(t, x) = R e^{-\omega r_d \tau} \left[\left(\frac{B}{x}\right)^{\frac{\theta_- + \vartheta_-}{\sigma}} \mathcal{N}(-\eta e_+) + \left(\frac{B}{x}\right)^{\frac{\theta_- - \vartheta_-}{\sigma}} \mathcal{N}(\eta e_-) \right]. \tag{1.118}$$

Note that $\vartheta_- = |\theta_-|$ for rebates paid at end ($\omega = 1$).

Greeks

We list some of the sensitivity parameters of the one-touch here, as they seem hard to find in the existing literature, but many people have asked me for them, so here we go.

Delta

$$v_x(t, x) = -\frac{R e^{-\omega r_d \tau}}{\sigma x} \left\{ \left(\frac{B}{x}\right)^{\frac{\theta_- + \vartheta_-}{\sigma}} \left[(\theta_- + \vartheta_-)\mathcal{N}(-\eta e_+) + \frac{\eta}{\sqrt{\tau}} n(e_+) \right] \right.$$

$$\left. + \left(\frac{B}{x}\right)^{\frac{\theta_- - \vartheta_-}{\sigma}} \left[(\theta_- - \vartheta_-)\mathcal{N}(\eta e_-) + \frac{\eta}{\sqrt{\tau}} n(e_-) \right] \right\} \tag{1.119}$$

Gamma can be obtained using $v_{xx} = \frac{2}{\sigma^2 x^2}[r_d v - v_t - (r_d - r_f)xv_x]$ and turns out to be:

$$v_{xx}(t, x) = \frac{2R e^{-\omega r_d \tau}}{\sigma^2 x^2} \cdot \tag{1.120}$$

$$\left\{ \left(\frac{B}{x}\right)^{\frac{\theta_- + \vartheta_-}{\sigma}} \mathcal{N}(-\eta e_+) \left[r_d(1 - \omega) + (r_d - r_f)\frac{\theta_- + \vartheta_-}{\sigma} \right] \right.$$

$$+ \left(\frac{B}{x}\right)^{\frac{\theta_- - \vartheta_-}{\sigma}} \mathcal{N}(\eta e_-) \left[r_d(1 - \omega) + (r_d - r_f)\frac{\theta_- - \vartheta_-}{\sigma} \right]$$

$$+ \eta \left(\frac{B}{x}\right)^{\frac{\theta_- + \vartheta_-}{\sigma}} n(e_+) \left[-\frac{e_-}{\tau} + \frac{r_d - r_f}{\sigma\sqrt{\tau}} \right]$$

$$\left. + \eta \left(\frac{B}{x}\right)^{\frac{\theta_- - \vartheta_-}{\sigma}} n(e_-) \left[\frac{e_+}{\tau} + \frac{r_d - r_f}{\sigma\sqrt{\tau}} \right] \right\}$$

Theta

$$v_t(t, x) = \omega r_d v(t, x) + \frac{\eta R e^{-\omega r_d \tau}}{2\tau} \left[\left(\frac{B}{x}\right)^{\frac{\theta_- + \vartheta_-}{\sigma}} n(e_+)e_- - \left(\frac{B}{x}\right)^{\frac{\theta_- - \vartheta_-}{\sigma}} n(e_-)e_+ \right]$$

$$= \omega r_d v(t, x) + \frac{\eta R e^{-\omega r_d \tau}}{\sigma \tau^{(3/2)}} \left(\frac{B}{x}\right)^{\frac{\theta_- + \vartheta_-}{\sigma}} n(e_+) \ln\left(\frac{B}{x}\right) \tag{1.121}$$

The computation exploits the identities (1.143), (1.144) and (1.145) derived below.
Vega requires the identities

$$\frac{\partial \theta_-}{\partial \sigma} = -\frac{\theta_+}{\sigma} \tag{1.122}$$

$$\frac{\partial \vartheta_-}{\partial \sigma} = -\frac{\theta_- \theta_+}{\sigma \vartheta_-} \tag{1.123}$$

$$\frac{\partial e_\pm}{\partial \sigma} = \pm \frac{\ln \frac{B}{x}}{\sigma^2 \sqrt{\tau}} + \frac{\theta_- \theta_+}{\sigma \vartheta_-} \sqrt{\tau} \tag{1.124}$$

$$A_\pm \overset{\Delta}{=} \frac{\partial}{\partial \sigma} \frac{\theta_- \pm \vartheta_-}{\sigma} = -\frac{1}{\sigma^2} \left[\theta_+ + \theta_- \pm \left(\frac{\theta_- \theta_+}{\vartheta_-} + \vartheta_- \right) \right] \tag{1.125}$$

and turns out to be

$$v_\sigma(t, x) = Re^{-\omega r_d \tau} . \tag{1.126}$$

$$\left\{ \left(\frac{B}{x} \right)^{\frac{\theta_- + \vartheta_-}{\sigma}} \left[\mathcal{N}(-\eta e_+) A_+ \ln \left(\frac{B}{x} \right) - \eta n(e_+) \frac{\partial e_+}{\partial \sigma} \right] \right.$$

$$\left. + \left(\frac{B}{x} \right)^{\frac{\theta_- - \vartheta_-}{\sigma}} \left[\mathcal{N}(\eta e_-) A_- \ln \left(\frac{B}{x} \right) + \eta n(e_-) \frac{\partial e_-}{\partial \sigma} \right] \right\} .$$

Vanna uses the identity

$$d_- = \frac{\ln \frac{B}{x} - \sigma \theta_- \tau}{\sigma \sqrt{\tau}} \tag{1.127}$$

and turns out to be

$$v_{\sigma x}(t, x) = \frac{Re^{-\omega r_d \tau}}{\sigma x} .$$

$$\left\{ \left(\frac{B}{x} \right)^{\frac{\theta_- + \vartheta_-}{\sigma}} \left[\mathcal{N}(-\eta e_+) A_+ \left(-\sigma - (\theta_- + \vartheta_-) \ln \left(\frac{B}{x} \right) \right) \right. \right.$$

$$\left. - \frac{\eta n(e_+)}{\sqrt{\tau}} \left(d_- \frac{\partial e_+}{\partial \sigma} + A_+ \ln \left(\frac{B}{x} \right) - \frac{1}{\sigma} \right) \right]$$

$$+ \left(\frac{B}{x} \right)^{\frac{\theta_- - \vartheta_-}{\sigma}} \left[\mathcal{N}(\eta e_-) A_- \left(-\sigma - (\theta_- - \vartheta_-) \ln \left(\frac{B}{x} \right) \right) \right.$$

$$\left. \left. + \frac{\eta n(e_-)}{\sqrt{\tau}} \left(d_- \frac{\partial e_-}{\partial \sigma} - A_- \ln \left(\frac{B}{x} \right) + \frac{1}{\sigma} \right) \right] \right\} \tag{1.128}$$

Volga uses the identities

$$g = \frac{1}{\sigma^2 \vartheta_-}\left[-\theta_+^2 - \theta_-^2 - \theta_+\theta_- + \frac{\theta_-^2\theta_+^2}{\vartheta_-^2}\right] \tag{1.129}$$

$$\frac{\partial^2 e_\pm}{\partial\sigma^2} = \mp \frac{2\ln\left(\frac{B}{x}\right)}{\sigma^3\sqrt{\tau}} + g\sqrt{\tau} \tag{1.130}$$

$$\frac{\partial A_\pm}{\partial\sigma} = \frac{\theta_+ + \theta_-}{\sigma^3} - \frac{2A_\pm \pm g}{\sigma} \tag{1.131}$$

and turns out to be

$$v_{\sigma\sigma}(t, x) = Re^{-\omega r_d \tau} \cdot$$

$$\left\{ \left(\frac{B}{x}\right)^{\frac{\theta_-+\theta_-}{\sigma}}\left[\mathcal{N}(-\eta e_+)\ln\left(\frac{B}{x}\right)\left(A_+^2\ln\left(\frac{B}{x}\right) + \frac{\partial A_+}{\partial\sigma}\right)\right.\right.$$

$$\left. -\eta n(e_+)\left(2\ln\left(\frac{B}{x}\right)A_+\frac{\partial e_+}{\partial\sigma} - e_+\left(\frac{\partial e_+}{\partial\sigma}\right)^2 + \frac{\partial^2 e_+}{\partial\sigma^2}\right)\right]$$

$$+\left(\frac{B}{x}\right)^{\frac{\theta_--\vartheta_-}{\sigma}}\left[\mathcal{N}(\eta e_-)\ln\left(\frac{B}{x}\right)\left(A_-^2\ln\left(\frac{B}{x}\right) + \frac{\partial A_-}{\partial\sigma}\right)\right.$$

$$\left.\left. +\eta n(e_-)\left(2\ln\left(\frac{B}{x}\right)A_-\frac{\partial e_-}{\partial\sigma} - e_-\left(\frac{\partial e_-}{\partial\sigma}\right)^2 + \frac{\partial^2 e_-}{\partial\sigma^2}\right)\right]\right\} \tag{1.132}$$

The risk-neutral probability of knocking out is given by

$$P[\tau_B \leq T]$$
$$= E\left[\mathbb{1}_{\{\tau_B \leq T\}}\right]$$
$$= \frac{1}{R}e^{r_d T}v(0, S_0) \tag{1.133}$$

Properties of the first hitting time τ_B

As derived, e.g., in [19], the first hitting time

$$\tilde{\tau} \stackrel{\Delta}{=} \inf\{t \geq 0 : \theta t + W(t) = x\} \tag{1.134}$$

of a Brownian motion with drift θ and hit level $x > 0$ has the density

$$P[\tilde{\tau} \in dt] = \frac{x}{t\sqrt{2\pi t}}\exp\left\{-\frac{(x-\theta t)^2}{2t}\right\}dt, \quad t > 0, \tag{1.135}$$

the cumulative distribution function

$$P[\tilde{\tau} \leq t] = \mathcal{N}\left(\frac{\theta t - x}{\sqrt{t}}\right) + e^{2\theta x}\mathcal{N}\left(\frac{-\theta t - x}{\sqrt{t}}\right), \quad t > 0, \tag{1.136}$$

the Laplace-transform

$$IE\,e^{-\alpha\tilde{\tau}} = \exp\left\{x\theta - x\sqrt{2\alpha + \theta^2}\right\}, \quad \alpha > 0, \; x > 0,$$

(1.137)

and the property

$$IP\left[\tilde{\tau} < \infty\right] = \begin{cases} 1 & \text{if } \theta \geq 0 \\ e^{2\theta x} & \text{if } \theta < 0 \end{cases}$$

(1.138)

For upper barriers $B > S_0$ we can now rewrite the first passage time τ_B as

$$\tau_B = \inf\{t \geq 0 : S_t = B\}$$
$$= \inf\left\{t \geq 0 : W_t + \theta_- t = \frac{1}{\sigma}\ln\left(\frac{B}{S_0}\right)\right\}.$$

(1.139)

The density of τ_B is hence

$$IP\left[\tilde{\tau}_B \in dt\right] = \frac{\frac{1}{\sigma}\ln\left(\frac{B}{S_0}\right)}{t\sqrt{2\pi t}} \exp\left\{-\frac{\left(\frac{1}{\sigma}\ln\left(\frac{B}{S_0}\right) - \theta_- t\right)^2}{2t}\right\}, \quad t > 0.$$

(1.140)

Derivation of the value function

Using the density (1.140) the value of the paid-at-end ($\omega = 1$) upper rebate ($\eta = -1$) option can be written as the the following integral.

$$v(T, S_0) = Re^{-r_d T}\,IE\left[I\!I_{\{\tau_B \leq T\}}\right]$$
$$= Re^{-r_d T}\int_0^T \frac{\frac{1}{\sigma}\ln\left(\frac{B}{S_0}\right)}{t\sqrt{2\pi t}} \exp\left\{-\frac{\left(\frac{1}{\sigma}\ln\left(\frac{B}{S_0}\right) - \theta_- t\right)^2}{2t}\right\} dt$$

(1.141)

To evaluate this integral, we introduce the notation

$$e_{\pm}(t) \overset{\Delta}{=} \frac{\pm\ln\frac{S_0}{B} - \sigma\theta_- t}{\sigma\sqrt{t}}$$

(1.142)

and list the properties

$$e_-(t) - e_+(t) = \frac{2}{\sqrt{t}}\frac{1}{\sigma}\ln\left(\frac{B}{S_0}\right),$$

(1.143)

$$n(e_+(t)) = \left(\frac{B}{S_0}\right)^{-\frac{2\theta_-}{\sigma}} n(e_-(t)),$$

(1.144)

$$\frac{\partial e_{\pm}(t)}{\partial t} = \frac{e_{\mp}(t)}{2t}.$$

(1.145)

We evaluate the integral in (1.141) by rewriting the integrand in such a way that the coefficients of the exponentials are the inner derivatives of the exponentials using properties (1.143), (1.144) and (1.145).

$$\int_0^T \frac{\frac{1}{\sigma} \ln\left(\frac{B}{S_0}\right)}{t\sqrt{2\pi t}} \exp\left\{ -\frac{\left(\frac{1}{\sigma}\ln\left(\frac{B}{S_0}\right) - \theta_- t\right)^2}{2t} \right\} dt$$

$$= \frac{1}{\sigma} \ln\left(\frac{B}{S_0}\right) \int_0^T \frac{1}{t^{(3/2)}} n(e_-(t))\, dt$$

$$= \int_0^T \frac{1}{2t} n(e_-(t))[e_-(t) - e_+(t)]\, dt$$

$$= -\int_0^T n(e_-(t))\frac{e_+(t)}{2t} + \left(\frac{B}{S_0}\right)^{\frac{2\theta_-}{\sigma}} n(e_+(t))\frac{e_-(t)}{2t}\, dt$$

$$= \left(\frac{B}{S_0}\right)^{\frac{2\theta_-}{\sigma}} \mathcal{N}(e_+(T)) + \mathcal{N}(-e_-(T)). \tag{1.146}$$

The computation for lower barriers ($\eta = 1$) is similar.

Quotation conventions and bid-ask spreads

If the payoff is at maturity, the undiscounted value of the one-touch is the touch probability under the risk-neutral measure. The market standard is to quote the price of a one-touch in percent of the payoff, a number between 0 and 100 %. The price of a one-touch depends on the theoretical value (TV) of the above formula, the overhedge (explained in Section 3.1) and the bid-ask spread. The spread in turn depends on the currency pair and the client. For interbank trading spreads are usually between 2 % and 4 % for liquid currency pairs, see Section 3.2 for details.

Two-touch

A two-touch pays one unit of currency (either foreign or domestic) if the underlying exchange rate hits both an upper and a lower barrier during its lifetime. This can be structured using basic touch options in the following way. The long two-touch with barriers L and H is equivalent to

1. a long single one-touch with lower barrier L,
2. a long single one-touch with upper barrier H,
3. a short double one-touch with barriers L and H.

This is easily verified by looking at the possible cases.

If the order of touching L and H matters, then the above hedge no longer works, but we have a new product, which can be valued, e.g., using a finite-difference grid or Monte Carlo Simulation.

Double-no-touch

The payoff

$$1\!\!1_{\{L \le \min_{[0,T]} S_t < \max_{[0,T]} S_t \le H\}} \tag{1.147}$$

of a double-no-touch is in units of domestic currency and is paid at maturity T. The lower barrier is denoted by L, the higher barrier by H.

Derivation of the value function

To compute the expectation, let us introduce the stopping time

$$\tau \stackrel{\triangle}{=} \min \{\inf \{t \in [0, T] | S_t = L \text{ or } S_t = H\}, T\} \tag{1.148}$$

and the notation

$$\tilde{\theta}_\pm \stackrel{\triangle}{=} \frac{r_d - r_f \pm \frac{1}{2}\sigma^2}{\sigma} \tag{1.149}$$

$$\tilde{h} \stackrel{\triangle}{=} \frac{1}{\sigma} \ln \frac{H}{S_t} \tag{1.150}$$

$$\tilde{l} \stackrel{\triangle}{=} \frac{1}{\sigma} \ln \frac{L}{S_t} \tag{1.151}$$

$$\theta_\pm \stackrel{\triangle}{=} \tilde{\theta}_\pm \sqrt{T - t} \tag{1.152}$$

$$h \stackrel{\triangle}{=} \tilde{h}/\sqrt{T - t} \tag{1.153}$$

$$l \stackrel{\triangle}{=} \tilde{l}/\sqrt{T - t} \tag{1.154}$$

$$y_\pm \stackrel{\triangle}{=} y_\pm(j) = 2j(h - l) - \theta_\pm \tag{1.155}$$

$$n_T(x) \stackrel{\triangle}{=} \frac{1}{\sqrt{2\pi T}} \exp \left(-\frac{x^2}{2T} \right) \tag{1.156}$$

$$n(x) \stackrel{\triangle}{=} \frac{1}{\sqrt{2\pi}} e^{-\frac{1}{2}x^2} \tag{1.157}$$

$$\mathcal{N}(x) \stackrel{\triangle}{=} \int_{-\infty}^{x} n(t) \, dt. \tag{1.158}$$

On $[t, \tau]$, the value of the double-no-touch is

$$v(t) = I\!E^t \left[e^{-r_d(T-t)} I\!I_{\{L \leq \min_{[0,T]} S_t < \max_{[0,T]} S_t \leq H\}} \right], \tag{1.159}$$

on $[\tau, T]$,

$$v(t) = e^{-r_d(T-t)} I\!I_{\{L \leq \min_{[0,T]} S_t < \max_{[0,T]} S_t \leq H\}}. \tag{1.160}$$

The joint distribution of the maximum and the minimum of a Brownian motion can be taken from [20] and is given by

$$I\!P \left[\tilde{l} \leq \min_{[0,T]} W_t < \max_{[0,T]} W_t \leq \tilde{h} \right] = \int_{\tilde{l}}^{\tilde{h}} k_T(x) \, dx \tag{1.161}$$

with

$$k_T(x) = \sum_{j=-\infty}^{\infty} \left[n_T(x + 2j(\tilde{h} - \tilde{l})) - n_T(x - 2\tilde{h} + 2j(\tilde{h} - \tilde{l})) \right]. \tag{1.162}$$

Hence the joint density of the maximum and the minimum of a Brownian motion with drift $\tilde{\theta}$, $W_t^{\tilde{\theta}} \triangleq W_t + \tilde{\theta}t$, is given by

$$k_T^{\tilde{\theta}}(x) = k_T(x) \exp\left\{\tilde{\theta}x - \frac{1}{2}\tilde{\theta}^2 T\right\}. \tag{1.163}$$

We obtain for the value of the double-no-touch on $[t, \tau]$

$$v(t) = e^{-r_d(T-t)} \, I\!E \, I\!I_{\{L \leq \min_{[0,T]} S_t < \max_{[0,T]} S_t \leq H\}}$$
$$= e^{-r_d(T-t)} \, I\!E \, I\!I_{\{\tilde{l} \leq \min_{[0,T]} W_t^{\tilde{\theta}_-} < \max_{[0,T]} W_t^{\tilde{\theta}_-} \leq \tilde{h}\}}$$
$$= e^{-r_d(T-t)} \int_{\tilde{l}}^{\tilde{h}} k_{(T-t)}^{\tilde{\theta}_-}(x)dx \tag{1.164}$$
$$= e^{-r_d(T-t)} \tag{1.165}$$
$$\cdot \sum_{j=-\infty}^{\infty} \left[e^{-2j\theta_-(h-l)} \{\mathcal{N}(h + y_-) - \mathcal{N}(l + y_-)\} \right.$$
$$\left. - e^{-2j\theta_-(h-l)+2\theta_-h} \{\mathcal{N}(h - 2h + y_-) - \mathcal{N}(l - 2h + y_-)\} \right]$$

and on $[\tau, T]$

$$v(t) = e^{-r_d(T-t)} I\!I_{\{L \leq \min_{[0,T]} S_t < \max_{[0,T]} S_t \leq H\}}. \tag{1.166}$$

Of course, the value of the double-one-touch on $[t, \tau]$ is given by

$$e^{-r_d(T-t)} - v(t). \tag{1.167}$$

Greeks

We take the space to list some of the sensitivity parameters I have been frequently asked about.

Vega

$$v_\sigma(t) = \frac{e^{-r_d(T-t)}}{\sigma} \cdot \sum_{j=-\infty}^{\infty}$$
$$\left\{ e^{-2j\theta_-(h-l)} \left[2j(h-l)(\theta_+ + \theta_-)\{\mathcal{N}(h + y_-) - \mathcal{N}(l + y_-)\} \right. \right.$$
$$\left. + n(h + y_-)(-h - y_+) - n(l + y_-)(-l - y_+) \right]$$
$$- e^{-2j\theta_-(h-l)+2\theta_-h} \left[2(\theta_+ + \theta_-)(j(h-l) - h)\{\mathcal{N}(-h + y_-) - \mathcal{N}(l - 2h + y_-)\} \right.$$
$$\left. \left. + n(-h + y_-)(h - y_+) - n(l - 2h + y_-)(-l + 2h - y_+) \right] \right\}$$

$$\tag{1.168}$$

Vanna

$$v_{\sigma S_t}(t) = \frac{e^{-r_d(T-t)}}{S_t\sigma^2\sqrt{T-t}}$$

$$\cdot \sum_{j=-\infty}^{\infty} \left\{ e^{-2j\theta_-(h-l)}(T_1-T_2) - e^{-2j\theta_-(h-l)+2\theta_-h}(T_3+T_4-T_5) \right\} \quad (1.169)$$

$$T_1 = n(h+y_-)\{1 - 2j(h-l)(\theta_+ +\theta_-) - (h+y_-)(h+y_+)\} \quad (1.170)$$

$$T_2 = n(l+y_-)\{1 - 2j(h-l)(\theta_+ +\theta_-) - (l+y_-)(l+y_+)\} \quad (1.171)$$

$$T_3 = 2(\theta_+ +\theta_-)[-2\theta_- j(h-l) + 2\theta_- h + 1]\{\mathcal{N}(-h+y_-)$$
$$-\mathcal{N}(l-2h+y-)\} \quad (1.172)$$

$$T_4 = n(-h+y_-)\{-2\theta_-(h-y_+) + 2(\theta_+ +\theta_-)(j(h-l)-h)$$
$$+(h-y_-)(h-y_+) - 1\} \quad (1.173)$$

$$T_5 = n(l-2h+y_-)\cdot$$
$$\{-2\theta_-(-l+2h-y_+) + 2(\theta_+ +\theta_-)(j(h-l)-h)$$
$$+(-l+2h-y_-)(-l+2h-y_+) - 1\} \quad (1.174)$$

Volga

$$v_{\sigma\sigma}(t) = \frac{e^{-r_d(T-t)}}{\sigma^2} \cdot \sum_{j=-\infty}^{\infty} \left\{ e^{-2j\theta_-(h-l)}(T_1+T_2) - e^{-2j\theta_-(h-l)+2\theta_-h}(T_3+T_4) \right\} \quad (1.175)$$

$$T_1 = (2j(\theta_+ +\theta_-)(h-l) - 3)\{2j(h-l)(\theta_+ +\theta_-)[\mathcal{N}(h+y_-) - \mathcal{N}(l+y_-)]\}$$
$$+(4j(\theta_+ +\theta_-)(h-l) - 1)[n(h+y_-)(-h-y_+)$$
$$-n(l+y_-)(-l-y_+)] \quad (1.176)$$

$$T_2 = n(h+y_-)(h+y_-)\left[1-(h+y_+)^2\right] - n(l+y_-)(l+y_-)$$
$$\left[1-(l+y_+)^2\right] \quad (1.177)$$

$$T_3 = (2(\theta_+ +\theta_-)(j(h-l)-h) - 3)\{2(\theta_+ +\theta_-)(j(h-l)-h)[\mathcal{N}(-h+y_-)]\}$$
$$-\mathcal{N}(l-2h+y-)]\} + (4(\theta_+ +\theta_-)(j(h-l)-h) - 1)[n(-h+y_-)(h-y_+)$$
$$-n(l-2h+y_-)(-l+2h-y_+)] \quad (1.178)$$

$$T_4 = n(-h+y_-)(h-y_-)\left[(h-y_+)^2 - 1\right]$$
$$-n(l-2h+y_-)(-l+2h-y_-)\left[(-l+2h-y_+)^2 - 1\right] \quad (1.179)$$

1.5.3 Compound and instalment

Compound options

A Compound call(put) option is the right to buy(sell) a vanilla option. It works similar to a vanilla call, but allows the holder to pay the premium of the call option spread over time. A first payment is made on inception of the trade. On the following payment day the holder of the compound call can decide to turn it into a plain vanilla call, in which case he has to pay the second part of the premium, or to terminate the contract by simply not paying any more.

Advantages

- Full protection against stronger EUR/weaker USD
- Maximum loss is the premium paid
- Initial premium required is less than in the vanilla call
- Easy termination process, specially useful if future cash flows are uncertain

Disadvantages

- Premium required as compared to a zero cost outright forward
- More expensive than the vanilla call

Example
A company wants to hedge receivables from an export transaction in USD due in 12 months time. It expects a stronger EUR/weaker USD. The company wishes to be able to buy EUR at a lower spot rate if the EUR becomes weaker on the one hand, but on the other hand be fully protected against a stronger EUR. The future income in USD is yet uncertain but will be under review at the end of the next half year.

In this case a possible form of protection that the company can use is to buy a EUR Compound call option with 2 equal semiannual premium payments as for example illustrated in Table 1.19.

The company pays 23,000 USD on the trade date. After a half year, the company has the right to buy a plain vanilla call. To do this the company must pay another 23,000 USD.

Of course, besides not paying the premium, another way to terminate the contract is always to sell it in the market or to the seller. So if the option is not needed, but deep in the money, the company can take profit from paying the premium to turn the compound into a plain vanilla call and then selling it.

If the EUR-USD exchange rate is above the strike at maturity, then the company can buy EUR at maturity at a rate of 1.1500.

If the EUR-USD exchange rate is below the strike at maturity the option expires worthless. However, the company would benefit from being able to buy EUR at a lower rate in the market.

Variations

Settlement As vanilla options compound options can be settled in the following two ways:

- Delivery settlement: Both parties deliver the cash flows.
- Cash settlement: the option seller pays cash to the buyer.

Table 1.19   Example of a Compound Call

Spot reference	1.1500 EUR-USD
Maturity	1 year
Notional	USD 1,000,000
Company buys	EUR call USD put strike 1.1500
Premium per half year of the Compound	USD 23,000.00
Premium of the vanilla call	USD 40,000.00

Distribution of payments The payments don't have to be equal. However, the rule is that the more premium is paid later, the higher the total premium. The cheapest distribution of payments is to pay the entire premium in the beginning, which corresponds to a plain vanilla call.

Exercise style Both the mother and the daughter of the compound option can be European and American style. The market default is European style.

Compound strategies One can think of a compound option on any structure, as for instance a compound put on a knock-out call or a compound call on a double shark forward.

Forward volatility

The daughter option of the compound requires knowing the volatility for its lifetime, which starts on the exercise date T_1 of the mother option and ends on the maturity date T_2 of the daughter option. This volatility is not known at inception of the trade, so the only proxy traders can take is the forward volatility $\sigma(T_1, T_2)$ for this time interval. In the Black-Scholes model the consistency equation for the forward volatility is given by Equation (1.102).

The more realistic way to look at this unknown forward volatility is that the fairly liquid market of vanilla compound options could be taken to back out the forward volatilities since this is the only unknown. These should in turn be consistent with other forward volatility sensitive products like forward start options, window barrier options or faders.

In a market with smile the payoff of the compound option can be approximated by a linear combination of vanillas, whose market prices are known. For the payoff of the compound option itself we can take the forward volatility as in Equation (1.102) for the at-the-money value and the smile of today as a proxy. More details on this can be found, e.g. in Schilling [21]. The actual forward volatility however, is a trader's view and can only be taken from market prices.

Instalment options

This section is based on Griebsch, Kühn and Wystup, see [22].

An instalment call option works similar to a compound call, but allows the holder to pay the premium of the call option in instalments spread over time. A first payment is made at inception of the trade. On the following payment days the holder of the instalment call can decide to prolong the contract, in which case he has to pay the second instalment of the premium, or to terminate the contract by simply not paying any more. After the last instalment payment the contract turns into a plain vanilla call. We illustrate two scenarios in Figure 1.27.

Example
A company wants to hedge receivables from an export transaction in USD due in 12 months time. It expects a stronger EUR/weaker USD. The company wishes to be able to buy EUR at a lower spot rate if the EUR becomes weaker on the one hand, but on the other hand be fully protected against a stronger EUR. The future income in USD is yet uncertain but will be under review at the end of each quarter.

In this case a possible form of protection that the company can use is to buy a EUR instalment call option with 4 equal quarterly premium payments as for example illustrated in Table 1.20.

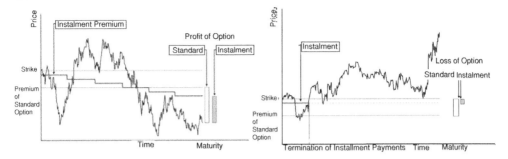

Figure 1.27   Comparison of two scenarios of an instalment option
The left hand side shows a continuation of all instalment payments until expiration. The right hand side shows a scenario where the instalment option is terminated after the first decision date.

The company pays 12,500 USD on the trade date. After one quarter, the company has the right to prolong the instalment contract. To do this the company must pay another 12,500 USD. After 6 months, the company has the right to prolong the contract and must pay 12,500 USD in order to do so. After 9 months the same decision has to be taken. If at one of these three decision days the company does not pay, then the contract terminates. If all premium payments are made, then the contract turns into a plain vanilla EUR call.

Of course, besides not paying the premium, another way to terminate the contract is always to resell it in the market. So if the option is not needed, but deep in the money, the company can take profit from paying the premium to prolong the contract and then selling it.

If the EUR-USD exchange rate is above the strike at maturity, then the company can buy EUR at maturity with a rate of 1.1500.

If the EUR-USD exchange rate is below the strike at maturity the option expires worthless. However, the company would benefit from being able to buy EUR at a lower rate in the market.

Compound options can be viewed as a special case of Instalment options, and the possible variations of compound options apply analogously to instalment options.

Reasons for trading compound and instalment options

We observe that compound and instalment options are always more expensive than buying a vanilla, sometimes substantially more expensive. So why are people buying them? The number one reason is an *uncertainty* about a future cash-flow in a foreign currency. If the cash-flow is certain, then buying a vanilla is, in principle, the better deal. An exception may be the situation in which a treasurer has a budget constraint, i.e. limited funds to spend for foreign exchange risk. With an instalment he can then split the premium over time. The main issue is however, if

Table 1.20   Example of an Instalment Call

Spot reference	1.1500 EUR-USD
Maturity	1year
Notional	USD 1,000,000
Company buys	EUR call USD put strike 1.1500
Premium per quarter of the Instalment	USD 12,500.00
Premium of the vanilla call	USD 40,000.00

a treasurer has to deal with an uncertain cash-flow, and buys a vanilla instead of an instalment, and then is faced with a far out of the money vanilla at time T_1, then selling the vanilla does not give him as much as the savings between the vanilla and the sum of the instalment payments.

The theory of instalment options

This book is not primarily on valuation of options. However, we do want to give some insight into selected topics that come up very often and are of particular relevance to foreign exchange options and have not been published in books so far. We will now take a look at the valuation, the implementation of instalment options and the limiting case of a continuous flow of premium payments.

Valuation in the Black-Scholes model

The intention of this section is to obtain a closed-form formula for the n-variate instalment option in the Black-Scholes model. For the cases $n = 1$ and $n = 2$ the Black-Scholes formula and Geske's compound option formula (see [23]) are already well known.

We consider an exchange rate process S_t modeled by a geometric Brownian motion,

$$S_{t_2} = S_{t_1} \exp((r_d - r_f - \sigma^2/2)\Delta t + \sigma\sqrt{\Delta t}Z) \quad \text{for } 0 \leq t_1 \leq t_2 \leq T, \quad (1.180)$$

where $\Delta t = t_2 - t_1$ and Z is a standard normal random variable independent of the past of S_t up to time t_1.

Let $t_0 = 0$ be the instalment option inception date and $t_1, t_2, \ldots, t_n = T$ a schedule of decision dates in the contract on which the option holder has to pay the premiums $k_1, k_2, \ldots, k_{n-1}$ to keep the option alive. To compute the price of the instalment option, which is the upfront payment V_0 at t_0 to enter the contract, we begin with the option payoff at maturity T

$$V_n(s) \stackrel{\Delta}{=} [\phi_n(s - k_n)]^+ \stackrel{\Delta}{=} \max[\phi_n(s - k_n), 0],$$

where $s = S_T$ is the price of the underlying asset at T and as usual $\phi_n = +1$ for a call option, $\phi_n = -1$ for a put option.

At time t_i the option holder can either terminate the contract or pay k_i to continue. Therefore by the risk-neutral pricing theory, the holding value is

$$e^{-r_d(t_{i+1}-t_i)} E[V_{i+1}(S_{t_{i+1}}) \mid S_{t_i} = s], \text{ for } i = 0, \ldots, n-1, \quad (1.181)$$

where

$$V_i(s) = \begin{cases} \left[e^{-r_d(t_{i+1}-t_i)} E[V_{i+1}(S_{t_{i+1}}) \mid S_{t_i} = s] - k_i\right]^+ & \text{for } i = 1, \ldots, n-1 \\ V_n(s) & \text{for } i = n \end{cases}. \quad (1.182)$$

Then the unique arbitrage-free value of the initial premium is

$$P \stackrel{\Delta}{=} V_0(s) = e^{-r_d(t_1-t_0)} E[V_1(S_{t_1}) \mid S_{t_0} = s]. \quad (1.183)$$

Figure 1.28 illustrates this context.

One way of pricing this instalment option is to evaluate the nested expectations through multiple numerical integration of the payoff functions via backward iteration. Alternatively, one can derive a solution in closed form in terms of the n-variate cumulative normal.

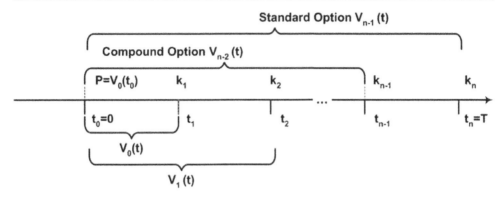

Figure 1.28   Lifetime of the Options V_i

The Curnow and Dunnett integral reduction technique

Denote the n dimensional multivariate normal integral with upper limits $h_1, \ldots, h_n$ and correlation matrix $R_n \overset{\Delta}{=} (\rho_{ij})_{i,j=1,\ldots,n}$ by $N_n(h_1, \ldots, h_n; R_n)$, and the univariate normal density function by $n(\cdot)$. Let the correlation matrix be non-singular and $\rho_{11} = 1$.

Under these conditions Curnow and Dunnett [24] derived the following reduction formula for multivariate normal integrals

$$N_n(h_1, \cdots, h_n; R_n) = \int_{-\infty}^{h_1} N_{n-1} \left(\frac{h_2 - \rho_{21} y}{(1 - \rho_{21}^2)^{1/2}}, \cdots, \frac{h_n - \rho_{n1} y}{(1 - \rho_{n1}^2)^{1/2}}; R_{n-1}^* \right) n(y) dy,$$

$$R_{n-1}^* \overset{\Delta}{=} (\rho_{ij}^*)_{i,j=2,\ldots,n},$$

$$\rho_{ij}^* \overset{\Delta}{=} \frac{\rho_{ij} - \rho_{i1}\rho_{j1}}{(1 - \rho_{i1}^2)^{1/2}(1 - \rho_{j1}^2)^{1/2}}. \tag{1.184}$$

A closed form solution for the value of an instalment option

Heuristically, the formula which is given in the theorem below has the structure of the Black-Scholes formula in higher dimensions, namely $S_0 N_n(\cdot) - k_n N_n(\cdot)$ minus the later premium payments $k_i N_i(\cdot)$ $(i = 1, \ldots, n-1)$. This structure is a result of the integration of the vanilla option payoff, which is again integrated minus the next instalment, which in turn is integrated with the following instalment and so forth. By this iteration the vanilla payoff is integrated with respect to the normal density function n times and the i-payment is integrated i times for $i = 1, \ldots, n-1$.

The correlation coefficients ρ_{ij} of these normal distribution functions contained in the formula arise from the overlapping increments of the Brownian motion, which models the price process of the underlying S_t at the particular exercise dates t_i and t_j.

Theorem 1.5.1   *Let $\vec{k} = (k_1, \ldots, k_n)$ be the strike price vector, $\vec{t} = (t_1, \ldots, t_n)$ the vector of the exercise dates of an n-variate instalment option and $\vec{\phi} = (\phi_1, \ldots, \phi_n)$ the vector of the put/call- indicators of these n options.*

The value function of an n-variate instalment option is given by

$$V_n(S_0, M, \vec{k}, \vec{t}, \vec{\phi}) = e^{-r_f t_n} S_0 \phi_1 \cdot \ldots \cdot \phi_n$$

$$\times N_n \left[\frac{\ln \frac{S_0}{S_1^*} + \mu^{(+)} t_1}{\sigma \sqrt{t_1}}, \frac{\ln \frac{S_0}{S_2^*} + \mu^{(+)} t_2}{\sigma \sqrt{t_2}}, \ldots, \frac{\ln \frac{S_0}{S_n^*} + \mu^{(+)} t_n}{\sigma \sqrt{t_n}}; R_n \right]$$

$$- e^{-r_d t_n} k_n \phi_1 \cdot \ldots \cdot \phi_n$$

$$\times N_n \left[\frac{\ln \frac{S_0}{S_1^*} + \mu^{(-)} t_1}{\sigma \sqrt{t_1}}, \frac{\ln \frac{S_0}{S_2^*} + \mu^{(-)} t_2}{\sigma \sqrt{t_2}}, \ldots, \frac{\ln \frac{S_0}{S_n^*} + \mu^{(-)} t_n}{\sigma \sqrt{t_n}}; R_n \right]$$

$$- e^{-r_d t_{n-1}} k_{n-1} \phi_1 \cdot \ldots \cdot \phi_{n-1}$$

$$\times N_{n-1} \left[\frac{\ln \frac{S_0}{S_1^*} + \mu^{(-)} t_1}{\sigma \sqrt{t_1}}, \frac{\ln \frac{S_0}{S_2^*} + \mu^{(-)} t_2}{\sigma \sqrt{t_2}}, \ldots, \frac{\ln \frac{S_0}{S_{n-1}^*} + \mu^{(-)} t_{n-1}}{\sigma \sqrt{t_{n-1}}}; R_{n-1} \right]$$

$$\vdots$$

$$- e^{-r_d t_2} k_2 \phi_1 \phi_2 N_2 \left[\frac{\ln \frac{S_0}{S_1^*} + \mu^{(-)} t_1}{\sigma \sqrt{t_1}}, \frac{\ln \frac{S_0}{S_2^*} + \mu^{(-)} t_2}{\sigma \sqrt{t_2}}; \rho_{12} \right]$$

$$- e^{-r_d t_1} k_1 \phi_1 N \left[\frac{\ln \frac{S_0}{S_1^*} + \mu^{(-)} t_1}{\sigma \sqrt{t_1}} \right], \tag{1.185}$$

where S_i^* $(i = 1, \ldots, n)$ is to be determined as the spot price S_t for which the payoff of the corresponding i-instalment option $(i = 1, \ldots, n)$ is equal to zero and $\mu^{(\pm)}$ is defined as $r_d - r_f \pm \frac{1}{2}\sigma^2$.

The correlation coefficients in R_i of the i-variate normal distribution function can be expressed through the exercise dates t_i,

$$\rho_{ij} = \sqrt{t_i/t_j} \text{ for } i, j = 1, \ldots, n \text{ and } i < j. \tag{1.186}$$

The proof is established with Equation (1.184). Formula (1.185) has been independently derived by Thomassen and Wouve in [25].

Valuation of instalment options with the algorithm of Ben-Ameur, Breton and François

The value of an instalment option at time t is given by the snell envelope of the discounted payoff processes, which is calculated with the dynamic programming method used by the algorithm of Ben-Ameur, Breton and François below. Their original work in [26] deals with instalment options with an additional exercise right at each instalment date. This means that at each decision date the holder can either exercise, terminate or continue.

We examine this algorithm now for the special case of zero value in case it is exercised at $t_1, \ldots, t_{n-1}$. The difference between the above mentioned types of instalment options consists in the (non-)existence of an exercise right at the instalment dates, but this does not change the algorithm in principle.

Model description

The algorithm developed by Ben-Ameur, Breton and François approximates the value of the instalment option in the Black-Scholes Model, which is the premium P paid at time t_0 to enter the contract.

The exercise value of an instalment option at maturity t_n is given by $V_n(s) \triangleq \max[0, \phi_n(s - k_n)]$ and zero at earlier times. The value of a vanilla option at time t_{n-1} is denoted by $V_{n-1}(s) = e^{-r_d \Delta t} I\!E[V_n(s) \mid S_{t_{n-1}} = s]$. At an arbitrary time t_i the holding value is determined as

$$V_i^h(s) = e^{-r_d \Delta t} I\!E[V_{i+1}(S_{t_{i+1}}) \mid S_{t_i} = s] \quad \text{for } i = 0, \ldots, n-1, \qquad (1.187)$$

where

$$V_i(s) = \begin{cases} V_0^h(s) & \text{for } i = 0, \\ \max[0, V_i^h(s) - k_i] & \text{for } i = 1, \ldots, n-1, \\ V_n^e(s) & \text{for } i = n. \end{cases} \qquad \text{(DP)} \qquad (1.188)$$

The function $V_i^h(s) - k_i$ is called net holding value at t_i, for $i = 1, \ldots, n-1$, which is shown in Figure 1.29.

The option value is the holding value or the exercise value, whichever is greater. The value function V_i, for $i = 0, \ldots, n-1$, is unknown and has to be approximated. Ben-Ameur, Breton and François propose an approximation method, which solves the above dynamic programming (DP)-equation (1.188) in a closed form for all s and i.

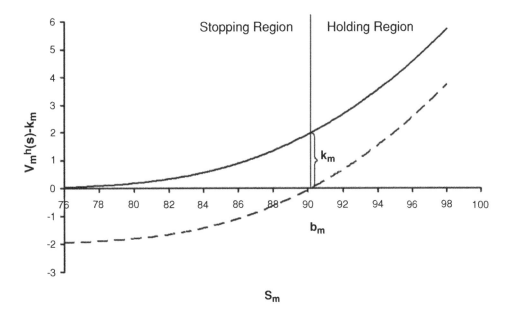

Figure 1.29   The holding value shortly before t_3 for an instalment option with 4 rates is shown by the solid line. The positive slope of this function is less than 1 and the function is continuous and convex. The net holding value of an instalment call option $V_m^h(s) - k_m$ for ($s > 0$) and a decision time m is presented by the dashed line. This curve intersects the x-axis in the point, where it divides the stopping region and the holding region. The value function is zero in the stopping region $(0, b_i)$ and equal to the net holding value in the holding region $[b_i, \infty)$, where b_i is a threshold for every time t_i, which depends on the parameters of the instalment option

Valuation of instalment options with stochastic dynamic programming

The idea of the above mentioned authors is to partition the positive real axis into intervals and approximate the option value through piecewise linear interpolation. Let $a_0 = 0 < a_1 < \ldots < a_p < a_{p+1} = +\infty$ be points in $I\!R_0^+ \cup \{\infty\}$ and $(a_j, a_{j+1}]$ for $j = 0, \ldots, p$ a partition of $I\!R_0^+$ in $(p+1)$ intervals.

Given approximations $\tilde{V}_i$ of option values V_i at supporting points a_j at the i-th step (at the beginning of the algorithm, at T, this is provided through the input values), this function is piecewise linearly interpolated by

$$\hat{V}_i(s) = \sum_{i=0}^{p} (\alpha_j^i + \beta_j^i s)\mathbf{II}_{\{a_j < s \le a_{j+1}\}}, \tag{1.189}$$

where $\mathbf{II}$ is the indicator function. The local coefficients of this interpolation in step i, the y-axis intercepts α_j^i and the slopes β_j^i, are obtained by solving the following linear equations

$$\tilde{V}_i(a_j) = \hat{V}_i(a_j) \text{ for } j = 0, \ldots, p-1. \tag{1.190}$$

For $j = p$, one chooses

$$\alpha_p^i = \alpha_{p-1}^i \text{ and } \beta_p^i = \beta_{p-1}^i. \tag{1.191}$$

Now it is assumed, that $\hat{V}_{i+1}$ is known. This is a valid assumption in this context, because the values $\hat{V}_{i+1}$ are known from the previous step. The mean value (1.187) is calculated in step i through

$$
\begin{aligned}
\tilde{V}_i^h(a_k) &= e^{-r_d \Delta t} I\!E[\hat{V}_{i+1}(S_{t_{i+1}})|S_{t_i} = a_k] \\
&\overset{(1.189)}{=} e^{-r_d \Delta t} \sum_{j=0}^{p} \alpha_j^{i+1} I\!E\left[\mathbf{II}_{\{\frac{a_j}{a_k} < e^{\mu \Delta t + \sigma \sqrt{\Delta t} z} \le \frac{a_{j+1}}{a_k}\}}\right] \\
&\quad + \beta_j^{i+1} a_k I\!E\left[e^{\mu \Delta t + \sigma \sqrt{\Delta t} z} \mathbf{II}_{\{\frac{a_j}{a_k} < e^{\mu \Delta t + \sigma \sqrt{\Delta t} z} \le \frac{a_{j+1}}{a_k}\}}\right],
\end{aligned} \tag{1.192}
$$

where $\mu \overset{\Delta}{=} r_d - r_f - \sigma^2/2$ and $\tilde{V}_i^h$ denotes the approximated holding value of the instalment option. Define

$$x_{k,j} \overset{\Delta}{=} \frac{\ln\left(\frac{a_j}{a_k}\right) - \mu \Delta t}{\sigma \sqrt{\Delta t}}, \tag{1.193}$$

so for $k = 1, \ldots, p$ and $j = 0, \ldots, p$ the first mean values in Equation (1.192), namely

$$A_{k,j} \overset{\Delta}{=} I\!E\left[\mathbf{II}_{\{\frac{a_j}{a_k} < e^{\mu \Delta t + \sigma \sqrt{\Delta t} z} \le \frac{a_{j+1}}{a_k}\}}\right] \tag{1.194}$$

can be expressed as

$$(1.194) = \begin{cases} N(x_{k,1}) & \text{for } j = 0, \\ N(x_{k,j+1}) - N(x_{k,j}) & \text{for } 1 \le j \le p-1, \\ 1 - N(x_{k,p}) & \text{for } j = p, \end{cases} \tag{1.195}$$

and similarly

$$B_{k,j} \triangleq I\!E\left[a_k e^{\mu\Delta t+\sigma\sqrt{\Delta t}z}\,I\!I_{\left\{\frac{a_j}{a_k}<e^{\mu\Delta t+\sigma\sqrt{\Delta t}z}\le\frac{a_{j+1}}{a_k}\right\}}\right]$$ (1.196)

can be expressed in the following way

$$(1.196)=\begin{cases}a_k\mathcal{N}(x_{k,1}-\sigma\sqrt{\Delta t})e^{(r_d-r_f)\Delta t} & \text{for } j=0,\\ a_k[\mathcal{N}(x_{k,j+1}-\sigma\sqrt{\Delta t})-\mathcal{N}(x_{k,j}-\sigma\sqrt{\Delta t})]e^{(r_d-r_f)\Delta t} & \text{for } 1\le j\le p-1,\\ a_k[1-\mathcal{N}(x_{k,p}-\sigma\sqrt{\Delta t})]e^{(r_d-r_f)\Delta t} & \text{for } j=p,\end{cases}$$ (1.197)

where $n(z)\triangleq\frac{1}{\sqrt{2\pi}}e^{-\frac{z^2}{2}}$ and $\mathcal{N}$ denotes the cumulative normal distribution function.

In the simplifying notation (1.195) and (1.197) the points a_i ($i=1,\dots,p$) can be understood as the quantiles of the log-normal distribution. These are not chosen directly, but are calculated as the quantiles of (e.g. equidistant) probabilities of the log-normal distribution. Thereby the supporting points lie closer together, in areas, where the modification rate of the distribution function is great. The number a_k in Equation (1.193) is the given exchange rate at time t_i and therefore constant. In the implementation it requires an efficient method to calculate the inverse normal distribution function. One possibility is to use the Cody-Algorithm taken from [27].

An algorithm in pseudo code

For a better understanding the described procedure (1.5.3) is sketched in form of an algorithm in this section. The algorithm works according to the dynamic programming principle backwards in time, based on the values of the exercise function of the instalment option at maturity T at predetermined supporting points a_j. Through linear connection of these points an approximation of the exercise function can be obtained. The exercise function at maturity is the payoff function of the vanilla option, which is constant up to the strike price K and in the region behind (i.e. $\ge K$) it is linear. The linear approximation at maturity T is therefore exact, except on the interval $K\in(a_l,a_{l+1})$, in case K does not correspond to one of these supporting points. For this reason the holding value of this linear approximation is calculated by the means of $A_{k,j}$ and $B_{k,j}$ from above. The transition parameters $A_{k,i}$ and $B_{k,i}$ can be calculated before the first iteration, because only values, which are known in the beginning, are required. The advantage of this approach is that the holding value needs only to be calculated at the supporting points a_j and because of linearity, the function values for all s are obtained. The values of the holding value at a_j are used again as approximations of the exercise values at time t_{n-1} and it is proceeded like in the beginning. The output of the algorithm is the value of the instalment option at time t_0.

A description in pseudo code

First the a_k are generated as quantiles of the distribution of the price at maturity of the exchange rate S_T and can be for example approximated by the Cody-Algorithm.

1. Calculate $q_1,\dots,q_p$-quantiles of the standard normal distribution via the inverse distribution function.

2. Calculate $a_1, \ldots, a_p$-quantiles of the log-normal distribution with mean $\log S_0 - \mu T$ and variance $\sigma \sqrt{T}$ by

$$\exp(q_i \sigma \sqrt{T} + \log S_0 + \mu T) = a_i.$$

In pseudo code the implementation of the theoretical consideration of Section 1.5.3 can be worked out in the following way. The principle of the backward induction is realized as a for-loop that counts backwards from $n - 1$ to 0.

1. Calculate $\hat{V}_n(s)$ for all s, using (1.189), i.e. calculate all α_i^n, β_i^n for $i = 0, \ldots, p$
2. For $j = n$ to 1
   a. Calculate $\tilde{V}_{j-1}^h(a_k)$ for a_k ($k = 1, \ldots, p$) in closed form using (1.192).
   b. Calculate $\tilde{V}_{j-1}(a_k)$ for $k = 1, \ldots, p$ using (DP) with $\tilde{V}_{j-1}^h(a_k)$ for $V_{j-1}^h(a_k)$.
   c. Calculate $\hat{V}_{j-1}(s)$ for all $s > 0$ using (1.189), i.e. calculate all α_i^{j-1}, β_i^{j-1} for $i = 1, \ldots, k$. Unless $j - 1$ is already equal to zero, calculate $\hat{V}_{j-1}(s)$ for $s = S_0$ and break the algorithm.
   d. Substitute $j \leftarrow j - 1$.

Repeat these steps until $\hat{V}_0(S_0)$ is calculated, which is the value of the instalment option at time 0.

This algorithm works with equidistant instalment dates, constant volatility and constant interest rates. Constant volatility and interest rates are assumptions of the applied Black-Scholes Model, but the algorithm would be extendable for piecewise constant volatility- and interest rate as functions of time, with jumps at the instalment dates. The interval length Δt in the calculation can be replaced in every period by arbitrary $t_{i+1} - t_i$. Furthermore the computational time could be decreased by omitting smaller supporting points in the calculation as soon as one of them generates a zero value in the maximum function.

Instalment options with a continuous payment plan

Let $g = (g_t)_{t \in [0,T]}$ be the stochastic process describing the discounted net payoff of an instalment option expressed as multiples of the domestic currency. If the holder stops paying the premium at time t, the difference between the option payoff and premium payments (all discounted to time 0) amounts to

$$g(t) = \begin{cases} e^{-r_d T}(S_T - K)^+ \mathbf{1}_{(t=T)} - \frac{p}{r_d}(1 - e^{-r_d t}) & \text{if } r_d \neq 0 \\ (S_T - K)^+ \mathbf{1}_{(t=T)} - pt & \text{if } r_d = 0 \end{cases}, \qquad (1.198)$$

where K is the strike. Given the premium rate p, there is a unique no-arbitrage premium P_0 to be paid at time 0 (supplementary to the rate p) given by

$$P_0 = \sup_{\tau \in \mathcal{T}_{0,T}} \mathbb{E}_Q(g_\tau). \qquad (1.199)$$

Ideally, p is chosen as the *minimal* rate such that

$$P_0 = 0. \qquad (1.200)$$

Note that P_0 from (1.199) can never become negative as it is always possible to stop payments immediately. Thus, besides (1.200), we need a minimality assumption to obtain a unique rate.

We want to compare the instalment option with the American contingent claim $f = (f_t)_{t \in [0,T]}$ given by

$$f_t = e^{-r_d t}(K_t - C_E(T - t, S_t))^+, \quad t \in [0, T], \tag{1.201}$$

where $K_t = \frac{p}{r_d}\left(1 - e^{-r_d(T-t)}\right)$ for $r_d \neq 0$ and $K_t = p(T - t)$ when $r_d = 0$. C_E is the value of a standard European call. Equation (1.201) represents the payoff of an American put on a European call where the variable strike K_t of the put equals the part of the instalments *not* to be paid if the holder decides to terminate the contract at time t. Define by $\tilde{f} = (\tilde{f}_t)_{t \in [0,T]}$ a similar American contingent claim with

$$\tilde{f}(t) = e^{-r_d t}\left[(K_t - C_E(T - t, S_t))^+ + C_E(T - t, S_t)\right], \quad t \in [0, T]. \tag{1.202}$$

As the process $t \mapsto e^{-r_d t} C_E(T - t, S_t)$ is a Q-martingale we obtain that

$$\sup_{\tau \in \mathcal{T}_{0,T}} I\!E_Q(\tilde{f}_\tau) = C_E(T, s_0) + \sup_{\tau \in \mathcal{T}_{0,T}} I\!E_Q(f_\tau). \tag{1.203}$$

The following theorem has been proved in [22] using earlier results of El Karoui, Lepeltier and Millet in [28].

Theorem 1.5.2 *An instalment option is the sum of a European call plus an American put on this European call, i.e.*

$$\underbrace{P_0 + p \int_0^T e^{-r_d s} \, ds}_{\text{total premium payments}} = C_E(T, s_0) + \sup_{\tau \in \mathcal{T}_{0,T}} I\!E_Q(f_\tau)$$

1.5.4 Asian options

This section is produced in conjunction with Silvia Baumann, Marion Linck, Michael Mohr and Michael Seeberg.

Asian Options are options on the average usually of spot fixings and are very popular and common hedging instruments for corporates. Average options belong to the class of path dependent options. The Term *Asian Options* comes from their origin in the Tokyo office of Banker's Trust in 1987.[5] The payoff of an Asian Option is determined by the path taken by the underlying exchange rate over a fixed period of time. We distinguish the four cases listed in Table 1.21 and compare values of average price options with vanilla options in Figure 1.30. Variations of Asian Options refer particularly to the way the average is calculated.

Kind of average   We find geometric, arithmetic or harmonic average of prices. Harmonic averaging originates from a payoff in *domestic* currency and will be treated in Section 1.6.9.

Time interval   We need to specify the period over which the prices are taken. The end of the averaging interval can be shorter than or equal to the option's expiration date, the starting value can be any time before. In particular, after an average option is traded, the beginning of the averaging period typically lies in the past, so that parts of the values contributing to the average are already known.

---

[5] see http://www.global-derivatives.com / Options/ Asian Options.

Table 1.21   Types of Asian Options for $T_0 \leq t \leq T$, where $[T_0, T]$ denotes the time interval over which the average is taken, K denotes the strike, S_T the spot price at expiration time and A_T the average

Product name	Payoff
average price call	$(A_T - K)^+$
average price put	$(K - A_T)^+$
average strike call	$(S_T - A_T)^+$
average strike put	$(A_T - S_T)^+$

Sampling style   The market generally uses discrete sampling, like daily fixings. In the literature we often find continuous sampling.

Weighting   Different weights may be assigned to the prices to account for a non-linear, i.e. skewed, price distribution, see [29], pp. 1116–1117, and the example below under 3.

Variations   The wide range of variations covers also the possible right for early execution, Asian options with barriers.

Asian Options are applied in risk management, especially for currencies, for the following reasons.

1. Protection against rapid price movements or manipulation in thinly traded underlyings at maturity, i.e. reduction of significance of the closing price through averaging.
2. Reduction of hedging cost through
   - the lower fair price compared to regular options since an average is less volatile than single prices, and
   - to achieve a similar hedging effect with vanilla options, a chain of such options would have to be bought – an obviously more expensive strategy.

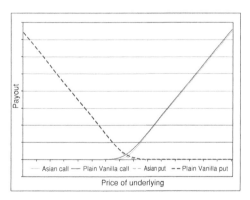
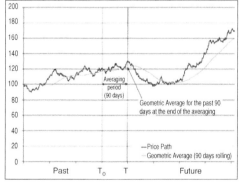

Figure 1.30   lhs: Comparing the value of average price options with vanillas, we see that average price options are cheaper. The reason is that averages are less volatile and hence less risky. rhs: Ingredients for average options: a price path, 90-days rolling price average (here: geometric), and an averaging period for an option with 90-days maturity

3. Adjustment of option payoff to payment structure of the firm
   - Average Price Options can be used to hedge a stream of (received) payments (e.g. a USD average call can be bought to hedge the ongoing EUR revenues of a US-based company). Different amounts of the payments can be reflected in flexible weights, i.e. the prices related to higher payments are assigned a higher weight than those related to smaller cash flows when calculating the average.
   - With Average Strike Options the strike price can be set at the average of the underlying price – a helpful structure in volatile or hardly predictable markets.

Valuation

The pricing approaches developed differ depending on the specific characteristics considered, e.g. averaging method, option style etc. In the following, we present the value formula for a *European Geometric Average Price Call*. Afterwards, two common approaches to evaluate Arithmetic Average Price Options are introduced. Henderson and Wojakowski prove the symmetry between Average Price Options and Average Strike Options in [30] allowing the use of the more established fixed-strike valuation methods to price *Floating Strike Asian Options*.

Geometric average options

Kemna and Vorst [31] derive a closed form solution for Geometric Average Price Options in a geometric Brownian motion model

$$dS_t = S_t[(r_d - r_f)dt + \sigma dW_t].$$
(1.204)

An extension for foreign exchange options can be found in Wystup [32]. A Geometric Average Price Call pays $(A_T - K)^+$, where A_T denotes the geometric average of the price of the underlying. In the discrete case, A_T is calculated as

$$A_T \stackrel{\Delta}{=} \sqrt[n+1]{\prod_{i=0}^{n} S_{t_i}},$$
(1.205)

in the continuous case as

$$A_T \stackrel{\Delta}{=} \exp\left\{ \frac{1}{T - T_0} \int_{T_0}^{T} \log S_t \, dt \right\}.$$
(1.206)

The random variable $\int_t^T W(u) \, du$ is normally distributed with mean zero variance

$$\Sigma^2 \stackrel{\Delta}{=} \frac{T^3}{3} + \frac{2t^3}{3} - t^2 T$$
(1.207)

for any $t \in [T_0, T]$. This can be calculated following the instructions in Shreve's lecture notes [19]. Therefore, the geometric average of a log-normally distributed random variable is log-normally distributed. In the continuous case, the distribution parameters can be derived as

$$\log A_T \sim \mathcal{N}\left[\frac{1}{2}\left(r_d - r_f - \frac{1}{2}\sigma^2\right)(T - T_0) + \log S_0; \frac{1}{3}\sigma^2(T - T_0) \right].$$
(1.208)

The interesting feature of these terms is the replacement of the geometric average by the underlying price S_0 smoothing the way to the option price determination. In the Black-Scholes model the value of the option can be computed as the expected payoff under the risk-neutral probability measure. Using the money market account $e^{-r_d(T-T_0)}$ as numeraire leads to the value of the continuously sampled geometric Asian fixed strike call,

$$C_{G-Asian} = I\!E\left[e^{-r_d(T-T_0)}(A_T - K)\mathbb{1}_{\{A_T>K\}}\right], \tag{1.209}$$

where we observe that the remaining computation works just like a vanilla. In order to derive a useful general result we need to generalize the payoff of the continuously sampled geometric Asian fixed strike option to

$$[\phi(A(-s,T) - K)]^+, \tag{1.210}$$

$$A(-s,T) \overset{\Delta}{=} \exp\left\{\frac{1}{T+s}\int_{-s}^{T} \log S(u)\,du\right\}, s \geq 0. \tag{1.211}$$

This definition includes the case where parts of the average is already known, which is important to value the option after it has been written.

With the abbreviations

- T for the expiration time (in years),
- s for the time before valuation date (in years), for which the values and average of the underlying is known,
- K for the strike of the option,
- ϕ taking the values $+1$ or -1 if the option is a call or a put respectively,
- $\alpha \overset{\Delta}{=} \frac{T}{T+s} \in [0,1]$,
- $\theta_\pm \overset{\Delta}{=} \frac{r_d-r_f}{\sigma} \pm \frac{\sigma}{2}$,
- $S_t = S_0 e^{\sigma W_t + \sigma\theta_- t}$ for the price of the underlying at time t,
- $d_\pm \overset{\Delta}{=} \frac{\ln\frac{S_0}{K}+\sigma\theta_\pm T}{\sigma\sqrt{T}}$,
- $n(t) \overset{\Delta}{=} \frac{1}{\sqrt{2\pi}}e^{-\frac{1}{2}t^2}$,
- $\mathcal{N}(x) \overset{\Delta}{=} \int_{-\infty}^{x} n(t)\,dt$,
- Vanilla$(S_0, K, \sigma, r_d, r_f, T, \phi) = \phi\left(S_0 e^{-r_f T}\mathcal{N}(\phi d_+) - K e^{-r_d T}\mathcal{N}(\phi d_-)\right)$,
- $H \overset{\Delta}{=} \exp\left\{-\frac{\alpha T}{2}\left(r_d - r_f + \frac{\sigma^2}{2}[1-\frac{2\alpha}{3}]\right)\right\}$,

the value of the continuously sampled geometric Asian fixed strike vanilla is then given by

$$\text{Asiangeo}(S_0,K,T,s,\sigma,r_d,r_f,\phi) = e^{(\alpha-1)r_d T} H \left(\frac{S_0}{A(-s,0)}\right)^{\alpha-1}$$
$$\text{Vanilla}\left(S_0, \frac{K}{H}\left(\frac{S_0}{A(-s,0)}\right)^{1-\alpha}, \frac{\alpha\sigma}{\sqrt{3}}, \alpha r_d, \alpha r_f, T, \phi\right). \tag{1.212}$$

This way a geometric Asian option with fixed strike can be viewed as a multiple of a vanilla option with the same spot and time to maturity but different parameters such as strike, volatility and interest rates. We observe in particular, that as time to maturity becomes smaller, the known part of the average becomes more prominent, α tends to zero and hence the volatility of the auxiliary vanilla option tends to zero. Moreover, the properties known for the function Vanilla carry over to the function Asiangeo. Greeks can also be derived from this relation.

Let us now consider the case, where averaging starts after T_0, i.e., the payoff is changed to

$$[\phi(A(t,T) - K)]^+, \tag{1.213}$$

$$A(t,T) \overset{\Delta}{=} \exp\left\{\frac{1}{T-t}\int_t^T \log S(u)\,du\right\}, \; t \in [0,T]. \tag{1.214}$$

Then the value becomes

$$\text{Asiangeowindow}(S_0, K, T, t, \sigma, r_d, r_f, \phi) =$$

$$H\,\text{Vanilla}\left(S_0, \frac{K}{H}, \frac{\Sigma\sigma}{(T-t)\sqrt{T}}, r_d, r_f, T, \phi\right), \tag{1.215}$$

$$H \overset{\Delta}{=} \exp\left\{-\frac{\sigma\theta_-}{2}(T-t) - \frac{\sigma^2}{2}(t - \frac{\Sigma}{T-t})\right\}. \tag{1.216}$$

Derivation of the value function

First we consider the call without history ($s = 0$). We rewrite the geometric average as

$$A(0,T) = \exp\left\{\frac{1}{T}\int_0^T \log S(u)\,du\right\}$$

$$= S_0 \exp\left\{\frac{\sigma}{2}\theta_- T + \frac{\sigma}{T}\int_0^T W(u)\,du\right\} \tag{1.217}$$

and compute the value function as

$$\text{Asiangeo}(S_0, K, T, 0, \sigma, r_d, r_f, \phi)$$

$$= e^{-r_d T}\,I\!E[(A(0,T) - K)^+]$$

$$= e^{-r_d T}\int_{-\infty}^{+\infty}\left(S_0 \exp\left\{\frac{\sigma}{2}\theta_- T + \sigma\sqrt{\frac{T}{3}}x\right\} - K\right)^+ n(x)\,dx$$

$$= S_0 e^{-r_f T} e^{-\frac{T}{2}(r_d - r_f + \frac{\sigma^2}{6})} \mathcal{N}\left(\frac{\ln\frac{S_0}{K} + \frac{\sigma}{2}\theta_- T}{\sigma\sqrt{\frac{T}{3}}} + \sigma\sqrt{\frac{T}{3}}\right)$$

$$- K e^{-r_d T}\mathcal{N}\left(\frac{\ln\frac{S_0}{K} + \frac{\sigma}{2}\theta_- T}{\sigma\sqrt{\frac{T}{3}}}\right), \tag{1.218}$$

which leads to the desired result. The analysis for the put option is similar. For $s > 0$ (real history) note that

$$A(-s,T) = A(-s,0)^{1-\alpha} A(0,T)^\alpha. \tag{1.219}$$

The first factor of this product is non-random at time 0, hence the value of a call with history is given by

$$
\begin{aligned}
& \text{Asiangeo}(S_0, K, T, s, \sigma, r_d, r_f, \phi) \qquad\qquad\qquad\qquad\qquad (1.220)\\
&= e^{-r_d T} \, I\!E[(A(-s, T) - K)^+]\\
&= e^{-r_d T} A(-s, 0)^{1-\alpha} I\!E\left[A(0, T)^\alpha - \frac{K}{A(-s, 0)^{1-\alpha}} \right)^+ \right]\\
&= e^{-r_d T} \int_{-\infty}^{+\infty} \left(S_0^\alpha \exp\left\{ \frac{\alpha\sigma}{2}\theta_- T + \alpha\sigma\sqrt{\frac{T}{3}} x \right\} - \frac{K}{A(-s, 0)^{1-\alpha}} \right)^+ n(x)\, dx.
\end{aligned}
$$

It is now an easy exercise to complete this calculation.

Arithmetic average options

Since the distribution of the arithmetic average of log-normally distributed random variables is not normal, a closed form solution for the frequently used Arithmetic Average Price Options is not immediately available. Some of the approaches to solve this valuation task are

1. Numerical approaches, e.g. Monte Carlo simulations work well, as one can take the geometric Asian option as a highly correlated control variate. Taking a PDE approach is equally fast as Večeř has shown how to reduce the valuation problem to a PDE in one dimension in [33].
2. Modifications of the geometric average approach;
3. Approximations of the density function for the arithmetic average, see [34] on p. 475.

For instance, Turnbull and Wakeman (see [35]) develop an approximation of the density function by defining an alternative distribution for the arithmetic average with moments that match the moments of the true distribution similarly as in Section 1.6.7. One can also match the cumulants up to fourth order: mean, variance, skew and kurtosis. The adjusted mean and variance are finally plugged into the general Black-Scholes formula. Lévy states in [34] that considering only the first two moments delivers acceptable results for typical ranges of volatility and simultaneously reduces the complexity of the Turnbull and Wakeman approach. Hakala and Perissé show in [3] how to include higher moments. We apply a Monte Carlo simulation of price paths to value arithmetic average price options. To improve the quality of the results, we take geometric average options with similar specifications as control variate, see [31], p. 124. For variance reduction techniques see [36], pp. 414–418. For further suggestions on the implementation of pricing models see e.g. [37], pp. 118–123. We show in Table 1.22 that the results are close to the analytical approximations provided by Turnbull and Wakeman as well as Lévy.

Sensitivity analysis

We analyse now the sensitivities of the values with respect to various input parameters and compare them with vanilla options. Throughout we will use the parameters $K = 1.2000$, $S_0 = 1.2000$, $r_d = 3\%$, $r_f = 2.5\%$, $\sigma = 10\%$, $T - T_0 = 3$ months (91 days). The similarity of vanilla and average options, and the effects from averaging prices, which already dominated the derivation of the value formula, are reflected in the *Greeks* as well. Both option types react

Table 1.22   Values of average options

Method	Ar. call	Ar. put	Geo. price call	Geo. price put	Geo. strike call	Geo. strike put
analytical	–	–	271.19	273.63	295.21	248.19
Monte Carlo	295.92	251.95	290.53	256.44	295.38	244.62
with control variate	276.57	269.14	–	–	–	–
Turnbull/Wakeman	276.36	269.02	–	–	–	–
Lévy	276.36	269.02	–	–	–	–

Input parameters are $K = 1.2000$, $S_0 = 1.2000$, $\sigma = 20\%$, $r_d = 3\%$, $r_f = 2.5\%$, $T - T_0 = 90\,\text{days} = 90/365$ years, 90 observations (implying a time step of 0.002739726 years), 10,000 price paths in the Monte Carlo simulation. The arithmetic average options are average price options. All values are in domestic pips.

in the same direction to parameter changes and differ only in the quantity of the option value change. This holds especially for delta, gamma, and vega. These sensitivities, which are related to the underlying, represent best the properties of average options, i.e. initially, the option is very sensitive to price changes in the underlying. Delta, gamma, and vega have accordingly high values. With decreasing time to maturity the impact of single prices on the final payoff diminishes, delta stabilizes, and gamma approaches zero, see [38], pp. 63–64. Figure 1.31 illustrates the similarity between vanilla and average price options with respect to delta and gamma.

For the same level of volatility in the underlying average options have a lower vega compared to vanilla options, because fluctuations of the underlying price are smoothed by the average. Note that the lower the volatility the smaller the value difference between average and vanilla options, see Figure 1.32.

Since single prices – especially at maturity – influence the payoff of average options less significantly than for vanilla options, time, i.e. the chance of a finally favorable performance, plays a less important role in determining the value of average options, leading to a lower theta. The interest rate sensitivity rho of average options is smaller than for vanilla options.

Hedging

With the sensitivity analysis in mind, the question arises, how the writer of an average option should deal with the risks of a short position.

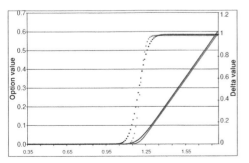 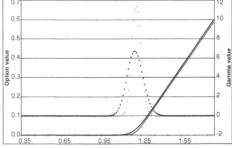

Figure 1.31   lhs: Option values and delta depending on the underlying price; rhs: Option values and gamma depending on the underlying price

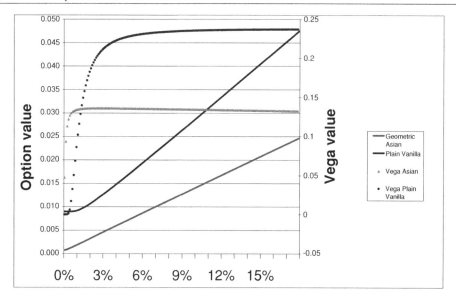

Figure 1.32 Option values and vega depending on volatility for at-the-money options

Dynamic hedging

For a call position, for instance, one way is the replication with an investment in the underlying that is funded by borrowing. The delta of the option suggests how many units of the underlying have to be bought. Since delta changes over time, the amount invested in the underlying has to be adjusted frequently. From the risk analysis it can be inferred that average options are easier to hedge than vanilla options, in particular the delta of average options stabilizes over time. Accordingly, the scope of required rebalancing of the hedge and the related transaction cost decrease over time. The costs of the hedge include interest payments as well as commissions and bid-ask-spreads due at every rebalancing transaction. See [39] and [38] for empirical analyses on the cost of dynamic and static hedging. Dynamic hedging neutralizes the delta exposure inherent in the option position. The volatility exposure has to be hedged with vanilla contracts.

Static hedging

Alternatively, a static hedge involving vanilla options can be set up. The position remains generally unchanged until maturity of the Average Option. Vanilla options are traded in liquid markets at relatively small bid-ask-spreads. Furthermore, not only the delta risk but also the gamma and volatility exposure can be reduced with options as hedge instrument. Static hedges with vanilla options have therefore become common market practice, see [40]. For instance, Lévy suggests in [40] as a rule of thumb to choose a vanilla call with a similar strike as a short average price call and an expiration that is one-third of the averaging period of the exotic, based on the appearance of the factor $\frac{T}{3}$ in Equation (1.218). As the right hand side of Figure 1.33 shows, the sensitivities of the short average price call are at their highest levels in the first third of the averaging period. Hedging with options only during this most critical time period already significantly reduces the sensitivity of the position to underlying price changes. Simultaneously, choosing vanilla calls with shorter maturity saves hedging costs. Nevertheless,

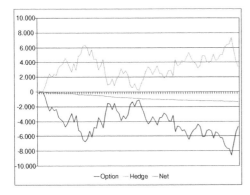 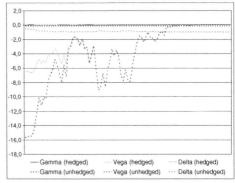

Figure 1.33   lhs: Dynamic hedging: Performance of option position and hedge portfolio; rhs: Static hedging: Comparison of hedged and unhedged "Greek" exposure. For both, sample prices were generated randomly

this approach leaves the option writer with an open position for the remaining time to maturity unless he or she decides to build up a new hedge portfolio (semi-static hedging strategy). Since the stabilized delta in the later life time of the average option reduces the rebalancing effort, a dynamic hedge could be an alternative to a renewed hedge with vanilla options.

1.5.5   Lookback options

This section is produced in conjunction with Silvia Baumann, Marion Linck, Michael Mohr and Michael Seeberg.

Lookback options are, as Asian options, path dependent. At expiration the holder of the option can "look back" over the life time of the option and exercise based upon the optimal underlying value (extremum) achieved during that period. Thus, Lookback options (like Asians) avoid the problem of European options that the underlying performed favorably throughout most of the option's lifetime but moves into a non-favorable direction towards maturity. Moreover, (unlike American Options) Lookback options optimize the market timing, because the investor gets – by definition – the most favorable underlying price. As summarized in Table 1.23 Lookback options can be structured in two different types with the extremum representing either the strike price or the underlying value. Figure 1.34 shows the development of the payoff of Lookback options depending on a sample price path. In detail we define

$$M_{t,T} \overset{\Delta}{=} \max_{t \leq u \leq T} S(u), \tag{1.221}$$

$$M_T \overset{\Delta}{=} M_{0,T}, \tag{1.222}$$

$$m_{t,T} \overset{\Delta}{=} \min_{t \leq u \leq T} S(u), \tag{1.223}$$

$$m_T \overset{\Delta}{=} m_{0,T}. \tag{1.224}$$

Variations of Lookback options include *Partial Lookback Options*, where the monitoring period for the underlying is shorter than the lifetime of the option. Conze and Viswanathan [41] present further variations like *Limited Risk* and *American Lookback Options*. Since the currency

Table 1.23   Types of lookback options

Payoff	Lookback type	Parameter
$M_T - S_T$	floating strike put	$\phi = -1, \bar{\eta} = -1$
$S_T - m_T$	floating strike call	$\phi = +1, \bar{\eta} = +1$
$(M_T - X)^+$	fixed strike call	$\phi = +1, \bar{\eta} = -1$
$(X - m_T)^+$	fixed strike put	$\phi = -1, \bar{\eta} = +1$

The contract parameters T and X are the time to maturity and the strike price respectively, and S_T denotes the spot price at expiration time. Fixed strike lookback options are also called *hindsight options*.

markets traded lookback options do not fit typical business needs, they are mainly used by speculators, see [42]. An often cited strategy is building *Lookback Straddles* paying

$$M_{t,T} - m_{t,T}, \tag{1.225}$$

(also called *range* or *hi-lo option*), a combination of Lookback put(s) and call(s) that guarantees a payoff equal to the observed range of the underlying asset. In theory, Garman pointed out in [43], that Lookback options can also add value for risk managers, because floating (fixed) strike lookback options are good means to solve the timing problem of market entries (exits), see [44]. For instance, a minimum strike call is suitable to avoid missing the best exchange rate in currency linked security issues. However, this right is very expensive. Since one buys a guarantee for the best possible exchange rate ever, lookback options are generally way too expensive and hardly ever trade. Exceptions are performance notes, where lookback and average features are mixed, e.g. performance notes paying say 50 % of the best of 36 monthly average gold price returns.

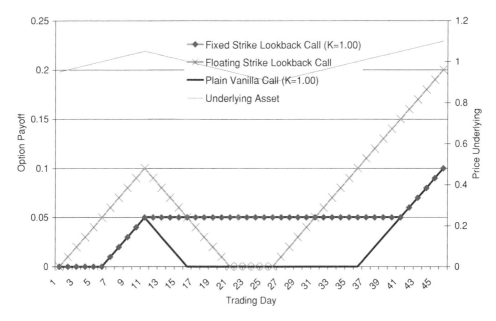

Figure 1.34   Payoff profile of Lookback calls (sample underlying price path, 20 trading days)

Valuation

As in the case of Asian options, closed form solutions only exist for specific products – in this case basically for any lookback option with continuously monitored underlying value. We consider the example of the floating strike lookback call. Again, the value of the option is given by

$$v(0, S_0) = I\!E \left[e^{-r_d T} (S_T - m_T) \right] \tag{1.226}$$
$$= S_0 e^{-r_f T} - e^{-r_d T} I\!E \left[m_T \right].$$

In the standard Black-Scholes model (1.1), the value can be derived using the reflection principle and results in

$$v(t, x) = \phi \left\{ x e^{-r_f \tau} \mathcal{N}(\phi b_1) - K e^{-r_d \tau} \mathcal{N}(\phi b_2) + \frac{1-\eta}{2} \phi e^{-r_d \tau} [\phi(R - X)]^+ \right.$$
$$\left. + \eta x e^{-r_d \tau} \frac{1}{h} \left[\left(\frac{x}{K} \right)^{-h} \mathcal{N}(-\eta \phi(b_1 - h\sigma \sqrt{\tau})) - e^{(r_d - r_f)\tau} \mathcal{N}(-\eta \phi b_1) \right] \right\}. \tag{1.227}$$

This value function has a removable discontinuity at $h = 0$ where it turns out to be

$$v(t, x) = \phi \left\{ x e^{-r_f \tau} \mathcal{N}(\phi b_1) - K e^{-r_d \tau} \mathcal{N}(\phi b_2) + \frac{1-\eta}{2} \phi e^{-r_d \tau} [\phi(R - X)]^+ \right.$$
$$\left. + \eta x e^{-r_d \tau} \sigma \sqrt{\tau} [-b_1 \mathcal{N}(-\eta \phi b_1) + \eta \phi n(b_1)] \right\}. \tag{1.228}$$

The abbreviations we use are

$$t : \text{running time (in years)}, \tag{1.229}$$

$$x \stackrel{\Delta}{=} S_t : \text{known spot at time of evaluation}, \tag{1.230}$$

$$\tau \stackrel{\Delta}{=} T - t : \text{time to expiration (in years)}, \tag{1.231}$$

$$n(t) \stackrel{\Delta}{=} \frac{1}{\sqrt{2\pi}} e^{-\frac{1}{2}t^2}, \tag{1.232}$$

$$\mathcal{N}(x) \stackrel{\Delta}{=} \int_{-\infty}^{x} n(t) \, dt, \tag{1.233}$$

$$h \stackrel{\Delta}{=} \frac{2(r_d - r_f)}{\sigma^2}, \tag{1.234}$$

$$K \stackrel{\Delta}{=} \begin{cases} R & \text{floating strike lookback } (X \leq 0) \\ \bar{\eta} \min(\bar{\eta} X, \bar{\eta} R) & \text{fixed strike lookback } \quad (X > 0) \end{cases}, \tag{1.235}$$

$$\eta \stackrel{\Delta}{=} \begin{cases} +1 & \text{floating strike lookback } (X \leq 0) \\ -1 & \text{fixed strike lookback } \quad (X > 0) \end{cases}, \tag{1.236}$$

$$b_1 \stackrel{\Delta}{=} \frac{\ln \frac{x}{K} + (r_d - r_f + \frac{1}{2}\sigma^2)\tau}{\sigma \sqrt{\tau}}, \tag{1.237}$$

$$b_2 \stackrel{\Delta}{=} b_1 - \sigma \sqrt{\tau}. \tag{1.238}$$

Note that this formula basically consists of that for a vanilla call (1st two terms) plus another term. Conze and Viswanathan also show closed form solutions for fixed strike lookback options and the variations mentioned above in [41]. Heynen and Kat develop equations for *Partial*

Table 1.24 Sample output data for lookback options

Payoff	Analytic model	Continuous
$M_T - S_T$	0.0231	0.0255
$S_T - m_T$	0.0310	0.0320
$(M_T - 0.99)^+$	0.0107	0.0131
$(0.97 - m_T)^+$	0.0235	0.0246

For the input data we used spot $S_0 = 0.8900$, $r_d = 3\%$, $r_f = 6\%$, $\sigma = 10\%$, $\tau = \frac{1}{12}$, running min $= 0.9500$, running max $= 0.9900$, $m = 22$. We find the analytic results in the continuous case in agreement with the ones published in [47]. We can also reproduce the numerical results for the discretely sampled floating strike lookback put contained in [48].

Fixed and Floating Strike Lookback Options in [45]. For those preferring the PDE-approach of deriving formulae, we refer to [46]. For most practical matters, where we have to deal with fixings and lookback features in combination with averaging, the only reasonable valuation technique is Monte Carlo simulation.

Example
We list some sample results in Table 1.24.

Sensitivity analysis

Delta

$$v_x(t, x) = \phi \left\{ e^{-r_f \tau} \mathcal{N}(\phi b_1) \right. \tag{1.239}$$
$$\left. + \eta e^{-r_d \tau} \frac{1}{h} \left[\left(\frac{x}{K}\right)^{-h} \mathcal{N}(-\eta\phi(b_1 - h\sigma\sqrt{\tau}))(1 - h) - e^{(r_d - r_f)\tau} \mathcal{N}(-\eta\phi b_1) \right] \right\}$$

At $h = 0$ this simplifies to

$$v_x(t, x) = \phi \left\{ e^{-r_f \tau} \mathcal{N}(\phi b_1) \right.$$
$$\left. + \eta e^{-r_d \tau} \left[\sigma\sqrt{\tau}[-b_1\mathcal{N}(-\eta\phi b_1) + \eta\phi n(b_1)] - \mathcal{N}(-\eta\phi b_1) \right] \right\} \tag{1.240}$$

Gamma

$$v_{xx}(t, x) = \frac{2e^{-r_f \tau}}{x\sigma\sqrt{\tau}} n(b_1) - \phi\eta e^{-r_d \tau} \frac{1 - h}{x} \mathcal{N}(-\phi\eta(b_1 - h\sigma\sqrt{\tau})) \tag{1.241}$$

Theta

We can use the Black-Scholes partial differential equation to obtain theta from value, delta and gamma.

vega

$$v_\sigma(t, x) = \phi\eta x e^{-r_d \tau} \frac{2}{\sigma} \left[\left(\frac{x}{K}\right)^{-h} \mathcal{N}(-\eta\phi(b_1 - h\sigma\sqrt{\tau})) \left(\frac{1}{h} + \ln\frac{x}{K}\right) \right.$$
$$\left. - e^{(r_d - r_f)\tau} \frac{1}{h} \mathcal{N}(-\eta\phi b_1) \right] \tag{1.242}$$

At $h = 0$ this simplifies to

$$v(t, x) = \phi \eta x e^{-r_d \tau} \sqrt{\tau} \left[-\sigma \sqrt{\tau} b_1 \mathcal{N}(-\eta \phi b_1) + 2\eta \phi n(b_1) \right] \qquad (1.243)$$

Discrete sampling

In practice, one cannot take the average over a continuum of exchange rates. The standard is to specify a *fixing calendar* and take only a finite number of fixings into account. Suppose there are m equidistant sample points left until expiration at which we evaluate the extremum. In this case the value can be determined by an approximation described in [49]. We set

$$\beta_1 = 0.5826 = -\zeta(1/2)/\sqrt{2\pi}, \qquad (1.244)$$

$$a = e^{\phi \beta_1 \sigma \sqrt{\tau/m}}, \qquad (1.245)$$

and obtain for fixed strike lookback options

$$v(t, x, r_d, r_f, \sigma, R, X, \phi, \bar{\eta}, m)$$
$$= v(t, x, r_d, r_f, \sigma, aR, aX, \phi, \bar{\eta})/a, \qquad (1.246)$$

and for floating strike lookback options

$$v(t, x, r_d, r_f, \sigma, R, X, \phi, \bar{\eta}, m)$$
$$= av(t, x, r_d, r_f, \sigma, R/a, X, \phi, \bar{\eta}) - \phi(a - 1)xe^{-r_f \tau}. \qquad (1.247)$$

One interesting observation is that when the options move deep in the money and have the same strike price, lookback options and vanilla options have the same value, except for extreme risk parameter inputs. This can be explained recalling that a floating strike lookback option has an exercise probability of 1 and buys (sells) at the minimum (maximum). When the strike price of a vanilla option equals the extremum of the exotic and is deep in the money, the holder of the option will also buy (sell) at the extremum with a probability very close to 1. Moreover, recall that the floating strike lookback option consists of a vanilla option and an additional term. Garman names this term a *strike-bonus option*, see [43]. It can be considered as an option that has an increased payoff whenever a new extremum is reached. When the underlying price moves very far away from the current extremum, the strike-bonus option has almost zero value.

The structure of the Greeks delta, rho, theta and vega is comparable for lookback and vanilla calls. Nonetheless, the intensity of these sensitivities against changes differs, see Figure 1.35. Close to or at the money, lookback calls have a significantly lower *delta* than their vanilla counterparts. The reason is that the strike-bonus option in the lookback call has a negative delta when the underlying value is close to the current extremum and a delta next to zero when it is far in the money. Intuitively, the lower Lookback delta is explained by the fact that the closer the current underlying value is to the extremum, the more likely is that the payoff of the lookback option remains unchanged, which is different for vanilla options where the payoff changes with every underlying movement. Note that whenever a new extremum is achieved, the payoff for a lookback option equals zero and remains unchanged until the underlying value moves into the adverse direction.

Floating strike lookback options have a lower *rho* than vanilla options (with equal strikes at the time of observation), which can be explained by the fact that the option holder needs to pay more up-front and thus has a lower principal profiting from favorable interest rate movements. As a rule of thumb, a floating strike lookback option is worth twice as much as a vanilla option.

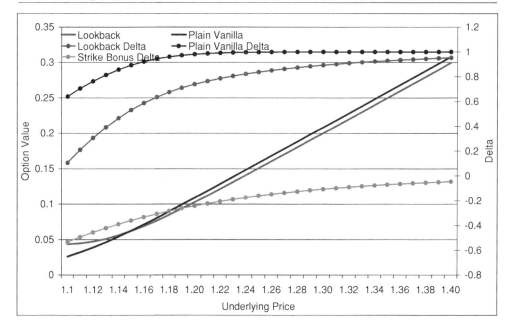

Figure 1.35   Vanilla and lookback call (left hand scale) with deltas (right hand scale) using $\min_t S_t =$ 1.00. The Lookback delta equals the sum of the delta of a vanilla option plus the delta of a strike bonus option.

The longer the time to maturity, the more intensively floating strike lookback options react compared to vanilla options.

The higher *theta* for lookback options reflects the fact that the optimal value achieved to date is "locked in" and the longer the time to maturity, the higher the chance to lock in an even better extremum.

Regarding the *vega*, lookback options show a stronger reaction than regular options. The higher the volatility of the underlying, the higher the probability to reach a new extremum. Moreover, having "locked in" this new extremum the option value can benefit even more from the higher chance of adverse price movements.

As pointed out by Taleb in [50], one particularly interesting risk parameter is the *gamma* since it is *one-sided*, while the vanilla gamma changes symmetrically for up- and down movements of the underlying, see Figure 1.36. A lookback option always has its maximum gamma at the extremum which can move over time. Vanilla options, however, have their maximum gamma at the strike price. The *lookback gamma asymmetry* indicates that gamma risk cannot be consistently (statically) hedged with vanilla options. The fact that gamma is considerably higher for lookback options implies that a frequent rebalancing of the hedging portfolio and hence high transaction costs are likely, see [51].

Hedging

Due to the maximum (minimum) function that allows the strike price to change there exists no pure static hedging strategy for floating strike lookback options. Instead, a *semi-static rollover*

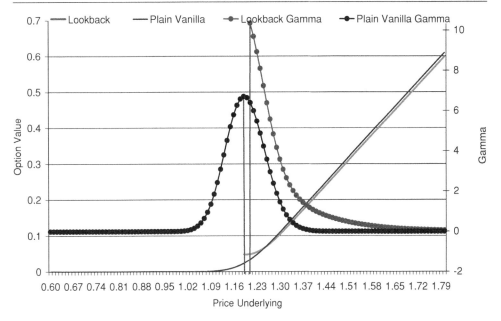

Figure 1.36   Value (left hand scale) and gamma (right hand scale) of an at-the-money floating strike lookback and a vanilla call

strategy can be applied, see [43]. As can be read from the value formula (1.227), we can hedge parts with a vanilla option. Whenever the maximum (minimum) changes, the writer of the option buys a new put (call) struck at the current market price and sells the old put (call). However, this does not work without costs. While the new put (call) is at-the-money, the old put (call) is out-of-the-money at the time of the sale and hence returns less money than the amount necessary to purchase the new option. We encounter vanilla option bid-ask spreads, and smile risk. The strike-bonus option returns exactly the money that is needed for the rollover. This approach, however, is rather theoretic, since strike-bonus options are hardly available in the market.

In practice, floating strike lookback options are usually hedged with a straddle, see Section 1.4.4. Cunningham and Karumanchi also explain a hedging strategy for fixed strike lookback options in [51]. The straddle to use is a combination of a vanilla put and a vanilla call, which have a term to maturity equal to that of the lookback option to be hedged, and a strike equal to the maximum (minimum) achieved by the underlying. At maturity T, the call (put) of this straddle becomes worthless since the strike is below (above) the terminal stock price S_T. The remaining put (call) exactly satisfies the obligation of the lookback option (see Figure 1.37). Over the lifetime of the option, the strike price of the straddle needs to be adapted if the current exchange rate S_t rises above (falls below) the current maximum (minimum). Regarding the intrinsic value, the holder of the hedging portfolio will not lose money since for instance the intrinsic value lost by the put will be exactly gained by the call. However, the deltas of the two options differ, not only in their sign. In addition, attempting to create a hedging portfolio with zero delta, the hedger has to buy a certain number of puts per one call. Figure 1.37 shows that for the latter two reasons this is not a self-financing hedging strategy.

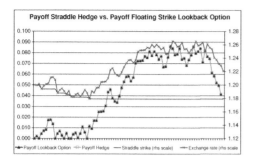
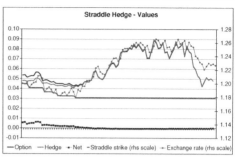

Figure 1.37 Comparison of the payoffs of a floating strike lookback option and a vanilla straddle (lhs) and the values of the positions (rhs) for a random time path (Exchange rate and straddle strike on the rhs scale)

Note that the strategy would not be self-financing even if the straddle was not adapted for a zero delta of the position. The definition of a *re-hedge threshold* and a maximum number of trades per period can help to balance the risk taken with transaction costs and administrative efforts.

Apart from this *semi-static*[6] hedge, a *dynamic hedge* using spot and money market is also possible. Due to the risk parameters, especially gamma and vega, which are difficult to hedge, the hedge appears to deviate considerably in value relative to the option over time.

1.5.6   Forward start, ratchet and cliquet options

A forward start vanilla option is just like a vanilla option, except that the strike is set on a future date t. It pays off

$$[\phi(S_T - K)]^+, \tag{1.248}$$

where K denotes the strike and ϕ takes the values $+1$ for a call and -1 for a put. The strike K is set as αS_t at time $t \in [0, T]$. Very commonly α is set to one.

Advantages

- Protection against spot market movement and against increasing volatility
- Buyer can lock in current volatility level
- Spot risk easy to hedge

Disadvantages

- Protection level not known in advance

---

[6] We refer to this technique as semi-static since the basic idea of the hedge is that of a static one: Initialize the hedge and wait until maturity. However, due to the changes of the extrema, the static hedge has to be adapted – a characteristic which is usually associated with dynamic hedging.

The value of forward start options

Using the abbreviations

- x for the current spot price of the underlying,
- $\tau \overset{\Delta}{=} T - t$,
- $F_s \overset{\Delta}{=} I\!E[S_s|S_0] = S_0 e^{(r_d - r_f)s}$ for the outright forward of the underlying,
- $\theta_\pm \overset{\Delta}{=} \frac{r_d - r_f}{\sigma} \pm \frac{\sigma}{2}$,
- $d_\pm \overset{\Delta}{=} \frac{\ln\frac{x}{K} + \sigma\theta_\pm\tau}{\sigma\sqrt{\tau}} = \frac{\ln\frac{f}{K} \pm \frac{\sigma^2}{2}\tau}{\sigma\sqrt{\tau}}$,
- $d_\pm^\alpha \overset{\Delta}{=} \frac{-\ln\alpha + \sigma\theta_\pm\tau}{\sigma\sqrt{\tau}}$,
- $n(t) \overset{\Delta}{=} \frac{1}{\sqrt{2\pi}} e^{-\frac{1}{2}t^2} = n(-t)$,
- $\mathcal{N}(x) \overset{\Delta}{=} \int_{-\infty}^x n(t)\,dt = 1 - \mathcal{N}(-x)$,

we recall the value of a vanilla option in Equation (1.7),

$$v(x, K, T, t, \sigma, r_d, r_f, \phi) = \phi e^{-r_d \tau}[f\mathcal{N}(\phi d_+) - K\mathcal{N}(\phi d_-)]. \tag{1.249}$$

For the value of a forward start vanilla option in a constant-coefficient geometric Brownian motion model we obtain

$$v = e^{-r_d t} I\!E\, v(S_t, K = \alpha S_t, T, t, \sigma, r_d, r_f, \phi) \tag{1.250}$$
$$= \phi e^{-r_d T}[F_T\mathcal{N}(\phi d_+^\alpha) - \alpha F_t\mathcal{N}(\phi d_-^\alpha)].$$

Noticeably, the value computation is easy here, because the strike K is set as a *multiple* of the future spot. If we were to choose to set the strike as a constant *difference* of the future spot, the integration would not work in closed form, and we would have to use numerical integration.

The crucial pricing issue here is that one needs to know the volatility, which is the *forward volatility*, i.e. the volatility that will materialize at the future time t for a maturity $T - t$. It is not at all clear in the market which proxy to take for this forward volatility. The standard is to use Equation (1.102).

Greeks

The Greeks are the same as for vanilla options after time t, when the strike has been set. Before time t they are given by

(Spot) delta

$$\frac{\partial v}{\partial S_0} = \frac{v}{S_0} \tag{1.251}$$

Gamma

$$\frac{\partial^2 v}{\partial x^2} = 0 \tag{1.252}$$

Theta

$$\frac{\partial v}{\partial t} = r_f v \tag{1.253}$$

Table 1.25   Value and Greeks of a forward start vanilla in USD on EUR/USD – spot of 0.9000, $\alpha = 99\,\%$, $\sigma = 12\,\%$, $r_d = 2\,\%$, $r_f = 3\,\%$, maturity $T = 186$ days, strike set at $t = 90$ days

	Call	Put
value	0.0251	0.0185
delta	0.0279	0.0206
gamma	0.0000	0.0000
theta	0.0007	0.0005
vega	0.1793	0.1793
rhod	0.1217	−0.1052
rhof	−0.1329	0.0950

Vega

$$\frac{\partial v}{\partial \sigma} = -\frac{e^{-r_d T}}{\sigma}[F_T n(d_+^\alpha)d_-^\alpha - \alpha F_t n(d_-^\alpha)d_+^\alpha] \tag{1.254}$$

Rho

$$\frac{\partial v}{\partial r_d} = \phi e^{-r_d T}\alpha F_t(T - t)\mathcal{N}(\phi d_-^\alpha) \tag{1.255}$$

$$\frac{\partial v}{\partial r_f} = -T v - \phi e^{-r_d T}\alpha F_t(T - t)\mathcal{N}(\phi d_-^\alpha) \tag{1.256}$$

Example
We consider an example in Table 1.25.

Reasons for trading forward start options

The key reason for trading a forward start is trading the forward volatility without any spot exposure. In quiet market phases with low volatility, buying a forward start is cheap. Keeping a long position will allow participation in rising volatility, independent of the spot level.

Variations

Forward start options can be altered in all kind of ways: they can be of American style, they can come with a deferred delivery or deferred premium, they can have barriers or appear as a strip.

A strip of forward start options is generally called a *Cliquet*.

A *Ratchet Option* consists of a series of forward start options, where the strike for the next forward start option is set equal to the spot at maturity of the previous.

1.5.7   Power options

This section is produced in conjunction with Silvia Baumann, Marion Linck, Michael Mohr and Michael Seeberg.

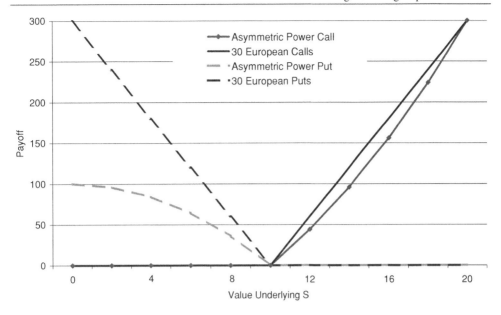

Figure 1.38   Payoff of asymmetric power options vs. vanilla options, using $K = 10, n = 2$

For power options, the vanilla option payoff function $[\phi(S_T - K)]^+$ is adjusted by raising the entire function or parts of the function to the n-th power, see, e.g. Zhang ([55]). The result is a non-linear profile with the potential of a higher payoff at maturity with a greater leverage than standard options. If the exponent n is exactly 1, the option is equal to a vanilla option. We distinguish between *asymmetric* and *symmetric* power options. Their payoffs in comparison with vanilla options are illustrated in Figures 1.38 and 1.39.

Asymmetric power options

With an asymmetric power option, the underlying S_T and strike K of a standard option payoff function are individually raised to the n-th power,

$$[\phi(S_T^n - K^n)]^+. \tag{1.257}$$

Figure 1.38 illustrates why this option type is called *asymmetric*. With increasing S_T, the convex call payoff grows exponentially. Given the limited and fixed profit potential of $K^2 = 10^2$, the concave put payoff decreases exponentially. It requires 30 vanilla options to replicate the call payoff if the underlying S_T moves to 20.

Asymmetric power options

In the symmetric type, the entire vanilla option payoff is raised to the n-th power,

$$[[\phi(S_T - K)]^+]^n, \tag{1.258}$$

see [52]. Figure 1.39 insinuates naming this option type *symmetric*, since put and call display the same payoff shape. Here, 10 vanilla options suffice to replicate the symmetric power option if the underlying S_T moves to 20.

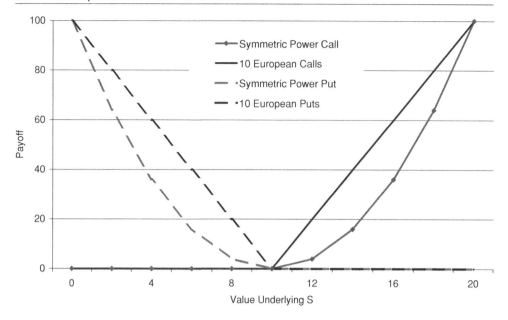

Figure 1.39   Payoff of symmetric power options vs. vanilla options, using $K = 10, n = 2$

Combining a symmetric power call and put as in Figure 1.39 leads to a symmetric power straddle, which pays

$$|S_T - K|^n. \tag{1.259}$$

Reasons for trading power options

Power options are often equipped with a payoff cap C to limit the short position risk as well as the option premium for the buyer. For example, the payments of the short position at $n = 3$ for $K = 10$ shoots to $2375(125)$ for the asymmetric (symmetric) power call if S_T moves to 15. Even with cap, the highly leveraged payoff motivates speculators to invest in the product that demands a considerably higher option premium than a vanilla option. Power options are mostly popular in the listed derivatives and retail market, due to their high leverage and due to their mere name. Besides this obvious reason additionally one can think of the following motives:

1. Hedging future levels of implied volatility. Vega, which is volatility risk, is extremely difficult to hedge as there is no directly observable measure available, see [53]. A power straddle is an effective instrument to do so as it preserves the volatility exposure better than a vanilla straddle when the price of the underlying moves significantly as shown below in the section on sensitivities to risk parameters.
2. Through their exponential, non-linear payoff, power options can hedge non-linear price risks. An example is an importer earning profits merely through a percentage mark-up on imported products. An exchange rate change will lead to a price change, which in turn may affect demand volumes. The importer faces a risk of non-linearly decreasing earnings, see [54].
3. With very large short positions in vanilla options, a rebalancing of a dynamic hedge may require such massive buying (selling) of the underlying that this impacts the price of the

underlying, which in turn requires further hedge adjustments and may "pin" the underlying to the strike price, see p. 37 in [52]. To *smooth this pin risk*, option sellers propose a *soft strike option* with a similarly smooth and continuous payoff curvature as power options. As we will show in the hedging analysis of this section, this payoff curvature can be effectively replicated using vanilla options with different strike prices. The *diversified* range of strikes then softens any effect of a move in the underlying price. For details on *soft strike options* see [52], pp. 37 and [54], pp. 51.

Valuation of the asymmetric power option

The value can be written as the expected payoff value under the risk neutral measure. Using the money market numeraire $e^{-r_d T}$ yields

$$\text{asymmetric power option value } v_{aPC} = e^{-r_d T}\, I\!E\left[\phi(S_T^n - K^n)I\!I_{\{\phi S_T > \phi K\}}\right]. \tag{1.260}$$

As K is a constant S_T is the only random variable which simplifies the equation to

$$v_{aPC} = \phi e^{-r_d T}\, I\!E\left[S_T^n I\!I_{\{\phi S_T > \phi K\}}\right] - \phi e^{-r_d T} K^n\, I\!E\left[I\!I_{\{\phi S_T > \phi K\}}\right]. \tag{1.261}$$

The expectation of an indicator function is just the probability that the event $\{S_T > K\}$ occurs. In the Black-Scholes model, S_T is log-normally distributed and evolves according to a geometric Brownian motion (1.1). Itô's Lemma implies that S_T^n is also a geometric Brownian motion following

$$dS_t^n = \left[n(r_d - r_f) + \frac{1}{2}n(n-1)\sigma^2\right]S_t^n\, dt + n\sigma\, S_t^n\, dW_t. \tag{1.262}$$

Solving the differential equation and calculating the expected value in Equation (1.261) leads to the desired closed form solution

$$v_{aPC} = \phi e^{-r_d T}\left[f^n e^{\frac{1}{2}n(n-1)\sigma^2 T}\mathcal{N}(\phi d_+^n) - K^n \mathcal{N}(\phi d_-)\right], \tag{1.263}$$

$$f \triangleq S_0 e^{(r_d - r_f)T},$$

$$d_- \triangleq \frac{\ln\frac{f}{K} - \frac{1}{2}\sigma^2 T}{\sigma\sqrt{T}},$$

$$d_+^n \triangleq \frac{\ln\frac{f}{K} + \left(n - \frac{1}{2}\sigma^2\right)T}{\sigma\sqrt{T}}.$$

Valuation of the symmetric power option

Due to the binomial term $(S_T - K)^n$ the general value formula derivation for the symmetric version looks more complicated. That is why a more intuitive approach is taken and the valuation logic is shown based on the asymmetric option discussed above. Taking the example of $n = 2$ the difference between asymmetric and symmetric call is

$$[S_T^2 - K^2] - [S_T^2 - 2S_T K + K^2] = 2K(S_T - K). \tag{1.264}$$

The symmetric version for $n = 2$ is thus exactly equal to the asymmetric power option minus $2K$ vanilla options. This way pricing and hedging the symmetric power option becomes a structuring exercise, see Figure 1.40.

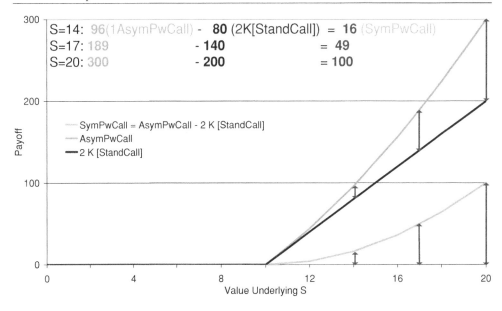

Figure 1.40 Symmetric power call replicated with asymmetric power and vanilla calls, using $K = 10$, $n = 2$

Tompkins and Zhang both discuss the more complicated derivation of the general formula for symmetric power options in [52] and [55]. Tompkins also presents a formula for symmetric power straddles for $n = 2$.

Sensitivity analysis

Looking at the *Greeks* of asymmetric power options compared to vanilla options, the exponential elements of power options are well reflected in the exposures. This is especially true for delta and gamma as can be seen in Figure 1.41, but is also valid for theta and vega. The power option rhos are very similar to the vanilla version.

Contrary to the asymmetric power option, the symmetric power option sensitivities exhibit new features that cannot be found with vanilla options, namely extreme delta values and a

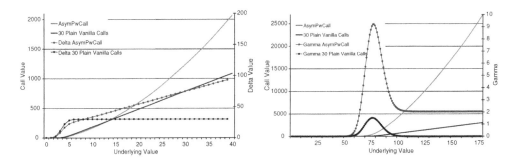

Figure 1.41 Asymmetric power call and vanilla call value and delta (lhs) and gamma (rhs) in relation to the underlying price, using $K = 10$, $n = 2$, $\sigma = 20\%$, $r_d = 5\%$, $r_f = 0\%$, $T = 90$ days

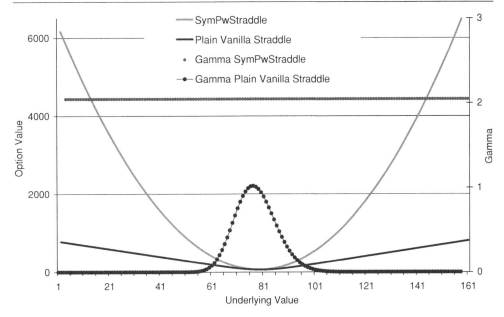

Figure 1.42   Gamma exposure of a symmetric power versus vanilla straddle, using $K = 80$ (at-the-money), $n = 2$, $\sigma = 20\%$, $r_d = 5\%$, $r_f = 0\%$, $T = 90$ days

gamma that resembles the plain vanilla delta. In the form of a straddle this creates a *constant gamma exposure*, see Figure 1.42.

At the same time, if the underlying increases significantly, the symmetric power straddle is able to preserve the exposure to volatility, whereas the vanilla straddle value becomes more and more invariant to the volatility input. Therefore, the power straddle is useful to hedge implied volatility, see Figure 1.43.

Hedging

The insights from the option payoffs, valuation, and the sensitivity analysis provide an effective static hedging strategy for both asymmetric as well as symmetric power options. The respective call values are considered as an example.

Static hedging

The continuous curvature of a power option can be approximated piecewise, adding up linear payoffs of vanilla options with different strike prices, see [52].

The symmetric power call for $n = 2$ is, as explained in the pricing section, just an asymmetric power call less $2K$ vanilla options.

The vanilla option hedge as a piecewise linear approximation is a natural upper boundary for the option price as it overestimates the option value, see Table 1.27. The complexity of a static hedge increases enormously with higher values of n. For the above example, a package of 25499 (3439) vanilla options is required to hedge one asymmetric (symmetric) power call. Overall, the static hedge strategy works very well as can be seen in Figure 1.44.

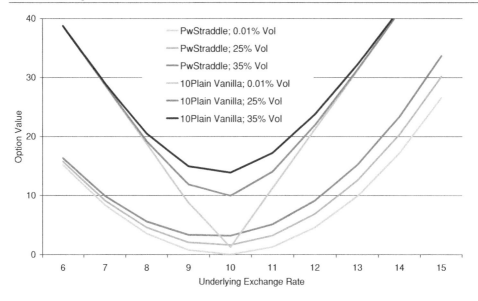

Figure 1.43   Vega exposure of a symmetric power versus vanilla straddle, using $K = 10$ (at-the-money), $n = 2, \sigma = 20\%, r_d = 5\%, r_f = 0\%, T = 90$ days

The static hedge of power options with vanillas takes into account the smile correctly, whence the price of the static hedge portfolio can serve as a market price of the power. All the sensitivities are automatically correctly hedged.

Dynamic hedging

A dynamic hedge involves setting up a position in the underlying and cash that offsets any value change in the option position. Usually the difficulty of dynamic hedging lies in second order, that is in gamma, and in vega risk. As the symmetric power straddle has a constant gamma, this simplifies delta hedging activities. In practice however, a static hedge is preferred

Table 1.26   Static hedging for the symmetric power call, using $K = 20, n = 2$

Underlying Price		10	11	12	13	14	15	16	17	18	19	20
Asym. Power Call		0	21	44	69	96	125	156	189	224	261	300
Vanilla Call Package	Sum	0	21	44	69	96	125	156	189	224	261	300
Package Components	Strike											
$2K$ Standard Calls	10		20	40	60	80	100	120	140	160	180	200
One Standard Call	10		1	2	3	4	5	6	7	8	9	10
Two Standard Calls	11			2	4	6	8	10	12	14	16	18
Two Standard Calls	12				2	4	6	8	10	12	14	16
Two Standard Calls	13					2	4	6	8	10	12	14
Two Standard Calls	14						2	4	6	8	10	12
Two Standard Calls	15							2	4	6	8	10
Two Standard Calls	16								2	4	6	8
Two Standard Calls	17									2	4	6
Two Standard Calls	18										2	4
Two Standard Calls	19											2

Table 1.27 Asymmetric power call hedge versus formula value, using $K = 10$ (at-the-money), $n = 2$, $\sigma = 15\%, r_d = 5\%, r_f = 0\%, T = 90$ days

Asym. Power Call	Formula Value	11.91
Vanilla Call Package	Sum	12
Package Components	Strike	
$2K$ Standard Calls	10	11.0354
One Standard Call	10	0.55177
Two Standard Calls	11	0.33257
Two Standard Calls	12	0.06928
Two Standard Calls	13	0.01034
Two Standard Calls	14	0.00116
Two Standard Calls	15	0.00010
Two Standard Calls	16	7.55E-06
Two Standard Calls	17	4.74E-07
Two Standard Calls	18	2.64E-08
Two Standard Calls	19	1.33E-09

as it allows banks packaging and thus hedging deeply out-of-the-money vanilla options, which are part of the options portfolio anyway.

1.5.8 Quanto options

A quanto option can be any cash-settled option, whose payoff is converted into a third currency at maturity at a pre-specified rate, called the *quanto factor*. There can be quanto plain vanilla,

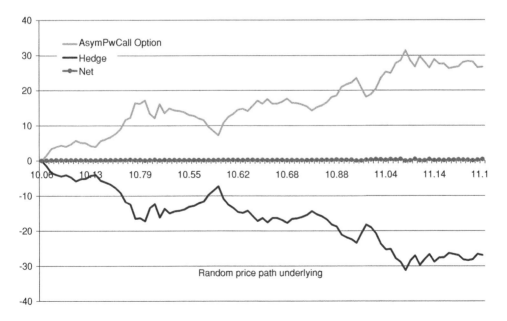

Figure 1.44 Static hedge performance of an asymmetric power call, using $K = 10, n = 2, \sigma = 150\%$, $r_d = 5\%, r_f = 0\%, T = 90$ days.

quanto barriers, quanto forward starts, quanto corridors, etc. The valuation theory is covered for example in [2] and [3]. We treat the example of a self-quanto forward in the exercises.

FX quanto drift adjustment

We take the example of a Gold contract with underlying XAU/USD in XAU-USD quotation that is quantoed into EUR. Since the payoff is in EUR, we let EUR be the numeraire or domestic or base currency and consider a Black-Scholes model

$$\text{XAU-EUR: } dS_t^{(3)} = (r_{EUR} - r_{XAU})S_t^{(3)}\, dt + \sigma_3 S_t^{(3)}\, dW_t^{(3)}, \tag{1.265}$$
$$\text{USD-EUR: } dS_t^{(2)} = (r_{EUR} - r_{USD})S_t^{(2)}\, dt + \sigma_2 S_t^{(2)}\, dW_t^{(2)}, \tag{1.266}$$
$$dW_t^{(3)} dW_t^{(2)} = -\rho_{23}\, dt, \tag{1.267}$$

where we use a minus sign in front of the correlation, because both $S^{(3)}$ and $S^{(2)}$ have the same base currency (DOM), which is EUR in this case. The scenario is displayed in Figure 1.45. The actual underlying is then

$$\text{XAU-USD: } S_t^{(1)} = \frac{S_t^{(3)}}{S_t^{(2)}}. \tag{1.268}$$

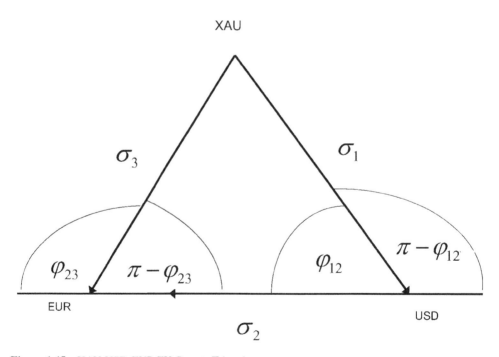

Figure 1.45   XAU-USD-EUR FX Quanto Triangle
The arrows point in the direction of the respective base currencies. The length of the edges represents the volatility. The cosine of the angles $\cos \phi_{ij} = \rho_{ij}$ represents the correlation of the currency pairs $S^{(i)}$ and $S^{(j)}$, if the base currency (DOM) of $S^{(i)}$ is the underlying currency (FOR) of $S^{(j)}$. If both $S^{(i)}$ and $S^{(j)}$ have the same base currency (DOM), then the correlation is denoted by $-\rho_{ij} = \cos(\pi - \phi_{ij})$.

Using Itô's formula, we first obtain

$$d\frac{1}{S_t^{(2)}} = -\frac{1}{(S_t^{(2)})^2} dS_t^{(2)} + \frac{1}{2} \cdot 2 \cdot \frac{1}{(S_t^{(2)})^3} (dS_t^{(2)})^2$$

$$= (r_{USD} - r_{EUR} + \sigma_2^2)\frac{1}{S_t^{(2)}} dt - \sigma_2 \frac{1}{S_t^{(2)}} dW_t^{(2)}, \qquad (1.269)$$

and hence

$$dS_t^{(1)} = \frac{1}{S_t^{(2)}} dS_t^{(3)} + S_t^{(3)} d\frac{1}{S_t^{(2)}} + dS_t^{(3)} d\frac{1}{S_t^{(2)}}$$

$$= \frac{S_t^{(3)}}{S_t^{(2)}}(r_{EUR} - r_{XAU}) dt + \frac{S_t^{(3)}}{S_t^{(2)}}\sigma_3 dW_t^{(3)}$$

$$+ \frac{S_t^{(3)}}{S_t^{(2)}}(r_{USD} - r_{EUR} + \sigma_2^2) dt + \frac{S_t^{(3)}}{S_t^{(2)}}\sigma_2 dW_t^{(2)} + \frac{S_t^{(3)}}{S_t^{(2)}}\rho_{23}\sigma_2\sigma_3 dt$$

$$= (r_{USD} - r_{XAU} + \sigma_2^2 + \rho_{23}\sigma_2\sigma_3)S_t^{(1)} dt + S_t^{(1)}(\sigma_3 dW_t^{(3)} + \sigma_2 dW_t^{(2)}).$$

Since $S_t^{(1)}$ is a geometric Brownian motion with volatility σ_1, we introduce a new Brownian motion $W_t^{(1)}$ and find

$$dS_t^{(1)} = (r_{USD} - r_{XAU} + \sigma_2^2 + \rho_{23}\sigma_2\sigma_3)S_t^{(1)} dt + \sigma_1 S_t^{(1)} dW_t^{(1)}. \qquad (1.270)$$

Now Figure 1.45 and the *law of cosine* imply

$$\sigma_3^2 = \sigma_1^2 + \sigma_2^2 - 2\rho_{12}\sigma_1\sigma_2, \qquad (1.271)$$

$$\sigma_1^2 = \sigma_2^2 + \sigma_3^2 + 2\rho_{23}\sigma_2\sigma_3, \qquad (1.272)$$

which yields

$$\sigma_2^2 + \rho_{23}\sigma_2\sigma_3 = \rho_{12}\sigma_1\sigma_2. \qquad (1.273)$$

As explained in Figure 1.45, ρ_{12} is the correlation between XAU-USD and USD-EUR, whence $\rho \stackrel{\Delta}{=} -\rho_{12}$ is the correlation between XAU-USD and EUR-USD. Inserting this into Equation (1.270), we obtain the usual formula for the drift adjustment

$$dS_t^{(1)} = (r_{USD} - r_{XAU} - \rho\sigma_1\sigma_2)S_t^{(1)} dt + \sigma_1 S_t^{(1)} dW_t^{(1)}. \qquad (1.274)$$

This is the risk-neutral process that can be used for the valuation of any derivative depending on $S_t^{(1)}$ which is quantoed into EUR.

Quanto vanilla

With these preparations we can easily determine the value of a vanilla quanto paying

$$Q[\phi(S_T - K)]^+, \qquad (1.275)$$

where K denotes the strike, T the expiration time, ϕ the usual put-call indicator, S the underlying in FOR-DOM quotation and Q the quanto factor from the domestic currency into the quanto currency. We let

$$\tilde{\mu} \stackrel{\Delta}{=} r_d - r_f - \rho\sigma\tilde{\sigma}, \qquad (1.276)$$

Table 1.28 Example of a quanto digital put

Notional	81,845 EUR
Maturity	3 months
European style Barrier	108.65 USD-JPY
Premium	60,180 EUR
including	1,000 EUR sales margin
Fixing source	ECB

The buyer receives 81,845 EUR if at maturity, the ECB fixing for USD-JPY (computed via EUR-JPY and EUR-USD) is below 108.65. Terms were created on January 12 2004

be the *adjusted drift*, where r_d and r_f denote the risk free rates of the domestic and foreign underlying currency pair respectively, σ the volatility of this currency pair, $\tilde{\sigma}$ the volatility of the currency pair DOM-QUANTO and ρ the correlation between the currency pairs FOR-DOM and DOM-QUANTO in this quotation. Furthermore we let r_Q be the risk free rate of the quanto currency.

Then the formula for the value can be written as

$$v = Q e^{-r_Q T} \phi [S_0 e^{\tilde{\mu} T} \mathcal{N}(\phi d_+) - K \mathcal{N}(\phi d_-)], \qquad (1.277)$$

$$d_\pm = \frac{\ln \frac{S_0}{K} + \left(\tilde{\mu} \pm \frac{1}{2}\sigma^2\right) T}{\sigma \sqrt{T}}. \qquad (1.278)$$

Example
We provide an example of European style digital put in USD/JPY quanto into EUR in Table 1.28.

Applications

The standard applications are performance linked deposit as in Section 2.3.2 or notes as in Section 2.5. Any time the performance of an underlying asset needs to be converted into the notional currency invested, and the exchange rate risk is with the seller, we need a quanto product. Naturally, an underlying like gold, which is quoted in USD, would be a default candidate for a quanto product, when the investment is in currency other than USD.

1.5.9 Exercises

1. Consider a EUR-USD market with spot at 1.2500, EUR rate at 2.5 %, USD rate at 2.0 %, volatility at 10.0 % and the situation of a treasurer expecting 1 Million USD in one year, that he wishes to change into EUR at the current spot rate ot 1.2500. In 6 months he will know if the company gets the definite order. Compute the price of a vanilla EUR call in EUR. Alternatively compute the price of a compound with two thirds of the total premium to be paid at inception and one third to be paid in 6 months. Do the same computations if the sales margin for the vanilla is 1 EUR per 1000 USD notional and for the compound is 2 EUR per 1000 USD notional. After six months the company ends up not getting the order and can waive its hedge. How much would it get for the vanilla if the spot is at 1.1500, at 1.2500 and at 1.3500? Would it be better for the treasurer to own the compound

and not pay the second premium? How would you split up the premia for the compound to persuade the treasurer to buy the compound rather than the vanilla? (After all there is more margin to earn.)

2. Find the fair price and the hedge of a *perpetual one-touch*, which pays 1 unit of the domestic currency if the barrier $H > S_0$ is ever hit, where S_0 denotes the current exchange rate. How about payment in the foreign currency? How about a *perpetual no-touch*? These thoughts are developed further to a *vanilla-one-touch duality* by Peter Carr [56].

3. Find the value of a *perpetual double-one-touch*, which pays a rebate R_H, if the spot reaches the higher level H before the lower level L, and R_L, if the spot reaches the lower level first. Consider as an example the EUR-USD market with a spot of S_0 at time zero between L and H. Let the interest rates of both EUR and USD be zero and the volatility be 10 %. The specified rebates are paid in USD. There is no finite expiration time, but the rebate is paid whenever one of the levels is reached. How do you hedge a short position?

4. A call (put) option is the right to buy (sell) one unit of an underlying asset (stock, commodity, foreign exchange) on a maturity date T at a pre-defined price K, called the strike price. An knock-out call with barrier B is like a call option that becomes worthless, if the underlying ever touches the barrier B at any time between inception of the trade and its expiration time. Let the market parameters be spot $S_0 = 120$, all interest and dividend rates be zero, volatility $\sigma = 10 \%$. In a liquid and jump-free market, find the value of a one-year *strike-out*, i.e. a down-and-out knock-out call, where $K = B = 100$.

   Suppose now, that the spot price movement can have downward jumps, but the forward price is still constant and equal to the spot (since there are no interest or dividend payments). How do these possible jumps influence the value of the knock-out call?

   The solution to this problem is used for the design of *turbo notes*, see Section 2.5.4.

5. Consider a regular down-and-out call in a Black-Scholes model with constant drift μ and constant volatility σ. Suppose you are allowed to choose time dependent deterministic functions for the drift $\mu(t)$ and the volatility $\sigma(t)$ with the constraint that their average over time coincides with their constant values μ and σ. How can the function $\mu(t)$ be shaped to make the down-and-out call more expensive? How can the function $\sigma(t)$ be shaped to make the down-and-out call more expensive? Justify your answer.

6. Consider a regular up-and-out EUR put USD call with maturity of 6 months. Consider the volatilities for all maturities, monthly up to 6 months. In a scenario with EUR rates lower than USD rates, describe the term structure of vega, i.e. what happens to the value if the k month volatility goes up for $k = 1, 2, \ldots, 6$. What if the rates are equal?

7. Suppose the EUR-USD spot is positively correlated with the EUR rates. How does this change the TV of a strike-out call?

8. What is the vega profile as a function of spot for a strike-out call?

9. Given Equation (1.165), which represents the theoretical value of a double-no-touch in units of domestic currency, where the payoff currency is also domestic. Let us denote this function by

$$v^d(S, r_d, r_f, \sigma, L, H),\tag{1.279}$$

where the superscript d indicates that the payoff currency is domestic. Using this formula, prove that the corresponding value in domestic currency of a double-no-touch paying one unit of *foreign* currency is given by

$$v^f(S, r_d, r_f, \sigma, L, H) = Sv^d\left(\frac{1}{S}, r_f, r_d, \sigma, \frac{1}{H}, \frac{1}{L}\right).\tag{1.280}$$

Assuming you know the sensitivity parameters of the function v^d, derive the following corresponding sensitivity parameters for the function v^f,

$$\frac{\partial v^f}{\partial S} = v^d \left(\frac{1}{S}, r_f, r_d, \sigma, \frac{1}{H}, \frac{1}{L} \right) - \frac{1}{S} \frac{\partial v^d}{\partial S} \left(\frac{1}{S}, r_f, r_d, \sigma, \frac{1}{H}, \frac{1}{L} \right), \qquad (1.281)$$

$$\frac{\partial^2 v^f}{\partial S^2} = \frac{1}{S^3} \frac{\partial^2 v^d}{\partial S^2} \left(\frac{1}{S}, r_f, r_d, \sigma, \frac{1}{H}, \frac{1}{L} \right),$$

$$\frac{\partial v^f}{\partial \sigma} = S \frac{\partial v^d}{\partial \sigma},$$

$$\frac{\partial^2 v^f}{\partial \sigma^2} = S \frac{\partial^2 v^d}{\partial^2 \sigma},$$

$$\frac{\partial^2 v^f}{\partial S \partial \sigma} = S \frac{\partial v^d}{\partial \sigma} \left(\frac{1}{S}, r_f, r_d, \sigma, \frac{1}{H}, \frac{1}{L} \right) - \frac{1}{S} \frac{\partial^2 v^d}{\partial S \partial \sigma} \left(\frac{1}{S}, r_f, r_d, \sigma, \frac{1}{H}, \frac{1}{L} \right),$$

$$\frac{\partial v^f}{\partial r_d} = \frac{\partial v^d}{\partial r_f},$$

$$\frac{\partial v^f}{\partial r_f} = \frac{\partial v^d}{\partial r_d}.$$

10. Suppose your front office application for double-no-touch options is out of order, but you can use double-knock-out options. Replicate a double-no-touch using two double-knock-out options. As shown in Figure 1.46, one can replicate a long double no-touch with

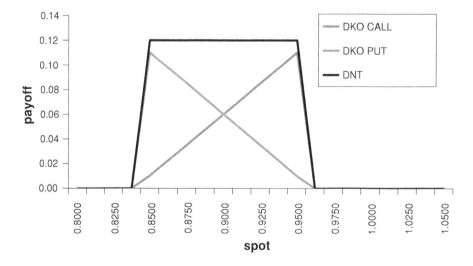

**Replicating a Double-No-Touch using
Double Knock-Out Calls and Puts**

barriers L and H using a portfolio of
(a) a long double-knock-out call with barriers L and H and strike L,
(b) a long double-knock-out put with barriers L and H and strike H.
The nominal amounts of the respective double-knock-out options depend on the currency
in which the payoff is settled. In case of a EUR-USD double-no-touch paying 1 USD
(domestic currency), show that the nominal amounts of the double-knock-out call and put
are both $\frac{1}{H-L}$.

Verify the following argument how to replicate a double-no-touch paying one unit of EUR
(foreign currency). More precisely, we can price this by taking a USD-EUR double-no-
touch with barriers $1/H$ and $1/L$. This double-no-touch can be composed as before using

$$\frac{1}{\frac{1}{L} - \frac{1}{H}} = \frac{LH}{H - L} \qquad (1.282)$$

DKO USD Calls with strike $1/H$ and DKO USD Puts with strike $1/L$, both with barriers
$1/H$ and $1/L$. Since furthermore

$$1 \text{ DKO USD Call with strike } 1/H \text{ and barriers } 1/H \text{ and } 1/L$$
$$= (1 \text{ DKO EUR Puts with strike } H \text{ and barriers } L \text{ and } H)/(H \cdot S),$$

and similarly

$$1 \text{ DKO USD Put with strike } 1/L \text{ and barriers } 1/H \text{ and } 1/L$$
$$= (1 \text{ DKO EUR Calls with strike } L \text{ and barriers } L \text{ and } H)/(L \cdot S),$$

we obtain for the EUR-USD double-no-touch paying one unit of EUR (foreign currency)

$$\frac{\text{DKOPut}(H, L, H) \cdot L + \text{DKOCall}(L, L, H) \cdot H}{(H - L) \cdot S}, \qquad (1.283)$$

where DKOPut(H, L, H) means a EUR Put with strike H and barriers L and H and
DKOCall(L, L, H) means a EUR Call with strike L and barriers L and H. The division
by EUR-USD Spot S must be omitted, if the price of the double-no-touch is to be quoted
in EUR. If it is quoted in USD, then the formula stays as it is.
11. Derive a closed form solution for the value of a continuously sampled geometric floating
   strike call and put. How are they related to the fixed strike formulae?
12. Discuss the settlement possibilities of Asian options, i.e. which type of average options
   can be settled in physical delivery, and which only in cash. In case of cash settlement,
   specify if both domestic and foreign currency can be paid or just one of them.
13. In theory, a lookback option can be replicated by a continuum of one-touch-options, see,
   for example, in Poulsen [57]. Find out more details and use this result to determine a
   market price of lookback options based on the liquid market of one-touch options. This
   can be approximated by methods of Section 3.1.
14. Implement a valuation of a forward start option (see Section 1.5.6) in a version where
   the strike K is set as $S_t + d$ at time $t \in [0, T]$. This has to be done using numerical
   integration. Compare the values you obtain with the standard forward start option values.
15. One can view a market of liquid forward start options as a source of information for the
   forward volatility. Using similar techniques as in the case of vanilla options, how would
   you back out the forward volatility smile?

16. Derive a closed form solution for a single barrier option where both the strike and the barrier are set as multiples of the spot S_t at the future time t, following the approach for forward start options.

17. In a standard annuity of n months, total loan amount K, monthly payments, the amount A paid back to the bank every month is constant and is the sum of the interest payment and the amortization. Payments happen at the end of each month, and the first payment is at the end of the first month. Clearly, as time passes the amortization rises. Assuming annual interest rate r compute the remaining debt R after n months. Furthermore, setting $R = 0$, find n. You may assume the time of one month being $1/12$ of a year and the monthly interest rate to be $R/12$. You may check your calculations at www.mathfinance.com/annuity.html.

18. The price of an ounce of Gold is quoted in USD. If the price of Gold drops by 5 %, but the price of Gold in EUR remains constant, determine the change of the EUR-USD exchange rate.

19. Suppose you are long a USD Put JPY Call quanto into AUD. What are the vega profiles of the positions in USD-JPY, USD-AUD and AUD-JPY?

20. Suppose you are short a double-no-touch. Draw the possible vega profiles as a function of the spot and discuss the possible scenarios.

21. Suppose you know the vega of a 2-month at-the-money vanilla. By what factor is the vega of a 4-month at-the-money vanilla bigger? How does this look for a 5-year vanilla in comparison to a 10-year vanilla?

22. Suppose the exchange rate S follows a Brownian motion without drift and constant volatility. How can you hedge a single-one-touch with digitals? Hint: Use the reflection principle.

23. Given vanillas and digitals, how can you structure European style barrier options?

24. Given the following market of bonds

Bond	Tenor in Years	Price	Notional	Coupon
ZeroBond 1	1	94	100	0 %
ZeroBond 2	2	88	100	0 %
CouponBond 1	3	100	100	7 %
CouponBond 2	4	100	100	8 %

write down the cash flows of the four bonds and determine the present value of the cash flow

t_0	1	2	3	4	years
	375	275	575	540	USD

in this market using both a replicating portfolio and a calculation of discount factors.

25. How would you find the Black-Scholes value of a EUR-USD *self-quanto forward* with strike K, which is cash-settled in EUR at maturity? Consider the two cases where either the conversion from USD into EUR of the payoff $S_T - K$ is done using S_T or using S_0.

26. Suppose a client believe very strongly that USD/JPY will reach a level of 120.00 in 3 months time. With a current spot level of 110.00, volatility of 10 %, JPY rate of 0 %,

USD rate of 3 %, find a product with maximum leverage and create a term sheet for the client explaining chances and risks.

27. Prove that a symmetric power straddle has a constant gamma. What does this imply for delta, vega, rhos and theta?

28. In Section 1.5.5 it was stated, that *as a rule of thumb, a floating strike lookback option is worth twice as much as a vanilla option.* Can you prove this rule? Discuss where it applies.

29. Let NT(B) and OT(B) denote the value of a no-touch and a one-touch with barrier B respectively, both paid at the end. Let KOPut(K, B) and KOCall(K, B) denote the value of a regular knock-out put and call with strike K and barrier B respectively. Let SOPut(K) and SOCall(K) denote the value of a strike-out put and call with strike K and barrier K respectively. Finally, let RKOPut(K, B) and RKOCall(K, B) denote the value of a reverse knock-out put and call with strike K and barrier B respectively. How can you replicate reverse knock-outs using touch-options, strike-outs and regular knock-outs? In particular, prove or verify the equation

$$\text{RKOCall}(K, B) = (B - K)\text{NT}(B) - \text{SOPut}(B) + \text{KOPut}(K, B). \qquad (1.284)$$

Support your answer with a suitable figure and state the corresponding equation for the RKOPut. This implies in particular that the market prices for reverse knock-outs can be implied from the market prices of touch and regular barrier options. Moreover, this result also shows how to hedge regular knock-out options.

30. Derive the value function of a quanto forward. Consider next a *self-quanto*, where in a EUR-USD market, a client does a forward where he agrees to receive $S_T - K$ in EUR rather than USD. If the amount he receives is negative, then he pays.

1.6 SECOND GENERATION EXOTICS

1.6.1 Corridors

A European corridor entitles its holder to receive a pre-specified amount of a currency (say EUR) on a specified date (maturity) proportional to the number of fixings inside a lower range and an upper range between the start date and maturity. The buyer has to pay a premium for this product.

Advantages

- High leverage product, high profit potential
- Can take advantage of a quiet market phase
- Easy to price and to understand

Disadvantages

- Not suitable for long-term
- Expensive product
- Price spikes and large market movements can lead to loss

Figure 2.12 shows a sample scenario for a corridor. At delivery, the holder receives $\frac{n}{N} \cdot$ notional, where n is the number of fixings between the lower and the upper range and N denotes to maximum number of fixing possible.

Types of corridors

European style corridor.   The corridor is *resurrecting*, i.e. all fixings inside the range count for the accumulation, even if some of the fixings are outside. Given a *fixing schedule* $\{S_{t_1}, S_{t_2}, \ldots, S_{t_N}\}$ the payoff can be specified by

$$\text{notional} \cdot \frac{1}{N} \sum_{i=1}^{N} I\!I_{\{S_{t_i} \in (L,H)\}}, \tag{1.285}$$

where N denotes the total number of fixings, L the lower barrier, H the higher barrier.

American style corridor.   The corridor is *non-resurrecting*, i.e. only fixings count for the accumulation that occurs before the first time the exchange rate leaves the range. In this case one needs to specify exactly the time the fixing is set. In particular, if on one day the exchange rate trades at or outside the range, does a fixing inside the range on this day still account for the accumulation? The default is that it does, if the range is left after the fixing time. In any case, the holder of the corridor keeps the accumulated amount.

Introducing the stopping time

$$\tau \stackrel{\Delta}{=} \inf\{t : S_t \notin (L, H)\}, \tag{1.286}$$

the payoff can be specified by

$$\text{notional} \cdot \frac{1}{N} \sum_{i=1}^{N} I\!I_{\{S_{t_i} \in (L,H)\}} I\!I_{\{t_i < \tau\}}. \tag{1.287}$$

As a variation, the fixing range and the knock-out range need not be identical, the ranges can be one-sided or only partially valid over time.

American style corridor with complete knock-out.   This is an American style corridor, where all of the accumulated amount is lost once the exchange rate trades at or outside the range. This is equivalent to a double-no-touch. The payoff can be specified by

$$\text{notional} \cdot \frac{1}{N} \sum_{i=1}^{N} I\!I_{\{S_{t_i} \in (L,H)\}} I\!I_{\{L < \min_{0 \le t \le T} S_t \le \max_{0 \le t \le T} S_t < H\}}, \tag{1.288}$$

where T denotes the expiration time. This type of corridor only makes sense if the range for the fixings is strictly smaller than the range for the knock-out.

American style corridor with discrete knock-out.   This is like an American style corridor where the knock-out occurs when the fixing is outside the range for the first time, i.e. we replace the stopping time by

$$\tau_d \stackrel{\Delta}{=} \min\{t_i : S_{t_i} \notin (L, H)\}. \tag{1.289}$$

Forward start corridor.   In this type, which can be European or American as before, the range will be set relative to a future spot level, see also Section 1.5.6.

Table 1.29   Example of a European corridor

Spot reference	1.1500 EUR-USD
Notional	1,000,000 EUR
Maturity	1 year
European style corridor	1.1000 - 1.18000 EUR-USD
Fixing schedule	monthly
Fixing source	ECB
Premium	500,000 EUR

To compare, the premium for the same corridor in American style would be 100,000 EUR.

Example
An investor wants to benefit from believing that the EUR-USD exchange rate will be often between two ranges during 12 months. In this case an advisable product to use is a European corridor as for example presented in Table 1.29.

If the investor's market expectation is correct, then it will receive 1 Mio EUR at delivery, twice the premium at stake.

Explanations

Fixings   are *official* exchange rate sources such as from the European Central Bank, the federal reserve bank or private banks, which takes place on each business day. For details on the impact on pricing see Section 3.4.

Fixing source   is the exact source of the fixing, for example Reuters page ECB37, OPTREF, or Bloomberg pages.

Fixing schedule   requires a start date, end date and a frequency such as daily, weekly or monthly. It can also be customized. Since there are often disputes about holidays, it is advisable to specify any fixing schedule explicitly in the deal confirmation.

Composition and applications

Obviously, a European style corridor is a sum of digital options. The only issue is that the expiration times are the fixing time and the delivery time is the same for all digital options.

Similarly, an American style corridor is a sum of double-barrier digitals with deferred delivery. We refer the reader to the exercises to work out the details.

Corridors occur very often as part of structured products such as a *range accrual forward* in Section 2.1.9 or a *corridor deposit* in Section 2.3.4.

1.6.2   Faders

Faders are options, whose nominal is directly proportional to the number of fixings the spot stays inside or outside a pre-defined range. A *fade-in option* has a progressive activation of the nominal. In a *fade-out option* the concept of a progressive activation of the nominal is changed to a progressive deactivation. We discuss as an example the fade-in put option, whose characteristics are the pre-defined range and the associated fixing schedule with the maximal number of fixing being M. For each fixing date with the fixing inside the pre-defined range the holder of a fade-in put option receives a vanilla put option with the notional

$$\frac{\text{number of fixings inside the range}}{M}. \tag{1.290}$$

Buying a fade-in put option provides protection against falling EUR and allows full participation in a rising EUR. The holder has to pay a premium for this protection. He will exercise the option only if at maturity the spot is below the strike. The seller of the option receives the premium, but is exposed to market movements and would need to hedge his exposure accordingly.

Advantages

• Protection against weaker EUR/stronger USD
• Premium not as high as for a Plain Vanilla Put option
• Full participation in a favorable spot movement

Disadvantages

• Selling amount depends on market movements
• No guaranteed worst case exchange rate for the full notional.

Example for the computation of the notional

We explain this product with a EUR Put-USD Call with strike K, which has two ranges and 6 fixings, in Figure 1.47.

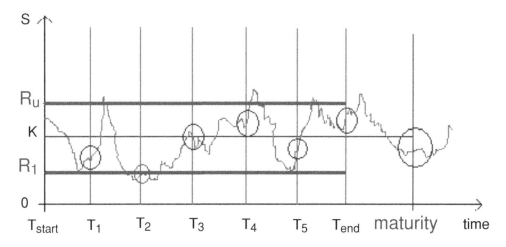

Figure 1.47   Notional of a fade-in put
At T_{end}, the holder would be entitled to sell $\frac{5}{6} \cdot 1$ Mio EUR, where 5 is the number of fixings between the lower and the upper range R_l and R_u on a resurrecting basis (here $n = 5$ because at T_2, the spot fixing is below the lower range). The total number of fixings inside the range will be known only at T_{end}. Hence, the notional of the put will only be known at T_{end}.

Table 1.30   Example of a fade-in put

Spot reference	1.1500 EUR-USD
Company buys	EUR put USD call
Fixing schedule	Monthly
Maturity	1 year
Notional amount	EUR 1,000,000
Strike	1.1600 EUR-USD
Lower Range	1.0000 EUR-USD
Upper Range	1.2000 EUR-USD
Premium	EUR 6,000.00

In comparison the corresponding vanilla put costs 50,000.00 EUR.

At maturity, the fade-in put works like a vanilla put. The holder would exercise the option and sell $\frac{5}{6}\cdot$ 1 Mio EUR at the strike K if the spot is below the strike. If it ends up above, the option would expire worthless. The overall loss of the buyer would be the option's premium.

Example
A company wants to hedge receivables from an export transaction in EUR due in 12 months time. It expects a weaker EUR/stronger USD. The company wishes to be able to sell EUR at a higher spot rate if the EUR becomes stronger on the one hand, but on the other hand be protected against a weaker EUR. The company finds the corresponding vanilla put too expensive and is prepared to take more risk. The treasurer believes that EUR/USD will not trade outside the range 1.1000–1.2000 for a significantly long time.

In this case a possible form of protection that the company can use is to buy a EUR fade-in put option, as for example presented in Table 1.30.
If the EUR-USD exchange rate is below the strike at maturity, then the company can sell EUR at maturity at the strike of 1.1600.

If the EUR-USD exchange rate is above the strike at maturity the option expires worthless. However, the company will benefit from a higher spot when selling EUR.

Variations

Besides puts, there are fade-in call or fade-in forwards, see Table 1.31 or the live trade in Table 2.3 in Section 2.1.3. Also more exotic types of faders can be created by taking exotic options and let them fade in or out.

Faders often have an additional knock-out range just like corridors, see Section 1.6.1. One then classifies faders into *resurrecting*, *non-resurrecting, keeping the accrued amount* and *non-resurrecting loosing parts of all of the accrued amount*.

Faders are most popularly applied in structuring *accumulative forwards*, see Section 2.1.10.

1.6.3   Exotic barrier options

Digital barrier options

Just like barrier options, which are calls or puts with knock-out or knock-in barriers, one can consider digital calls and puts with additional American style knock-out or knock-in barriers.

Table 1.31   Example of a fade-in forward. In comparison the corresponding fade-in call costs 27,000.00 EUR

Spot reference	1.1500 EUR-USD
Company buys	EUR-USD forward
Fixing schedule	Monthly
Maturity	1 year
Notional amount	EUR 1,000,000
Strike	1.0000 EUR-USD
Lower Range	1.0000 EUR-USD
Upper Range	1.1800 EUR-USD
Premium	EUR 9,000.00

Knowing the digitals, we can derive the knock-in digitals form the knock-out digitals. The knock-out digitals can be viewed as the delta of the knock-out vanilla options, and hence the values, prices and hedges from there.

The motivation for such products is to make betting on events cheaper.

Window barriers

Barriers need not be active for the entire lifetime of the option. Window Barrier Options are European Plain Vanilla or Binary Options with Barriers where the Barriers are active during a period of time which is shorter than the whole lifetime of the option. For example only the first 3 months from a 6 months maturity option. One can specify arbitrary time ranges with piecewise constant barrier levels or even non-constant barriers. See Figure 1.48 for the value function of a window barrier option. Linear and exponential barriers are useful if there is a certain drift in the exchange rate caused, e.g., by a high interest rate differential (high swap points).

Step and soft barriers

In case of a knock-out event, a client might argue: "Come on, the spot only crossed the barrier for a very short moment, can't you make an exception and not let my option knock out?" This is a very common concern: how to get protection against price spikes. Such a protection is certainly possible, but surely has its price. One way is to measure the time the spot spends opposite the knock-out barrier and let the option knock out gradually. For instance one could agree that the option's nominal is decreased by 10 % for each day the exchange rate fixing is opposite the barrier. This can be done linearly or exponentially. Such contracts are also referred to as *occupation time derivatives*.

Fluffy barriers

Fluffy Barrier Options are European Options with a Fluffy Barrier which knocks-in or -out in a non-digital way. The knock-in or knock-out is generally linear between the minimum and maximum Fluffy Barrier levels. For instance one can specify a barrier range of 2.20 to 2.30 where the option loses 25 % of its nominal when 2.20 is breached, 50 % when 2.25 is breached, 75 % when 2.275 is breached and 100 % when 2.30 is breached.

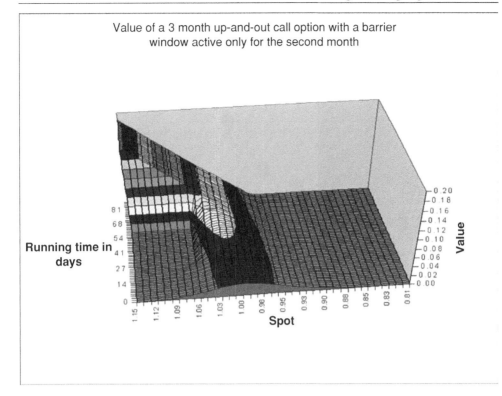

Value of a 3 month up-and-out call option with a barrier
window active only for the second month

Figure 1.48   Value function $v(t, x)$ of an up-and-out call option with window barrier active only for the second month, with strike $K = 0.9628$, knock-out barrier $B = 1.0590$ and maturity 3 months. We used the interest rates $r_d = 6.68\%$, $r_f = 5.14\%$, volatility $\sigma = 11.6\%$ and $R = 0$

Parisian and Parasian barriers

Another way to get price spike protection is to let the option knock out only if the spot spends a certain pre-specified length of time opposite the barrier – either in total (Parasian) or in a row (Parisian). Clearly the plain barrier option is the least expensive, followed by the Parasian, then the Parisian barrier option and finally the corresponding vanilla contract. See Figure 1.49.

Resetable barriers

This is a way to give the holder of a barrier option a chance to reset the barrier during the life of the option n times at a priori determined N times in the future $(N \geq n)$. This kind of extra protection also makes the barrier option more expensive.

Quanto barriers

In foreign exchange options markets option payoffs are often paid in a currency different from the underlying currency pair. For instance a USD/JPY call is designed to be paid in EUR, where the exchange rate for EUR/JPY is determined a priori. Surely such features can be applied to barrier options as well.

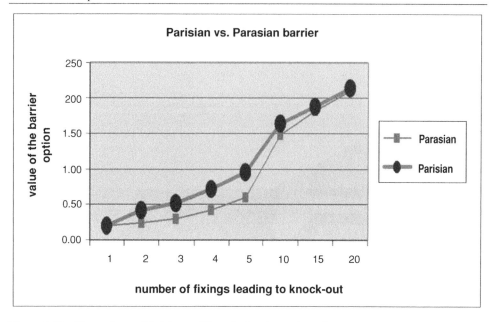

Figure 1.49   Comparison of Parisian and Parasian barrier option values

Transatlantic barrier options

For Transatlantic barrier options one barrier is of American style, the other one of European style. Naturally, the European style barrier is in-the-money, the American style barrier usually out-of-the-money. Therefore, there are essentially two versions,

1. a call with strike K, a European style up-and-out $H > K$ and an American style down-and-out at $L \leq K$,
2. a put with strike K, a European style down-and-out $L < K$ and an American style up-and-out $H \geq K$.

The motivation for such products is of course the savings effect in comparison to vanilla or single barrier options on the one hand and the fear of price spikes and a resulting preference for European style barriers on the other.

   The pricing and hedging is comparatively easy provided we have regular and digital barrier options available as basic products. Then we can structure the transatlantic barrier option just like in Equation (3.31), with an additional out-of-the-money knock-out barrier.

Outside barrier options

Outside barrier options are options in one currency pair with one or several barriers or window barriers in another currency pair. In general form the payoff can be written as

$$[\phi (S_T - K)]^+ \, I\!\!I_{\{\min_{0 \leq t \leq T} (\eta R(t)) > \eta B\}}. \tag{1.291}$$

This is a European put or call with strike K and a knock-out barrier H in a second currency pair, called the *outer* currency pair. As usual, the binary variable ϕ takes the value $+1$ for a call and -1 for a put and the binary variable η takes the value $+1$ for a lower barrier and -1 for an upper barrier. The positive constants σ_i denote the annual volatilities of the i-th asset or foreign currency, ρ the instantaneous correlation of their log-returns, r the domestic risk free rate and T the expiration time in years. In a risk-neutral setting the drift terms μ_i take the values

$$\mu_i = r - r_i \tag{1.292}$$

where r_i denotes the risk free rate of the i-th foreign currency. Knock-in outside barrier options prices can be obtained by the standard relationship *knock-in plus knock-out = vanilla*.

In the standard two-dimensional Black-Scholes model

$$dS_t = S_t \left[\mu_1 dt + \sigma_1 dW_t^{(1)} \right], \tag{1.293}$$

$$dR_t = R_t \left[\mu_2 dt + \sigma_2 dW_t^{(2)} \right], \tag{1.294}$$

$$\mathbf{Cov}\left[W_t^{(1)}, W_t^{(2)} \right] = \sigma_1 \sigma_2 \rho t, \tag{1.295}$$

Heynen and Kat derive the value in [45].

$$\begin{aligned}
V_0 &= \phi S_0 e^{-r_1 T} \mathcal{N}_2(\phi d_1, -\eta e_1; \phi\eta\rho) \\
&\quad -\phi S_0 e^{-r_1 T} \exp\left(\frac{2(\mu_2 + \rho\sigma_1\sigma_2)\ln(H/R_0)}{\sigma_2^2} \right) \mathcal{N}_2(\phi d_1', -\eta e_1'; \phi\eta\rho) \\
&\quad -\phi K e^{-rT} \mathcal{N}_2(\phi d_2, -\eta e_2; \phi\eta\rho) \\
&\quad +\phi K e^{-rT} \exp\left(\frac{2\mu_2 \ln(H/R_0)}{\sigma_2^2} \right) \mathcal{N}_2(\phi d_2', -\eta e_2'; \phi\eta\rho),
\end{aligned} \tag{1.296}$$

$$d_1 = \frac{\ln(S_0/K) + (\mu_1 + \sigma_1^2)T}{\sigma_1 \sqrt{T}}, \tag{1.297}$$

$$d_2 = d_1 - \sigma_1 \sqrt{T}, \tag{1.298}$$

$$d_1' = d_1 + \frac{2\rho \ln(H/R_0)}{\sigma_2 \sqrt{T}}, \tag{1.299}$$

$$d_2' = d_2 + \frac{2\rho \ln(H/R_0)}{\sigma_2 \sqrt{T}}, \tag{1.300}$$

$$e_1 = \frac{\ln(H/R_0) - (\mu_2 + \rho\sigma_1\sigma_2)T}{\sigma_2 \sqrt{T}}, \tag{1.301}$$

$$e_2 = e_1 + \rho\sigma_1 \sqrt{T}, \tag{1.302}$$

$$e_1' = e_1 - \frac{2\ln(H/R_0)}{\sigma_2 \sqrt{T}}, \tag{1.303}$$

$$e_2' = e_2 - \frac{2\ln(H/R_0)}{\sigma_2 \sqrt{T}}. \tag{1.304}$$

The bivariate standard normal distribution $\mathcal{N}_2$[7] and density functions n_2 are defined by

$$n_2(x, y; \rho) \triangleq \frac{1}{2\pi\sqrt{1-\rho^2}} \exp\left(-\frac{x^2 - 2\rho xy + y^2}{2(1-\rho^2)}\right),$$ (1.305)

$$\mathcal{N}_2(x, y; \rho) \triangleq \int_{-\infty}^{x} \int_{-\infty}^{y} n_2(u, v; \rho)\, du\, dv.$$ (1.306)

For the Greeks, most of the calculations of partial derivatives can be simplified substantially by the homogeneity method described in [6], which states for instance, that

$$V_0 = S_0 \frac{\partial V_0}{\partial S_0} + K \frac{\partial V_0}{\partial K}.$$ (1.307)

We list some of the sensitivities for reference.

delta(inner spot)

$$\frac{\partial V_0}{\partial S_0} = \phi e^{-r_1 T} \mathcal{N}_2(\phi d_1, -\eta e_1; \phi\eta\rho)$$ (1.308)

$$-\phi e^{-r_1 T} \exp\left(\frac{2(\mu_2 + \rho\sigma_1\sigma_2)\ln(H/R_0)}{\sigma_2^2}\right) \mathcal{N}_2(\phi d_1', -\eta e_1'; \phi\eta\rho)$$

dual delta(inner strike)

$$\frac{\partial V_0}{\partial K} = -\phi e^{-rT} \mathcal{N}_2(\phi d_2, -\eta e_2; \phi\eta\rho)$$ (1.309)

$$+\phi e^{-rT} \exp\left(\frac{2\mu_2 \ln(H/R_0)}{\sigma_2^2}\right) \mathcal{N}_2(\phi d_2', -\eta e_2'; \phi\eta\rho)$$

gamma(inner spot)

$$\frac{\partial^2 V_0}{\partial S_0^2} = \frac{e^{-r_1 T}}{S_0\sigma_1\sqrt{T}}\left[n(d_1)\mathcal{N}\left(\frac{-\phi\rho d_1 - \eta e_1}{\sqrt{1-\rho^2}}\right)\right.$$ (1.310)

$$\left.- \exp\left(\frac{2(\mu_2 + \rho\sigma_1\sigma_2)\ln(H/R_0)}{\sigma_2^2}\right) n(d_1')\mathcal{N}\left(\frac{-\phi\rho d_1' - \eta e_1'}{\sqrt{1-\rho^2}}\right)\right]$$

The standard normal density function n and its cumulative distribution function $\mathcal{N}$ are defined in (1.316) and (1.323). Furthermore, we use the relations

$$\frac{\partial}{\partial x}\mathcal{N}_2(x, y; \rho) = n(x)\mathcal{N}\left(\frac{y - \rho x}{\sqrt{1-\rho^2}}\right),$$ (1.311)

$$\frac{\partial}{\partial y}\mathcal{N}_2(x, y; \rho) = n(y)\mathcal{N}\left(\frac{x - \rho y}{\sqrt{1-\rho^2}}\right).$$ (1.312)

[7] See http://www.mathfinance.com/frontoffice.html for a source code to compute $\mathcal{N}_2$.

dual gamma(inner strike) Again, the homogeneity method described in [6] leads to the result

$$S^2 \frac{\partial^2 V_0}{\partial S_0^2} = K^2 \frac{\partial^2 V_0}{\partial K^2}. \tag{1.313}$$

In order to derive the value function we start with a triple integral. We treat the up-and-out call as an example. The value of an outside up-and-out call option is given in Section 24 in [19] by the integral

$$V_0 \stackrel{\Delta}{=} \frac{e^{-rT}}{\sqrt{T}} \int_{\hat{m}=0}^{\hat{m}=m} \int_{\hat{b}=-\infty}^{\hat{b}=\hat{m}} \int_{\tilde{b}=-\infty}^{\tilde{b}=\infty} F(\hat{b}, \tilde{b}) n(\frac{\tilde{b}}{\sqrt{T}}) f(\hat{m}, \hat{b}) \, d\tilde{b} \, d\hat{b} \, d\hat{m}, \tag{1.314}$$

where the payoff function F, the normal density function n, the joint density function f and the parameters $m, b, \hat{\theta}, \gamma$ are defined by

$$F(\hat{b}, \tilde{b}) \stackrel{\Delta}{=} \left(S_0 e^{\gamma \sigma_2 T + \rho \sigma_2 \hat{b} + \sqrt{1-\rho^2}\sigma_2 \tilde{b}} - K \right)^+ \tag{1.315}$$

$$n(t) \stackrel{\Delta}{=} \frac{1}{\sqrt{2\pi}} e^{-\frac{1}{2}t^2}, \tag{1.316}$$

$$f(\hat{m}, \hat{b}) \stackrel{\Delta}{=} \frac{2(2\hat{m} - \hat{b})}{T\sqrt{2\pi T}} \exp \left\{ -\frac{(2\hat{m} - \hat{b})^2}{2T} + \hat{\theta}\hat{b} - \frac{1}{2}\hat{\theta}^2 T \right\}, \tag{1.317}$$

$$m \stackrel{\Delta}{=} \frac{1}{\sigma_1} \ln \frac{L}{Y_0}, \tag{1.318}$$

$$b \stackrel{\Delta}{=} \frac{1}{\sigma_2} \ln \frac{L}{S_0}, \tag{1.319}$$

$$\hat{\theta} \stackrel{\Delta}{=} \frac{r}{\sigma_1} - \frac{\sigma_1}{2}, \tag{1.320}$$

$$\gamma \stackrel{\Delta}{=} \frac{r}{\sigma_2} - \frac{\sigma_2}{2} - \rho\hat{\theta}. \tag{1.321}$$

The goal is to write the above integral in terms of the bivariate normal distribution function (1.306). For easier comparison we use the identification Table 1.32.

Table 1.32 Relating the notation of Heynen and Kat to the one by Shreve

Heynen/Kat	Shreve
S_0	S_0
R_0	Y_0
σ_1	σ_2
σ_2	σ_1
H	L
K	K
μ_1	$r - \frac{\sigma_2^2}{2}$
μ_2	$r - \frac{\sigma_1^2}{2}$

The solution can be obtained by following the steps

(a) Use a change of variables to prove the identity

$$\int_{-\infty}^{x} \mathcal{N}(az + B)n(z)\,dz = \mathcal{N}_2\left(x, \frac{B}{\sqrt{1+a^2}}; \frac{-a}{\sqrt{1+a^2}}\right), \tag{1.322}$$

where the cumulative normal distribution function $\mathcal{N}$ is defined by

$$\mathcal{N}(x) \overset{\Delta}{=} \int_{-\infty}^{x} n(t)\,dt. \tag{1.323}$$

A probabilistic proof is presented in [58].

(b) Extend the identity (1.322) to

$$\int_{-\infty}^{x} e^{Az}\mathcal{N}(az + B)n(z)\,dz = e^{\frac{A^2}{2}}\mathcal{N}_2\left(x - A, \frac{aA + B}{\sqrt{1+a^2}}; \frac{-a}{\sqrt{1+a^2}}\right). \tag{1.324}$$

(c) Change the order of integration in Equation (1.314) and integrate the $\hat{m}$ variable.
(d) Change the order of integration to make $\tilde{b}$ the inner variable and $\hat{b}$ the outer variable. Then use the condition $F(\hat{b}, \tilde{b}) \geq 0$ to find a lower limit for the range of $\tilde{b}$. This will enable you to skip the positive part in F and write Equation (1.314) as a sum of four integrals.
(e) Use (1.322) and (1.324) to write each of these four summands in terms of the bivariate normal distribution function $\mathcal{N}_2$.
(f) Compare your result with the one provided by Heynen and Kat using the identification table given above.

The solution of the integral works like this.

(a) To prove the identity

$$\int_{-\infty}^{x} \mathcal{N}(az + B)n(z)\,dz = \mathcal{N}_2\left(x, \frac{B}{\sqrt{1+a^2}}; \frac{-a}{\sqrt{1+a^2}}\right),$$

we must show that for $\rho = \frac{-a}{\sqrt{1+a^2}}$

$$\int_{v=-\infty}^{x} \int_{u=-\infty}^{av+B} \exp\left(-\frac{1}{2}(u^2 + v^2)\right) du\,dv \tag{1.325}$$

$$= \frac{1}{\sqrt{1-\rho^2}} \int_{v=-\infty}^{x} \int_{u=-\infty}^{\frac{B}{\sqrt{1+a^2}}} \exp\left(-\frac{u^2 - 2\rho uv + v^2}{2(1-\rho^2)}\right) du\,dv. \tag{1.326}$$

We start with (1.325), do the change of variable $u = (\tilde{u} - \rho v)/\sqrt{1 - \rho^2}$ and obtain

$$\frac{1}{\sqrt{1 - \rho^2}} \int_{v=-\infty}^{x} \int_{\tilde{u}=-\infty}^{\sqrt{1-\rho^2}(av+B)+\rho v} \exp\left(-\frac{\tilde{u}^2 - 2\rho\tilde{u}v + v^2}{2(1 - \rho^2)}\right) d\tilde{u}\, dv. \quad (1.327)$$

The choice $\rho = \frac{-a}{\sqrt{1+a^2}}$ produces the upper limit of integration $\frac{B}{\sqrt{1+a^2}}$ for $\tilde{u}$ and this leads to (1.326).

(b) Extend the identity (1.322) to

$$\int_{-\infty}^{x} e^{Az}\mathcal{N}(az + B)n(z)\,dz = e^{\frac{A^2}{2}}\mathcal{N}_2\left(x - A, \frac{aA + B}{\sqrt{1 + a^2}}; \frac{-a}{\sqrt{1 + a^2}}\right).$$

We complete the square, substitute $z - A = u$, use identity (1.322) and obtain

$$\int_{-\infty}^{x} e^{Az}\mathcal{N}(az + B)n(z)\,dz = e^{\frac{A^2}{2}} \int_{-\infty}^{x} \mathcal{N}(az + B)n(z - A)\,dz$$

$$= e^{\frac{A^2}{2}} \int_{-\infty}^{x-A} \mathcal{N}(au + aA + B)n(u)\,du$$

$$= e^{\frac{A^2}{2}}\mathcal{N}_2\left(x - A, \frac{aA + B}{\sqrt{1 + a^2}}; \frac{-a}{\sqrt{1 + a^2}}\right).$$

(c) Change the order of integration in Equation (1.314) and integrate the $\hat{m}$ variable.

$$V_0 = \frac{e^{-rT - \frac{1}{2}\theta^2 T}}{\sqrt{T}} \int_{\tilde{b}=-\infty}^{\tilde{b}=\infty} n\left(\frac{\tilde{b}}{\sqrt{T}}\right) \int_{\hat{b}=-\infty}^{\hat{b}=m} e^{\theta\hat{b}} F(\hat{b}, \tilde{b}) \int_{\hat{m}=\hat{b}\vee 0}^{\hat{m}=m} f(\hat{m}, \hat{b})\, d\hat{m}\, d\hat{b}\, d\tilde{b}$$

$$= \frac{e^{-rT - \frac{1}{2}\theta^2 T}}{T} \int_{\tilde{b}=-\infty}^{\tilde{b}=\infty} n\left(\frac{\tilde{b}}{\sqrt{T}}\right) \int_{\hat{b}=-\infty}^{\hat{b}=m} e^{\theta\hat{b}} F(\hat{b}, \tilde{b}) \left[n\left(\frac{\hat{b}}{\sqrt{T}}\right) - n\left(\frac{2m - \hat{b}}{\sqrt{T}}\right)\right] d\hat{b}\, d\tilde{b}.$$

(d) Change the order of integration to make $\tilde{b}$ the inner variable and $\hat{b}$ the outer variable. Then use the condition $F(\hat{b}, \tilde{b}) \geq 0$ to find a lower limit for the range of $\tilde{b}$. This will enable you to skip the positive part in F and write Equation (1.314) as a sum of four integrals.

The condition $F(\hat{b}, \tilde{b}) \geq 0$ is satisfied if and only if

$$\tilde{b} \geq \frac{b - \rho\hat{b} - \gamma T}{\sqrt{1 - \rho^2}}. \quad (1.328)$$

We may now proceed in our calculation as follows.

$$
V_0 = \frac{e^{-rT - \frac{1}{2}\hat{\theta}^2 T}}{T} \int_{\hat{b}=-\infty}^{\hat{b}=m} \int_{\tilde{b}=\frac{b-\rho\hat{b}-\gamma T}{\sqrt{1-\rho^2}}}^{\tilde{b}=\infty} n\left(\frac{\tilde{b}}{\sqrt{T}}\right) e^{\hat{\theta}\hat{b}} F\left(\hat{b}, \tilde{b}\right) \left[n\left(\frac{\hat{b}}{\sqrt{T}}\right) - n\left(\frac{2m-\hat{b}}{\sqrt{T}}\right) \right] d\tilde{b}\, d\hat{b}
$$

$$
= \frac{S_0 e^{-rT - \frac{1}{2}\hat{\theta}^2 T}}{T} \int_{\hat{b}=-\infty}^{\hat{b}=m} \int_{\tilde{b}=\frac{b-\rho\hat{b}-\gamma T}{\sqrt{1-\rho^2}}}^{\tilde{b}=\infty} n\left(\frac{\tilde{b}}{\sqrt{T}}\right) e^{\hat{\theta}\hat{b}} e^{\gamma\sigma_2 T + \rho\sigma_2\hat{b} + \sqrt{1-\rho^2}\sigma_2\tilde{b}} n\left(\frac{\hat{b}}{\sqrt{T}}\right) d\tilde{b}\, d\hat{b}
$$

$$
- \frac{S_0 e^{-rT - \frac{1}{2}\hat{\theta}^2 T}}{T} \int_{\hat{b}=-\infty}^{\hat{b}=m} \int_{\tilde{b}=\frac{b-\rho\hat{b}-\gamma T}{\sqrt{1-\rho^2}}}^{\tilde{b}=\infty} n\left(\frac{\tilde{b}}{\sqrt{T}}\right) e^{\hat{\theta}\hat{b}} e^{\gamma\sigma_2 T + \rho\sigma_2\hat{b} + \sqrt{1-\rho^2}\sigma_2\tilde{b}} n\left(\frac{2m-\hat{b}}{\sqrt{T}}\right) d\tilde{b}\, d\hat{b}
$$

$$
- \frac{K e^{-rT - \frac{1}{2}\hat{\theta}^2 T}}{T} \int_{\hat{b}=-\infty}^{\hat{b}=m} \int_{\tilde{b}=\frac{b-\rho\hat{b}-\gamma T}{\sqrt{1-\rho^2}}}^{\tilde{b}=\infty} n\left(\frac{\tilde{b}}{\sqrt{T}}\right) e^{\hat{\theta}\hat{b}} n\left(\frac{\hat{b}}{\sqrt{T}}\right) d\tilde{b}\, d\hat{b}
$$

$$
+ \frac{K e^{-rT - \frac{1}{2}\hat{\theta}^2 T}}{T} \int_{\hat{b}=-\infty}^{\hat{b}=m} \int_{\tilde{b}=\frac{b-\rho\hat{b}-\gamma T}{\sqrt{1-\rho^2}}}^{\tilde{b}=\infty} n\left(\frac{\tilde{b}}{\sqrt{T}}\right) e^{\hat{\theta}\hat{b}} n\left(\frac{2m-\hat{b}}{\sqrt{T}}\right) d\tilde{b}\, d\hat{b}
$$

$$
= S_0 e^{(-r - \frac{1}{2}\hat{\theta}^2 + \gamma\sigma_2 + \frac{1}{2}(1-\rho^2)\sigma_2^2)T}
$$

$$
\int_{y=-\infty}^{y=\frac{m}{\sqrt{T}}} e^{(\hat{\theta}+\rho\sigma_2)\sqrt{T}y} \mathcal{N}\left(\frac{\rho}{\sqrt{1-\rho^2}}y + \frac{-b+\gamma T + (1-\rho^2)\sigma_2 T}{\sqrt{1-\rho^2}\sqrt{T}}\right) n(y)\, dy
$$

$$
- S_0 e^{(-r - \frac{1}{2}\hat{\theta}^2 + \gamma\sigma_2 + \frac{1}{2}(1-\rho^2)\sigma_2^2)T} e^{(\hat{\theta}+\rho\sigma_2)2m}
$$

$$
\int_{y=-\infty}^{y=-\frac{m}{\sqrt{T}}} e^{(\hat{\theta}+\rho\sigma_2)\sqrt{T}y} \mathcal{N}\left(\frac{\rho}{\sqrt{1-\rho^2}}y + \frac{-b+2\rho m + \gamma T + (1-\rho^2)\sigma_2 T}{\sqrt{1-\rho^2}\sqrt{T}}\right) n(y)\, dy
$$

$$
- K e^{(-r - \frac{1}{2}\hat{\theta}^2)T}
$$

$$
\int_{y=-\infty}^{y=\frac{m}{\sqrt{T}}} e^{\hat{\theta}\sqrt{T}y} \mathcal{N}\left(\frac{\rho}{\sqrt{1-\rho^2}}y + \frac{-b+\gamma T}{\sqrt{1-\rho^2}\sqrt{T}}\right) n(y)\, dy
$$

$$
+ K e^{(-r - \frac{1}{2}\hat{\theta}^2)T} e^{2m\hat{\theta}}
$$

$$
\int_{y=-\infty}^{y=-\frac{m}{\sqrt{T}}} e^{\hat{\theta}\sqrt{T}y} \mathcal{N}\left(\frac{\rho}{\sqrt{1-\rho^2}}y + \frac{-b+2m\rho + \gamma T}{\sqrt{1-\rho^2}\sqrt{T}}\right) n(y)\, dy.
$$

(e) Use (1.322) and (1.324) to write each of these four summands in terms of the bivariate normal distribution function $\mathcal{N}_2$.

We take $a = \frac{\rho}{\sqrt{1-\rho^2}}$ in all four summands which implies that $\frac{-a}{\sqrt{1+a^2}} = -\rho$. We choose A and B as suggested by Equation (1.324) and obtain

$$V_0 = S_0 \mathcal{N}_2 \left(\frac{\ln \frac{L}{Y_0} - (r - \frac{\sigma_1^2}{2})T}{\sigma_1 \sqrt{T}} - \rho \sigma_2 \sqrt{T}, \; \frac{\ln \frac{S_0}{K} + (r + \frac{\sigma_2^2}{2})T}{\sigma_2 \sqrt{T}}; -\rho \right)$$

$$- S_0 e^{2m(\hat{\theta} + \rho \sigma_2)} \mathcal{N}_2 \left(\frac{-\ln \frac{L}{Y_0} - (r - \frac{\sigma_1^2}{2})T}{\sigma_1 \sqrt{T}} - \rho \sigma_2 \sqrt{T}, \; \frac{\ln \frac{S_0}{K} + (r + \frac{\sigma_2^2}{2})T}{\sigma_2 \sqrt{T}} + \frac{2m\rho}{\sqrt{T}}; -\rho \right)$$

$$- K e^{-rT} \mathcal{N}_2 \left(\frac{\ln \frac{L}{Y_0} - (r - \frac{\sigma_1^2}{2})T}{\sigma_1 \sqrt{T}}, \; \frac{\ln \frac{S_0}{K} + (r - \frac{\sigma_2^2}{2})T}{\sigma_2 \sqrt{T}}; -\rho \right)$$

$$+ K e^{-rT} e^{2m\hat{\theta}} \mathcal{N}_2 \left(\frac{-\ln \frac{L}{Y_0} - (r - \frac{\sigma_1^2}{2})T}{\sigma_1 \sqrt{T}}, \; \frac{\ln \frac{S_0}{K} + (r - \frac{\sigma_2^2}{2})T}{\sigma_2 \sqrt{T}} + \frac{2m\rho}{\sqrt{T}}; -\rho \right).$$

(f) Compare your result with the one provided by Heynen and Kat using the identification table given above.

This comparison can be done instantly. We just note that $\mathcal{N}_2(x, y; \rho) = \mathcal{N}_2(y, x; \rho)$.

Inside barrier options can be viewed as a special case. The formula for the (inside) up-and-out call option can be deduced from this result simply by choosing $Y_0 = S_0, \sigma_1 = \sigma_2 \stackrel{\Delta}{=} \sigma$, $\hat{\theta} = \theta_-, \rho = 1$ and using the identity $\mathcal{N}_2(x, y; -1) = \mathcal{N}(x) - \mathcal{N}(-y) = \mathcal{N}(y) - \mathcal{N}(-x)$. Denoting $\theta_\pm \stackrel{\Delta}{=} \frac{r}{\sigma} \pm \frac{\sigma}{2}$, it follows that

$$V_0 = S_0 \left[\mathcal{N} \left(\frac{m - \theta_+ T}{\sqrt{T}} \right) - \mathcal{N} \left(\frac{b - \theta_+ T}{\sqrt{T}} \right) \right]$$

$$- S_0 e^{2m\theta_+} \left[\mathcal{N} \left(\frac{m + \theta_+ T}{\sqrt{T}} \right) - \mathcal{N} \left(\frac{2m - b + \theta_+ T}{\sqrt{T}} \right) \right]$$

$$- K e^{-rT} \left[\mathcal{N} \left(\frac{m - \theta_- T}{\sqrt{T}} \right) - \mathcal{N} \left(\frac{b - \theta_- T}{\sqrt{T}} \right) \right]$$

$$+ K e^{-rT} e^{2m\theta_-} \left[\mathcal{N} \left(\frac{m + \theta_- T}{\sqrt{T}} \right) - \mathcal{N} \left(\frac{2m - b + \theta_- T}{\sqrt{T}} \right) \right].$$

Knock-in-knock-out options

Knock-In-Knock-Out Options are barriers with both a knock-out and a knock-in barrier. However, it is not so simple, because there are three fundamentally different types, namely,

1. the knock-out can happen *any time*,
2. the knock-out can happen only *after* the knock-in,
3. the knock-out can happen only *before* the knock-in.

The first one is the market standard, but when dealing one should always clarify which type of knock-in-knock-out is agreed upon. For example, let the lower barrier L be a knock-out barrier and the upper barrier U be a knock-out barrier. Standard type 1 KIKO can only be exercised if L is never touched *and* U has been touched at least once. This can be replicated by standard barrier options via

$$\text{KIKO}(L, U) = \text{KO}(L) - \text{DKO}(L, U). \tag{1.329}$$

Therefore, pricing and hedging of this KIKO is straightforward.

The second type is a special case of a *knock-in on strategy* option. Any structure can be equipped with a *global* knock-in barrier, that has to be touched before the structure becomes alive. Knock-out events in the structure are only active *after* the structure knocks in. This is a product of its own and requires an individual valuation, pricing and hedging approach.

In the third type of KIKO a knock-out can only happen before the knock-in. Once the option is knocked in, the knock-out barrier is no longer active. This is also a product of its own and requires an individual valuation, pricing and hedging approach.

James Bond Range

As James Bond can only live twice, the *James Bond Range* is a double-no-touch type of an option. Given an upper barrier H and a lower barrier L, it pays one unit of currency, if the spot remains inside (L, H) at all times until expiry T, or if the spot hits L the spot thereafter remains in a new range to be set around L or similarly if the spot hits H the spot thereafter remains in a new range to be set around H.

1.6.4 Pay-later options

A pay-later option is a vanilla option, whose premium is only paid if the option is exercised, i.e. if the spot is in-the-money at the expiration time. If the spot is not in-the-money, the holder of the option cannot exercise the option, and will end up not having paid anything. However, if the spot is in-the-money, the holder of the option has to pay the option premium, which will then be noticeably higher than the plain vanilla. For this reason pay-later options are not traded very often.

Advantages

- Full protection against spot market movement
- Premium is only paid if the options ends up in-the-money
- Premium is paid only at maturity

Disadvantages

- More expensive than a plain vanilla
- Credit risk for the seller as payoff can be negative

The valuation for the pay-later option

The payoff of pay-later option is defined as

$$[\phi(S_T - K) - P] \, I\!I_{\{\phi S_T \geq \phi K\}} \tag{1.330}$$

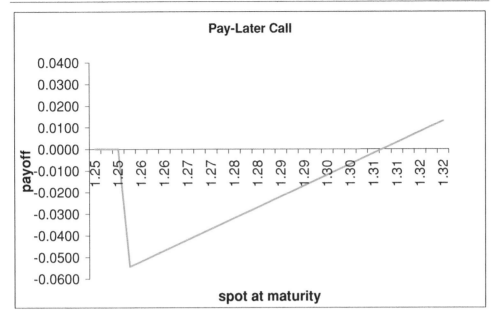

Figure 1.50 Payoff of a pay-later EUR call USD put
We use the market input spot $S_0 = 1.2000$, volatility $\sigma = 10\%$, EUR rate $r_f = 2\%$, USD rate $r_d = 2.5\%$, strike $K = 1.2500$, time to maturity $T = 0.5$ years. The vanilla value is 0.0158 USD, the digital value is 0.2781 USD, the resulting pay-later price is 0.0569 USD, which is substantially higher than the plain vanilla value. Consequently the break-even point is at 1.3075, which is quite far off. For this reason pay-later type structures do not trade very often.

and illustrated in Figure 1.50. As usual, the binary variable ϕ takes the value $+1$ for a call and -1 for a put, K the strike in units of the domestic currency, and T the expiration time in years. The *price P* of the pay-later option is paid at time T, but it is set at time zero in such a way that the time zero *value* of the above payoff is zero. Take care to notice the difference between price and value. After the option is written, the price P does not change anymore.

We denote the current spot by x and the current time by t and define, furthermore, the abbreviations

$$n(t) \triangleq \frac{1}{\sqrt{2\pi}} e^{-\frac{1}{2}t^2}, \tag{1.331}$$

$$N(x) \triangleq \int_{-\infty}^{x} n(t)\,dt, \tag{1.332}$$

$$\tau \triangleq T - t, \tag{1.333}$$

$$f = xe^{(r_d - r_f)\tau}, \tag{1.334}$$

$$d_\pm \triangleq \frac{\log\frac{f}{K} \pm \frac{1}{2}\sigma^2\tau}{\sigma\sqrt{\tau}}, \tag{1.335}$$

$$\text{vanilla}(x, K, T, t, \sigma, r_d, r_f, \phi) = \phi e^{-r_d\tau}[fN(\phi d_+) - KN(\phi d_-)], \tag{1.336}$$

$$\text{digital}(x, K, T, t, \sigma, r_d, r_f, \phi) = e^{-r_d\tau}N(\phi d_-). \tag{1.337}$$

The formulae of vanilla and digital options have been derived in Sections 1.2 and 1.5.2.

The payoff can be rewritten as

$$[\phi(S_T - K)]^+ - P\,\mathbb{1}_{\{\phi S_T \geq \phi K\}}, \tag{1.338}$$

whence the value of the pay-later option in the Black-Scholes model

$$dS_t = S_t\left[(r_d - r_f)dt + \sigma\, dW_t\right] \tag{1.339}$$

is easily read as

$$\text{paylater}(x, K, P, T, t, \sigma, r_d, r_f, \phi) = \text{vanilla}(x, K, T, t, \sigma, r_d, r_f, \phi) \tag{1.340}$$
$$-P \cdot \text{digital}(x, K, T, t, \sigma, r_d, r_f, \phi).$$

In particular, this leads to a quick implementation of the value and all the Greeks having the functions vanilla and digital at hand.

For the *pay-later price* setting

$$\text{paylater}(x, K, P, T, 0, \sigma, r_d, r_f, \phi) = 0 \tag{1.341}$$

yields

$$P = \frac{\text{vanilla}(x, K, T, 0, \sigma, r_d, r_f, \phi)}{\text{digital}(x, K, T, 0, \sigma, r_d, r_f, \phi)} \tag{1.342}$$

$$= \text{vanilla}(x, K, T, 0, \sigma, r_d, r_f, \phi)\frac{e^{r_d T}}{\mathcal{N}(\phi d_-)}. \tag{1.343}$$

This can be interpreted as follows. The value P is like the value of a vanilla option, except that

- we must pay interest $e^{r_d T}$, since the premium is due only at time T and
- the premium only needs to be paid if the option is exercised, which is why we divide by the (risk-neutral) probability that the option is exercised $\mathcal{N}(\phi d_-)$.

We observe that the pay-later option can be viewed as a *structured product*. All we need are vanilla and digital options. The structurer will easily replicate a short pay-later with a long vanilla and a short digital. We learn that several types of options can be composed from existing ones, which is the actual job of structuring. This way it is also straightforward to determine a market price, given a vanilla market.

Variations

Pay-later options are an example of the family of contingent or deferred payment options. We can also simply defer the payment of a vanilla without any conditions on the moneyness. Another variation is paying back the vanilla premium if the spot stays inside some range, see the exercises in Section 2.1.19. Naturally, the pay-later effect can be extended beyond vanilla options to all kind of options.

1.6.5   Step up and step down options

The Step Option is an option where the strike of the option is readjusted at predefined fixing dates, but only if the spot is more favorable than that of the previous fixing date. The step option can either be a plain vanilla option or single barrier option. The concept of a progressive *step up* or *step down* could be changed also to a progressive *step up* or *step down* for a forward rate.

1.6.6   Spread and exchange options

A spread option compensates a spread in exchange rates and pays off

$$\left[\phi\left(aS_T^{(1)} - bS_T^{(2)} - K\right)\right]^+. \tag{1.344}$$

This is a European spread put ($\phi = -1$) or call ($\phi = +1$) with strike $K > 0$ and the expiration time in years T. We assume without loss of generality that the weights a and b are positive. These weights are needed to make the two exchange rates comparable, as USD-CHF and USD-JPY differ by a factor of the size of 100. A standard for the weights are the reciprocals of the initial spot rates, i.e. $a = \frac{1}{S_0^{(1)}}$ and $b = \frac{1}{S_0^{(2)}}$.

Spread options are not traded very often in FX markets. If they are they are usually cash-settled. Exchange options come up more often as they entitle the owner to exchange one currency for another, which is very similar like a vanilla option, which is reflected in the valuation formula.

In the two-dimensional Black-Scholes model

$$dS_t^{(1)} = S_t^{(1)}\left[\mu_1 dt + \sigma_1 dW_t^{(1)}\right], \tag{1.345}$$

$$dS_t^{(2)} = S_t^{(2)}\left[\mu_2 dt + \sigma_2 dW_t^{(2)}\right], \tag{1.346}$$

$$\mathbf{Cov}\left[W_t^{(1)}, W_t^{(2)}\right] = \rho t, \tag{1.347}$$

with positive constants σ_i denoting the annual volatilities of the i-th foreign currency, ρ the instantaneous correlation of their log-returns, r the domestic risk free rate and risk-neutral drift terms

$$\mu_i = r - r_i, \tag{1.348}$$

where r_i denotes the risk free rate of the i-th foreign currency, the value is given by (see [59])

$$\text{spread} = \int_{-\infty}^{+\infty} \text{vanilla}\left(S(x), K(x), \sigma_1\sqrt{1 - \rho^2}, r, r_1, T, \phi\right) n(x)\, dx \tag{1.349}$$

$$S(x) \stackrel{\Delta}{=} aS_0^{(1)} e^{\rho\sigma_1\sqrt{T}x - \frac{1}{2}\sigma_1^2\rho^2 T} \tag{1.350}$$

$$K(x) \stackrel{\Delta}{=} bS_0^{(2)} e^{\sigma_2\sqrt{T}x + \mu_2 T - \frac{1}{2}\sigma_2^2 T} + K. \tag{1.351}$$

Notes

1. The integration can be done by the Gauß-Legendre-algorithm using integration limits -5 and 5. A corresponding source code and sample figures can be found in the Front Office section of www.mathfinance.com. The function vanilla (European put and call) can be found in Section 1.2.
2. The integration can be done analytically if $K = 0$. This is the case of *exchange options*, the right to exchange one currency for another.
3. To compute Greeks one may want to use homogeneity relations as discussed in [6].
4. In a foreign exchange setting, the correlation can be computed in terms of known volatilities. This can be found in Section 1.6.7.

Derivation of the value function

We use Equation (1.7) for the value of vanilla options along with the abbreviations thereafter.
    We rewrite the model in terms of independent new Brownian motions $W^{(1)}$ and $W^{(2)}$ and get

$$S_T^{(1)} = S_0^{(1)} \exp\left[\left(\mu_1 - \frac{1}{2}\sigma_1^2\right)T + \sigma_1\rho W_T^{(2)} + \sigma_1\sqrt{1 - \rho^2}W_T^{(1)}\right], \tag{1.352}$$

$$S_T^{(2)} = S_0^{(2)} \exp\left[\left(\mu_2 - \frac{1}{2}\sigma_2^2\right)T + \sigma_2 W_T^{(2)}\right]. \tag{1.353}$$

This allows us to write $S_T^{(1)}$ in terms of $S_T^{(2)}$, i.e.,

$$S_T^{(1)} = \exp\left[\hat{\mu}_1 + \frac{\sigma_1\rho}{\sigma_2}\left(\ln S_T^{(2)} - \hat{\mu}_2\right) + \sigma_1\sqrt{1 - \rho^2}W_T^{(1)}\right], \tag{1.354}$$

$$\hat{\mu}_i \triangleq \ln S_0^{(i)} + \left(\mu_i - \frac{1}{2}\sigma_i^2\right)T, \tag{1.355}$$

which shows that given $S_T^{(2)}$, $\ln S_T^{(1)}$ is normally distributed with mean and variance

$$\mu = \hat{\mu}_1 + \frac{\sigma_1\rho}{\sigma_2}\left(\ln S_T^{(2)} - \hat{\mu}_2\right), \tag{1.356}$$

$$\sigma^2 = \sigma_1^2(1 - \rho^2)T. \tag{1.357}$$

We recall from the derivation of the Black-Scholes formula for vanilla options that (and in fact, for $\rho = 0$ this *is* the Black-Scholes formula)

$$IE\left[\left(\phi\left(S_T^{(1)} - K\right)\right)^+\right] \tag{1.358}$$

$$= \phi\left[e^{\mu + \frac{\sigma^2}{2}}\mathcal{N}\left(\phi\frac{-\ln K + \mu + \sigma^2}{\sigma}\right) - K\mathcal{N}\left(\phi\frac{-\ln K + \mu + \sigma^2}{\sigma}\right)\right],$$

which allows to compute the value of a spread option as

$$e^{-rT} IE\left[\left(\phi\left(aS_T^{(1)} - bS_T^{(2)} - K\right)\right)^+\right] \tag{1.359}$$

$$= aIE\left[e^{-rT} IE\left[\left(\phi\left(S_T^{(1)} - \left(\frac{b}{a}S_T^{(2)} + \frac{K}{a}\right)\right)\right)^+\bigg| S_T^{(2)}\right]\right] \tag{1.360}$$

$$= a \cdot IE\left[\text{vanilla}\left(S_0^{(1)}\exp\left\{\frac{\sigma_1\rho}{\sigma_2}\left(\ln S_T^{(2)} - \hat{\mu}_2\right) - \frac{1}{2}\sigma_1^2\rho^2 T\right\},\right.\right.$$
$$\left.\left.\frac{b}{a}S_T^{(2)} + \frac{K}{a}, \sigma_1\sqrt{1 - \rho^2}, r, r_1, T, \phi\right)\right] \tag{1.361}$$

$$= \int_\infty^\infty \text{vanilla}\left(aS_0^{(1)}\exp\left\{\sigma_1\rho\sqrt{T}x - \frac{1}{2}\sigma_1^2\rho^2 T\right\},\right.$$
$$\left. b\exp\{\sigma_2\sqrt{T}x + \hat{\mu}_2\} + K, \sigma_1\sqrt{1 - \rho^2}, r, r_1, T, \phi\right)n(x)\,dx$$

$$= \int_{-\infty}^{+\infty} \text{vanilla}\left(S(x), K(x), \sigma_1\sqrt{1 - \rho^2}, r, r_1, T, \phi\right)n(x)\,dx. \tag{1.362}$$

Table 1.33   Example of a spread option

	EUR	GBP
Spot in USD	1.2000	1.8000
Interest rates	2 %	4 %
Volatility	10 %	9 %
Weights	1/1.2000	1/1.8000
USD rate	3 %	
Correlation	20 %	
Maturity	0.5 years	
Strike	0.0020	
Value	0.0375 USD	

Example

We consider the example in Table 1.33. An investor or corporate believes that EUR/USD will out perform GBP/USD in 6 months. To make it concrete we first normalize both exchange rates by dividing by their current spot and then want to reward the investor one pip for each pip the normalized EUR/USD will be more than 20 pips higher than normalized GBP/USD.

1.6.7   Baskets

This section is produced jointly with Jürgen Hakala and appeared first in [60].

In many cases corporate and institutional currency managers are faced with an exposure in more than one currency. Generally these exposures would be hedged using individual strategies for each currency. These strategies are composed of spot transactions, forwards, and in many cases options on a single currency. Nevertheless, there are instruments that include several currencies, and these can be used to build a multi-currency strategy that is almost always cheaper than the portfolio of the individual strategies. As a prominent example we now consider basket options in detail.

Protection with currency baskets

Basket options are derivatives based on a common base currency, say EUR, and several other risky currencies. The option is actually written on the basket of risky currencies. Basket options are European options paying the difference between the basket value and the strike, if positive, for a basket call, or the difference between strike and basket value, if positive, for a basket put respectively at maturity. The risky currencies have different weights in the basket to reflect the details of the exposure.

For example, a basket call on two currencies USD and JPY pays off

$$\max\left(a_1\frac{S_1(T)}{S_1(0)} + a_2\frac{S_2(T)}{S_2(0)} - K, 0\right) \tag{1.363}$$

at maturity T, where $S_1(t)$ denotes the exchange rate of EUR-USD and $S_2(t)$ denotes the exchange rate of EUR-JPY at time t, a_i the corresponding weights and K the basket strike. A basket option protects against a drop in both currencies at the same time. Individual options on each currency cover some cases that are not protected by a basket option (shaded triangular areas in Figure 1.51) and that's why they cost more than a basket.

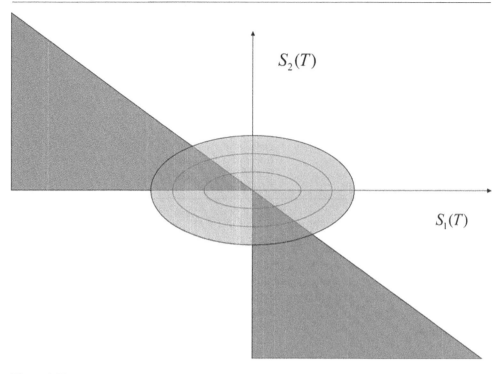

Figure 1.51   Protection with a basket option in two currencies
The ellipsoids connect the points that are reached with the same probability assuming that the forward prices are at the center.

Pricing basket options

Basket options should be priced in a consistent way with plain vanilla options. In the Black-Scholes model we assume a log-normal process for the individual correlated basket constituents. A decomposition into uncorrelated constituents of the exchange rate processes

$$dS_i = \mu_i S_i \, dt + S_i \sum_{j=1}^{N} \Omega_{ij} \, dW_j \qquad (1.364)$$

is the basis for pricing. Here μ_i denotes the difference between the foreign and the domestic interest rate of the i-th currency pair, dW_j the j-th component of independent Brownian increments. The covariance matrix is given by

$$C_{ij} = (\Omega\Omega^T)_{ij} = \rho_{ij}\sigma_i\sigma_j. \qquad (1.365)$$

Here σ_i denotes the volatility of the i-th currency pair and ρ_{ij} the correlation coefficients.

Exact Method. Starting with the uncorrelated components the pricing problem is reduced to the N-dimensional integration of the payoff. This method is accurate but rather slow for more than two or three basket components.

A Simple Approximation method assumes that the basket spot itself is a log-normal process with drift μ and volatility σ driven by a Wiener Process $W(t)$,

$$dS(t) = S(t)[\mu\,dt + \sigma\,dW(t)] \tag{1.366}$$

with solution

$$S(T) = S(t)e^{\sigma W(T-t)+(\mu-\frac{1}{2}\sigma^2)(T-t)}, \tag{1.367}$$

given we know the spot $S(t)$ at time t. It is a fact that the sum of log-normal processes is not log-normal, but as a crude approximation it is certainly a quick method that is easy to implement. In order to price the basket call the drift and the volatility of the basket spot need to be determined. This is done by matching the first and second moment of the basket spot with the first and second moment of the log-normal model for the basket spot. The moments of log-normal spot are

$$I\!E[S(T)] = S(t)e^{\mu(T-t)}, \tag{1.368}$$
$$I\!E[S(T)^2] = S(t)^2 e^{(2\mu+\sigma^2)(T-t)}. \tag{1.369}$$

We solve these equations for the drift and volatility,

$$\mu = \frac{1}{T-t}\ln\left(\frac{I\!E[S(T)]}{S(t)}\right), \tag{1.370}$$

$$\sigma = \sqrt{\frac{1}{T-t}\ln\left(\frac{I\!E[S(T)^2]}{S(t)^2}\right)}. \tag{1.371}$$

In these formulae we now use the moments for the basket spot,

$$I\!E[S(T)] = \sum_{j=1}^{N}\alpha_j S_j(t)e^{\mu_j(T-t)}, \tag{1.372}$$

$$I\!E[S(T)^2] = \sum_{i,j=1}^{N}\alpha_i\alpha_j S_i(t)S_j(t)e^{\left(\mu_i+\mu_j+\sum_{k=1}^{N}\Omega_{ki}\Omega_{jk}\right)(T-t)}. \tag{1.373}$$

The value is given by the well-known Black-Scholes-Merton formula for plain vanilla call options,

$$v(0) = e^{-r_d T}(f\mathcal{N}(d_+) - K\mathcal{N}(d_-)), \tag{1.374}$$
$$f = S(0)e^{\mu T}, \tag{1.375}$$
$$d_\pm = \frac{\ln\frac{f}{K} \pm \frac{1}{2}\sigma^2 T}{\sigma\sqrt{T}}, \tag{1.376}$$

where $\mathcal{N}$ denotes the cumulative standard normal distribution function and r_d the domestic interest rate.

A more accurate and equally fast approximation. The previous approach can be taken one step further by introducing one more term in the Itô-Taylor expansion of the basket spot, which results in

$$v(0) = e^{-r_d T} \left(F \mathcal{N}(d_1) - K \mathcal{N}(d_2) \right), \tag{1.377}$$

$$F = \frac{S(0)}{\sqrt{1 - \lambda T}} e^{\left(\mu - \frac{\lambda}{2} + \frac{\lambda \sigma^2}{2(1 - \lambda T)} \right) T}, \tag{1.378}$$

$$d_2 = \frac{\sigma - \sqrt{\sigma^2 + \lambda \left(\left(1 + \frac{\lambda}{1 - \lambda T} \right) \sigma^2 T - 2 \ln \frac{F \sqrt{1 - \lambda T}}{K} \right)}}{\lambda \sqrt{T}}, \tag{1.379}$$

$$d_1 = \sqrt{1 - \lambda T} d_2 + \frac{\sigma \sqrt{T}}{\sqrt{1 - \lambda T}}. \tag{1.380}$$

The new parameter λ is determined by matching the third moment of the basket spot and the model spot. For details see [3]. Most remarkably this major improvement in the accuracy only requires a marginal additional computation effort.

Correlation risk

Correlation coefficients between market instruments are usually not obtained easily. Either historical data-analysis or implied calibrations need to be done. However, in the foreign exchange market the cross instrument is traded as well, for the example above the USD-JPY spot and options are traded, and the correlation can be determined from this contract. In fact, denoting the volatilities as in the tetrahedron in Figure 1.52, we obtain formulae for the correlation coefficients in terms of known market implied volatilities

$$\rho_{12} = \frac{\sigma_3^2 - \sigma_1^2 - \sigma_2^2}{2 \sigma_1 \sigma_2}, \tag{1.381}$$

$$\rho_{34} = \frac{\sigma_1^2 + \sigma_6^2 - \sigma_2^2 - \sigma_5^2}{2 \sigma_3 \sigma_4}. \tag{1.382}$$

This method also allows hedging correlation risk by trading FX implied volatility. For details see [3].

Pricing basket options with smile

The previous calculations are all based on the Black-Scholes model with constant market parameters for rates and volatility. This can all be made time-dependent and can then include the term structure of volatility. If we wish to include the smile in the valuation, then we can either switch to a more appropriate model or perform a Monte Carlo simulation where the probabilities of the exchange rate paths are computed in such a way that the individual vanilla prices are correctly determined. This *weighted Monte Carlo approach* has been discussed by Avellaneda et al. in [61].

Practical Example
We want to find out how much one can save using a basket option. We take EUR as a base currency and consider a basket of three currencies USD, GBP and JPY. We list the contract data and the amount of option premium one can save using a basket call rather than three individual call options in Table 1.34 and the market data in Table 1.35.

The amount of premium saved essentially depends on the correlation of the currency pairs. In Figure 1.53 we take the parameters of the previous scenario, but restrict ourselves to the currencies USD and JPY.

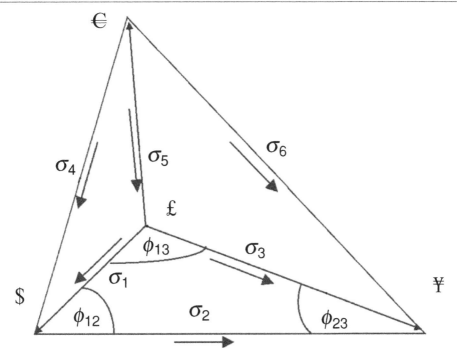

Figure 1.52 Relationship between volatilities σ(edges) and correlations ρ (cosines of angles) in a tetrahedron with 4 currencies and 6 currency pairs. The arrows mark the market standard quotation direction, i.e. in EUR-USD the base currency is USD and the arrow points to USD

Conclusions

Many corporate clients are exposed to multi-currency risk. One way to turn this fact into an advantage is to use multi-currency hedge instruments. We have shown that basket options are convenient instruments protecting against exchange rates of most of the basket components changing in the same direction. A rather unlikely market move of half of the currencies' exchange rates in opposite directions is not protected by basket options, but when taking this residual risk into account the hedging cost is reduced substantially. Another example how to use currency basket options is discussed in Section 2.5.2.

Table 1.34 Sample contact data of a EUR call basket put

Contract data	Strikes	Weights	Single option Prices
EUR/USD	1.1390	33.33 %	4.94 %
EUR/GBP	0.7153	33.33 %	2.50 %
EUR/JPY	125.00	33.33 %	3.87 %
sum		100 %	3.77 %
basket price			2.90 %

The value of the basket is noticeably less than the value of 3 vanilla EUR calls

Table 1.35 Sample market data of 21 October 2003 of four currencies EUR, GBP, USD and JPY

Vol	Spot	Correlation ccy pair	GBP/USD	USD/JPY	GBP/JPY	EUR/USD	EUR/GBP	EUR/JPY
8.80	1.6799	GBP/USD	1.00	−0.49	0.42	0.72	−0.15	0.29
9.90	109.64	USD/JPY	−0.49	1.00	0.59	−0.55	−0.21	0.41
9.50	184.17	GBP/JPY	0.42	0.59	1.00	0.09	−0.35	0.70
10.70	1.1675	EUR/USD	0.72	−0.55	0.09	1.00	0.58	0.54
7.50	0.6950	EUR/GBP	−0.15	−0.21	−0.35	0.58	1.00	0.42
9.80	128.00	EUR/JPY	0.29	0.41	0.70	0.54	0.42	1.00

The correlation coefficients are implied from the volatilities based on Equations (1.381) and (1.382).

1.6.8 Best-of and worst-of options

Options on the maximum or minimum of two or more exchange rates pay in their simple version

$$\left[\phi \left(\eta \min \left(\eta S_T^{(1)}, \eta S_T^{(2)} \right) - K \right) \right]^+. \tag{1.383}$$

This is a European put or call with expiration time T in years on the minimum ($\eta = +1$) or maximum ($\eta = -1$) of the two underlyings $S_T^{(1)}$ and $S_T^{(2)}$ with strike K. As usual, the binary variable ϕ takes the value $+1$ for a call and -1 for a put.

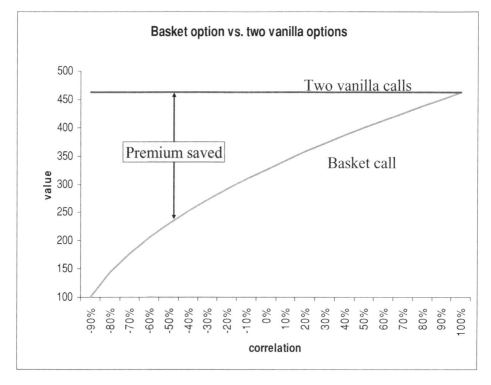

Figure 1.53 Amount of premium saved in a basket of two currencies compared to two single vanillas as a function of correlation: The smaller the correlation, the higher the premium savings effect

Valuation in the Black Scholes model

In the two-dimensional Black-Scholes model

$$dS_t^{(1)} = S_t^{(1)}\left[\mu_1 dt + \sigma_1 dW_t^{(1)}\right], \tag{1.384}$$

$$dS_t^{(2)} = S_t^{(2)}\left[\mu_2 dt + \sigma_2 dW_t^{(2)}\right], \tag{1.385}$$

$$\mathbf{Cov}\left[W_t^{(1)}, W_t^{(2)}\right] = \sigma_1\sigma_2\rho t, \tag{1.386}$$

we let the positive constants σ_i denote the volatilities of the i-th foreign currency, ρ the instantaneous correlation of their log-returns, r the domestic risk free rate. In a risk-neutral setting the drift terms μ_i take the values

$$\mu_i = r - r_i, \tag{1.387}$$

where r_i denotes the risk free rate of the i-th foreign currency.

The value has been published originally by Stulz in [62] and happens to be

$$
\begin{aligned}
&v\left(t, S_t^{(1)}, S_t^{(2)}, K, T, r_1, r_2, r, \sigma_1, \sigma_2, \rho, \phi, \eta\right) \\
&= \phi\left[S_t^{(1)}e^{-r_1\tau}\mathcal{N}_2(\phi d_1, \eta d_3; \phi\eta\rho_1)\right. \\
&\quad + S_t^{(2)}e^{-r_2\tau}\mathcal{N}_2(\phi d_2, \eta d_4; \phi\eta\rho_2) \\
&\quad \left. - Ke^{-r\tau}\left(\frac{1-\phi\eta}{2} + \phi\eta\mathcal{N}_2(\eta(d_1 - \sigma_1\sqrt{\tau}), \eta(d_2 - \sigma_2\sqrt{\tau}); \rho)\right)\right],
\end{aligned} \tag{1.388}
$$

$$\sigma^2 \stackrel{\Delta}{=} \sigma_1^2 + \sigma_2^2 - 2\rho\sigma_1\sigma_2, \tag{1.389}$$

$$\rho_1 \stackrel{\Delta}{=} \frac{\rho\sigma_2 - \sigma_1}{\sigma}, \tag{1.390}$$

$$\rho_2 \stackrel{\Delta}{=} \frac{\rho\sigma_1 - \sigma_2}{\sigma}, \tag{1.391}$$

$$\tau \stackrel{\Delta}{=} T - t, \tag{1.392}$$

$$d_1 \stackrel{\Delta}{=} \frac{\ln\left(S_t^{(1)}/K\right) + \left(\mu_1 + \frac{1}{2}\sigma_1^2\right)\tau}{\sigma_1\sqrt{\tau}}, \tag{1.393}$$

$$d_2 \stackrel{\Delta}{=} \frac{\ln\left(S_t^{(2)}/K\right) + \left(\mu_2 + \frac{1}{2}\sigma_2^2\right)\tau}{\sigma_2\sqrt{\tau}}, \tag{1.394}$$

$$d_3 \stackrel{\Delta}{=} \frac{\ln\left(S_t^{(2)}/S_t^{(1)}\right) + \left(r_1 - r_2 - \frac{1}{2}\sigma^2\right)\tau}{\sigma\sqrt{\tau}}, \tag{1.395}$$

$$d_4 \stackrel{\Delta}{=} \frac{\ln\left(S_t^{(1)}/S_t^{(2)}\right) + \left(r_2 - r_1 - \frac{1}{2}\sigma^2\right)\tau}{\sigma\sqrt{\tau}}. \tag{1.396}$$

The bivariate standard normal distribution and density functions $\mathcal{N}_2$ and n_2 are defined in Equations (1.306) and (1.305).

Greeks

Most of the calculations of partial derivatives can be simplified substantially by the homogeneity method described in [6], which states for instance, that

$$v = S_t^{(1)} \frac{\partial v}{\partial S_t^{(1)}} + S_t^{(2)} \frac{\partial v}{\partial S_t^{(2)}} + K \frac{\partial v}{\partial K}. \tag{1.397}$$

Using this equation we can immediately write down the deltas.

deltas

$$\frac{\partial v}{\partial S_t^{(1)}} = \phi e^{-r_1 \tau} \mathcal{N}_2(\phi d_1, \eta d_3; \phi \eta \rho_1) \tag{1.398}$$

$$\frac{\partial v}{\partial S_t^{(2)}} = \phi e^{-r_2 \tau} \mathcal{N}_2(\phi d_3, \eta d_4; \phi \eta \rho_2) \tag{1.399}$$

dual delta (strike)

$$\frac{\partial v}{\partial K} = -\phi e^{-r\tau} \left(\frac{1 - \phi \eta}{2} + \phi \eta \mathcal{N}_2(\eta(d_1 - \sigma_1 \sqrt{\tau}), \eta(d_2 - \sigma_2 \sqrt{\tau}); \rho) \right) \tag{1.400}$$

gammas We use the identities

$$\frac{\partial}{\partial x} \mathcal{N}_2(x, y; \rho) = n(x) \mathcal{N} \left(\frac{y - \rho x}{\sqrt{1 - \rho^2}} \right), \tag{1.401}$$

$$\frac{\partial}{\partial y} \mathcal{N}_2(x, y; \rho) = n(y) \mathcal{N} \left(\frac{x - \rho y}{\sqrt{1 - \rho^2}} \right), \tag{1.402}$$

and obtain

$$\frac{\partial^2 v}{\partial (S_t^{(1)})^2} = \frac{\phi e^{-r_1 \tau}}{S_t^{(1)} \sqrt{\tau}} \left[\frac{\phi}{\sigma_1} n(d_1) \mathcal{N} \left(\eta \sigma \frac{d_3 - d_1 \rho_1}{\sigma_2 \sqrt{1 - \rho^2}} \right) \right. \tag{1.403}$$
$$\left. - \frac{\eta}{\sigma} n(d_3) \mathcal{N} \left(\phi \sigma \frac{d_1 - d_3 \rho_1}{\sigma_2 \sqrt{1 - \rho^2}} \right) \right],$$

$$\frac{\partial^2 v}{\partial (S_t^{(2)})^2} = \frac{\phi e^{-r_2 \tau}}{S_t^{(2)} \sqrt{\tau}} \left[\frac{\phi}{\sigma_2} n(d_2) \mathcal{N} \left(\eta \sigma \frac{d_4 - d_2 \rho_2}{\sigma_1 \sqrt{1 - \rho^2}} \right) \right. \tag{1.404}$$
$$\left. - \frac{\eta}{\sigma} n(d_4) \mathcal{N} \left(\phi \sigma \frac{d_2 - d_4 \rho_2}{\sigma_1 \sqrt{1 - \rho^2}} \right) \right],$$

$$\frac{\partial^2 v}{\partial S_t^{(1)} \partial S_t^{(2)}} = \frac{\phi \eta e^{-r_1 \tau}}{S_t^{(2)} \sigma \sqrt{\tau}} n(d_3) \mathcal{N} \left(\phi \sigma \frac{d_1 - d_3 \rho_1}{\sigma_2 \sqrt{1 - \rho^2}} \right). \tag{1.405}$$

sensitivity with respect to correlation Direct computations require the identity

$$\frac{\partial}{\partial \rho} \mathcal{N}_2(x, y; \rho) = \frac{1}{\sqrt{1 - \rho^2}} n(y) n\left(\frac{x - \rho y}{\sqrt{1 - \rho^2}}\right) \qquad (1.406)$$

$$= \frac{1}{\sqrt{1 - \rho^2}} n(x) n\left(\frac{y - \rho x}{\sqrt{1 - \rho^2}}\right) \qquad (1.407)$$

$$= n_2(x, y, \rho). \qquad (1.408)$$

However, it is easier to use the following identity relating correlation risk and cross gamma outlined in [6].

$$\frac{\partial v}{\partial \rho} = \sigma_1 \sigma_2 \tau S_t^{(1)} S_t^{(2)} \frac{\partial^2 v}{\partial S_t^{(1)} \partial S_t^{(2)}} \qquad (1.409)$$

vegas Again, we refer to [6] to get the following formulas for the vegas.

$$\frac{\partial v}{\partial \sigma_1} = \frac{\rho v_\rho + \sigma_1^2 \tau (S_t^{(1)})^2 v_{S_t^{(1)} S_t^{(1)}}}{\sigma_1} \qquad (1.410)$$

$$= S_t^{(1)} e^{-r_1 \tau} \sqrt{\tau} \left[\rho_1 \phi \eta n(d_3) \mathcal{N}\left(\phi \sigma \frac{d_1 - d_3 \rho_1}{\sigma_2 \sqrt{1 - \rho^2}}\right) \right. \qquad (1.411)$$

$$\left. + n(d_1) \mathcal{N}\left(\eta \sigma \frac{d_3 - d_1 \rho_1}{\sigma_2 \sqrt{1 - \rho^2}}\right) \right]$$

$$\frac{\partial v}{\partial \sigma_2} = \frac{\rho v_\rho + \sigma_2^2 \tau (S_t^{(2)})^2 v_{S_t^{(2)} S_t^{(2)}}}{\sigma_2} \qquad (1.412)$$

$$= S_t^{(2)} e^{-r_2 \tau} \sqrt{\tau} \left[\rho_2 \phi \eta n(d_4) \mathcal{N}\left(\phi \sigma \frac{d_2 - d_4 \rho_2}{\sigma_1 \sqrt{1 - \rho^2}}\right) \right. \qquad (1.413)$$

$$\left. + n(d_2) \mathcal{N}\left(\eta \sigma \frac{d_4 - d_2 \rho_2}{\sigma_1 \sqrt{1 - \rho^2}}\right) \right]$$

rhos Again, we refer to [6] to get the following formulas for the rhos.

$$\frac{\partial v}{\partial r_1} = -S_t^{(1)} \tau \frac{\partial v}{\partial S_t^{(1)}} \qquad (1.414)$$

$$\frac{\partial v}{\partial r_2} = -S_t^{(2)} \tau \frac{\partial v}{\partial S_t^{(2)}} \qquad (1.415)$$

$$\frac{\partial v}{\partial r} = -K \tau \frac{\partial v}{\partial K} \qquad (1.416)$$

theta Among the various ways to compute theta one may use the one based on [6].

$$\frac{\partial v}{\partial t} = -\frac{1}{\tau} \left[r_1 v_{r_1} + r_2 v_{r_2} + r v_r + \frac{\sigma_1}{2} v_{\sigma_1} + \frac{\sigma_2}{2} v_{\sigma_2} \right] \qquad (1.417)$$

More general results about best-of and worst of options can be found in detail in Chapter 7 of [3].

Variations

Options on the maximum and minimum generalize in various ways. For instance, they can be quantoed or have individual strikes for each currency pair. We consider some examples.

Multiple strike option

This variation of best-of/worst-of options deals with individual strikes, i.e. they pay off

$$\max_i \left[0; M_i(\phi(S_T^{(i)} - K_i)) \right].$$
(1.418)

Madonna option

This one pays the *Euclidian distance*,

$$\max \left[0; \sqrt{\sum_i (S_T^{(i)} - K_i)^2} \right].$$
(1.419)

Pyramid option

This one pays the *maximum norm*,

$$\max \left[0; \sum_i |S_T^{(i)} - K_i| - K \right].$$
(1.420)

Mountain range and Himalaya option. This type of option comes in various flavors and is rather popular in equity markets, whence we will not discuss them here. A reference is the thesis by Mahomed [63].

Quanto best-of/worst-of options. These options come up naturally if an investor wants to participate in several exchange rate movements with a payoff in other than the base currency.

Barrier best-of/worst-of options. One can also add knock-out and knock-in features to all the previous types discussed.

Application for re-insurance

Suppose you want to protect yourself against a weak USD compared to several currencies for a period of one year. As USD seller and buyer of EUR, GBP and JPY you need simultaneous protection of all three rising against the USD. Of course, you can buy three put options, but if you only need one of the three, then you can save considerably on the premium, as shown in Table 1.36. We can imagine a situation like this if a re-insurance company insures ships in various oceans. If a ship sinks near the coast of Japan, the client will have to be paid an amount in JPY. The re-insurance company is long USD and assumes only one ship to sink at most in one year and ready to take the residual risk of more than one sinking.

Table 1.36   Example of a triple strike best-of call (American style) with 100 M USD notional and one year maturity. Compared to buying vanilla options one saves 800,000 USD or 20 %

Currency pair	Spot	Strikes	Vanilla premium	Best-of premium
EUR/USD	0.9750	1.0500	1.4 M	
USD/JPY	119.00	110.00	1.7 M	
GBP/USD	1.5250	1.6300	0.9 M	
		Total in USD	4.0 M	3.2 M

Since the accidents can occur any time, all options are of American style, i.e. they can be exercised any time. The holder of the option can choose the currency pair to exercise. Hence, he can decide for the one with the highest profit, even if the currency of accident is a different one. It would be difficult to incorporate and hedge this event insurance into the product, whence the protection needs to assume the worst case scenario that is still acceptable to the re-insurance company. For example, if the re-insurance needs GBP and the spots at exercise time are at EUR/USD $= 1.1200$, USD/JPY $= 134.00$ and GBP/USD $= 1.6400$, you will find both the EUR and GBP constituents in-the-money. However, exercising in GBP would pay a net of 613,496.93 USD, in EUR 6,666,666.67 USD. The client would then exercise in EUR, buy the desired GBP in the EUR/GBP spot market and keep the rest of the EUR.

Application for corporate and retail investors

Just like a *dual currency deposit* described in Section 2.3.1, one can use a worst-of put to structure a *multi-currency deposit* with a coupon even higher. We refer the reader to the exercises.

1.6.9   Options and forwards on the harmonic average

Let there be a time schedule of observation times $t_1, \ldots, t_n$ of some underlying. Options and Forwards on the arithmetic average

$$\frac{1}{n} \sum_{i=1}^{n} S(t_i) \tag{1.421}$$

have been analyzed and traded for some time, see Section 1.5.4. The geometric average

$$\sqrt[n]{\prod_{i=1}^{n} S(t_i)} \tag{1.422}$$

has often been used as control variate for the arithmetic average, whose distribution in a multiplicative model like Black-Scholes is cumbersome to deal with. The *harmonic average*

$$\frac{n}{\sum_{i=1}^{n} \frac{1}{R(t_i)}} \tag{1.423}$$

comes up if a client wants to exchange an amount of *domestic* currency into the *foreign* currency at an average rate of the currency pair FOR-DOM, e.g. wants to exchange USD into EUR at a rate, which is an average of observed EUR-USD rates. In this case the USD is the base or numeraire currency and we need to actually look at the exchange rate of $R = 1/S$ in DOM-FOR quotation in order to allow the domestic currency as a notional amount. As in the case of standard Asian contracts, there can be forwards and options on the harmonic average, both with fixed and floating strike. We treat one possible example in the next section.

Harmonic Asian swap

We consider a EUR-USD market with spot reference 1.0070, swap points for time T_1 of -45, swap points for time $T_2 > T_1$ of -90. As a contract specification, the client buys N USD at the daily average of the period of one months before T_1, denoted by A_1. Then the client sells N USD at the daily average of a period of one month before T_2, denoted by A_2. The payoff in EUR of this structure (cash settled two business days after T_2) is

$$\frac{N}{A_2} - \frac{N}{A_1}. \tag{1.424}$$

To replicate this using the fixed strike Asian Forward we can decompose it as follows.

1. We sell to the client the payoff $1 - \frac{1}{A_1}$ (using strike 1 by default) with notional N.
2. We buy from the client the payoff $1 - \frac{1}{A_2}$ (using strike 1 by default) with notional N.

On a notional of $N = 5$ million USD this could have a theoretical value of -23.172 EUR. This is what we should charge the client in addition to overhedge and sales margin. One problem is that the structure is very transparent for the client. If we take the forward for mid February, we have -45 swap points, for mid June -90 swap points. This means that the client would know that in a first order approximation he owes the bank 45 swap points, which is

$$5 \text{ MIO USD} \cdot 0.0045 = 22{,}500 \text{EUR}.$$

If the swap ticket requires entering a strike, one can use 1.0000 in both tickets, but this value does not influence the value of the swap.

1.6.10   Variance and volatility swaps

A variance swap is a contract that pays the difference of a pre-determined fixed variance (squared volatility), which is usually determined in such a way that the trading price is zero, and a realized historic annualized variance, which can be computed only at maturity of the trade. Therefore, the variance swap is an ideal instrument to hedge volatility exposure, a need for funds and institutional clients. Of course one can hedge vega with vanilla options, but is then also subject to spot movements and time decay of the hedge instruments. The variance swap also serves as a tool for speculating on volatility.

Advantages

- Insurance against changing volatility levels
- Independence of spot
- Zero cost product
- Fixed volatility (break-even point) easy to approximate as average of smile

Table 1.37   Example of a Variance Swap in EUR-USD

Spot reference	1.0075 EUR-USD
Notional M	USD 10,000,000
Start date	19 November 2002
Expiry date	19 December 2002
Delivery of cash settlement	23 December 2002
Fixing period	Every weekday from 19-Nov-02 to 19-Dec-02
Fixing source	ECB fixings $F_0, F_1, \ldots, F_N$
Number of fixing days N	23 (32 actual days)
Annualization factor B	$262.3 = 23/32 * 365$
Fixed strike K	85.00 % % corresponding to a volatility of 9.22 %
Payoff	$M * (\text{realized variance} - K)$
Realized variance	$\frac{B}{N-1}\sum_{i=1}^{N}(r_i - \bar{r})^2; \bar{r} = \frac{1}{N}\sum_{i=1}^{N} r_i; r_i = \ln \frac{F_i}{F_{i-1}}$
Premium	none

The quantity r_i is called the log-return from fixing day $i - 1$ to day i and the average log-return is denoted by $\bar{r}$. The notation % % means a multiplication with 0.0001. It is also sometimes denoted as %^{2}.

Disadvantages

- Difficult to understand
- Many details in the contract to be set
- Variance harder to capture than volatility
- Volatility swaps are harder to price than variance swaps

Example
Suppose the 1-month implied volatility for EUR/USD at-the-money options are close to its one-year historic low. This can easily be noticed by looking at *volatility cones*, see Section 1.3.10. Suppose further that you are expecting a period of higher volatility during the next month. Your are looking for a zero cost strategy, where you would be rewarded if your expectation turns out to be correct, but you are ready to encounter a loss otherwise. In this case an advisable strategy to trade is a variance or volatility swap. We consider an example of a variance swap in Table 1.37.

To make this clear we consider the following two scenarios with possible fixing results listed in Table 1.38 and Figure 1.54.

- If the realized variance is 0.41 % (corresponding to a volatility of 6.42 %), then the market was quieter than expected and you need to pay 10 MIO USD * (0.85 % – 0.41 %) = 44,000 USD.
- If the realized variance is 1.15 % (corresponding to a volatility of 10.7 %), then your market expectation turned out to be correct and you will receive 10 MIO USD * (1.15 %–0.85 %) = 30,000 USD.

A volatility swap trades

$$\sqrt{\frac{B}{N-1}\sum_{i=1}^{N}(r_i - \bar{r})^2} \tag{1.425}$$

Table 1.38   Example of two variance scenarios in EUR-USD

Date	Fixing (low vol)	Fixing (high vol)
19/11/02	1.0075	1.0075
20/11/02	1.0055	1.0055
21/11/02	1.0111	1.0111
22/11/02	1.0086	1.0086
25/11/02	1.0027	1.0027
26/11/02	1.0019	1.0067
27/11/02	1.0033	0.9997
28/11/02	1.0096	1.0113
29/11/02	1.0077	1.0062
2/12/02	1.0094	1.0094
3/12/02	1.0029	0.9999
4/12/02	1.0043	1.0043
5/12/02	0.9977	0.9977
6/12/02	0.9953	1.0037
9/12/02	0.9966	0.9962
10/12/02	0.9986	0.9986
11/12/02	1.0003	0.9907
12/12/02	0.9956	1.0018
13/12/02	0.9981	1.0000
16/12/02	0.9963	0.9963
17/12/02	1.0040	1.0040
18/12/02	1.0045	1.0017
19/12/02	1.0085	1.0114
variance	0.41 %	1.15 %
volatility	6.42 %	10.70 %

The left column shows a possible fixing set with a lower realized variance, the right column a scenario with a higher variance.

against a fixed volatility, which is usually determined in such a way that the trading price is zero. Since the square root is not a linear function of the variance, this product is more difficult to price than a standard variance swap. For details on pricing and hedging we refer to [64]. As a rule of thumb, the fixed variance or volatility to make the contract worth zero is the average of the volatilities in the volatility smile matrix for the maturity under consideration as there exists a static hedging portfolio consisting of vanilla options with the same maturity.

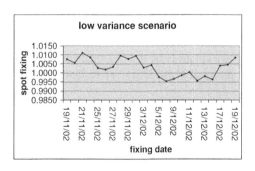 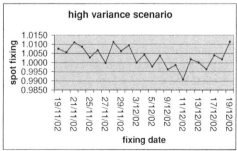

Figure 1.54   Comparison of scenarios for a low variance (left column) and a higher variance (right column)

Forward variance swap

In a standard variance swap, the first spot fixing is at inception of the trade or two business days thereafter. However, there may be situations where a client needs to hedge a forward volatility exposure that originates from a compound, instalment, forward start, cliquet or other exotic option with a significant forward volatility dependence. We will illustrate now how to structure a forward variance swap, where the first fixing is at some time in the future, using standard variance swaps. Let there be J fixings in the initial period and M fixings in the second period. The total number of Fixings is hence $M + J$. We can then split the payoff

$$\frac{B}{M-1} \sum_{i=J+1}^{J+M} (r_i - \bar{r})^2 - K \qquad (1.426)$$

into the two parts

$$\frac{B}{M-1} \sum_{i=1}^{J+M} (r_i - \bar{r})^2 - K - \left[\frac{B}{M-1} \sum_{i=1}^{J} (r_i - \bar{r})^2 - 0 \right] \qquad (1.427)$$

$$= \frac{C}{J+M-1} \sum_{i=1}^{J+M} (r_i - \bar{r})^2 - K - \left[\frac{D}{J-1} \sum_{i=1}^{J} (r_i - \bar{r})^2 - 0 \right]$$

and find as the only solution for the numbers C and B

$$C = \frac{(J+M-1)B}{M-1},$$

$$D = \frac{(J-1)B}{M-1}. \qquad (1.428)$$

Modifications

When computing the variance of a random variable X whose mean is small, we can take the second moment $I\!E X^2$ as an approximation of the variance

$$\mathbf{var}(X) = I\!E X^2 - (I\!E X)^2. \qquad (1.429)$$

Following this idea and keeping in mind that the average of log-returns of FX fixings is indeed often close to zero, the variance swap is sometimes understood as a second moment swap rather than an actual variance swap. To clarify traders specify in their dialogue whether the product is *mean subtracted* or not. We have presented here the variance swap with the mean subtracted.

1.6.11 Exercises

1. Sometimes buyers of options prefer to pay for their option only at the delivery date of the contract, rather than the spot value date, which is by default two business days after the trade date. How do the value formulae for say vanilla options change if we include this *deferred payment* style? You need to consider carefully the currency in which the premium is paid. To be precise, let the sequence of dates $t_0 < t_{sv} < t_e < t_d$ and t_{pv} denote the *trade date*, the *spot value date*, *expiration date*, *delivery date* and the *premium value date* respectively,

with all of the dates generally having different interest rates. How does the vanilla formula generalize?

2. Starting with the value for digital options, derive exactly the value of a European style corridor in the Black-Scholes model. Discuss how to find a market price based on the market of vanilla options. How does this extend to American style corridors?

3. How would you structure a *fade-out call* that starts with a nominal amount of M. As the exchange rate evolves, the notional will be decreased by $\frac{M}{N}$ for each of the N fixings that is outside a pre-defined range?

4. Similar to the corridors in Section 1.6.1 write down the exact payoff formulae for the various variations of faders in Section 1.6.2.

5. Describe a possible client view that could lead to trading a fade-in forward in Table 1.31.

6. What is wrong in Equation (1.427) in the decomposition of the forward variance swap? How can we fix it?

7. Implement the static hedge for a variance swap following [64] using the approximation of the logarithm by vanilla options. Then take the current smile of USD-JPY and find the fair fixed variance of a variance swap for 6 months maturity. How does the fixed variance change if the seller wants to earn a sales margin of 0.1 % of the notional amount? Compare the fixed strike with the average of the implied volatilities for 6 months. Discuss the impact of changing interest rates on the price and on the hedge.

8. Compute the integral in Equation (1.349) to get a closed form solution for the exchange option.

9. The value of a spread option presented in Section 1.6.6 works for the case of a joint base currency, like USD/CHF and USD/JPY. How does the formula extend if the quotation differs, like USD-CHF and EUR-USD, so there is a joint currency in both exchange rates, but the base currencies are different? More generally, consider arbitrary exchange rate pairs like EUR-GBP and USD-JPY.

10. How would delivery-settlement of a spread option work in practice?

11. Compute the correlation coefficients implied from the volatilities in Table 1.39 based on Equations (1.381) and (1.382). What are the upper and lower limits for the EUR/USD volatility to guarantee all correlation coefficients being contained in the interval $[-1, +1]$, assuming all the other volatilities are fixed?

12. As a variation of the James Bond range in Section 7, we consider barriers A, B, C, D as illustrated in Figure 1.55.

   A rather *tolerant double no-touch* knocks out after the second barrier is touched or crossed. How would you hedge it statically using standard barrier and touch options?

Table 1.39   Sample market data of four currencies EUR, GBP, USD and CHF

ccy pair	Volatility
GBP/USD	9.20 %
USD/CHF	11.00 %
GBP/CHF	8.80 %
EUR/USD	10.00 %
EUR/GBP	7.80 %
EUR/CHF	5.25 %

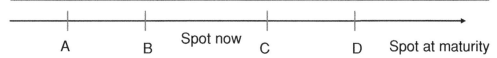

Figure 1.55   Nested double-no-touch ranges

13. Derive closed form solutions to all knock-in-knock-out types of barrier options in the Black-Scholes model.
14. The formula for the theoretical value of outside barrier options in Section 1.6.3 only works for two currency pairs with the same base or domestic currency such as for example EUR-USD and GBP-USD. Why? How does it extend if the second currency pair is USD-JPY? And how does it extend if the second currency pair is AUD-JPY?
15. The pricing of Parisian barrier options can be done with Monte Carlo and PDE methods. Implement the approach by Bernard, le Courtois and Quittard-Pinon using characteristic functions described in [65].
16. The pay-later price in Equation (1.342) is measured in units of domestic currency. Does this change if the premium is specified to be paid in foreign currency? If no, argue why. If yes, specify how.
17. Derive the pay-later price of a digital option.
18. Derive the pay-later price of a call spread.
19. How would you structure an up-and-out call whose premium is only paid if the spot is in-the-money at the expiration time?
20. A *chooser option* lets the buyer decide at expiration time, if he wants to either exercise α calls with strike K_c or β puts with strike K_p. Discuss how to find a market price and how to statically hedge it. (Hint: Straddle.). Moreover, if the decision of which option to take is taken at time t strictly before the expiration time T, how would you price and hedge the chooser? How does it simplify if $\alpha = \beta = 1$ and $K_c = K_p$?

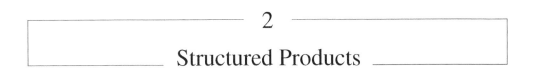

2

Structured Products

2.1 FORWARD PRODUCTS

This section deals with various ways to enhance forward rates. We start by explaining the outright or vanilla forward. Enhancements can then be done in various ways and can be classified in forward products with guaranteed worst case and forward products without such a guaranteed worst case. While the former usually allow hedge-accounting in the IAS 39 sense, the latter are rather speculative in nature, but can produce more significant enhancements.

The products with worst case all work the same way. The corporate client engages into a forward contract with a strike that is worse than the market. Hence, he has some money left to invest in an option. The option is then chosen to match the client's view on the future development of the underlying exchange rate. There is unlimited freedom to choose. We explain many popular structures.

Naturally, the forward products address corporate treasurers in the first place, companies with international business and cash flows. However, the real target group are mid-size companies, because the large global players usually have enough knowledge, infrastructure and staff to buy the components of the structures separately, whereas the mid-size corporate often prefers packaged solutions.

For the private or institutional investor, the forward products are only of limited use as they normally do not have the foreign exchange cash flow behind their investments. For this group similar strategies can be used by omitting the basic forward contracts with worst case and quanto the structures into the respective domestic currency with cash settlement.

2.1.1 Outright forward

The outright forward is a zero cost strategy to fix the exchange rate at a future date. It forms a risk-free basis of the budget calculations. On the other hand it does not leave any room for participation in any direction. The contract parameters of an outright forward are

1. Currency pair
2. Amount and currency to be sold or bought
3. Settlement date
4. Forward Rate F

For example, a company agrees to sell 1 Million EUR in 6 months and buys 1.18 Million USD. In this case the currency pair is EUR/USD and forward rate is 1.1800. Both parties have to stick to their agreement, However, one can of course unwind a forward contract at any time. If S_t denotes the price of the underlying exchange rate, the payoff of the forward contract at time T is

$$S_T - f. \tag{2.1}$$

Hence the value at time zero is

$$e^{-r_f T} S_0 - e^{-r_d T} f. \tag{2.2}$$

The outright forward rate f is the rate that makes this zero cost, i.e.,

$$f = e^{(r_d - r_f)T} S_0, \tag{2.3}$$

which corresponds to the expected value of S_T under the risk-neutral measure. This is not a prediction of the spot rate at time T.

As time passes, the value of the forward contract is no longer necessarily zero. So one of the two counterparts is always in debt. This should be taken into consideration when computing the credit line for the counterpart.

Backwardation and contango

The function that maps the maturity T to the outright forward rate for this maturity is called the forward curve. A decreasing curve is called backwardation and an increasing forward curve is called a contango situation. There can be forward curves with humps, in which case neither of the two scenarios apply.

Put-call parity

It is well known, that a long forward can be replicated by a long call and a short put with the same strike and same notional. This replication is often called a *synthetic forward*. While an outright forward contract is usually zero cost for both parties, the synthetic forward can be used to generate a premium for the forward: The counterpart buying a forward at a rate below the outright forward rate should be paid a premium. In practice, this premium is often replaced by giving the counterpart another option to participate in his market view.

FX swap

An FX swap is a combination of a spot deal and a forward contract. A client agrees to buy 1 million EUR now at spot S_0 and sell it again on a pre-determined date at the outright forward rate f. Both trades are zero cost. The difference $f - S_0$ is called the FX swap rate. The first leg on an FX swap can also be a forward contract, with the second leg a forward contract on a later date.

The FX swap rate $f - S_0$ is usually multiplied by a factor of 10,000 to produce the so-called swap points f if the exchange rate is quoted to four decimal places. For example, assuming the spot rate for EUR/USD at 1.1800, the forward rate at 1.1750, then the swap points are -50. We are in a backwardation scenario. If the exchange rate is quoted to two decimal places as in USD/JPY, then the FX swap rate is multiplied by a factor of 100 to get the swap points.

Non-deliverable forward

The non-deliverable forward (NDF) is a forward with cash settlement, i.e. instead of exchanging two currencies at maturity, the net value $S_T - f$ (in domestic currency) or $(S_T - f)/S_T$ (in foreign currency) of this exchange is computed and the winner of the trade receives this net value as cash from the loser. It is possible in all traded underlyings, but most common in emerging markets.

2.1.2 Participating forward

The participating forward is like a synthetic forward (see Section 2.1.1), except that the notionals are different. In a more general manner, the strikes can also be different.

It is also very similar to a risk reversal. A participating forward entitles the holder to buy an agreed amount (notional of the Call option) of a currency (say EUR) on a specified date (maturity) at a pre-determined rate (long strike) if the exchange rate is above it at maturity. If the exchange rate is below the strike of the short put at this time, the holder must buy a second agreed amount (notional of the Put option) in EUR at the short strike. Therefore, buying a participating forward provides full protection against rising EUR. The holder will exercise the option only if at maturity the spot is above the long strike at maturity.

Advantages

• Full protection against stronger EUR/weaker USD
• Zero cost product

Disadvantages

• Participation in weaker EUR/stronger USD is limited

The participating forward can be composed in several ways. In the low risk style, the notional of the sold put is smaller than the notional of the bought call. In this case, the risk on the downside is comparatively small and hence the strike on the upside will normally not look like the greatest deal that comes down the pike. In a high risk style, the notional of the sold put is higher than the notional of the bought call, say by a factor of 2. In this case the risk on the

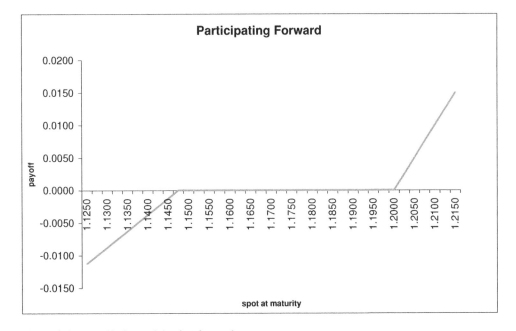

Figure 2.1 Payoff of a participating forward

downside is substantial and the strike of the call can be set much lower. Engaging in a product like this usually requires a strong bullish view of the counterparty. This high risk style product is also sometimes called *leveraged forward*.

For example a company wants to sell 1 Million USD (notional of the Call option). At maturity:

1. If $S_T < K_1$, it is obliged to buy the notional of the Put option at K_1.
2. If $K_1 < S_T < K_2$, it will not exercise the call option. The company can trade at spot.
3. If $S_T > K_2$, it will exercise the EUR call option and buy EUR at strike K_2.

Example
A company wants to hedge receivables from an export transaction in USD due in 12 months' time. It expects a stronger EUR/weaker USD. The company wishes to be fully protected against a stronger EUR. But it finds that the corresponding plain vanilla is too expensive and is prepared to take more risk in selling a Put option.

In this case a possible form of protection that the company can use is to buy a participating forward, for example:

Table 2.1   Example of a participating forward

Spot reference	1.1500 EUR-USD
Company buys	EUR call USD put
Company sells	EUR put USD call
Maturity	1 year
Notional of the Call option	EUR 1,000,000
Notional of the Put option	EUR 500,000
Strike of the long Call option	1.2000 EUR-USD
Strike of the short Put option	1.1475 EUR-USD
Premium	0.00

If company's market expectation is correct, it can buy EUR at maturity at the strike of 1.2000. Its risk is that, if the EUR-USD exchange rate will be below the strike of 1.1475 at maturity, it will be obliged to buy 500,000 EUR at the strike of 1.1475. The company can buy the other 500,000 EUR at the spot market and hence participate partially in a falling EUR (hence the name participating forward).

2.1.3   Fade-in forward

The fade-in forward works similar to a participating forward. The EUR buyer/USD seller buys a EUR call with strike K_2, sells a EUR put with strike $K_1 < K_2$ and buys a EUR put with the same strike K_1 with a fade-in range $[R_L, R_H]$ and possible knock out levels $B_L \leq R_L$ and $B_H \geq R_H$ (see Section 1.6.2). The expiration and delivery date and the notionals of all three components are the same. This way, at the end of the contract, the result is going to be a participating forward as described above, where the participation level is determined by the ratio of the number of fixings inside the range and the total number of fixings. If all fixings are inside the range, then the client holds only a long EUR call, whereas the short EUR put has been netted by the long fade-in EUR put. Conversely, if none of the fixings turn out to be in

Table 2.2   Terms and conditions of a fade-in forward as of 27 May 2004

Company buys	USD
Company sells	EUR
Expiry Date	1 July 2005
Delivery Date	5 July 2005 (delivery settled)
Notional Amount	USD 5,000,000
Corridor	1.1200–1.2600 EUR-USD
Fixing Calendar	all 286 week days starting from 28 May 2004 ending on 1 July 2005
Guaranteed worst case	1.1800 EUR-USD
Participation level P	$\frac{\text{fixings inside range}}{\text{all fixings}} \cdot 100\%$
Premium	0.00

the fade-in range, or we encounter a complete knock out, then the final position at maturity is a risk reversal.

Advantages

- Full protection against stronger EUR/weaker USD
- Participation in weaker EUR/stronger USD possible up to 100% (better than in the risk reversal or participating forward)
- Zero cost product

Disadvantages

- Participation in weaker EUR/stronger USD unknown at inception and at worst zero

Example
For example, we consider a fade-in forward traded buy a USD buying company on 27 May 2004, whose terms and conditions are listed in Table 2.2.

The seller pays the notional amount to the company on the delivery date. The company pays the EUR amount to the seller on the delivery date. This EUR amount is determined as follows.

If the spot at maturity is at or below the worst case, then the entire USD amount is converted into EUR using the worst case.

If the spot at maturity is above the worst case, the company participates with $P\%$ in the favorable spot movement, i.e. $P\%$ of the USD amount are converted at the spot at maturity and $(1 - P\%)$ of the USD amount are converted at the worst case.

The reference spot at maturity is the in-house fixing of the selling bank. For week days, where there is no EUR-USD fixing, the fixing of the previous weekday is used.

To decompose this structure, we refer the reader to the exercises.

2.1.4   Knock-out forward

The knock-out forward is one of the many possibilities to improve the outright forward rate at zero cost by taking some risk. Instead of the company buying a long call and selling a short put with the same strike, notional and maturity we attach one or two knock-out barriers for both. For the EUR buyer the scenario could be the following

Table 2.3   Example of a knock-out forward

Spot reference	1.1500 EUR-USD
Outright forward reference	1.1400 EUR-USD
Notional	EUR 1,000,000
Maturity	1 year
Strike	1.1000 EUR-USD
American style knock-out	1.2900 EUR-USD
Premium	0.00

Advantages

- Corporate buys EUR at 300 pips below the outright
- Zero cost product

Disadvantages

- Hedge is lost in case of knock-out
- No worst case scenario
- No participation in weaker EUR/stronger USD

The most noticeable risk factor here is the lack of a worst case. We only know a best case in advance. A EUR rising to 1.5000 would cause substantial trouble to the corporate. Buying this product requires a strong view of a rising EUR with an upper bound at the knock-out barrier. Nevertheless, this strategy is actively traded in the market.

2.1.5   Shark forward

The shark forward is also called *forward plus* or *forward extra* or enhanced forward or forward with profit potential. It is suitable for companies that want to fix a forward price while

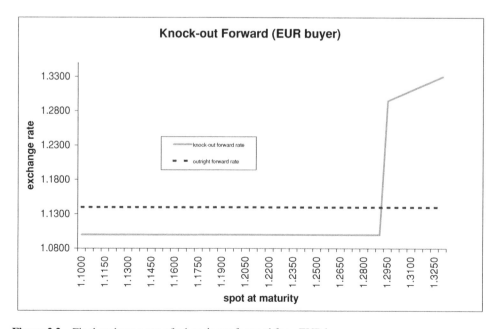

Figure 2.2   Final exchange rate of a knock-out forward for a EUR buyer

benefiting from a spot movement they believe in. It gives a certain range of profit potential, while *maintaining a worst case level* near the forward rate. It is composed of a forward contract with a forward price as the worst case and a reverse knock-out, whose payoff profile looks like a shark fin. We distinguish two kinds of shark forward contracts.

(shark) forward plus: the buyer benefits from a favorable spot movement.

(shark) forward extra: the buyer benefits from a spot movement against his position.

Shark forward plus

We consider the following example. Spot EUR/USD = 1.1200, 3 months maturity, outright forward rate 1.1164, volatility 10.30 %.

The seller of 1 MIO USD, who needs protection against a falling USD, but expects the USD to rise, can get a worst case of 1.1200, equal to the current spot and only slightly worse than the outright forward rate, a participation level of 1.1200 and an American (European) style knock out trigger of 1.0772 (1.0951). The bid-ask prices of this strategy are 0.2075 – 0.0000 % USD, i.e. the client buys the shark forward plus for zero cost and in case of unwind would have to pay 0.2075 % of the USD notional. The exchange rate the client gets is min(worst case, spot at maturity), as we are looking at the following scenarios.

- If the spot at maturity is above 1.1200, then the client must sell 1 MIO USD at the worst case.
- If the spot at maturity is below 1.1200 and the trigger has not been touched, then the client can sell 1 MIO USD at the spot.
- If the trigger has been touched, then the client must sell 1 MIO USD at the worst case.

The buyer of 1 MIO USD, who needs protection against a rising USD, but expects the USD to weaken, can get a worst case of 1.1100, one big figure below the current spot and only slightly below the outright forward rate, a participation level of 1.1100 and an American (European) style knock out trigger of 1.1712 (1.1495). The price of this strategy is 0.2425 – 0.0000 % USD, i.e. the client buys the shark forward plus for zero cost and in case of unwind would have to pay 0.2425 % of the USD notional. The exchange rate the client gets is max(worst case, spot at maturity), as we are looking at the following scenarios.

- If the spot at maturity is below 1.1100, then the client must buy 1 MIO USD at the worst case.
- If the spot at maturity is above 1.1100 and the trigger has not been touched, then the client can buy 1 MIO USD at the spot.
- If the trigger has been touched, then the client must buy 1 MIO USD at the worst case.

In both cases the client has a guaranteed worst case protection at zero cost and can participate in a favorable spot movement. The margin for this structure is 500.00 EUR.

More generally, one can allow participation levels P different from the worst case W. This is sometimes called *forward plus plus* or *forward super plus* or *forward plus with extra strike*. The seller of 1 MIO USD, who needs protection against a falling USD, but expects the USD to rise *significantly*, can get a worst case of $W = 1.1200$, equal to the current spot and only slightly worse than the outright forward rate, a participation level of $P = 1.1000$ and an American (European) style knock out trigger of 1.0582 (1.0744). The bid-ask prices of this strategy are 0.2475 – 0.0000 % USD, i.e. the client buys the shark forward plus for zero cost and in case of

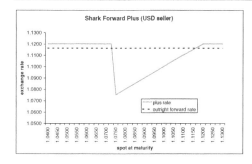 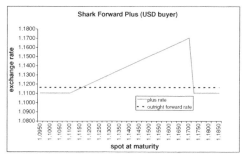

Figure 2.3 Comparison of final exchange rates for a shark forward plus: outright forward versus forward plus rate

unwind would have to pay 0.2475 % of the USD notional. The exchange rate the client gets is

$$\min\left(W, \frac{1}{\frac{1}{S_T} + \frac{1}{W} - \frac{1}{P}}\right), \tag{2.4}$$

as we are looking at the following scenarios. Here S_T denotes the spot at maturity.

- If the spot at maturity is above the participation level 1.1000, then the client must sell 1 MIO USD at the worst case.
- If the spot at maturity is below 1.1000 and the trigger has not been touched, then the client can sell 1 MIO USD at the rate

$$\frac{1}{\frac{1}{S_T} + \frac{1}{W} - \frac{1}{P}}. \tag{2.5}$$

- If the trigger has been touched, then the client must sell 1 MIO USD at the worst case.

The buyer of 1 MIO USD, who needs protection against a rising USD, but expects the USD to remain above the current spot, can get a worst case of 1.1100, one big figure below the current spot and only slightly below the outright forward rate, a participation level of 1.1200 and an American (European) style knock out trigger of 1.1830 (1.1632). The bid-ask prices of this strategy are 0.2900 – 0.0000 % USD, i.e. the client buys the shark forward plus for zero cost and in case of unwind would have to pay 0.2900 % of the USD notional. The exchange rate the client gets is

$$\max\left(W, \frac{1}{\frac{1}{S_T} + \frac{1}{W} - \frac{1}{P}}\right), \tag{2.6}$$

as we are looking at the following scenarios. Here S_T denotes the spot at maturity.

- If the spot at maturity is below 1.1200, then the client must buy 1 MIO USD at the worst case.
- If the spot at maturity is above 1.1200 and the trigger has not been touched, then the client can buy 1 MIO USD at the rate

$$\frac{1}{\frac{1}{S_T} + \frac{1}{W} - \frac{1}{P}}. \tag{2.7}$$

- If the trigger has been touched, then the client must buy 1 MIO USD at the worst case.

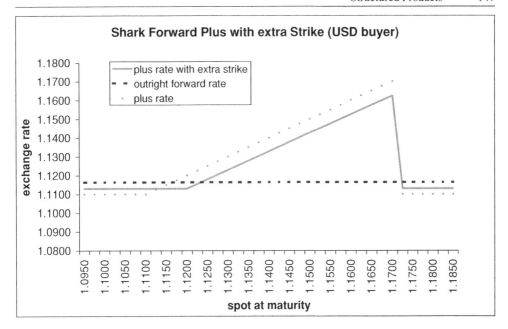

Figure 2.4 Comparison of final exchange rates for a shark forward plus: The forward plus worst case is the lowest. Using on extra strike or participation, one can increase either the knock-out barrier or – as shown here – move the worst case closer to the outright forward of the same price and allow less participation on the upside.

In both cases the client has a guaranteed worst case protection at zero cost and can participate in a favorable spot movement. The margin for this structure is 500.00 EUR. The benefit of these participation levels are barriers that are further away from the current spot.

If the notional is specified in EUR rather than in USD, then the exchange rate

$$\frac{1}{\frac{1}{S_T} + \frac{1}{W} - \frac{1}{P}} \tag{2.8}$$

in Equations (2.4)–(2.7) must be replaced by

$$S_T + W - P. \tag{2.9}$$

A more aggressive version of the shark forward is discussed in Section 2.1.14 about the *Double Shark Forward*.

2.1.6 Fader shark forward

A *fader forward plus* is a forward plus where the trigger/reset risk fades out linearly with the passage of time. The benefit over a standard forward plus is that the participation is proportionately retained on favorable spot moves up until the trigger event occurs.

Analysis

Compared to a Forward Plus, the Fader Forward Plus seeks to mitigate the participation loss if the reset trigger trades. This is illustrated in the following example scenarios for a 12 months Fader Forward Plus.

Table 2.4   Example of a fader forward plus

Spot reference	1.2150 EUR-USD
Outright forward reference	1.2152 EUR-USD
Client sells Notional	USD 1,000,000
Maturity	1 year
Worst Case EUR Buy (USD Sell) on 100 %	1.2250 EUR-USD
Best Case EUR Buy (USD Sell) on 100 %	1.1690 EUR-USD
Premium	0.00

Scenario 1: EUR/USD trades below 1.1690 in month 6 and fixes below 1.1690 on expiry. Result: 50 % notional can be bought at 1.1690 and the remaining 50 % at the worst case protection rate 1.2250.

Scenario 2: EUR/USD trades below 1.1690 in Month 9 and fixes below 1.1690 on expiry. Result: 75 % notional can be bought at 1.1690 and the remaining 25 % at the worst case protection rate 1.2250.

Scenario 3: EUR/USD trades below 1.1690 in Month 9 and fixes at 1.1800 on expiry. Result: 75 % notional can be bought at 1.1800 and the remaining 25 % at the worst case protection rate 1.2250.

Alternative

An alternative could be a 50 % Fader Forward Plus, where the client participates on 50 % of notional.

- Improve the worst case on 100 % to 1.2200
- Or improve the best case on 50 % to 1.1390
- Maintain net zero cost

The details of this structure are

- The client buys EUR (Sell USD) Forward at 1.2250
- The client buys a 1.2250–1.1690 Fader EUR Put Spread (USD Call Spread) with a lower corridor and knock-out barrier at 1.1689.

Advantages

- Absolute protection at 1.2250 on 100 % of the notional
- The client can take advantage of favorable market movements down to a pre-determined level
- The participation will lock-in with the passage of time
- A best case EUR buying (USD selling) rate of 1.1690
- Zero cost

Disadvantages

- If the pre-determined knock-out level trades relatively early in the tenor period with minimal accrual the net achieved rate will only be slightly better than the worst case rate.

Table 2.5 Example of a fader forward extra

Trade date	Oct 9 2004
Spot reference	1.2165 EUR-USD
Outright forward reference	1.2159 EUR-USD
Swap points reference	−6 EUR-USD
EUR interest rate	2.32 %
USD interest rate	2.26 %
ATM reference volatility	10.35 %
Client sells Notional	USD 4,800,000
Maturity date	Jul 27 2005
Delivery date	Jul 29 2005
Fixing on each business day	from trade date to maturity date
Worst Case EUR Buy (USD Sell) on 100 %	1.2300 EUR-USD
Upper corridor and corridor	1.2801 EUR-USD
Fader style	keep 100 % of the accrued amount
Client buys fader EUR call spread	1.2300–1.2800 EUR-USD
Premium	0.00
Sales margin	EUR 13,205
Delta hedge: the bank buys	EUR 3,768,784

Summary

This hedge has been designed to provide an absolute level of protection with a potential to benefit from favorable moves in the spot market to a pre-determined level. This benefit accrues with time, such that even if the pre-determined level trades the net achieved exchange rate will be better than the outright forward.

The fader forward plus allows participation in favorable spot movements. Similarly, the *fader forward extra* allows participation if the spot moves against the client's position. In this case, the client trades a synthetic forward and buys a fader EUR call spread as for example indicated in Table 2.5.

For information we list the details of the structure and the prices of the components in Table 2.6.

2.1.7 Butterfly forward

A butterfly forward entitles the holder to buy a specified amount of a currency (say EUR) on a specified date (expiry) at a non-fixed preferential rate if the spot rate will be within a pre-defined range at any time during the entire period until expiry. A butterfly forward allows the holder to take advantage of both an appreciation and depreciation of EUR-USD up to the pre-defined trigger levels. The butterfly forward is a zero cost strategy like the outright

Table 2.6 Pricing details of a fader forward extra

Product	Strike	Barrier	Bank	Upper corridor	Price in EUR
forward	1.2300		sells		−43,187.23
fader call	1.2300	1.2801	sells	1.2801	47,257.87
fader call	1.2800	1.2801	buys	1.2801	−17,275.91

forward. The worst-case exchange rate is absolutely guaranteed but always slightly worse than the outright forward rate. It is suitable for the corporate treasurer who can't make up his mind whether to trade a shark forward plus or extra, i.e. his only view on the future development of the exchange rate is movement.

Advantages

- Worst case W is guaranteed
- Zero cost product

Disadvantages

- If the exchange rate will be out of the range $[L, H]$ at expiry, the final exchange rate will be worse than the outright forward rate

For example the company wants to buy 10 Mio EUR. At maturity:

1. If $S_T > H$ or if $S_T < L$, the company would buy 10 Million EUR at strike W (Worst Case).
2. If $H > S_T > L$, the company would buy 10 Million EUR at strike S_T if $S_T \leq W$ or $2W - S_T$ if $S_T > W$.

Composition

In the butterfly forward the corporate buys a synthetic forward (see Section 2.1.1) with strike at the worst case and buys a double-knock-out call and a double-knock-out put with the same

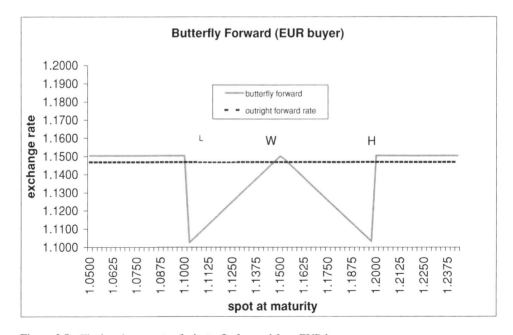

Figure 2.5   Final exchange rate of a butterfly forward for a EUR buyer

strike and barriers. Knock-out barriers can be either American or European style or Bermudan or windows.

Example
A company wants to hedge receivables from an export transaction in USD due in 3 months time and is considering hedging the currency risk. It expects that EUR-USD to either move up or down but remain within a predefined range for the entire period.

In this case a possible form of protection that the company can use is to buy a butterfly forward, for example:

Table 2.7   Example of a butterfly forward

Spot reference S_0	1.1500 EUR-USD
Outright forward reference	1.1468 EUR-USD
Notional	EUR 10,000,000
Maturity T	3 months
Worst case W	1.1503 EUR-USD
Upper trigger (American style) H	1.2000 EUR-USD
Lower trigger (American style) L	1.1000 EUR-USD
Final exchange rate	$W - |W - S_T|$ EUR-USD
Premium	0.00

The final exchange rate is stated under the condition that the spot rate does not trade at or through either the 1.2000 EUR-USD or 1.1000 EUR-USD triggers at any time during the entire period until expiry.

The butterfly forward enables the company to buy its USD-receivables in 3 months time at a rate of 1.1503 EUR-USD. This exchange rate is 35 points above the current forward rate of 1.1468 EUR-USD and represents its worst-case scenario. This rate shall be its final exchange rate if the prevailing exchange rate at expiry is equal to the worst case of 1.1503 EUR-USD and/or if the spot rate reaches either trigger level of 1.2000 EUR-USD or 1.1000 EUR-USD at any time during the entire period until expiry.

If the prevailing exchange rate at expiry is above or below the worst case of 1.1503 EUR-USD and it never reaches the trigger levels during the entire period until expiry, then the company's final exchange rate will be calculated by subtracting the positive difference between the worst case and the spot reference at expiry from the worst case level. In this case the company takes advantage of both lower and higher exchange rates.

2.1.8   Range forward

The range or bonus forward is another forward enhancement with guaranteed worst case. It entitles the holder to buy an agreed amount of a currency (say EUR) on a specified date (expiry) at a preferential rate (which will represent its best-case scenario) if the spot rate is within a predefined range at expiry. Range forwards provide full protection for a foreign exchange transaction. The range forward is a zero cost strategy like an outright forward. The holder will benefit from a best case scenario if the spot rate is within a predefined range. However, if the spot rate is outside this predefined range, the holder will buy EUR at another rate, which represents the holder's worst-case scenario. The worst-case exchange rate is absolutely guaranteed but always slightly worse than the outright forward rate.

Advantages

- Worst case guaranteed
- Zero cost product

Disadvantages

- If the exchange rate will be out of the range at expiry, the final exchange rate will be worse than the outright forward rate

For example the company wants to buy 10 Mio EUR. At maturity:

1. If $H < S_T$ or if $S_T < L$, the company would buy 10 Mio EUR at strike W (Worst Case).
2. If $H > S_T > L$, the company would buy 10 Mio EUR at strike B (Best Case).

Composition

In the range forward the corporate buys a synthetic forward (see Section 2.1.1) with strike at the worst case and buys a double-no-touch.

Example

A company wants to hedge receivables from an import transaction in USD due in 3 months time and is considering hedging the current risk. It expects that EUR-USD will end within a predefined range.

In this case a possible form of protection that the company can use is to buy a range forward as for example in Table 2.8.

The range forward enables the holder to buy his EUR-liability in 3 months time at a rate of 1.1600 EUR-USD. This exchange rate represents his worst-case scenario. This rate will be his final exchange rate if the spot rate reaches or crosses either trigger levels of 1.1100 or 1.1700 at expiry.

If the spot rate is within the pre-defined range of 1.1100 and 1.1700 at expiry then the final exchange rate will be the best case rate of 1.1303 EUR-USD at expiry.

Alternatives

The barriers can be American style barriers. Then the best-case scenario happens only if the spot rate stays within the predefined range during the entire period until expiry. Usually this will lead to a wider range or a better best case. One can also think of one-sided touch options,

Table 2.8   Example of a range or bonus forward

Spot reference	1.1500 EUR-USD
Outright forward reference	1.1471 EUR-USD
Notional	EUR 10,000,000
Maturity	3 months
Worst case	1.1600 EUR-USD
Best case	1.1303 EUR-USD
Range	1.1100–1.1700 EUR-USD
Premium	0.00

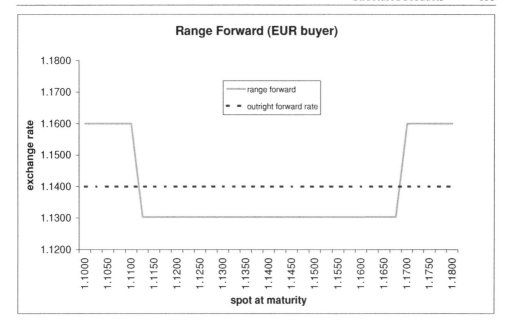

Figure 2.6   Final exchange rate of a range forward for a EUR buyer

window touch options, transatlantic touch options, touch options with rebates. The principle is always the same.

2.1.9   Range accrual forward

A range accrual or corridor or simply accrued forward is a forward contract in a currency pair, say EUR/USD, with a guaranteed worst case exchange rate. The worst case improves by a specified number of pips for each day between trade date and maturity the EUR/USD fixing is inside a pre-determined range. In the standard resurrecting or European style range, the improvement does not happen on days, when the fixing is outside the range, but the improvement can continue in the future. If all EUR/USD fixings are inside the range, then the exchange rate improves to the best case, which is above the outright forward rate. The standard range accrual forward is a zero-cost product and the worst case is worse than the outright forward rate. Betting on a quiet market phase can lead to an exchange rate which is much better than the outright forward.

Advantages

- Worst case guaranteed
- Zero cost product

Disadvantages

- No participation if the EUR/USD rate moves in the company's favor
- Many fixings outside the range lead to an exchange rate which is worse than the outright forward rate

Table 2.9   Example of a range accrual forward

Spot reference	1.1500 EUR-USD
Outright forward reference	1.1470 EUR-USD
Company	buys EUR sells USD
Notional	USD 1,000,000
Maturity	3 months
Worst case W	1.1550 EUR-USD
Best case	1.1265 EUR-USD
Resurrecting Range	1.1400–1.1600 EUR-USD
USD pips per day (ppd)	3.49
Final Exchange Rate	$W/(1 + W *$ days within the range $*$ ppd/10,000)
Premium	0.00

Composition

The range accrual forward works similar like the range forward. The corporate client buys a synthetic forward (see Section 2.1.1) with strike at the worst case, and instead of buying a double-no-touch, the client buys a corridor, see Section 1.6.1 and Figure 2.12.

Example
A company wants to hedge receivables from an export transaction in USD due in 3 months time. It expects the EUR/USD exchange rate to stay near the current spot over the next 3 months. The company wishes to use this view to enhance its exchange rate, but would like to have a guaranteed worst case scenario.

In this case a possible form of protection that the company can use is to enter into a range accrual forward as for example listed in Table 2.9.

The range accrual forward enables the company to sell 1 MIO USD in 3 months time at a rate of 1.1550 EUR-USD. This rate is 80 points above the current forward rate of 1.1470 EUR-USD and represents the worst-case scenario. This rate is the final exchange rate if the spot is fixed outside the predefined range of 1.1400–1.1600 EUR-USD on every day until expiry.

If the spot is fixed inside the range on some or all days until expiry, the worst case rate W will improve to the final exchange rate E, which is calculated by the following formula:

$$\frac{W}{1 + \frac{W N_r p}{10,000}}, \tag{2.10}$$

where N_r denotes the number of days when the spot was fixed within the range and p the pips per day. If the spot is fixed on 18 days within the predefined range until expiry, the final exchange rate will be

$$\frac{1.1550}{1 + 1.1550 \cdot 18 \cdot 3.49/10,000} = 1.1467 \text{ EUR-USD}.$$

This rate is equal to the current forward rate so that 18 days represents the break-even level. If for example spot is fixed on 50 days within the predefined range, the final exchange rate will be

$$\frac{1.1550}{1 + 1.1550 \cdot 50 \cdot 3.49/10,000} = 1.1322 \text{ EUR-USD}.$$

This is an improvement by 228 points compared to the worst-case scenario and by 148 points compared to the current forward rate.

Alternatives

Noticeably, the accrual range is very small, whence this product appears difficult to sell from a psychological view point. The reason is the resurrecting style range. If one changes this to a non-resurrecting style range or American style, the improvement stops at the first time the spot leaves the range. However, the company keeps the already accrued pips. This is more risky, but the range can be set wider.

Other alternatives are of course to modify the start and the end date of the range. For longer tenors it is advisable to use a series of forward start corridors, so the range will be reset around the future spot in say a quarterly schedule. This will give the client always fresh chances to accumulate forward enhancement pips even if the spot will move to a new level.

One important point to mention is to assure the schedule of fixings (daily, weekly, monthly, quarterly, ...) is fully agreed with the client. The safest way to go about it is to state the exact list of fixing days and agree before trading the contract. The other important issue is to clarify what happens if the fixing happens to be exactly on the lower or upper range. While a fair financial institution should treat such an instant always in favor of the client, the front office systems are sometimes programmed in a different way, namely counting fixings on the

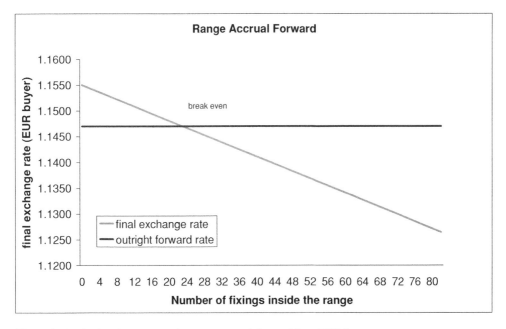

Figure 2.7   Final exchange rate of a range accrual forward for a EUR buyer

range as outside the range. For pricing it is of course irrelevant because in most continuous time models such an event has zero probability. However, a mismatch of agreement with the client and internal implementation can lead to losses in the options portfolio after the fixing is entered.

2.1.10 Accumulative forward

An accumulative forward is a (usually) zero cost forward enhancement without a guaranteed worst case, a product of rather speculative nature. It is popular in France, Italy and the United Kingdom among many corporates. The trading parties agree on a payoff, say a plain forward, and specify ranges; with each fixing inside such a range a pre-determined notional amount of a specified currency for this payoff accumulates. There are many ways to build these contracts.

As an example we take an accumulative forward in EUR/USD, spot ref 1.1500. We let the expiry and delivery date be 12 months and take 250 ECB fixings. The client sells 200,000 USD at 1.1000 for each day the EUR/USD fixing is between 1.1000 and 1.2000. The client sells 400,000 USD at 1.1000 for each day the EUR/USD fixing is below 1.1000. In the extreme case of all fixing below 1.1000 the total amount accumulated would be 100 million USD. If the non-resurrecting knock out level of 1.2000 is ever traded, then the accumulation stops, but the client keeps 100 % of the accumulated amount. This means that the amount accumulated becomes the notional of a forward contract with the pre-determined delivery date. It is up to the client to either keep or unwind the position and take the profit.

We notice here that there are many things to design.

Ranges. In principle many ranges can be set arbitrarily and for each range there is a notional amount that should be specified. They can even be overlapping. In our example we have three ranges, one from 0.0000 to 1.1000 with 2 times the notional, one from 1.1000 to 1.2000 with one times the notional, and one from 1.2000 to infinity with zero times the notional.

Knock-out Ranges. Knock-out ranges can be set anywhere and need not agree with the fade-in ranges.

Leverage. Usually the amount the client wishes to hedge is the basic notional. In our example it is 200,000 USD per business day. The client improves his exchange rate by taking risk if the spot moves against him, i.e. for the USD seller we consider here, a spot lower than 1.1000 would hurt. This loss is multiplied with a factor of 2 in our example. It is called the leverage of the accumulative forward. Any positive number is possible, common leverage factors are 1 and 2. One can be rather aggressive here to improve the desired low rate even more.

Resurrecting/non-resurrecting. Each range should be declared either resurrecting or non-resurrecting.

Amount kept in case of knock out. For resurrecting ranges, there is no knock-out. This is also commonly traded. However, the conditions are usually a bit worse than in the non-resurrecting case. Here the rate would be about 1.1250 instead of the 1.1000. We need to implement the two cases of *keep all* and *keep nothing* as they are different products. For general amounts to keep the *keep all* and *keep nothing* can be mixed by using appropriate notional amounts.

Fixings. We need to specify the exact fixing schedule and the fixing source. We also need to clarify if the daily amount on a day when the accumulative forward knocks out counts for the accumulated amount. The standard is that it does if the fixing is before the knock-out event on this day and it does not if the fixing is at or after the knock-out event.

Advantages

- Noticeable improvement of exchange rate
- Zero cost product
- Allows numerous tailor-made features

Disadvantages

- No guaranteed worst case
- The amount traded is not fixed but depends on the spot movements, so it can't be considered as a hedge and is unlikely to be eligible for hedge accounting in the IAS 39 sense.
- Generally risky product, entire hedge amount can be lost.

Composition

The accumulative forward consists of fade-in calls and fade-in puts, possibly with extra knock-out ranges.

Comment

Since this product is risky it is usually just a part of a corporate hedging strategy along with outright forward or other enhanced forwards with guaranteed worst case. In case of a continuously rising exchange rate, the client keeps getting knocked out, may keep some of the accumulated amount as a forward contract, and can engage in a new accumulative forward with higher strike and ranges. This way the client always buys EUR at a rate less than the market at zero cost. So as an alternative to doing nothing the accumulative forward is quite attractive. Compared to the outright forward, however, it can hurt the corporate budget a lot. So this may be a good add-on to more conservative hedging.

Conversely if the spot moves in the client's favor, the client is penalized, often in a multiple amount. Hence, it appears advisable to restructure the accumulative forward as soon as the spot moves below the strike. This means that this product needs a rather active treasurer watching the market or a bank helping him or her to do this.

Extra features

Rebates. Like in the case of barrier options, one can pay a rebate amount in case of knock out. Of course, this makes the product more expensive. On the other hand, it makes it easier to sell a new product to the client who gets hurt by the knock-out event.

Fees. An accumulative forward need not necessarily trade at zero cost. A client can pay to improve the conditions or opt for a rather aggressive arrangement and get a cash payment up-front.

Stripped Settlement. It is possible to settle the accumulated amounts at pre-determined intermediate settlement dates. This basically means stripping the accumulative forward into a series.

Bounds on Amounts. There are ways to place upper bounds on the accumulated amount. In the example above, one could agree on the accumulation to stop when 75 Million USD have accumulated. This is a *Parasian style* knock-out event.

Validity of Knock-out Barriers. Like in the shark forward, one can think of partial knock-out barriers.

Improved Rate on early Knock-out. It usually feels awkward to report a knock-out event to the client soon after inception of the trade. To avoid this one can agree on an exchange rate even below the improved one, say 1.0500 if the knock out happens during the first month. Of course, this exchange rate is only valid for the amount accumulated up to the knock-out event. This can be included in the structure by the client buying a fade-in EUR call with *keep all* in case of knock-out and selling the same fade-in EUR call with *keep nothing*. Hence, if there is no knock-out, the two positions net each other, and conversely, if there is a knock-out, only the client receives a forward contract. The ranges should be chosen identical as for the basic version of the accumulative forward.

Digital Events. To improve the final exchange rate, one can include a digital event by agreeing to double the accumulated amount if the spot at expiration time is below the strike (and the accumulative forward has not knocked out until then). This can be achieved by the client selling another EUR put with the same specifications and ranges as the basic version and keep nothing in case of knock-out. More generally, one can agree to an arbitrary multiple of the daily amount rather then doubling. And even more generally the digital strike may differ from the strike of the accumulative forward. For example, consider the following zero-cost structure for a EUR buyer/USD seller on spot reference of 1.2000 with a tenor of 5 months. The client buys one fold the EUR amount at 1.1700 between 1.1500 and 1.2500 and 2.3 fold below 1.1500, keeps 100 % of the accumulated amount and converts twice the accumulated amount, if the spot is below 1.2000 at expiration time.

A note on pricing

Fader contracts can be priced in closed form in the Black-Scholes model, see [3] for details. A trading price can be obtained by an approximate hedge consisting of liquid first generation exotics, whose prices we know. The difference between the theoretical value in the Black-Scholes model and the trading mid price is called the *overhedge*. We then compose an approximate hedge, compute its overhedge and take this overhedge as a proxy for the overhedge of the fader contract. This is very common practice of traders. In the simple case of a resurrecting fader, the contract merely consists of a sum of knock-out calls or puts, whose prices are known in the market. For the non-resurrecting faders, the story is slightly more complicated, because the amount accumulated at knock out is not known in advance, but has to be estimated.

As an example we take an accumulative forward in EUR/USD, at a spot reference of 0.9800 of September 24 2002. We let the tenor be 15 months. The client buys a total of 28 million EUR at an improved rate of 0.9150 with value date in 15 months. For each EUR/USD fixing

Table 2.10 Overhedge of RKO EUR calls and KO EUR puts

Tenor	Basis Points (in EUR) RKO calls	Basis Points (in EUR) KO puts
6 months	+25	−5
9 months	+40	−10
12 months	+40	−20
15 months	+40	−20
average	+36	−12

between 0.9150 and 1.0500 the client accumulates 28 million EUR divided by the number of fixing days. For each EUR/USD fixing below 0.9150 the client accumulates twice this daily amount, such that in the extreme case of all fixing below 0.9150 the total amount accumulated would be 56 million EUR. If the non-resurrecting knock out level of 1.0500 is ever traded, then the accumulation stops, but the client keeps 100 % of the accumulated amount.

The TV (theoretical value) of this structure can be calculated. Based on the volatility and interest rates term structure at that time it was about 400,000 EUR, which the client would have to receive. However, the hedge of the structure has a massive overhedge, which can be computed as follows.

For the 0.9150 EUR calls reverse knock out (RKO) at 1.0500 we determine the overhedge as the average of the maturities 6 to 15 months. We do the same for the 0.9150 EUR puts knock out at 1.0500. The details are listed in Table 2.10.

On 28 million EUR 36 basis points (bps) are 101,000 EUR, which is the overhedge for buying the RKO calls in the hedge. Similarly on 56 million EUR 12 bps are 68,000 EUR, which is the overhedge for selling the KO puts. Both are priced at mid market, so are fairly aggressive.

Next we need to worry about the cost of knock out. If the knock out level of 1.0500 is reached, the client has the right to buy the accumulated EUR amount at 0.9150 (with the pre-determined value date), even though the spot is then at 1.0500. For the bank selling the accumulative forward this is substantial risk, which can be hedged by buying a 1.0500 one-touch with 15 months maturity. The only thing is the notional of this one-touch has to be approximated. First of all the amount at risk, called the *parity risk* is

$$1.0500 - 0.9150 = 0.1350 \text{ USD per EUR}$$
$$= 0.1286 \% \text{ EUR}. \tag{2.11}$$

We approximate the time it takes to reach the parity level of 0.9150 by 7 months and take from the market that the price of a 7 month 0.9150 one-touch is 40 % . So say 40 % chance below 0.9150, accumulating 22.23 million EUR and 60 % chance above 0.9150, accumulating 16.8 million EUR. The sum of these two amounts may be the total of 39.03 million EUR accumulated. The 15 months 1.0500 one-touch would cost 53.5 %, whence the parity risk amount equals 39.03 mio * 53.5 % * 12.86 % = 2.7 million EUR. The one-touch overhedge would be 2.7 mio * 3 % (mid market) = 81,000 EUR.

Finally, to hedge the vega of 206,000 EUR, we take the bid-offer spread of the price in volatilities and arrive at 206,000 * 0.15 vols (bid-offer) = 31,000 EUR.

The total overhedge is now 101,000 + 68,000 + 81,000 + 31,000 = 281,000 EUR. This method is surely not fully exact, but gives a very good approximating hedge and along its market price, which may be better than any more complicated model.

Table 2.11   Terms and conditions of an accumulated forward in GBP-EUR

Period	122 days
Start date	08-Apr-03
End date	24-Sep-03
Delivery date	26-Sep-03
Strike	1.4200
Knock-out barrier	1.5000
Client	sells EUR (buys GBP) at the strike
Notional	EUR 7,500,000.00
Notional per business day	EUR 61,475.41
Premium	Zero
EUR/GBP spot reference	1.4535 GBP-EUR
12mth outright forward	1.4463 (GBP 3.53 %, EUR 2.45 %)

The main risk in the accumulative forward to capture is the forward smile dynamics. A more scientific approach has been worked out by Baker, Beneder and Zilber in [66].

Example
We consider an example of a GBP-EUR Accumulative Forward, whose terms and conditions are listed in Table 2.11. The ranges are illustrated in Figure 2.8.

Notional is computed by

$$\text{Notional} \cdot \left[\frac{\text{RangeDays}}{\text{Days}} + 2\frac{\text{TopDays}}{\text{Days}} \right], \tag{2.12}$$

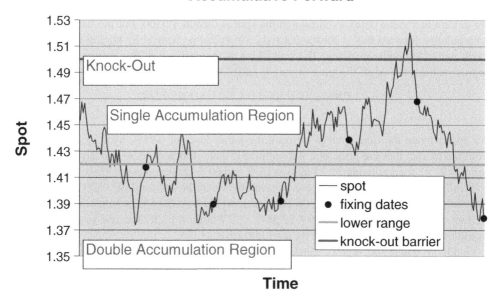

Figure 2.8   Ranges for an accumulative forward in EUR/GBP in GBP-EUR quotation

Days is the number of all business days in the period,

RangeDays is the number of business days in the period that the reference rate fixes between strike and knock-out barrier,

TopDays is the number of business days in the period that the reference rate fixes below the strike,

Reference Rate is the EUR/GBP rate in GBP-EUR quotation by the European Central Bank published on Reuters page ECB37,

Settlement is physical on the delivery date.

Knock-Out Condition: If GBP-EUR trades at or above the knock-out level at any time, then the transaction terminates and the client sells 50 % of the accumulated EUR amount up to the knock-out date if the knock-out occurs after 14h15 Frankfurt Time. The GBP-EUR daily trading range will be determined by the bank and should a rate query arise, can be cross-referenced with three market making banks.

Example
If the GBP-EUR reference rate fixing remains in the range 1.4200 and 1.5000 for 110 days of the business days before trading at 1.5000, then the contract would terminate at that point with a notional of EUR 3,381,147.55, which the client sells at 1.4200 for settlement on the delivery date (26-Sep-03).

2.1.11 Boomerang forward

The following zero cost product could serve as alternative for corporates, particularly those who trade accumulators. Here is an example for a EUR buyer (USD seller) for a spot reference of 1.2000 and 1 year outright forward reference of 1.2000.

- If EUR/USD remains above $B = 1.1349$ for the $T = 1$ year period, the bank will pay the counterparty $(S(T) - 1.1790) \cdot 10$ million EUR. Or in the case of delivery settlement, the client can buy EUR at 1.1790, which is much better than the spot and the outright forward rate.
- If EUR/USD trades below B at any time during that year period, the counterparty pays the bank $(1.2190 - S(T)) \cdot 10$ million EUR, unless spot is above 1.2190 at maturity, in which case the bank pays the counterparty $(S(T) - 1.2190) \cdot 10$ million EUR. In other words, in case of knock-in at B the client is locked into a forward contract with strike 1.2190. This is also his guaranteed worst case.

The boomerang forward can be structured as follows. The client

1. buys 1Y 1.1790 EUR Call (USD Put) KO at 1.1349,
2. sells 1Y 1.2190 EUR Put (USD Call) RKI at 1.1349,
3. buys 1Y 1.2190 EUR Call (USD Put) KI 1.1349.

The good feature here as compared to accumulators is a guaranteed worst case. The zero cost strategy only hurts the client if the spot falls significantly, so the barrier is hit and the client is faced with a much higher exchange rate than the spot.

2.1.12 Amortizing forward

A treasurer can enhance a company's foreign exchange rate at zero cost by taking a risk, but still participate in the exchange rate moving in its favor. One of the possible solutions can be an amortizing forward, which provides the client with a worst case exchange rate, but if the spot rate moves against him or her the notional of the forward contract decreases.

For contract parameters maturity in years T, strike K and knock-out barrier B, notional of the underlying N, payment schedule $0 = t_0 < t_1 < t_2 \ldots, t_n = T$, the payoff is

$$F(S, K, B, t_i, N) \stackrel{\Delta}{=} N \sum_{m=1}^{n} (S_{t_m} - K) \prod_{i=1}^{m-1} \left[\min \left[1, \left(\frac{S_{t_i} - B}{K - B} \right)^{+} \right] \right]. \qquad (2.13)$$

We denote by $v(t, x)$ the value of the amortizing forward at time t if the spot S_t takes the value x. The value at time zero is given by

$$v(0, S_0) = I\!E[e^{-r_d \tau} F(S, K, B, t_i, N)], \qquad (2.14)$$

A closed-form solution or numerical integration are both possible in the Black-Scholes model. A straightforward exercise to determine the value as a benchmark would be a Monte Carlo simulation. The standard trading convention is to determine B for a desired worst case K in such a way that the value is zero.

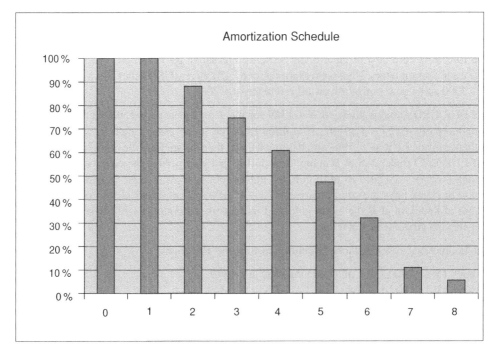

Figure 2.9 Amortization schedule of an amortizing forward contract for a EUR buyer/USD seller

Table 2.12 Example of an amortizing forward

Spot reference	1.1500 EUR-USD
Outright forward reference	1.1566 EUR-USD
Notional	USD 10,000,000
Maturity	2 years
Worst case	1.1650 EUR-USD
Barrier	0.8700 EUR-USD
Schedule	Quarterly
Premium	0.00

Example

We consider a EUR buyer/USD seller for a total initial notional of $N = 10$ Million USD for a period of 2 years with quarterly settlements. This means that at the end of each following 8 quarters the corporate sells USD. A worst case $K = 1.1650$ is guaranteed and is taken slightly worse than the 2-year outright forward rate. If the spot moves up over the next 2 years, then the corporate can benefit from the guaranteed worst case. The worst case exchange rate is always going to be the rate at which the notional is traded. The only changing parameter is the notional. If the spot goes up, the full notional is traded. If the spot moves down, then the notional decreases proportional to the distance of the spot from the worst case, i.e. by the factor

$$\left(\frac{S_{t_i} - B}{K - B} \right), \tag{2.15}$$

but only if the spot at time t_i is below the worst case K and above the barrier B. If any of the S_{t_i} is below B then all the future notionals are zero, thus the contract can be considered as terminated. Consequently, when the exchange rate depreciates, the worst case is binding, but only for a smaller notional, and the more the spot movement hurts the corporate, the less notional it is required to trade.

We illustrate a possible scenario in Table 2.13 and Figure 2.9. At the last quarter for example, the corporate is obliged to sell 600,000 USD at 1.1650 even though the market spot is at 1.0200. However, the corporate can trade the remaining 9,4 Million USD at spot.

2.1.13 Auto-renewal forward

Once more, we consider a client who wants to enhance his or her forward exchange rate at zero cost by taking a risky position. The auto-renewal forward is a strategy consisting of a series of forward contracts, which is automatically renewed.

Table 2.13 Possible amortization schedule

Quarter	1	2	3	4	5	6	7	8
Spot reference	1.18	1.13	1.12	1.11	1.10	1.07	0.97	1.02
Notional traded in %	100	88	75	61	47	32	11	6

For contract parameters maturity in years T, strikes K_1 and K_2, renewal barrier B, payment schedule $0 = t_0 < t_1 < t_2 \ldots, t_n = T$, the payoff is

$$F(S, K_1, K_2, B, \{t_i\}, N) \stackrel{\Delta}{=} \sum_{N=1}^{J} \prod_{n=0}^{N-1} \mathbb{1}_{\{S_{t_{ln}} > B\}} H(K_1, K_2, \{S\}_{t_{ln+1} \ldots t_{ln+l}}),$$

$$H(K_1, K_2, \{S\}_{t_j \ldots t_k}) \stackrel{\Delta}{=} \sum_{i=j}^{k} \left[(K_1 - S_{t_i})^+ + (K_2 - S_{t_i})^+ \mathbb{1}_{\{S_{t_j} > K_1\}} - 2(S_{t_i} - K_2)^+ \right]. \quad (2.16)$$

We denote by $v(t, x)$ the value of the auto-renewal forward at time t if the spot S_t takes the value x. It is well known that the value at time zero is given by

$$v(0, S_0) = I\!\!E[e^{-r_d T} F(S, K_1, K_2, B, t_i, N)]. \quad (2.17)$$

The contract parameters K_1, K_2 and B are usually determined in such a way that the value at inception of the contract is zero.

Example
Taking a USD/JPY spot ref 120.00, we consider a company receiving 1 million USD per quarter for the next three years. The company wishes to exchange the USD into JPY at a suitable rate, i.e. the higher the better. However, a worst case exchange rate for the USD seller should be guaranteed. In this case the conditions of the auto-renewal forward could be set like this.

- the company sells 1 million USD at the end of each quarter of the first year.
- if the exchange rate at the end of the quarter is below 110.00, then the company sells at 110.00.
- if the exchange rate at the end of the quarter is between 110.00 and 125.00, then the company sells at 125.00.
- if the exchange rate at the end of the quarter is above 125.00, then the company sells twice the amount at 125.00.
- if at the end of the first year, the exchange rate is above 120.00, then the strategy is automatically renewed for another year.
- the maximum number of years will be 3.

In this example, the contract parameters are $K_1 = 110.00$, $K_2 = 125.00$, $B = 120.00$, $J = 3$, $l = 4$. Usually, J denotes the number of years and l the number of delivery dates per year. So if $l = 4$, then the company has agreed on quarterly delivery.

2.1.14 Double shark forward

The double shark forward is structured just like a shark forward (see Section 2.1.5). In the case of a USD buyer, the corporate buys a EUR put with strike equal to the worst case and sells a reverse knock-in EUR call. It happens frequently that the barrier of the reverse knock-in is too close to the spot and therefore likely to be hit. In this case the corporate would be left with the worst case. If we want to move away the knock-in barrier and still have a zero cost product, we can increase the notional of the reverse knock-in, commonly by a factor of 2.

Table 2.14   Example of a double forward plus

Spot reference	1.1500 EUR-USD
Outright forward reference	1.1460 EUR-USD
Notional	USD 10,000,000
Maturity	8 months
Worst case	1.1250 EUR-USD
Knock-in barrier (European style)	1.3080 EUR-USD
Premium	0.00

Example
We consider a company that needs to buy 10 Million USD in 8 months due to an import transaction. A double forward plus scenario is presented in Table 2.14.

This means that the corporate is protected against falling EUR with a worst case of 1.1250 at no cost. At the same time, the corporate can participate in a rising EUR all the way up to 1.3080. The only crucial risk is that the amount will be doubled if EUR/USD trades above 1.3080 on the expiration date. This event is considered extremely unlikely, but if it happens, then the corporate has to pay a high penalty. For example, if the spot ends at 1.3250, the corporate is obliged to buy 20 USD at 1.1250 even though the market is a 1.3250. This causes a loss of 2,683,438 EUR or 3,555,555 USD. Thus, if the unlikely knock-in event happens, the damage is disastrous.

2.1.15   Forward start chooser forward

Another possible forward enhancement with guaranteed worst case would be to trade a synthetic forward with worst case as strike, pretty much like most of the forward catalogue products. Here the client buys a forward start chooser option, i.e. the strike will be set in the future on the forward start date and the client can decide to take either a call or a put. One can additionally allow forward starting barriers. This product is useful if the corporate thinks to have a view on the underlying exchange rate at a later stage, namely at the forward start date.

2.1.16   Free style forward

If the corporate has no view on the exchange rate at all and is willing to leave the profit maximization to the bank, then the corporate can trade a worst case forward contract with the bank. In turn, the bank is taking proprietary trading positions on behalf of the corporate client and lets him or her participate in any gains created from there. This requires a substantial trust factor, as the client has no way to double-check what the bank has done. The bank would in turn try to maximize the payoff to the client to keep him or her happy and ready for the next trade.

2.1.17   Boosted spot/forward

The boosted spot/forward is a zero cost spot/forward deal with a rate better than the market, which is financed by selling an option, usually an out-of-the money vanilla. The improved spot/forward rate is often chosen to match the strike of the sold vanilla.

Table 2.15   Example of a boosted spot

Spot reference	1.1500 EUR-USD
Improved spot rate	1.1200 EUR-USD
Client sells	USD 1,000,000
Client sells	EUR put USD call
Notional	750,000 EUR
Maturity	12 months
Strike	1.1200 EUR-USD
Premium	0.00

Advantages

- Improved exchange rate for spot/forward deal
- Zero cost product

Disadvantages

- Client needs a credit line go short the option
- Unlimited risk in the short option position

This is a product that usually looks good in the beginning and after that it becomes a continuous worry about the option staying out of the money. It is not suitable for hedge-accounting, but a rather speculative strategy.

Example

We consider a EUR buyer, USD seller, who gains three big figures in his spot deal by selling a 12 month EUR put, see Table 2.15.

Clearly the cost of the spot deal is

$$1,000,000 \left(\frac{1}{1.1200} - \frac{1}{1.1500} \right) \text{EUR} = 23,292 \text{ EUR}.$$

On a 10 % volatility, 1 % USD interest rate and 2 % EUR interest rate, the EUR put pays 23,433 EUR, so the sales margin would be 141 EUR.

The philosophy behind this structure is that the client wants to buy EUR, so the salesperson argues accordingly. If the spot moves up, then the client should be happy having bought the EUR for less than the market at no cost. If the spot moves down below 1.1200, then the client just gets a few more EUR at the improved rate. For large downward movements, however, this can't really be called an improvement anymore. One could limit the risk on the downside by introducing a floor or a barrier. However, we would then have to increase the notional or the strike.

We see this type of structure traded in the inter bank market rather than as a corporate hedging strategy.

2.1.18   Time option

A time option or American style forward contract entitles *and* requires the holder to buy/sell a pre-determined amount of a currency at a pre-determined strike K within a given time period

$[T_1, T_2]$ in the future. The holder can choose times in this period to exercise parts of the total amount, where he or she shouts, which is why this type of contract is also called a *shout forward*. The time option is just like an American style call, except that the entire amount must be exercised. Obviously, the optimal exercise time would apply to the entire amount.

Mathematically, the value at time zero is given by

$$v(0) = \sup_{\tau \in [T_1, T_2]} I\!E \left[e^{-r_d \tau} \phi(S_\tau - K) \right], \tag{2.18}$$

where τ is a stopping time. As in the case of the outright forward, the strike K^* is usually determined by requiring $v(0) = 0$. Now, based on a simple arbitrage argument, taking EUR/USD as a default exchange rate, we observe

$$K^* \geq \max_{t \in [T_1, T_2]} f(t) \text{ for the EUR buyer} \tag{2.19}$$

$$K^* \leq \min_{t \in [T_1, T_2]} f(t) \text{ for the EUR seller}, \tag{2.20}$$

where $f(t)$ denotes the outright forward rate for value date t. In fact, the inequalities can be strict. However, it is advisable to verify that the front office system contains a suitable implementation of this product.

Advantages

- Complete flexibility in the exercise schedule
- Zero cost product
- Guaranteed worst case

Disadvantages

- Worst case is not better than any outright forward rate over the time horizon
- No participation in the spot moving in the client's favor
- Cumbersome for the client to determine the optimal exercise region

2.1.19   Exercises

1. Write a Monte Carlo pricer to compute the value of an amortizing forward of Section 2.1.12.
2. Write a Monte Carlo pricer to compute the value of an auto-renewal forward of Section 2.1.13.
3. Write a binomial tree pricer to compute the value of a time option of Section 2.1.18. Find a parameter set, for which

$$K^* > \max_{t \in [T_1, T_2]} f(t) \text{ for the EUR buyer.}$$

4. Consider the case of a resurrecting style accumulative forward with maturity T. Now at some time $0 < t_1 < T$ during the lifetime of the contract the client has the right to cancel the contract at zero cost. So if the client is a EUR buyer (USD seller), and a lot of notional has accumulated before time t_1 and the EUR-USD spot depreciates, then the client would typically want to cancel. How would you go about finding the value of such a contract? Describe where the problem is in case of Monte Carlo simulations, argue why partial

Table 2.16   Terms and conditions of a *contingent rebate* structure

Currency pair	EUR-USD
Nominal	USD 1,000,000.00
Maturity	4 months from now
Strike	0.9000
Range	0.8500 0.9200
Type of barrier	American
Premium	EUR 28,000 to be paid after two working days

differential equations would be problematic and come up with a suggestion how to fix the problems.

5. Given a market situation of EUR-USD spot 0.9000 and 4-months forward of 0.8960 and terms listed in Table 2.16.

   For your EUR buy/USD sale in 4 months you have guaranteed a worst case scenario of 0.9000 EUR-USD. This rate is 0.40 USD-cents above the current outright forward of 0.8960 EUR-USD.

   In case the EUR-USD exchange rate at maturity is above 0.9000, you exercise your right to sell your USD at 0.9000.

   You may participate arbitrarily, if the EUR-USD exchange rate decreases.

   If the EUR-USD exchange rate stays within the specified range for the entire life time of the structure, you will be returned your premium.

   How would you structure this product? And how much sales margin would it generate for a volatility of 10 %, EUR interest rate of 3 % and USD interest rates such that the forward comes out correctly, if it is priced in the Black-Scholes model?

6. Given a market situation of EUR-USD spot 0.9000 and 4-months forward of 0.8960 and terms listed in Table 2.17.

   You have ensured a worst case of 0.9060 EUR-USD for your EUR purchase/USD sale in 4 months. This exchange rate is 1.00 USD-cents above the current outright forward of 0.8960 EUR-USD. The worst case will be used in one of the following cases.

   - If at maturity the EUR-USD exchange rate is below 0.9060 EUR-USD, then the USD notional will be exchanged into EUR with the worst case rate of 0.9060 EUR-USD.
   - If the EUR-USD exchange rate ever trades once at or above the trigger of 0.9300 EUR-USD, then the strategy changes into the obligation to buy EUR and sell USD at a rate of 0.9060 EUR-USD.

Table 2.17   Terms and conditions of a structured forward

Currency pair	EUR-USD
Nominal	$N =$ USD 1,000,000.00
Maturity	$T = 4$ months from now
Worst case exchange rate	$W = 0.9060$
Trigger	$B = 0.9300$
Trigger type	American
Final realized exchange rate	Nominal/final amount of EUR
Final amount of EUR	$N\left[\frac{1}{W} + \left(\frac{1}{W} - \frac{1}{S_T}\right)\right]$

The final amount of EUR is only correct, if the reference spot at maturity is above 0.9060 EUR-USD and the trigger 0.9300 has not been touched or crossed during the lifetime of the structure.

Table 2.18 Terms and conditions of a structured forward

Currency pair	EUR-USD
Nominal	USD 1,000,000.00
Maturity	4 months from now
Preliminary exchange rate	0.8850
Worst case	0.9050
Trigger	0.9200
Trigger type	European – only valid at maturity

- If until maturity the exchange rate EUR-USD never touches or crosses 0.9300 EUR-USD and if at maturity the spot reference is above 0.9060, then the final exchange rate is computed using the above formula.

How would you structure this product? And how much sales margin would it generate for a volatility of 10 %, EUR interest rate of 3 % and USD interest rates such that the forward comes out correctly, if it is priced in the Black-Scholes model?

7. Given a market situation of EUR-USD spot 0.9000 and 4-months forward of 0.8960 and terms listed in Table 2.18.

   For your EUR-purchase/USD-sale in 4 months you have a preliminary exchange rate of 0.8850. This rate is 1.10 USD-cents better than the outright forward 0.8960 EUR-USD and will be used if the trigger is not touched or crossed at maturity.

   If the EUR-USD exchange rate touches or crosses the trigger on the maturity date then you must sell your USD at a rate of 0.9050.

   How would you structure this product? And how much sales margin would it generate for a volatility of 10 %, EUR interest rate of 3 % and USD interest rates such that the forward comes out correctly, if it is priced in the Black-Scholes model?

8. Given a market situation of EUR-USD spot 0.8900 and 6-months forward of 0.8850 and terms listed in Table 2.19.

   You have locked your USD-sale in 6 months at a rate of 0.8850 EUR-USD. This is your worst case scenario. This rate is also identical with today's outright forward.

   The potential forward rate of 0.8850 EUR-USD will be used if one of the following cases will occur.

- The EUR-USD-exchange rate at maturity is below 0.8850 EUR-USD. In this case you just exercise your forward agreement and buy USD 1,000,000 at a rate of 0.8850 EUR-USD.
- The EUR-USD-exchange rate touches or crosses the trigger 0.9850 EUR-USD at some time before maturity. In this case you are bound to a forward contract with the worst case rate of 0.8850 EUR-USD.

Table 2.19 Terms and conditions of a structured forward with *doubling option*: the bank has the right to double the notional at maturity

Nominal	USD 1,000,000.00
Maturity	6 months from now
Worst case	0.8850 EUR-USD
American style knock-in Trigger K	0.9850 EUR-USD

If the EUR-USD-exchange rate never touches or crosses the trigger 0.9850 EUR-USD until maturity and if at maturity the exchange rate is above 0.8850, you don't use the forward contract but buy the USD at the exchange rate spot at maturity. This way you can participate in a rising exchange rate up to a maximal level of 0.9849 EUR-USD.

At maturity the bank has the right to double the nominal amount, if EUR-USD has ever traded above the trigger 0.9850 EUR-USD before maturity *and* EUR-USD trades above 0.8850 EUR-USD at maturity. In this case you would buy USD 2,000,000 at the rate of 0.8850 EUR-USD.

How would you structure this product? And how much sales margin would it generate for a volatility of 10 %, EUR interest rate of 3 % and USD interest rates such that the forward comes out correctly, if it is priced in the Black-Scholes model?

9. Discuss how to structure a *chooser forward*, which is a shark forward, where the client can decide at some time *t* before expiration time *T* whether to go for a favorable participation (forward plus) or for a non-favorable participation (forward extra). How does it work if the worst case and both the participation strikes are all different? How does it simplify if they are all equal?

10. You might be tempted to replicate a long time option as a long American style call and a short European style put. Convince yourself that this is wrong by stating an example where the replication and the time option differ.

11. What are the options needed to structure the fade-in forward listed in Table 2.2? Try to find the relevant market data for this day and re-evaluated this deal to find out how much margin the bank made.

2.2   SERIES OF STRATEGIES

Series of strategies are often applied when the corporate expects regular cash flows over a period of time. Essentially all structured products can be composed as a series version. Everything is possible, so that we can't really present a complete list of series structures. It starts with a simple series of forward contracts, continued with series of vanillas, spreads, risk reversals, straddles, strangles, seagulls etc. For the forward series in turn, one can just package a series of say 12 outright forward contracts for one year, with monthly settlement dates. The individual legs would be all zero cost, hence the entire series would also be zero cost. The alternative is to find the average strike that works for all and still produces a zero cost structure. In case of the forwards, the average is just the arithmetic average of the outright forward rates.

For a zero cost series of risk reversals for example, where we want to use only one and the same strike for all the calls and one strike for all the puts, we need to find these strikes by iteration. In the following we would like to give a few examples how these series can be worked out and what the alternatives are.

2.2.1   Shark forward series

For the shark forward series many different ways to do this are possible.

Identical shark forwards

Here we do a shark forward series, whose parameters for each tenor are the same except the maturity date. This is sometimes called the *Milano strategy*. So, for example, we take

12 shark forwards, one maturing and settling in each month. The major disadvantage of this is that the barrier for the shorter maturities is comparatively far away from the spot, so the components with short maturity in the structure become unreasonably expensive. There are ways to circumvent this weakness as we show now.

Identical shark forwards with time dependent barriers

Here we can simply design a step function for the knock-out barrier, starting with a barrier closer to the spot for the first leg and then move the barrier further away from the spot with longer maturities. To keep it simple for the client, the steps of the barrier moves are usually kept constant.

Window shark forwards

Another common way to structure series of shark forwards is to use window barriers for the knock-out barrier components. This means that the barrier is only valid for the time between the last maturity and the actual maturity of the leg. Of course, window barriers and stepping barriers can be combined.

Forwards with single compensation payment

This is more than just stripping existing structures with varying maturities. Here we take a series of synthetic forward contracts, usually with the same strike and notional amounts. The strike chosen represents the guaranteed worst case scenario for the client. The value of the entire series leaves money to invest into an option representing the client's market view. In the case of a shark forward the structure contains a reverse knock-out. The entire structure is usually zero cost.

As an example we consider an exporter in the EUR zone expecting incoming cash flow of 1 Million USD at the end of each month for the following 20 months, representing a total notional amount of 20 Million USD. The client seeks a low exchange rate to buy EUR.

In this concrete case the outright forward rates for EUR/USD as of May 3rd 2004 are listed in Table 2.20.

We consider the following alternatives.

Wait for better times. This means that the client does not do any hedge, but waits for the spot to come down. This strategy is free of cost, but carries enormous risk. Suppose the average exchange rate during the following 20 months is at 1.2500 on average, then the corporate encounters a total loss of 867,660 EUR. On the other hand, the corporate can fully participate in a falling EUR.

20 outright forward contracts. This is the zero cost fully safe hedging strategy. However, the corporate can not benefit from a falling EUR.

20 EUR call options. This is the full coverage solution with full participation in a falling EUR. However, the drawback is of course, that it is expensive. For strike 1.2000 for instance this would cost 550,000 EUR.

Table 2.20   EUR/USD outright forward rates as of
May 3rd 2004 for spot reference 1.1900

Value date	Outright forward rate
5/31/04	1.1892
6/30/04	1.1882
7/30/04	1.1873
8/31/04	1.1866
9/30/04	1.1860
10/29/04	1.1856
11/30/04	1.1852
12/31/04	1.1849
1/31/05	1.1847
2/28/05	1.1845
3/31/05	1.1844
4/29/05	1.1844
5/31/05	1.1844
6/30/05	1.1845
7/29/05	1.1847
8/31/05	1.1850
9/30/05	1.1854
10/31/05	1.1858
11/30/05	1.1864
12/30/05	1.1870

20 risk reversals. This covers the corporate's risk of a rising EUR and allows some decent participation in a falling EUR at zero cost. For instance one could set the strike of the EUR calls at 1.2500 and the strike of the EUR puts at 1.1300.

Series of forwards with a single compensation payment. Here we could generate a worst case of 1.2000, which is only 143 pips worse than the average outright forward rate. By giving up these 143 pips the corporate would buy an EUR put with strike 1.2000 and American style barrier 1.0500. We let the notional of this reverse knock-out coincide with the total notional amount of 20 Million USD, although this is in no regards binding. Even the strike could be lowered to allow for a lower knock-out trigger if needed. Now, if the trigger is ever touched, the EUR put is knocked out, and the client is left with the guaranteed worst case. If the trigger is not touched, then the client participates in a cheaper EUR and receives a compensation payment. As a result his overall exchange rate is approximately equal to the EUR/USD spot at maturity. This strategy is free of cost, a well-balanced mixture of safety and participation opportunities, allows for hedge-accounting, can be confirmed as a forward contract and can be unwound any time at market conditions.

2.2.2   Collar extra series

Let us assume a corporate treasurer who needs to buy EUR in 3 months and in 6 months from an income in JPY. He would like to hedge against rising EUR/JPY and have a worst case of 130.00 EUR-JPY guaranteed. However, if EUR-JPY trades at least once below 128.00 in each respective time period, he is willing to buy EUR at a rate below the worst case but near the

Table 2.21 Example of a collar extra series

Spot reference	133.00 EUR-JPY
3 month outright forward	132.30 EUR-JPY
6 month outright forward	131.60 EUR-JPY
Client sells	JPY
Client buys	10,000,000.00 EUR per maturity
Guaranteed worst case	133.00 EUR-JPY
3 month improved case	132.30 EUR-JPY
6 month improved case	131.60 EUR-JPY
Knock-in condition for improved case	128.00 EUR-JPY (American style)
Premium	0.00

current outright forward rate. He finds buying two vanilla calls too expensive and is looking for a zero-cost strategy. We list the indication in Table 2.21.

We note that this is a series of two collar extras. The knock-in barrier is valid for each tenor individually. The knock-in event happens if at least once between trade time and expiry EUR/JPY trades at or below 128.00. If the knock-in event occurs, the client has locked in a forward with the improved case. It is called improvement, because it is better than the guaranteed worst case. However, it is worse than trading a new outright forward at the time of knock-in. This feature makes the structure zero cost. If the knock-in event does not occur, then the client participates in a falling EUR/JPY rate until 128.01.

Composition

For each tenor, the client

1. buys a EUR call with strike at the worst case, down-and-out at 128.00,
2. sells a EUR put with strike at the improved case, down-and-in at 128.00,
3. buys a EUR call with strike at the improved case, down-and-in at 128.00.

2.2.3 Exercises

1. Compose a strip of EUR put USD call vanillas for one year, one for each month with the same strike K. Assume a flat interest rate of 3 % for USD and 2.5 % for EUR, a volatility of 10 % and a current spot of 1.2000. Let the monthly amount be 200,000.00 USD. The client is willing to pay 30,000 EUR premium for the strip. Where should the strike be for a sales margin of 2,000 USD? What is the delta hedge you as a seller have to do? Where should the spot go if you are greedy and want a sales margin of 3,000 USD?
2. Given the following indicative terms and conditions for an importer in the EUR zone against USD in Table 2.22. It is a series of contracts with a EUR bearish participation, where the corporate client
   - expects quarterly incoming USD over a time period of 5 years,
   - expects a EUR depreciation and wants to participate in it,
   - needs a protection against a rising EUR,
   - prefers a zero cost strategy.

Table 2.22   Sample term sheet of a series of structured risk reversals. S_T denotes the spot at cutoff time of the respective quarter

Time to maturity	5 years
Notional amount	1,000,000 USD each quarter
Settlements	quarterly
Spot reference	1.1350
5 year outright forward reference	1.1500
Upper trigger	1.2300
Lower trigger	1.0500
Exchange rate for EUR-USD	
Best case	$\min(S_T, 1.1400)$
Downside case	1.1400
Upside case	$\min(S_T, 1.1500)$
Combined case	$\max(1.1400, \min(S_T, 1.1500))$
Resulting worst case	1.1500 EUR/USD

Best Case occurs if the continuously observed EUR-USD exchange rate remains below the upper trigger and above the lower trigger from inception of the trade until the maturity of the respective quarter.

Downside Case occurs if the continuously observed EUR-USD exchange rate trades at or below the lower trigger at least once from inception of the trade until the maturity of the respective quarter.

Upside Case occurs if the continuously observed EUR-USD exchange rate trades at or above the upper trigger at least once from inception of the trade until the maturity of the respective quarter.

Combined Case occurs if the continuously observed EUR-USD exchange rate trades at or above the upper trigger and at or below the lower trigger at least once from inception of the trade until the maturity of the respective quarter.

Cutoff The cutoff time for each quarter is 10:00 a.m. New York time two business days before the delivery date.

Find out the ingredients of this structure, i.e. which standard products are used to structure this deal? Under current market conditions, what is its value?

2.3   DEPOSITS AND LOANS

There is a huge market for deposits and loans both on the corporate side as well as on the retail side. With permanently low interest rates for the major currencies many investors seek ways to enhance coupons by taking a speculative position in the financial markets. Deposits can be linked to many underlyings. Convertible and reverse convertible bonds are popular structures linking deposits to equity markets. *Deutsche Postbank*, for example, offers a savings account where the interest rate is linked to the result of a lottery. *Hypovereinsbank* has come up with a coupon linked to the result of soccer matches. We also find inflation or weather linked notes.

In this book we present structured deposits and loans linked to the foreign exchange markets. All of them trade and more are expected to join as the hunger for coupon enhancements is never ending.

Deposits can be generally categorized in *capital guaranteed* and *non-capital-guaranteed* products. In the latter the investor waives part of the coupon the money market would pay and buys a derivative matching his or her market view. In the former, the investor usually sells an option to increase the coupon and then hopes that the holder of the option cannot exercise the option.

2.3.1 Dual currency deposit/loan

A dual currency deposit (DCD) is a very popular and liquidly traded standard FX-linked investment, that works like a *reverse convertible bond* in the equity markets. Investors searching for higher yields are selling a vanilla call on the deposit currency, which is also a put on another currency, to receive a higher coupon and then hope that the option they sold will be out-of-the-money at maturity. Some banks also name it *enhanced deposit*.

The product works like this. An investor deposits an amount in say EUR for a fixed time horizon, usually from one day up to one year, and instead of the market interest rate she receives a higher coupon. For example, she invests 5 million EUR for 1 month (we take 30/360 years here), where the market rate is 3.00 %, which would return 12,500 EUR interest payment. The higher and fully guaranteed coupon is then for example 5.00 % = 20,833 EUR. For this can't be a free lunch, the investor is taking the following risk. At a EUR-CHF spot reference of 1.4662 he chooses a strike of 1.4700. If at maturity the spot stays below 1.4700 (strong CHF), then the investor is paid back the full notional in EUR. Conversely, if the spot at maturity is above 1.4700 (weak CHF), then the notional is converted into CHF 7.35 Million. So the investor is always paid back the weaker currency. The interest rate with the enhanced coupon of 5.00 % is paid in either case.

Advantages

- Guaranteed higher coupon than market
- Liquid product, whence sales margins are comparatively small
- An exporting company in the country of the other currency needs to buy the other currency anyway and can use the strike as a budget rate
- Investor can take a short option position

Disadvantages

- No capital guarantee: if the other currency becomes worthless, then the investor can lose the entire capital
- The investor receives a higher coupon at the cost of taking *unlimited* exchange rate risk, see Figure 2.10
- Investor has to pay tax on the enhanced coupon, but cannot tax-deduct the risk on the upside

Composition

- The investor deposits 5 M EUR for 1 month
- The investor sells a EUR call CHF put

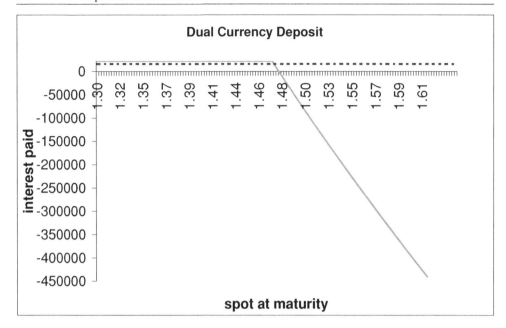

Figure 2.10   Comparing the market interest rate (dotted line) with the enhanced interest rate of a dual currency deposit

- Spot reference 1.4662 Strike 1.4700
- Premium: 11,631 EUR (deferred to end of the deposit)
- This yields 12,500 EUR + 11,631 EUR = 24,131 EUR
- The bank pays only 20,833 EUR
- → Margin: 3,298 EUR

In general, the formula relating the notional amount N, the bid deferred premium of the vanilla in units of the underlying P, the sales margin M, the market interest rate r_M (bid side) and the enhanced interest rate r_E, the deposit horizon of d days is given by

$$N \cdot r_E \cdot \frac{d}{360} = N \cdot r_M \cdot \frac{d}{360} + P - M, \tag{2.21}$$

which can be solved easily for any quantity desired. Note that for GBP the daycount convention for deposits is 365 days rather than 360.

The premium of the short option must be paid at delivery of the deposit. The DCD is an ideal way for a bank to buy options from their clients without taking any credit risk. Since the bank has the deposit amount, it can never get into a situation of a defaulting client. Conversely, the investor is taking the credit default risk of the issuer as in any other deposit. Surely, the better the rating of the issuer, the lower the coupon. This extends to the DCD. The exchange rate risk can be reduced by taking a strike sufficiently far away from the spot. However, selling such a far out-of-the-money option will not enhance the coupon significantly. The unlimited risk on the upside can be limited by selling an up-and-out call (see Section 1.5.1) or a call spread (see Section 1.4.1) rather than a vanilla call. But even that would give only a small coupon enhancement. Yet another alternative would be take a smaller notional for the option, so the conversion risk would only apply to say 50 % of the invested capital. Again lowering risk would imply a smaller coupon.

The investor is obviously taking risk on the upside. What if the investor believes in an upward trend and would rather take risk on the downside? One can then take the other currency. But if she wants to invest in the same currency, a similar structure as in the dual currency deposit does not work in a sellable way. Of course, the investor can always sell a put on the deposit currency. However, at maturity, the payoff of the put would have to be cash-settled in the deposit currency and this payoff then subtracted from the deposit amount. An alternative might be the *turbo deposit* as explained in Section 2.3.5. The case of unwinding such a dual currency deposit is treated in the exercises.

One can turn this deposit into a loan, where the client borrows EUR at a subsidized interest rate, but has to pay back the other currency if the EUR decreases below the pre-defined strike. So in case of a dual currency loan, the client would bet on a strengthening loan currency. She would sell a EUR put. This product is by far less popular as the issuers are taking the credit default risk of both the loan as well as of the long option position. An example can be worked out in the exercises.

2.3.2 Performance linked deposits

A performance linked deposit is a deposit with a participation in an underlying market. The standard is that a GBP investor waives her coupon that the money market would pay and instead buys a EUR-GBP call with the same maturity date as the coupon, strike K and notional N in EUR. These parameters have to be chosen in such a way that the offer price of the EUR call equals the money market interest rate plus the sales margin. The strike is often chosen to be the current spot. The notional is often a percentage p of the deposit amount A, such as 50 % or 25 %. The coupon paid to the investor is then a pre-defined minimum coupon plus the participation

$$ p \cdot \frac{\max[S_T - S_0, 0]}{S_0}, \tag{2.22} $$

which is the return of the exchange rate viewed as an asset, where the investor is protected against negative returns. So, obviously, the investor buys a EUR call GBP put with strike $K = S_0$ and notional $N = pA$ GBP or $N = pA/S_0$ EUR. So if the EUR goes up by 10 % against the GBP, the investor gets a coupon of 10p % in addition to the minimum coupon.

Advantages

- Possible higher coupon than market
- Liquid product, whence sales margins are comparatively small
- Capital is guaranteed
- Worst case coupon is known up-front

Disadvantages

- Possible lower coupon than market
- Investor has to pay tax on the best case coupon, but can not tax-deduct the risk on receiving the worst case coupon
- Participation formulae can often appear misleading to investors

Table 2.23   Example of a performance linked deposit, where the investor is paid 30 % of the EUR-GBP return

Notional	5,000,000 GBP
Start date	3 June 2005
Maturity	2 Sept 2005 (91 days)
Number of days	91
Money market reference rate	4.00 % act/365
EUR-GBP spot reference	0.7000
Minimum rate	2.00 % act/365
Additional coupon	$30\% \cdot \frac{100 \max[S_T - 0.7000, 0]}{0.7000}$ act/360
S_T	EUR-GBP fixing on 31 August 2005 (88 days)
Fixing source	ECB

Example

We consider the example shown in Table 2.23. This means for example that if the EUR-GBP spot fixing is 0.7200, the additional coupon would be 0.8571 %. The break-even point is at 0.7467, so this product is advisable for a very strong EUR bullish view. For a weakly bullish view an alternative would be to buy an up-and-out call with barrier at 0.7400 and 75 % participation, where we would find the best case to be 0.7399 with an additional coupon of 4.275 %, which would lead to a total coupon of 6.275 %.

Composition

- From the money market we get 49,863.01 GBP at the maturity date.
- The investor buys a EUR call GBP put with strike 0.7000 and with notional 1.5 Million GBP.
- The offer price of the call is 26,220.73 GBP, assuming a volatility of 8.0 % and a EUR rate of 2.50 %.
- The deferred premium is 24,677.11 GBP.
- The investor receives a minimum payment of 24,931.51 GBP.
- Subtracting the deferred premium and the minimum payment from the money market leaves a sales margin of 254.40 GBP (awfully poor I admit).
- Note that the option the investor is buying must be cash-settled.

Variations

There are many variations of the performance linked notes. Of course, one can think of European style knock-out calls, or window-barrier calls. For a participation in a downward trend, the investor can buy puts. One of the frequent issues in Foreign Exchange, however, is the deposit currency being different from the domestic currency of the exchange rate, which is quoted in FOR-DOM (foreign-domestic), meaning how many units of domestic currency are required to buy one unit of foreign currency. So if we have a EUR investor who wishes to participate in a EUR-USD movement, we have a problem, the usual *quanto confusion* that can drive anybody up the wall in FX at various occasions. What is the problem? The payoff of the EUR call USD put

$$[S_T - K]^+ \tag{2.23}$$

is in domestic currency (USD). Of course, this payoff can be converted into the foreign currency (EUR) at maturity, but at what rate? If we convert at rate S_T, which is what we could do in the spot market at no cost, then the investor buys a vanilla EUR call. But here, the investor receives a coupon given by

$$p \cdot \frac{\max[S_T - S_0, 0]}{S_T}. \tag{2.24}$$

If the investor wishes to have performance of Equation (2.22) rather than Equation (2.24), then the payoff at maturity is converted at a rate of 1.0000 into EUR, and this rate is set at the beginning of the trade. This is the *quanto factor*, and the vanilla is actually a *self-quanto* vanilla, i.e., a EUR call USD put, cash-settled in EUR, where the payoff in USD is converted into EUR at a rate of 1.0000. This self quanto vanilla can be valued by inverting the exchange rate, i.e., looking at USD-EUR. This way the valuation can incorporate the smile of EUR-USD. Similar considerations need to be done if the currency pair to participate in does not contain the deposit currency at all. A typical situation is a EUR investor, who wishes to participate in the gold price, which is measured in USD, so the investor needs to buy a XAU call USD put quantoed into EUR. So the investor is promised a coupon as in Equation (2.22) for a XAU-USD underlying, where the coupon is paid in EUR, this implicitly means that we must use a quanto plain vanilla with a quanto factor of 1.0000. For the valuation of quantos see Hakala and Wystup [3] of Section 1.5.8.

2.3.3 Tunnel deposit/loan

Unlike the dual currency deposit, the *tunnel deposit* or *double-no-touch linked deposit* or *range deposit* is fully capital guaranteed. The maturities vary from one month up to one year. The investor receives a minimum coupon below the market, which is often taken to be 0.00 %, if the underlying exchange rate leaves a pre-defined range at least once between trade time and expiration time. Conversely, if the exchange rate stays inside the pre-defined range at all times, then the investor receives a coupon above the market rate. Hence, the tunnel deposit is a bet on a sidewards movement of the underlying exchange rate. The investor waives parts of her market coupon and goes long a double-no-touch, whose notional is in the deposit currency , and the amount is the difference between the best case and the worst case interest rate payments. Usually, the exchange rate contains the currency of the deposit and another currency. If the deposit currency is not in the exchange rate, then the payoff has to be quantoed into the deposit currency, which is possible, but not very common.

Advantages

- Possible higher coupon than market
- Liquid product, whence sales margins are comparatively small
- Capital is guaranteed
- Worst case coupon is known up-front

Disadvantages

- Possible lower coupon than market
- Investor has to pay tax on the best case coupon, but can not tax-deduct the risk on receiving the worst case coupon

Table 2.24 Example of a tunnel deposit

Notional	2,000,000 EUR
Start date	3 June 2005
Maturity	5 Sept 2005
Number of days	94
Money market reference rate	2.50 % act/360
Minimum rate	1.00 % act/360
Maximum rate	4.20 % act/360
Range	1.1750–1.3000 EUR-USD
Range valid up to	1 Sept 2005 10:00 a.m. N.Y.

The minimum rate is paid if EUR-USD leaves the range, the maximum rate is paid if EUR-USD stays inside the range

Example

We consider the example shown in Table 2.24 and illustrate the interest rate payments in Figure 2.11.

Composition

- We obtain 13,056.67 EUR from the money market.
- The investor buys a EUR-USD double-no-touch with range 1.1750–1.3000 and with payout 16,711.11 EUR. This notional must match the interest rate difference of the maximum and the minimum rate, which is

$$2,000,000.00 \cdot (4.20\% - 1.00\%) \cdot \frac{94}{360} = 16,711.11.$$

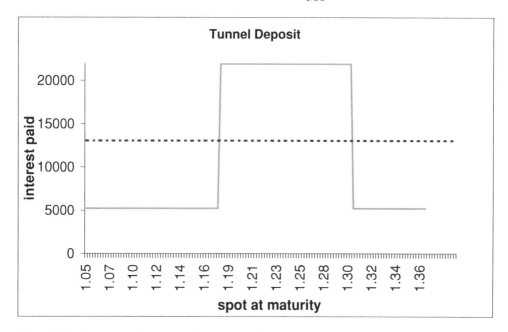

Figure 2.11 Best case and worst case interest rate of a tunnel deposit compared with the market interest rate (dotted line)

- The offer price of the double-no-touch is 37.00 %, assuming a volatility of 10.0 % and a USD rate of 2.70 %.
- To defer the premium to the maturity date we use the rate 2.65 %.
- The deferred premium becomes 37.2506 %, which is 6,225.89 EUR.
- The investor receives a minimum payment of 5,222.22 EUR.
- Subtracting the deferred premium and the minimum payment from the money market leaves a sales margin of 1,608.56 EUR.
- The investor receives a maximum payment of 21,933.33 EUR.

In general, the formula relating the notional deposit amount N, the offer deferred premium of the double-no-touch in units of the underlying P, the sales margin M, the market interest rate r_M (bid side), the minimum interest rate r_0 and the deposit horizon of d days is given by

$$N \cdot (r_M - r_0) \cdot \frac{d}{360} = M + P, \tag{2.25}$$

which can be solved easily for any quantity desired. Note that for GBP the daycount convention for deposits is 365 days rather than 360.

Variations and remarks

This tunnel deposit can be altered in various ways. Instead of a double-no-touch the investor could go long any type of range bet, such as a single-no-touch, a single-one-touch, a window double-one-touch, a digital call or put or European style double-no-touch.

One can also design this as a loan, where the client is charged a best case interest rate below market if the underlying exchange rate remains inside a range, but a worst case interest rate above market otherwise. We refer the reader to the exercises.

2.3.4 Corridor deposit/loan

The corridor deposit works very similar to a tunnel deposit. The capital is guaranteed, the investor is also guaranteed a worst case coupon, which is often taken to be 0 %. The investor then bets on a currency pair trending sideways, i.e. she chooses a currency pair out of which one is the deposit currency. Then the investor and the issuer agree on a fixing schedule, usually consisting of N business days, and a fixing source such as ECB or FED. At maturity, the number of fixings inside a pre-defined range k will be counted. The coupon paid to the investor will then be $\frac{k}{N}$ times the maximum coupon C. So the worst case is $k = 0$, where the investor is left with the minimum coupon. The best case is $k = N$, where the investor gets the full coupon C.

Advantages

- Possible higher coupon than market
- Capital is guaranteed
- Worst case coupon is known up-front
- Unlike the tunnel deposit, price spikes beyond the range do not result in the worst case coupon, but will lead only to loosing $\frac{1}{N}$ of the coupon

Table 2.25 Example of a corridor deposit

Notional	5,000,000 GBP
Start date	3 June 2005
Maturity	2 Sept 2005 (91 days)
Number of days	91
Money market reference rate	4.00 % act/365
Minimum rate	2.00 % act/365
Maximum rate	6.00 % act/360
Range	1.7750–1.8250 GBP-USD
Range style	resurrecting
First fixing	6 June 2005
Last fixing	31 August 2005
Total number of fixings N	61
Fixing source	ECB using the ratio of EUR-USD and EUR-GBP

The minimum rate is paid in any case. The coupon paid at maturity in GBP is $(6\% - 2\%)\frac{k}{N}$, where k is the number of fixings inside the range.

Disadvantages

- Possible lower coupon than market
- Investor has to pay tax on the best case coupon, but can not tax-deduct the risk on receiving a coupon below market
- Since resurrecting style corridors are expensive, the range or the maximum coupon often do not appear to be overwhelmingly attractive to the investor

Example
We consider the example shown in Table 2.25 and illustrate the interest rate payments in Figure 2.12.

Composition

- Money from the money market is 49,863.01 GBP.
- The investor buys a GBP-USD resurrecting corridor with range 1.7750–1.8250 and with notional 49,863.01 GBP. This notional must match the interest rate difference of the maximum and the minimum rate, which is

$$5,000,000.00 \cdot (6.00\% - 2.00\%) \cdot \frac{91}{365} = 49,863.01.$$

- The offer price of the corridor is 40.00 %, assuming a volatility of 9.0 % and a USD rate of 2.50 %.
- To defer the premium to the maturity date we use the rate 4.00 %.
- The deferred premium becomes 40.3989 %, which is 20,144.11 GBP.
- The investor receives a minimum payment of 24,931.51 GBP.
- Subtracting the deferred premium and the minimum payment from the money from the money market leaves a sales margin of 4,787.40 GBP.
- The investor receives a maximum payment of 74,794.52 EUR.
- The amount of interest paid per fixing inside the range is 817.43 GBP.

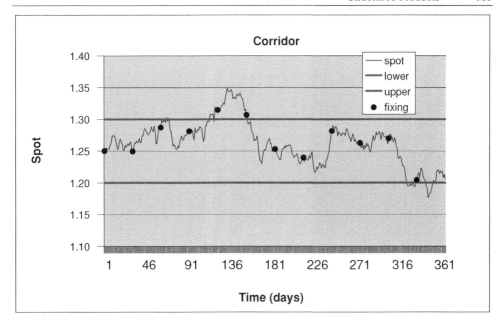

Figure 2.12 Example of a corridor with spot 1.2500, domestic interest rate 3.00 %, foreign interest rate 2.75 %, volatility 10 %, for a maturity of 1 year with 12 monthly fixings indicated by the dots. The range is 1.2000–1.3000. In a resurrecting corridor, the investor would accumulate 10 out of 12 fixings. In a non-resurrecting corridor, the investor would accumulate 4 out of 12 fixings as the fifth is outside the range

In general, the formula relating the notional deposit amount N, the offer deferred premium of the corridor in units of the underlying P, the sales margin M, the market interest rate r_M (bid side), the minimum interest rate r_0 and the deposit horizon of d days is given by

$$N \cdot (r_M - r_0) \cdot \frac{d}{360} = M + P, \tag{2.26}$$

which can be solved easily for any quantity desired. Note that for GBP the day-count convention for deposits is 365 days rather than 360.

Variations and remarks

This corridor deposit can be altered in various ways. Instead of a two-sided range the investor could go long any type of range bet, such a one-sided corridor or a non-resurrecting style corridor, where the number of fixings inside the range will stop to increase if the continuously observed exchange rate or the first fixing is at or outside the range. The ranges can also be set afresh at fixed times in the future depending on the spot in the future, so the investor would be long a series of forward start corridors. Generally, bands need not be constant, but can be functions of time, mostly linear or exponential in practice.

One can also design this as a loan, where the client is charged a best case interest rate below market if all the fixings of the underlying exchange rate remain inside a range, but a worse

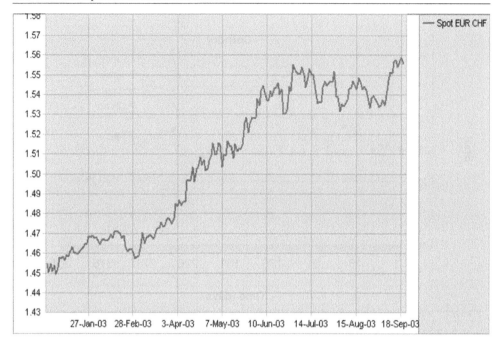

Figure 2.13   EUR-CHF spot during the first three quarters of 2003
Source: SuperDerivatives.

case interest rate above market otherwise, where the interest rate to be paid increases linearly with the number of fixings outside the pre-defined range. We refer the reader to the exercises.

2.3.5 Turbo deposit/loan

The trend is your friend. We are looking at an up-trend market such as EUR-CHF displayed in Figure 2.13 and would like to invest EUR in a strategy which could generate an interest rate higher than the market if the trend persists. This can be done with the Turbo Deposit.

At maturity, the investor then receives his capital plus

- a minimum rate (usually 0 %) if the EUR-CHF spot at cutoff time is below a level K_1,
- the EUR market rate if the EUR-CHF spot at cutoff time is between K_1 and K_2,
- twice the EUR market rate if the EUR-CHF spot at cutoff time is above K_2.

Example
We display an example term sheet of a turbo deposit in Table 2.26.

The way this works is that the market interest rate payment for the EUR deposit is not paid to the investor, but is split up in a sales margin and the premia for two digital call options, one with strike K_1 and one with strike K_2, which the investor is long. The notional of the digital calls is in the deposit currency. The amount is the interest payment in EUR, which is here equal to

$$5,000,000.00 \cdot 0.0211 \cdot \frac{180}{360} = 52,750.00.$$

Table 2.26 Example of a turbo deposit

Spot reference	1.5550 EUR-CHF
6-months reference deposit rate	2.11 % p.a. act/360
Notional	EUR 5,000,000
Start value date	24-Sep-2003
Expiration date	22-Mar-2004, 10:00 a.m. New York time
Maturity date	24-Mar-2004
Lower level K_1	1.5100 EUR-CHF
Upper level K_2	1.5800 EUR-CHF
Double interest rate	4.22 % p.a. act/360
Single interest rate	2.11 % p.a. act/360
Minimum interest rate	0.00 % p.a. act/360
Interest rate payment currency	EUR

The premia for the digital calls is paid at the maturity date of the deposit, since we do not have any cash-flow other than the notional of the deposit at the beginning. This product will usually look attractive if the forward curve is decreasing, because then the two digital calls are comparatively cheap. Similar types of structures are popular in conjunction with interest rate swaps, see for example Section 2.4.3. Similarly, to bet on a downward trend, one can flip the structure, so the investor would buy two digital put options.

2.3.6 Tower deposit/loan

The tower deposit takes the idea of the tunnel deposit and develops it further for the investor with a higher risk appetite. The investor receives a guaranteed capital and a worst case coupon below market, which is often taken to be 0 %, and then builds up higher coupons like in a tower depending on which range the underlying exchange rate remains. Hence, the tunnel deposit is a bet on a sidewards movement of the underlying exchange rate. The investor waives parts of her market coupon and goes long a portfolio of nested double-no-touch contracts, whose notional is in the deposit currency, and the amount is the difference between the interest rate payments of two successive coupons. Usually, the exchange rate contains the currency of the deposit and another currency. If the deposit currency is not in the exchange rate, then the payoff has to be quantoed into the deposit currency, which is possible, but not very common. Figure 2.14 shows an example of three ranges in a tower shape. Since the ranges are nested, there are other

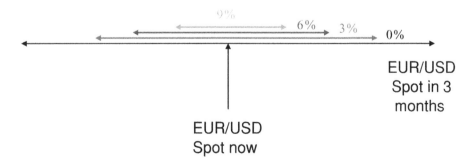

Figure 2.14 Design of a tower deposit with three ranges

names for this structured deposit such as *multiple range deposit* or *onion deposit* or *tetris bond* or *wedding cake*.

Advantages

- Possible much higher coupon than market
- Capital is guaranteed
- Worst case coupon is known up-front

Disadvantages

- Possible lower coupon than market
- Investor has to pay tax on the best case coupon, but can not tax-deduct the risk on receiving the worst case coupon
- Since the investor buys a portfolio of first generation exotics, the sales margins tend to be higher as for a dual currency deposit or a tunnel deposit
- Looks attractive only if the time to maturity is at least 3 months and the interest rate of the deposit currency is already high enough, say at least 3.0 %

Example
We consider the example shown in Table 2.27.

Composition

- Money from the money market is 25,328 EUR.
- The investor buys 3 EUR-USD double-no-touch contracts with payoff 22,750 EUR. This notional matches the interest rate differences of 3.00 %, which is for example

$$3,000,000.00 \cdot (9.00\% - 6.00\%) \cdot \frac{91}{360} = 22,750. \qquad (2.27)$$

- The deferred offer prices of the double-no-touch contracts are
  1. Range 0.8650–0.9000: 1,149 EUR
  2. Range 0.8600–0.9050: 2,948 EUR
  3. Range 0.8500–0.9150: 7,873 EUR
  assuming a volatility of 10.0 % and a USD rate of 2.70 %.

Table 2.27 Example of tower deposit

Notional	3,000,000 EUR
Tenor	3 months (91 days)
EUR-USD spot reference	0.8800
Market reference rate	3.34 % act/360
Minimum rate	0.00 % act/360
Rate for range 0.8500–0.9150	3.00 % act/360
Rate for range 0.8600–0.9050	6.00 % act/360
Rate for range 0.8650–0.9000	9.00 % act/360

The minimum rate is paid if EUR-USD leaves the widest range, the rates for the ranges are paid if EUR-USD stays inside the respective range.

- The total price to pay for the portfolio of the three double-no-touch contracts is hence 11,970 EUR.
- Subtracting this price from the money from the money market leaves a sales margin of 13,358 EUR.

Modifications

There are many ways to modify the tower deposit.

1. The portfolio can be composed of an arbitrary number of double-no-touch contracts, but also single-touch or touch contracts with partial barriers are possible.
2. One can think of a partial (99 %) capital guarantee, which would yield higher coupons.
3. One can use forward start barriers or reset barriers.
4. The same structure works for a loan.
5. The tower deposit usually does not work well for low yield currencies. If the investor is willing to take risk on the capital, then one can combine the dual currency deposit with the tower deposit (see Exercise 11).

Tower deposit as a note

As an example of a yield enhancement we consider a 1 year tower note in EUR, which is just a listed version of the tower deposit. It is designed for investors who believe EUR/USD will trade in a range during the next year.

The investor prefers to have a note issued by a AA bank under the *European Medium Term Note (EMTN)* program. The indicative terms are listed in Table 2.28.

2.3.7 Exercises

1. For a dual currency loan in EUR against GBP, with 180 days time to maturity, EUR borrowing rate of 4.00 %, EUR-GBP spot of 0.7000, find out what delta EUR put to take to offer the client an enhanced interest rate of 2.00 % and a sales margin of 0.10 % of the deposit notional. You may assume a EUR-GBP volatility of 8.50 %. In order to limit the risk on the downside, it might be better to trade a down-and-out EUR put. With the same strike, find the barrier so the enhanced rate is 3.00 %.

Table 2.28 Example of a tower note. Ranges are American style

Spot reference	1.2350 EUR-USD
1 year EUR rate reference	2.20 %
Payment date	1 month after the trade date
Maturity date	1 year after the payment date
Principal amount	EUR 3,000,000
Issue Price	99.00 %
Redemption price	100 %
Coupon 4.00 % p.a.	if EUR-USD stays inside the range 1.1500–1.3200
Coupon 2.28 % p.a.	if EUR-USD stays inside the range 1.1300–1.3500
Coupon 1.50 % p.a.	if EUR-USD stays inside the range 1.1100–1.4000
Coupon 0.00 % p.a.	if EUR-USD trades outside the range 1.1100–1.4000
Basis	act/360

2. Consider a client who has traded a dual currency deposit, notional in USD 1 million, against CHF, with a conversion strike of 1.2000 USD-CHF. He has agreed on a coupon of 6.00 %. Now there are 60 days left to go until maturity, the spot has gone up to 1.2200, volatility to 9.50 %–9.70 %, 60 days USD interest rate is 3.00 %–3.10 %, 60 days CHF interest rate is 1.20 %–1.30 %. The investor is afraid of the USD further rising and wants to unwind his dcd. Compute how much the bank can pay the client if the bank wants to charge a sales margin of 1,000.00 USD, carefully distinguishing which bid and ask rate to use.

3. Consider the performance linked deposit in Section 2.3.2. Assuming a minimum interest rate of 0 % and a desired sales margin of 3,000.00 GBP, what would be the percentage of the participation p? If instead of the call the client would buy a call spread with upper strike 0.7500 to cap the participation, what would be the participation p? What would you suggest to an investor who insists on a 100 % participation ($p = 100$ %)? How about a *super call spread*, where the notional of the sold EUR call is twice than the notional of the bought EUR call, which means that the participation actually goes down after the upper strike and becomes 0 % for a strike of 0.8000. Is this still capital guaranteed?

4. Design a deposit linked to the gold price S_T (in USD), where a EUR investor receives an annual coupon of

$$-10.00\% + p \max[S_T - S_0,0]\%$$ (2.28)

in EUR. This means, that the capital is only 90 % guaranteed, and the investor participates in an upward movement of the Gold price. For instance, if $p = 100$ % and if the gold price rises by 10 USD per ounce, then the coupon will be zero.[1] If the gold price rises by 40 USD per ounce, then the coupon will be 30 %. You may assume current market data or (if unavailable) $T = 1$ year, $r_{EUR} = 3$ %, $r_{USD} = 2$ %, $r_{XAU} = 0.25$ %, $S_0 = 400$, EUR-USD spot $= 1.2500$, EUR-USD volatility $= 10$ %, XAU-USD volatility $= 12$ %, XAU-EUR volatility $= 11$ %. Which products do we need to structure this deposit? How do we hedge it? Suppose you want to include a sales margin of 2 % of the EUR notional, find a suitable value for p.

5. Performance linked deposits need not be restricted to FX. For example, *Deutsche Postbank* offers a savings account with a guaranteed interest rate of say 1 % p.a. act/360, plus 50 % participation in the rising DAX, where the strike is set equal to spot at the beginning of each month and the interest is paid monthly. Describe the composition of this product and try to find out the sales margin for the bank. More information is available on the webpage www.postbank.de.

6. Design a tunnel loan for the size of 20 million USD for the period of 12 months. Assume the market data for USD offer rate of 3.50 %, a worst case of 4.50 %, a desired best case of 1.90 %, a sales margin of 2,500 USD, a USD-JPY spot of 105.00, volatility of 10.0 %, JPY rate of 0.1 %. Find a suitable range. Generally derive a formula like Equation (2.25) for the tunnel deposit, that relates the relevant parameters.

7. Consider the example of the corridor deposit in Table 2.25 and compute how the range can be widened if the corridor is non-resurrecting, i.e. if any of the bands is ever touched, then

---

[1] The price of Gold is usually measured in USD per ounce and quoted in XAU-USD notation (Reuters RIC **XAU**=). The letter **X** is for exchange and **AU** for the latin name *aurum* for gold. Silver is noted in FX markets as XAG-USD, the letters **AG** from the latin *argentum*.

Table 2.29   12m GBP-denominated Structured Deposit – GOLD Windowed Knock-out Range Accrual, where d is the number of business days that the Gold reference price fixes within the barriers and N is the number of business days in the deposit period

Principal amount	GBP 10,000,000
Issue date	TBA
Final maturity date	12 months after the issue date
Up-front fee to client	75 bps
Gold reference price	The London a.m. gold fixing
Fixing source	Reuters Page **GOFO**
Lower barrier	USD 296 oz
Upper barrier	USD 338 oz
KO barrier start date	3 months
Coupon	$7.75\% \cdot \frac{d}{N}$ (annual, 30/360)
Assumption	$N = 253$ business days per period
Calculation agent	Deutsche Bank AG, London
Market data	
12-month GBP deposit	3.98 % money market rate
Gold spot price	USD 319.50 oz

Knock-out provision: After the KO barrier start date, if gold (Reuters RIC **XAU=**) ever trades outside the barriers then the coupon stops accruing immediately from that point and for the rest of the term of the transaction. The accrual fraction to date is paid at maturity. For the avoidance of doubt, coupon is not accrued on the business day on which gold first trades outside the barriers, regardless of that day's gold reference price.

the investor keeps only the accumulated interest rate, but can not accumulate any further. If we go one step further and consider the case of a complete loss of past and future interest payments in case of either of the bands being touched, then the range should be even wider. Find out the range and an equivalent product.

8. How would you structure the following *12m GBP-denominated Structured Deposit – GOLD Windowed Knock-out Range Accrual*, whose indicative terms and conditions are listed in Table 2.29?

    The investor's objectives are

    • The client invests in a short term deposit with guaranteed principal.
    • Currently, Money Market yields are low and the client wants to invest into a structure that has the potential to earn a 7.75 % coupon.
    • The client takes the view that gold is range bound within a 296/338 range.

9. Design a turbo deposit for an investment of 10 Million USD for 12 months. Consider a market USD interest rate of 2.5 %. The investor believes in a downward trend of XAU-USD. For your computations take the current spot of XAU-USD, the strikes 7.5 % above and below the spot. Look up the XAU-USD volatility and the XAU deposit rate from a suitable market screen.

10. Consider a tower note with a portfolio of double-no-touch contracts. If we want to approximate the coupon to grow linearly with the size of the range, then we need many double no-touch-contracts. If the double-no-touches are of European style, then the cost of such a portfolio easily becomes way too large due to the fixed costs of each ticket. To what portfolio of vanilla contracts does this approximation converge? You may call the resulting structure a *butterfly deposit*. Describe how this works in detail. If the double-no-touch contracts are of American style, then the limiting exotic option would be a type of an occupation time derivative. Find out what can be used and what literature is available.

Table 2.30 Sample market data to structure a triple currency deposit

currency pair	spot	volatility
EUR-GBP	0.7000	8%
GBP-USD	1.8000	10%
USD-CHF	1.2500	11%

11. Consider a EUR-USD market with 3.00% in both EUR and USD for 6 months, spot at 1.2000, volatility at 10.20%. We want to combine a dual currency deposit with a tower deposit with 2 double-no-touch contracts with ranges 1.1500–1.2500 and 1.1000–1.3000. An investor seeks coupons 2.0%, 5.0% and 8.0% on his USD notional. The bank wants to make 0.2% of the USD amount as a sales margin. Compute the market price of the 2 double-no-touch contracts using the traders' rule of thumb of Section 3.1. Then determine strike to convert the USD amount into a EUR amount to be paid back if the spot at maturity is below this strike. Implement this structure in such a way that the sales person can solve for any of the coupons, the sales margin and the strike.

12. A dual currency deposit enhances the coupon for sure and transfers the risk of getting the weaker of two currencies paid back to the investor. One can now consider more than two currencies and pay back the weakest of all and enhance the coupon even more. How would you structure this? This is called a *triple or multi-currency deposit*. Take an example of a USD investor with market rate of 3% p.a. and a maturity of one year. Assume the other currencies being GBP and CHF with rates 4% and 1% p.a. respectively. Take the market data from Table 2.30 and assume the investor deposits 10 million USD, and the bank has the right to choose to pay either 10 million USD or 5.55 million GBP or 12.5 million CHF in one year. Assuming a zero sales margin, what coupon would the investor receive if we only consider GBP in a standard dual currency deposit format? What coupon would the investor receive if we use all the currencies?

2.4   INTEREST RATE AND CROSS CURRENCY SWAPS

An interest rate swap is a very common bank product. Two counterparties agree on a currency and a notional amount in this currency and on a schedule of payment dates. On these payment dates there will be cash flows between the counterparties. The standard is that one pays a fixed coupon and the other pays a floating coupon based on the LIBOR (London Interbank Offer Rate). This standard interest rate swap is a tool to hedge uncertainties of future interest rates. The fixed rate is normally chosen in such a way that the total value of the swap is zero (or leaves some margin for the bank). There can also be floating payments for both the counterparties, if for example A pays to B quarterly and B to A annually. Relevant for each swap contract is the exact specification of the payment schedules (interest rate fixing dates and value dates), the interest rate and day-count convention, the source of the LIBOR rate, possible fees, exchange of notional amounts. However, this is not a book about interest rate products or the valuation or modeling issues of the very same. The contribution of this book is about how to link such swaps to foreign exchange products. This combination becomes then an FX-linked swap if the FX part of the combination is just an add-on or a true hybrid FX-IR product if the FX and IR (interest rate) part can not be separated. In the following we concentrate on some popular FX-linked swaps.

2.4.1 Cross currency swap

In a cross currency swap the two cash-flow schedules and notional amounts are in different currencies. Other than that, a cross currency swap is just like an interest rate swap. The key reference for the valuation cross currency swaps is [67]. The default motivation to enter into a cross currency swap is the desire to pay interest in a currency with lower rates such as JPY or CHF and receive interest in a currency with higher rates (see Figure 2.15). This is free of cost! However, it works only if the notional amounts are agreed to be exchanged at the maturity date of the swap, so both counterparties have an open foreign exchange position, namely a long-term FX forward. Low interest rates are hence bought by taking this risk.

Advantages

- Beneficial interest rate payments, i.e. receiving higher coupons or paying lower coupons than market
- Liquid and transparent product, whence sales margins are comparatively small
- Zero cost product
- (Partial) protection of the notional possible

Disadvantages

- Long term FX forward risk
- Long term view on the FX rate impossible

Example
We consider a situation where

- EUR interest rates are higher than JPY interest rates,
- a treasurer expects the EUR-JPY exchange rate to be near the current spot or even higher in 5 years,
- the treasurer is looking for an opportunity to receive EUR payments at zero cost.

The terms of a cross currency swap to reflect this are listed in Table 2.31.

If the treasurer's market expectation is correct, then she receives 1.90 % of the EUR notional every year for free. In case of a stronger EUR in 5 years there are chances of additional profit, if EUR-JPY will be above 135.50.

Table 2.31   Example of a cross currency swap in EUR-JPY

Currency pair	EUR-JPY
Current Spot	135.50 EUR-JPY
notional	EUR 10,000,000 and JPY 1,355,000,000
Exchange of notionals	Only at maturity
Maturity	5 years from now
You receive EUR interest rates	1.90 % annually
You pay JPY interest rates	0.00 % annually
Notional for Protection	JPY 1,355,000,000
Strike for protection	100.00
You receive for protection	EUR Put JPY Call Expiring 5 years

Her risk is that if the EUR-JPY exchange rate will be below 135.50 at expiry and she is bound to buy 1,355 MIO JPY at the EUR-JPY spot. However, the bank guarantees a worst case exchange rate of 100.00.

If she is willing to give up this worst case protection, the bank will pay annual interest rates of 2.50 % in EUR instead of the 1.90 %.

We will deal with a more realistic example about how to protect the final exchange rate risk in the next section.

2.4.2   Hanseatic swap

The *Hanseatic Swap* is a cross currency swap with a partial protection of the final exchange notional, an idea to lower interest rate payments. As we have seen above the standard cross currency swap carries a lot of exchange rate risk at the end. This product helps to reduce this risk at zero cost and still allows lowering interest rate payments. A bit of the upside participation is given up and used to finance a downside protection.

Advantages

- Beneficial interest rate payments, i.e. receiving higher coupons or paying lower coupons than market
- Zero cost product
- (Partial) protection of the notional included

Disadvantages

- Final exchange rate risk not *fully* covered
- Long term view on the FX rate impossible, i.e. suitable for rather short term contracts

Example
We take EUR-CHF and show in Figure 2.15 and Table 2.32 how a corporate client can lower his interest rate payments in EUR obligations by 1.05 % for 6 months, as long as EUR-CHR stays in a range around the current spot.

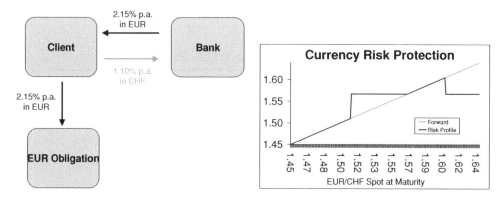

Figure 2.15   Cash flows and currency risk protection for a Hanseatic cross currency swap

Table 2.32   Example of a Hanseatic cross currency swap in EUR-CHF

Period	6 months
Notional	EUR 5,000,000 CHF 7,835,000
The client receives	2.15 % p.a. in EUR 30/360
Fixing and payment	quarterly
The client pays	1.10 % p.a. in CHF 30/360
Fixing and payment	quarterly
Spot reference	1.5624 EUR-CHF
Currency protection	
Strike	1.5670 EUR-CHF
Upper knock-in-limit (American style)	1.6050 EUR-CHF
Lower knock-out-limit (American style)	1.5100 EUR-CHF
Premium	0.00 EUR

- If the exchange rate EUR-CHF stays below the upper knock-in level of 1.6050 during the next 6 months, the client can participate in the exchange rate and obtain an interest rate advantage of 1.05 % p.a.
- If the exchange rate EUR-CHF ever touches or crosses 1.6050 during the next 6 months, the client is obliged to buy CHF at 1.5670 and can no more participate in a rising EUR.
- If the exchange rate EUR-CHF remains above the lower knock-out level of 1.5100 during the next 6 months, the client is entitled to buy CHF at 1.5670. This is his protection against currency losses.
- If the exchange rate EUR-CHF ever trades at or below the lower knock-out level of 1.5100 during the next 6 months, the client's protection is lost and he needs to buy CHF at the spot.
- In summary, if the exchange rate EUR-CHF stays inside the range 1.5100–1.6050, the client's interest rate is reduced by 1.05 % for 6 months. Additionally he may participate in a rising EUR.

Composition

1. The basis for this structure is a 6 months cross currency swap in EUR-CHF with strike 1.5670 worth 32,000 EUR.
2. The client sells a 6 months EUR call CHF put with strike 1.5670, up-and-in at 1.6050 and receives a premium of 26,375 EUR (=0.5275 % EUR).
3. The client buys a 6 months EUR put CHF call with strike 1.5670, down-and-out at 1.5100 and pays a premium of 30,875 EUR (=0.6175 % EUR).
4. Overall the structure is offered at zero cost to the client, whence the sales margin is 27,500 EUR.

2.4.3   Turbo cross currency swap

The turbo cross currency swap is a cross currency swap *without* any protection of the final exchange notional. It doubles the participation on the upside as well as the risk on the downside. Hence it is a hedging instrument for those who are seriously betting on a rising exchange rate. So as in the *turbo deposit* described in Section 2.3.5 the client chooses three ranges, a lower range with a worst case interest rate payment, a middle range – usually around the current spot – with an interest rate payment attractive enough to enter into the swap and an upper range with very low, ideally zero interest rate. These ranges are valid at each interest cash flow date. This product usually works well in a forward backwardation market such as EUR-CHF or EUR-JPY and can be marketed easily in situations where exchange rates are near their historic low, because then it appears likely to be on a rising exchange rate in the long run. The product generates attractive coupons for the client and worthwhile margins for the bank for long tenors.

Advantages

- Beneficial interest rate payments, i.e. receiving higher coupons or paying lower coupons than market
- Zero cost product
- Turbo effect can bring the coupon down to zero or close to zero

Disadvantages

- Very risky as final exchange rate risk not covered
- Long term view on the FX rate impossible, i.e. once the exchange rate moves far into the worst case range, then it is likely to stay there

Example
We take EUR-CHF and show in Figure 2.16 and Table 2.33 how a corporate client can lower his interest rate payments in EUR obligations to 0.5 % for 4 years, as long as EUR-CHF moves and stays in a range above the current spot.

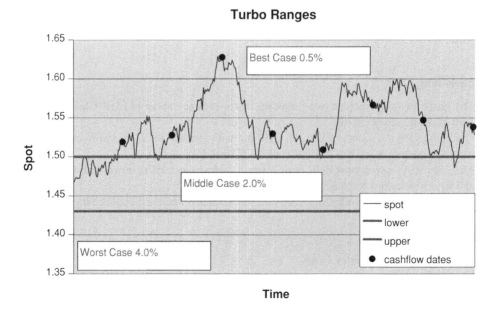

Figure 2.16   Three ranges for a turbo cross currency swap in EUR-CHF
In this sample path the structure works out well for the client as all the future spot fixings are in the upper range, whence he would pay the best case interest rate of only 0.50 % in all of the eight periods.

Table 2.33 Example of a turbo cross currency swap in EUR-CHF

Maturity	4 years
Notional	2,500,000 EUR/3,670,000 CHF
Strike	1.4680
Spot reference	1.4677
4 Year par interest rate	1.72 % in CHF
Amortization	none
The bank pays in EUR	fix 3.20 %
The bank receives in CHF	fix 4.00 % if EUR-CHF < 1.4300
	fix 2.00 % if EUR-CHF is between 1.4300 and 1.5000
	fix 0.50 % if EUR-CHF ≥ 1.5000
Fixing of the FX options	10:00 a.m. N.Y. time
	two business days before the end of each period
Coupon payments	semiannually
Basis	30/360, modified following, unadjusted
Premium	none

Composition

1. The basic product is a 4 year EUR-CHF cross currency swap with final exchange of the notionals. This is at par with CHF semiannual rate at 1.72 %. To structure this deal, we start with a swap that pays the worst case 4.00 % in CHF to the bank, whence the swap should be worth more than zero. In fact, the swap is worth, say, 240,000 EUR. From this amount the bank provides the turbo participation and takes a sales margin, so the turbo cross currency swap can be offered at zero cost to the client.
2. The client goes long a strip of 8 European digital EUR calls with strike 1.4300, two for each of the four years. The notional of the digital calls must be in CHF and the amount must be the cash flow to get from the worst case 4.00 % down to the middle case 2.00 %, so it must be 3,670,000 CHF * (4.00–2.00) %*180/360 = 36,700 CHF.
3. Furthermore, the client goes long a strip of another 8 European digital EUR calls with strike 1.5000. Their notional is computed similarly by 3,670,000 CHF * (2.00–0.50) %*180/360 = 27,525 CHF.
4. The total offer price for these strips is 170,000 EUR, whence there are 70,000 EUR left for the bank as a sales margin. The trader needs to buy 1,800,000 EUR from the spot desk, and trade the cross currency swap with worst case with the swap desk.

Variations

Obviously, there can be many ways to vary this type of a swap, e.g.

- The swap itself can have floating rates on the payer as well as on the receiver side, and the worst and best cases can be built as absolute differences from these floating rates.
- The swap itself can be amortizing. Consequently the notionals of the digital EUR calls are no more constant, but rather decreasing with maturity. Very small notional amounts of each ticket can make the overall structure unattractive, as the fixed costs for each ticket lead to a high offer price of the strip.
- There is no restriction to have three ranges: there can be two, in which case we are dealing with a *flip swap* as in Section 2.4.5, or more than three. The only issue is that if we increase

the number of ranges, then the notional amounts for the digital calls becomes very small and the costs for each ticket can lead to the strips being very expensive.

• Instead of simple digital options, one can use more exotic options, such as digital options with additional (window) knock-out barriers, which would make the ranges or the interest rates even more attractive. One can also imagine forward start digital options, where ranges are set afresh at each cash flow date. Of course, the strikes need not be constant over time. If the client wishes to incorporate a (linear) trend, this can easily be done. However, the structure with *constant* strikes usually works out attractive, *because* the forward curve tends downwards, so placing the ranges along the forward rate will make the structure unattractive, as the digital options would then become more expensive.

2.4.4   Buffered cross currency swap

While the turbo cross currency swap double the benefit from a rising exchange rate, the buffered cross currency swap buffers the effect of a falling exchange rate. If the exchange rate depreciates, then the client gets caught at the end. If this happens, he wants to at least pay less interest. The overall reason for a client to enter a cross currency swap is saving on the interest payments. This is achieved by taking a final exchange rate risk. Thus, the client bets against the forward. If this bet turns out to be correct, then the turbo cross currency swap adds a higher leverage. If the bet goes wrong, then the buffered cross currency swap compensates for the pain of a loss.

This effect is achieved by the client buying two strips of digital puts rather than digital calls. The rest of the structure is identical to the turbo cross currency swap.

Of course, for a downward sloping forward curve, structuring a turbo is much easier than structuring a buffered cross currency swap, because the swap with the worst case costs the same in both types, whereas the digital put strips are significantly more expensive than the digital call strips. For this reason they are not traded very often. An upward sloping forward curve would make it unreasonable to enter into a cross currency swap in the first place, because the interest rates would then be higher and the client hence not motivated.

2.4.5   Flip swap

A flip swap can be a single currency swap or a cross currency swap where the client receives a fixed or floating interest rate and pays either a best case below par or a worst case above par. The worst and best case depend on a foreign exchange rate to trade below or above a pre-specified strike and will be set at the end of each period. As in the turbo or buffered cross currency swap the structure works best if the client bets against the outright forward curve, i.e. if the forward curve is sloping downwards, then he would pay the best case if the exchange rate is *above* the strike and worst case otherwise.

Advantages

• Beneficial interest rate payments, i.e. receiving higher coupons or paying lower coupons than market
• Zero cost product
• Worst case known in advance

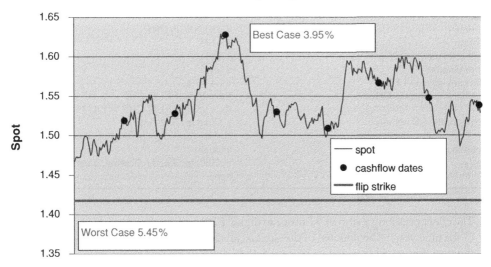

Figure 2.17   Two ranges for a flip swap in EUR-CHF
In this sample path the structure works out well for the client as all the future spot fixings are in the upper range, whence he would pay the best case interest rate of only 3.95 % in all periods.

Disadvantages

- Drastic interest payment improvement difficult, if the client wants to have a strike such that at inception of the trade she is deep in the best case
- Long term view on the FX rate impossible, i.e. once the exchange rate moves far into the worst case range, then it is likely to stay there

Example
We take EUR-CHF and show in Figure 2.17 and Table 2.34 how a corporate client can lower his interest rate payments in CHF obligations by 0.5 % for 9 years, as long as EUR-CHR stays above a strike significantly below the current spot. This flip swap is usually added to an existing interest rate payment plan, that can be lowered if the client is willing to take a certain long term FX view. It is attractive as we are starting in a best case region, the worst case region appears far away (in our example near the historic low of EUR-CHF) and even if the exchange rate falls below the strike, the interest rate burden is just 1.0 % higher than what the client receives.

Composition

1. The basic product is a 9 year CHF swap with two fixed legs, where – assuming a worst case – the bank receives more than it pays, whence the swap should be worth more than zero. In fact, the swap is worth, say, 335,000 CHF, which is about 228,000 EUR. From this amount the bank provides the possibility to reduce the worst case to the best case and takes a sales margin, so the flip swap can be offered at zero cost to the client.

Table 2.34   Example of a flip swap in EUR-CHF

Maturity	9 years
Notional	4,420,200.00 CHF
Strike	1.4175
Spot reference	1.4671
Amortization	none
The bank pays in CHF	fix 4.45 %
The bank receives in CHF	fix 5.45 % if EUR-CHF < 1.4175
	fix 3.95 % if EUR-CHF $\geq$ 1.4175
Fixing of the FX options	10:00 a.m. N.Y. time
	two business days before the end of each period
Coupon payments	annually
Basis	30/360, modified following, unadjusted
Premium	none

2. The client goes long a strip of 9 European digital EUR calls with strike 1.4175, one for each of the nine years. The notional of the digital calls must be in CHF and the amount must be the cash flow to get from the worst case 5.45 % down to the best case 3.95 %, so it must be 4,420,200 CHF * (5.45–3.95) %*360/360 = 66,303 CHF.
3. The total offer price for this strip is 196,000 EUR, whence there are 32,000 EUR left for the bank as a sales margin. The trader needs to buy 1,400,000 EUR from the spot desk, and trade the CHF swap with worst case with the swap desk.

Variations

Obviously, there can be many ways to vary this type of a swap, e.g.

- The swap itself can have floating rates on the payer as well as on the receiver side, and the worst and best cases can be built as absolute differences from these floating rates.
- The swap itself can be amortizing. Consequently the notionals of the digital EUR calls are no more constant, but rather decreasing with maturity. Very small notional amounts of each ticket can make the overall structure unattractive, as the fixed costs for each ticket lead to a high offer price of the strip.
- There is no restriction to have two cases: there can be three, in which case we are dealing with a *turbo* or a *buffered* (cross currency) swap as in Sections 2.4.3 and 2.4.4 or more than three. The only issue is that if we increase the number of cases, then the notional amounts for the digital calls becomes very small and the costs for each ticket can lead to the strips to be very expensive.
- Instead of simple digital options, one can use more exotic options, such as digital options with additional (window) knock-out barriers, which would make the strike or the interest rates even more attractive. One can also imagine forward start digital options, where the strike is set afresh at each cash flow date. Of course, the strike need not be constant over time. If the client wishes to incorporate a (linear) trend, this can easily be done.

2.4.6   Corridor swap

The corridor swap or *bonus* swap (compare with the *bonus forward* in Section 2.1.8) is very similar to the turbo or buffered (cross currency) swap. In all the three products, there are three ranges. In the corridor swap the client pays a best case interest rate below par if an exchange rate is inside a pre-specified corridor and a worst case above par otherwise.

Advantages

- Beneficial interest rate payments, i.e. receiving higher coupons or paying lower coupons than market
- Zero cost product
- Start in the best case

Disadvantages

- Very risky as final exchange rate risk not covered
- Long term view on the FX rate impossible, i.e. once the exchange rate moves far into the worst case range, then it is likely to stay there
- Ranges are often unattractive as betting is only halfway against the forward curve

Example
We take EUR-CHF and show in Figure 2.18 and Table 2.35 how a corporate client can lower his interest rate payments in EUR obligations to 0.8 % for 3 years, as long as EUR-CHF stays inside a range around the current spot. The attractive part of this deal is that the worst case is not as far away from the par rate as the best case.

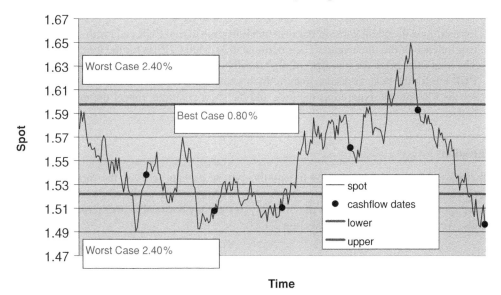

Figure 2.18   Corridor ranges for a corridor cross currency swap in EUR-CHF
In this sample path the structure works out well for the client for three future spot fixings where she would pay the best case and not so well for the other three spot fixings where she would pay the worst case.

Table 2.35   Example of a corridor cross currency swap in EUR-CHF

Maturity	3 years
Notional	3,942,500 CHF/2,500,000 EUR
Strike	1.5770
Spot reference	1.5770
3 Year par interest rate	1.72 % in CHF
Amortization	none
The bank pays in EUR	fix 2.80 %
The bank receives in CHF	fix 2.40 % if EUR-CHF $\notin$ [1.5220, 1.5975]
	fix 0.80 % if EUR-CHF $\in$ [1.5220, 1.5975]
Fixing of the FX options	10:00 a.m. N.Y. time
	two business days before the end of each period
Coupon payments	semiannually
Basis	30/360, modified following, unadjusted
Premium	none

Composition

1. The basic product is a 3 year EUR-CHF cross currency swap with final exchange of the notionals. This is at par with CHF semiannual rate at 1.72 %. To structure this deal, we start with a swap that pays the worst case 2.40 % in CHF to the bank, whence the swap should be worth more than zero. In fact, the swap is worth, say, 72,000 EUR. From this amount the bank provides the corridor participation and takes a sales margin, so the corridor currency swap can be offered at zero cost to the client.
2. The client goes long a strip of 6 European digital EUR calls with strike 1.5220, two for each of the three years. The notional of the digital calls must be in CHF and the amount must be the cash flow to get from the worst case 2.40 % down to the best case 0.80 %, so it must be 3,942,500 CHF * (2.40–0.80) % * 180/360 = 31,5400 CHF.
3. Furthermore, the client goes short a strip of 6 European digital EUR calls with strike 1.5975, two for each of the three years. Their notional is 31,5400 CHF as for the long digital calls.
4. The total offer price for this strip of digital calls is 52,000 EUR, whence there are 30,000 EUR left for the bank as a sales margin. In this case there is only a small or no delta hedge for the FX options required as the long and the short positions cancel the necessary spot hedges.

Variations

Obviously, there can be many ways to vary this type of a swap, see, e.g. the variations of the *turbo cross currency swap* of Section 2.4.3. One variation is to reset the ranges depending on future spot levels. This overcomes the difficulty to state any reasonable long term view on FX levels. We discuss an example in Section 2.4.8.

2.4.7   Double-no-touch linked swap

The double-no-touch linked swap picks up the idea of a *tunnel deposit* of Section 2.3.3. A swap or cross currency swap is set up as a basic product and the interest rate payments for the client are a worst case above par if a currency pair ever hits or leaves a pre-specified range between inception of the trade and maturity time and a best case below par otherwise.

Table 2.36   Example of a EUR-CHF 9-month-double-no-touch linked 2 year swap in EUR

Maturity	2 years
Notional	5,000,000 EUR
Spot reference	1.5388
Amortization	none
The bank pays in EUR	fix 2.60 % p.a.
The bank receives in EUR	fix 3.70 % p.a. if EUR-CHF $\notin$ [1.4990, 1.5810]
	fix 1.00 % p.a. if EUR-CHF $\in$ [1.4990, 1.5810]
Range valid up to	10:00 a.m. N.Y. time in 9 months
Coupon payments	annually
Basis	act/360, modified following, adjusted
Premium	none

Advantages

- Beneficial interest rate payments, i.e. receiving higher coupons or paying lower coupons than market
- Zero cost product
- Start in the best case
- Guaranteed worst case known in advance

Disadvantages

- Long term view on the FX rate impossible, i.e. suitable only for maturities up to one year
- Tunnel sometimes unattractive as betting is only halfway against the forward curve

Example
We take EUR-CHF and show in Table 2.36 how a corporate client can lower his interest rate payments in EUR obligations from 2.60 % to 1.00 % for 1 year, if EUR-CHF stays inside a range around the current spot for the next 9 months. The attractive part of this deal is that the worst case is not as far away from the par rate as the best case.

Composition

1. The basic product is a 2 year EUR swap, where the bank pays a fixed rate of 2.60 % and receives a worst case fixed rate of 3.70 %, which is worth, say, 107,000 EUR. From this amount the bank provides the tunnel participation and takes a sales margin, so the swap can be offered at zero cost to the client.
2. The client goes long two 9-month EUR-CHF double-no-touch with range 1.4990–1.5810, with *deferred* EUR cash settlement one in 1 year and the other one in 2 years. The notional of each double-no-touch must be in EUR and the amount must be the cash flow to get from the worst case 3.70 % down to the best case 1.00 %, so it must be 5,000,000 EUR * (3.70–1.00) % * 365/360 = 136,875 EUR.
3. The total offer price of the two double-no-touch options is 71,000 EUR, whence there are 36,000 EUR left for the bank as a sales margin.
4. Pricing the double-no-touch options with deferred delivery may not be available in some front office applications. However, one can price the double-no-touch with standard

non-deferred delivery and take this as a super-replication, because the options desk can keep the potential payoff for free between expiration and delivery and would thus make some extra profit. However, the booking of the trades should have the correct delivery dates of the double-no-touch options.
5. In this case the FX Options desk buys 400,000 EUR from the spot desk to delta hedge the double-no-touch options. This EUR swap is fixed-fixed with practically no risk, whence the valuation is easy and the hedge is not urgent.

Variations

With this basic idea laid out one can think of a whole bunch of variations. We can take other touch options instead of a double-no-touch. We can apply the idea to swaps with a floating leg, to cross currency swaps, swaps with amortization. The only constraint is that the first interest rate payment must be after the expiration of the double-no-touch. Using a deferred delivery allows a combination of rather long term products such as swaps with rather short term products such as double-no-touch options. One can also think of nested ranges with corresponding coupons just like the tower deposits in Section 2.3.6.

2.4.8 Range reset swap

The range reset swap is based on the idea of a *corridor swap* as explained in Section 2.4.6. Investors betting on FX rates remaining inside a pre-defined range are often hit by unexpected market moves, specially if the time intervals are long. For this reason range bets are often more attractive if the range is reset around future spot levels in the future. This is implemented in the range reset swap, which is an interest rate swap where the investor pays Libor or a fixed rate in one currency and receives a best case or a worst case interest payment in another (or the same) currency depending on whether the FX spot remains inside a range for the time interval under consideration. Resetting the ranges is usually only marginally more expensive than fixing the range for all times, but gives a lot more security to the investor. We consider an example listed in Table 2.37.

The way this works is that we price a swap floating leg against a zero fixed leg to get the amount of EUR we can spend. From this amount the bank subtracts the sales margin and buys 6 EUR-USD forward start corridors.

2.4.9 Exercises

1. Consider the cross currency swap in Table 2.31. Compute the break-even point in the EUR-JPY rate, i.e. at which EUR-JPY rate at maturity would the treasurer lose all the interest rate she received in EUR, because she would have to buy EUR at 135.50 even though the spot (the one you are asked to compute) is below 135.50? Secondly, what is the worst case scenario and what is the corresponding maximum loss?
2. Consider a hanseatic cross currency swap as in Section 2.4.2 and assume current market conditions of EUR-JPY. For a notional of 10 Million EUR, 1 year tenor, quarterly payments find suitable conditions for a partial protection if the goal is zero interest payment in JPY and a sales margin of 50,000 EUR. What is the delta hedge in case of a trade? If you do not have access to market data, you may assume a flat term structure of 3.0 % for EUR, 0.1 % for JPY, volatility of 10 % for EUR-JPY, spot and strike of 130.00 for EUR-JPY.

Table 2.37 Indicative Terms and Conditions as of 11 August 2004 or a EUR-USD range reset swap

Spot reference	1.2700 EUR-USD
1 year EUR rate reference	2.20 %
Trade date	11 August 2004
Start date	13 August 2004
Maturity date	13 August 2007
Principal amount	USD 10,000,000
Up-front fee	1.85 % of the Notional
Redemption price	100 %
The bank receives	6 Month Libor – 2bps, act/360
The bank pays best case	5.00 % p.a. semianually, 30/360
The bank pays worst case	0.00 %
Fixing of the barriers (pre-defined range)	At fixing date
Upper barrier	108 % of the fixing spot
Lower barrier	92 % of the fixing spot
	Fixing date and Expiry date
Period 1	11 Aug 2004–10 Feb 2005
Period 2	10 Feb 2005–11 Aug 2005
Period 3	11 Aug 2005–9 Feb 2006
Period 4	9 Feb 2006–10 Aug 2006
Period 5	10 Aug 2006–9 Feb 2007
Period 6	9 Feb 2007–9 Aug 2007
Fixing spot	Reuters ECB37
Fixing and payment business days	London & New York

Ranges are American style. The best case is paid for each period in which EUR/USD stays inside the pre-defined range between the fixing date and the expiry date.

3. Consider a turbo cross currency swap as in Section 2.4.3 in EUR-JPY. Let us take a maturity of 5 years, annual cash flows, 10 Million EUR notional, and a market of EUR-JPY spot 130.00, volatility 10 %, EUR rate 4.0 %, JPY rate 0.5 % constant over time. Let us assume further that the bank wants to earn 100,000 EUR sales margin on this trade. Compute the outright forward rates for each year. Then compute the value of the cross currency swap with strike 130.00 and where the bank pays 4.0 % in EUR and a worst case of 4.0 % in JPY. Let the middle case be 2.0 % and the best case be 0.0 %. What constant ranges can the bank offer the client? What is the impact on the sales margin if we make the ranges symmetric around the forward rates?

4. Structure a *Basket Spread Swap*, where the client receives EURIBOR semi-annually for 3 years and pays a worst case fixed rate w. The fixed rate goes down to the best case b (often zero) linear with the performance of a currency basket, but not below b. Obviously, the client trades a swap with worst case b and goes long a basket call spread. Compose a basket of your choice and determine the details of the trade, i.e. maturities, notionals, prices, hedges. Try to generate a suitable parameter scenario that would sell well under current market conditions.

2.5 PARTICIPATION NOTES

Participation or *performance* notes are usually listed and capital guaranteed products, where the investor invests a certain amount of a currency, waives parts of the market interest and participates in a certain market sector. These type of notes are generally more popular in equity and index markets, where even retail investors have a view. Foreign Exchange is only recently being discovered as an *asset class*. Only very commonly known exchange rates like EUR/USD or the Gold price XAU/USD are considered suitable from a marketing point of view. We discuss a few examples.

2.5.1   Gold participation note

We consider a capital guaranteed 5-year note in EUR with a coupon based on the gold price (XAU/USD). Let us assume an investor believes in a rising gold price and wishes to invest an amount N in EUR. At maturity the investor receives

* 100 % of the invested capital,
* +95 % participation via Min(gold price return, 60 %) in USD.

Figure 2.19   Gold bars of Commerzbank

This type of participation specification usually causes a lot of confusion or discussion since in FX it is never so clear which currency we are talking about. Generally, only a formula helps, which makes these notes a bit difficult to retail. In our case the payoff formula is

$$N \cdot \left[100\% + 95\% \frac{\max(0, \min (\text{XAU-USD}(T) - \text{XAU-USD}(0), 60))\%}{\text{EUR-USD}(T)} \right]. \quad (2.29)$$

This means for instance that if we start with a gold price of 400 USD per ounce and end with 450 USD per ounce, and the EUR/USD exchange rate at maturity T is 1.0000, then the investor receives the invested capital and 95% of 50%, i.e. 47.5% one-time coupon, which is quite a good deal. The maximum loss is missing out on the market interest rate, which happens if the gold price does not rise. The maximum gain in this case is 95% of 60%, which is 57%. An additional confusion is caused by the conversion into EUR. In this case, the conversion is taken at the maturity date T, which means that the investor is taking chances and risks of EUR/USD spot movements. Other offers could be a EUR/USD exchange rate to be fixed in advance, which would make the structure a *quanto* capped call performance note, and the EUR/USD exchange rate risk rests with the issuer. The terms and conditions are summarized in the term sheet in Table 2.38. Overall, as you can see this is not so easy to explain to a retail client. To support it, one can use historic time series as in Figure 2.20.

Here are some arguments for a possible rising Gold price.

1. The price of gold has moved above a **25 year low** and is now expected to break out to the upside.
2. Consumption of gold has exceeded production for the past 10 years, and when the low price of gold fell below production cost, many **gold mines reduced production**.
3. Gold price is highly **de-correlated from the equity and bond markets**: the correlation between gold price and the DJI index is equal to -0.30 over the last 4 years.
4. In a such a climate of market uncertainty, gold constitutes a good way to **diversify your investments**.

Table 2.38   Sample indicative terms and conditions of a gold performance note as of 21 February 2003

Investment type	Bond
Issuer	to be specified
First trading day	to be set
Fixing of the initial spot reference	on the first trading day
Maturity	5 years after the first trading day
Notional N	EUR 10,000,000.00
Initial price	100%
Capital guarantee	100%
Underlying	Gold price XAU-USD
Gold price source	Reuters RIC XAU=
EUR-USD fixing source	Reuters page OPTREF
Payoff at maturity	Formula (2.29)
XAU-USD(0)	Gold price on the first trading day
XAU-USD(T)	Gold price one week before maturity
EUR-USD(T)	EUR-USD spot reference one week before maturity

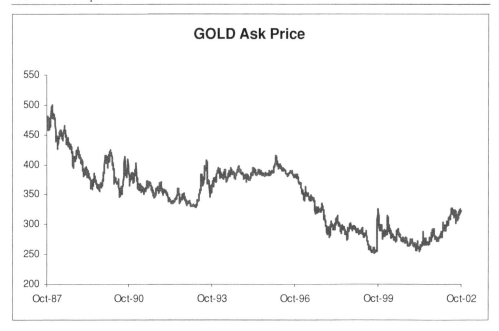

Figure 2.20   History of the ask price of Gold in USD from 1987 to 2002. *Source*: Bloomberg.

Of course, it is matter of the quality of the market research groups to underline such arguments, and at the very end, it is a matter of belief for the investor.

2.5.2   Basket-linked note

Now we analyze how to structure a USD-denominated note, where the investor participates in the performance of a currency basket of the four currencies EUR, AUD, GBP and CHF against the USD. Following the basket payoff in Equation (1.363) we use the weights and normalizers in Table 2.39.

This way we form an index $I(t)$, and the note could look like this. The issuer pays

$$\min[1.18; \max[0; I(T) - 1.06]] \tag{2.30}$$

Table 2.39   Currency pairs, normalizers, weights, sample spots and values of a basket of four used to structure a basket-linked performance note

Currency pairs	Sample spots $S_j(T)$	Weights a_j	Normalizers $S_j(0)$	Summands
EUR/USD	0.9800	25 %	1.0400	0.265306122
AUD/USD	0.5610	25 %	0.6500	0.289661319
GBP/USD	1.5300	25 %	1.6000	0.261437908
CHF/USD	0.6725	25 %	0.7000	0.260223048
			Index	107.66 % USD

The summands are computed as $a_j \frac{S_j(T)}{S_j(0)}$, the index value $I(T)$ being the sum of these four summands, the basket payoff following Equation (1.363).

times the notional, which is essentially a capped basket call. Taking a maturity of one year and a notional of 10,000,000.00 USD, we obtain 220,000.00 USD from the money market, assuming a USD rate of 2.20 %. The basket with strike 1.06 would cost 1.4 % USD, the one with strike 1.18 would generate 0.1 % USD, which leaves us with a total cost of 1.3 % USD. Since the USD interest is not paid to the investor, the issuer makes 0.9 % USD sales margin out of this structure. Alternatively, he could guarantee a minimum interest rate of 0.5 % and only keep 0.4 % of sales margin.

In the sample spot scenario of Table 2.39, the client would be paid an interest of 1.66 %, which is below money market and hence an effective loss. If the index shoots up to 118 % or more, the investor is paid an interest of 12 %, which is way above money market.

2.5.3 Issuer swap

An issuer swap is not a structured product. The issuer of a bond or a note or any listed derivative is usually a bank or corporate. Along with the issuer goes its credit default risk. A low rated bank or a small cap will tend to have a higher default risk than a central bank. Therefore, coupons of low rated issuers will be higher than coupons of high rated issuers. It can happen that a bank wants to issue a bond or a note, but can not do this, because either its credit rating is too low or because of legal or marketing constraints is not allowed to issue a certain note. In this case the product can still be sold, however, under the name of another issuer. In this case the issuers have to be swapped and the *credit spread* has to be paid from the lower rated to the higher rated issuer. In such a case the entire product of a bank is sold to the issuer, and the bank then buys it back for distribution. This swap of issuers is called an *issuer swap*.

2.5.4 Moving Strike Turbo Spot unlimited

The Moving Strike Turbo Spot is a product, which is often issued as a certificate or listed note. It is automatically renewed at pre-specified times, say monthly, unless it is canceled. It can be canceled by the holder or the issuer at these renewal dates. If the contract is canceled, it pays to the holder

$$[\phi(S - K_t)]^+,\qquad(2.31)$$

where K_t denotes a moving strike and as usual $\phi = +1$ in case of a call and $\phi = -1$ in case of a put. The strike is updated due to the rule

$$K_{t_{i+1}} = K_{t_i} e^{(r_d + \phi r - r_f)(t_{i+1} - t_i)}.\qquad(2.32)$$

where r_d, r_f are the domestic and foreign continuously compounded rates and r is some positive rate.

As soon as the strike K_t is touched, the product is exercised with value 0.

The idea behind this product is to give an investor the possibility to invest into the spot of an underlying in a note format. The investor participates linear in rising and falling spot rates. The alternative would be to buy the underlying with a stop-loss strategy if the spot moves down to K_t. However, this would require a lot of cash and short selling the underlying in case of a desired participation in a downward movement. In the certificate format only a quantity of the size of the payoff needs to be invested. Besides that the default risk is also minimized for both parties. These features combined with the simple payoff structure have made this product extremely popular, not only in foreign exchange markets.

Pricing of a Moving Strike Turbo Spot unlimited

Given that in t_1 the contract can be canceled, the price in t_1 must be

$$[\phi(S_{t_1} - K_{t_1})]^+ \tag{2.33}$$

unless K_t has been touched. As an example we consider the call version. In $t_0 < t_1$ the value of a down-and-out call with a barrier equal to the strike can be determined in the case of zero drift $r_d - r_f$, because a forward contract with strike K_{t_1} would be a perfect static hedge. For this reason the adjustment rate r is introduced to generate a zero drift. The value of the forward contract is

$$v_{t_0} = e^{-r_d(t_1-t_0)} I\!E \left(S_{t_1} - K_{t_1} \right) = S_{t_0} e^{-r_f(t_1-t_0)} - K_{t_0} e^{(r-r_f)(t_1-t_0)} . \tag{2.34}$$

Provided $r_f \geq 0$ and r is chosen greater than 0 we have

$$v_{t_0} < (S_{t_0} - K_{t_0}) . \tag{2.35}$$

The right side of this inequality is the quoted offer price.

Hedging the Moving Strike Turbo

In a backwardation scenario of the forward curve, the issuer does not need to worry, as earning sales margin comes for free, because the hedge of the down-and-out call using the forward is cheaper than the down-and-out call even in the case of $r = 0$. The issuer just pockets the cost of carry. However, in a contango situation the use of r becomes crucial as the issuer would otherwise pay the cost of carry. It has been interesting to observe how much time it took for various banks in 2003/2004, when the EUR-USD forward curve switched from backwardation to contango, to discover the reasons for their losses in dealing with the turbo notes.

2.6   HYBRID FX PRODUCTS

A real hybrid FX product involves more than one market instrument where the components of the markets cannot be isolated. We have seen that forwards, deposits and swaps can be enhanced by starting with a worst case and then buying FX options or series of these to participate in certain FX market movements. These structures have an FX component that is separable from the basic product. Examples for real hybrid FX products are

Long term FX options. The interest rate risk of long term FX options is so prominent that we can no longer work with the Black-Scholes model assuming deterministic interest rates. We need to rather model the future interest rates in the two currencies as a stochastic process. Modeling both rates along with the exchange rates requires at least a three-factor model.

Options with deferred delivery. Usually the delivery date of options are two business days after the maturity date. However, it can happen that we need the payoff of an option to be delivered at a much later date. For example, if a client buys a 6-month double-no-touch, whose payoff is supposed to enhance the interest rates of a 5 year swap with semi-annual cash flows. In such a case the delivery date may be four and a half years after the maturity of the double-no-touch. This cash on hold is subject to interest rates in the future, whence modeling the value of such a deferred delivery double-no-touch is no longer just dependent on the exchange rate.

Table 2.40   Example of a dual asset range accrual note

Spot reference	1.5300 EUR-CHF
EUR rate reference	2.20 %
Issue price	100 %
Capital guarantee	100 %
Notional	10,000,000 EUR
Maturity	13 months
Coupon	3.75 % $\cdot \frac{n}{d}$ p.a., paid once at maturity
Total number of fixing days	d
Conventions	30/360, Modified Following, Adjusted
12 month Euribor corridor	2.25 %–3.25 %
EUR-CHF corridor	1.5100–1.5700
EUR-CHF fixing source	Reuters page ECB37
Euribor fixing source	Reuters page Euribor01

The number of fixing days, where both EUR-CHF and 12 month Euribor are fixed inside the corridor is denoted by n.

Interest rate products with a knock-in or knock-out barrier in FX.

Equity products with a knock-in or knock-out barrier in FX.

Credit products with a knock-in or knock-out barrier in FX.

Derivatives in a non-FX market quantoed into another currency.

Power Reverse Dual Currency Bonds (PRDC). A PRDC is an overall name for an entire class of bonds. In principle, it works like a dual currency deposit in bond format, where the coupons can also be paid in different currencies or be quantoed into other currencies. A detailed overview can be found, e.g. in [68].

As an example we consider a 13 month dual asset range accrual note in Table 2.40.

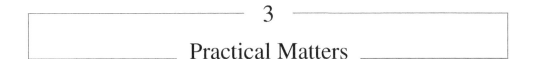
Practical Matters

3.1   THE TRADERS' RULE OF THUMB

The traders' rule of thumb is a method used by traders to determine the cost of risk managing the volatility risk of exotic options with vanilla options. This cost is then added to the theoretical value in the Black-Scholes model and is called the *overhedge*. The method has been described in [69] and [70]. We explain the rule and then consider the example of a one-touch, introduced in Section 1.5.2.

The Traders' Rule of Thumb is also sometimes called *Vanna-Volga Pricing*. Delta and vega are the most relevant sensitivity parameters for foreign exchange options maturing within one year. A delta-neutral position can be achieved by trading the spot. Changes in the spot are explicitly allowed in the Black-Scholes model. Therefore, model and practical trading have very good control over spot change risk. The more sensitive part is the vega position. This is taken care of in the Black-Scholes model. Market participants need to trade other options to obtain a vega-neutral position. However, even a vega-neutral position is subject to changes of spot and volatility. For this reason, the sensitivity parameters *vanna* (change of vega due to change of spot) and *volga* (change of vega due to change of volatility) are of special interest. The plots for vanna and volga for a vanilla are displayed in Figures 3.1 and 3.2. In this section we outline how the cost of such a vanna- and volga- exposure can be used to obtain prices for options that are closer to the market than their theoretical Black-Scholes value.

3.1.1   Cost of vanna and volga

We fix the rates r_d and r_f, the time to maturity T and the spot x and define

$$\text{cost of vanna} \triangleq \text{Exotic Vanna Ratio} \times \text{value of RR}, \tag{3.1}$$

$$\text{cost of volga} \triangleq \text{Exotic Volga Ratio} \times \text{value of BF}, \tag{3.2}$$

$$\text{Exotic Vanna Ratio} \triangleq B_{\sigma x}/\text{RR}_{\sigma x}, \tag{3.3}$$

$$\text{Exotic Volga Ratio} \triangleq B_{\sigma \sigma}/\text{BF}_{\sigma \sigma}, \tag{3.4}$$

$$\text{value of RR} \triangleq [\text{RR}(\sigma_\Delta) - \text{RR}(\sigma_0)], \tag{3.5}$$

$$\text{value of BF} \triangleq [\text{BF}(\sigma_\Delta) - \text{BF}(\sigma_0)] \tag{3.6}$$

where σ_0 denotes the at-the-money (forward) volatility and σ_Δ denotes the wing volatility at the delta pillar Δ, B denotes the value function of a given exotic option. The values of risk

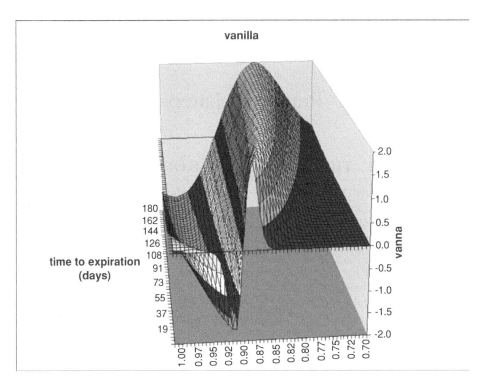

Figure 3.1 Vanna of a vanilla option as a function of spot and time to expiration, showing the skew symmetry about the at-the-money line

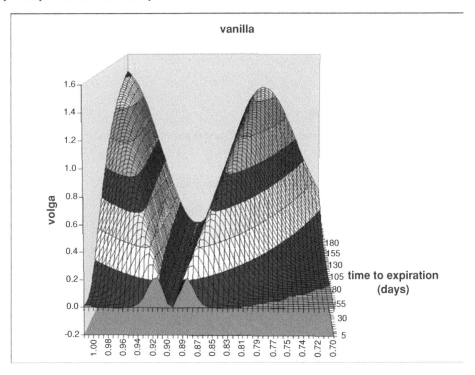

Figure 3.2 Volga of a vanilla option as a function of spot and time to expiration, showing the symmetry about the at-the-money line

reversals and butterflies are defined by

$$RR(\sigma) \overset{\Delta}{=} call(x, \Delta, \sigma, r_d, r_f, T) - put(x, \Delta, \sigma, r_d, r_f, T), \tag{3.7}$$

$$BF(\sigma) \overset{\Delta}{=} \frac{call(x, \Delta, \sigma, r_d, r_f, T) + put(x, \Delta, \sigma, r_d, r_f, T)}{2}$$

$$- \frac{call(x, \Delta_0, \sigma_0, r_d, r_f, T) + put(x, \Delta_0, \sigma_0, r_d, r_f, T)}{2}, \tag{3.8}$$

where vanilla$(x, \Delta, \sigma, r_d, r_f, T)$ means vanilla$(x, K, \sigma, r_d, r_f, T)$ for a strike K chosen to imply $|vanilla_x(x, K, \sigma, r_d, r_f, T)| = \Delta$ and Δ_0 is the delta that produces the at-the-money strike. To summarize we abbreviate

$$c(\sigma_\Delta^+) \overset{\Delta}{=} call(x, \Delta^+, \sigma_\Delta^+, r_d, r_f, T), \tag{3.9}$$

$$p(\sigma_\Delta^-) \overset{\Delta}{=} put(x, \Delta^-, \sigma_\Delta^-, r_d, r_f, T), \tag{3.10}$$

and obtain

$$\text{cost of vanna} = \frac{B_{\sigma x}}{c_{\sigma x}(\sigma_\Delta^+) - p_{\sigma x}(\sigma_\Delta^-)} \left[c(\sigma_\Delta^+) - c(\sigma_0) - p(\sigma_\Delta^-) + p(\sigma_0) \right], \tag{3.11}$$

$$\text{cost of volga} = \frac{2B_{\sigma\sigma}}{c_{\sigma\sigma}(\sigma_\Delta^+) + p_{\sigma\sigma}(\sigma_\Delta^-)} \left[\frac{c(\sigma_\Delta^+) - c(\sigma_0) + p(\sigma_\Delta^-) - p(\sigma_0)}{2} \right], \tag{3.12}$$

where we note that volga of the butterfly should actually be

$$\frac{1}{2} \left[c_{\sigma\sigma}(\sigma_\Delta^+) + p_{\sigma\sigma}(\sigma_\Delta^-) - c_{\sigma\sigma}(\sigma_0) - p_{\sigma\sigma}(\sigma_0) \right], \tag{3.13}$$

but the last two summands are close to zero. The *vanna-volga adjusted value* of the exotic is then

$$B(\sigma_0) + p \times [\text{cost of vanna} + \text{cost of volga}]. \tag{3.14}$$

A division by the spot x converts everything into the usual quotation of the price in % of the underlying currency. The cost of vanna and volga is often adjusted by a number $p \in [0, 1]$, which is often taken to be the risk-neutral no-touch probability. The reason is that in the case of options that can knock out, the hedge is not needed anymore once the option has knocked out. The exact choice of p depends on the product to be priced, see Table 3.2. Taking $p = 1$ to be default would lead to overestimated overhedges for double-no-touch options as pointed out in [69].

The values of risk reversals and butterflies in Equations (3.11) and (3.12) can be approximated by a first order expansion as follows. For a risk reversal we take the difference of the call with correct implied volatility and the call with at-the-money volatility minus the difference of the put with correct implied volatility and the put with at-the-money volatility. It is easy to see that this can be well approximated by the vega of the at-the-money vanilla times the risk reversal in terms of volatility. Similarly the cost of the butterfly can be approximated by the vega of the at-the-money volatility times the butterfly in terms of volatility. In formulae this is

$$c(\sigma_\Delta^+) - c(\sigma_0) - p(\sigma_\Delta^-) + p(\sigma_0)$$
$$\approx c_\sigma(\sigma_0)(\sigma_\Delta^+ - \sigma_0) - p_\sigma(\sigma_0)(\sigma_\Delta^- - \sigma_0)$$
$$= \sigma_0[p_\sigma(\sigma_0) - c_\sigma(\sigma_0)] + c_\sigma(\sigma_0)[\sigma_\Delta^+ - \sigma_\Delta^-]$$
$$= c_\sigma(\sigma_0)RR \tag{3.15}$$

and similarly

$$\frac{c(\sigma_\Delta^+) - c(\sigma_0) + p(\sigma_\Delta^-) - p(\sigma_0)}{2}$$

$$\approx c_\sigma(\sigma_0)\text{BF}. \tag{3.16}$$

With these approximations we obtain the formulae

$$\text{cost of vanna} \approx \frac{B_{\sigma x}}{c_{\sigma x}(\sigma_\Delta^+) - p_{\sigma x}(\sigma_\Delta^-)} c_\sigma(\sigma_0)\text{RR}, \tag{3.17}$$

$$\text{cost of volga} \approx \frac{2B_{\sigma\sigma}}{c_{\sigma\sigma}(\sigma_\Delta^+) + p_{\sigma\sigma}(\sigma_\Delta^-)} c_\sigma(\sigma_0)\text{BF}. \tag{3.18}$$

3.1.2   Observations

1. The price supplements are linear in butterflies and risk reversals. In particular, there is no cost of vanna supplement if the risk reversal is zero and no cost of volga supplement if the butterfly is zero.
2. The price supplements are linear in the at-the-money vanilla vega. This means supplements grow with growing volatility change risk of the hedge instruments.
3. The price supplements are linear in vanna and volga of the given exotic option.
4. We have not observed any relevant difference between the exact method and its first order approximation. Since the computation time for the approximation is shorter, we recommend using the approximation.
5. It is not clear up front which target delta to use for the butterflies and risk reversals. We take a delta of 25 % merely on the basis of its liquidity.
6. The prices for vanilla options are consistent with the input volatilities as shown in Figures 3.3, 3.4 and 3.5.
7. The method assumes a zero volga of risk reversals and a zero vanna of butterflies. This way the two sources of risk can be decomposed and hedged with risk reversals and butterflies. However, the assumption is actually not exact. For this reason, the method should be used with a lot of care and causes traders and financial engineers to keep adding exceptions to the standard method.

3.1.3   Consistency check

A minimum requirement for the vanna-volga pricing to be correct is the consistency of the method with vanilla options. We show in Figure 3.3, Figure 3.4 and Figure 3.5 that the method does in fact yield a typical foreign exchange smile shape and produces the correct input volatilities at-the-money and at the delta pillars. We will now prove the consistency in the following way. Since the input consists only of three volatilities (at-the-money and two delta pillars), it would be too much to expect that the method produces correct representation of the entire volatility matrix. We can only check if the values for at-the-money and target-Δ puts and calls are reproduced correctly. In order to verify this, we check if the values for an at-the-money call, a risk reversal and a butterfly are priced correctly. Surely we only expect approximately correct results. Note that the number p is taken to be one, which agrees with the risk-neutral no-touch probability for vanilla options.

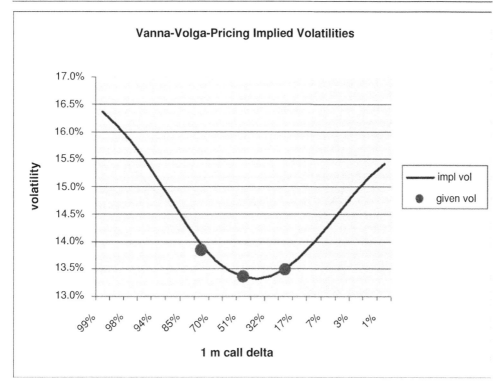

Figure 3.3   Consistency check of vanna-volga-pricing
Vanilla option smile for a one month maturity EUR/USD call, spot $= 0.9060$, $r_d = 5.07\%$, $r_f = 4.70\%$, $\sigma_0 = 13.35\%$, $\sigma_\Delta^+ = 13.475\%$, $\sigma_\Delta^- = 13.825\%$

For an at-the-money call vanna and volga are approximately zero, whence there are no supplements due to vanna cost or volga cost.
For a target-Δ risk reversal

$$c(\sigma_\Delta^+) - p(\sigma_\Delta^-) \tag{3.19}$$

we obtain

$$\text{cost of vanna} = \frac{c_{\sigma x}(\sigma_\Delta^+) - p_{\sigma x}(\sigma_\Delta^-)}{c_{\sigma x}(\sigma_\Delta^+) - p_{\sigma x}(\sigma_\Delta^-)} \left[c(\sigma_\Delta^+) - c(\sigma_0) - p(\sigma_\Delta^-) + p(\sigma_0) \right],$$

$$= c(\sigma_\Delta^+) - c(\sigma_0) - p(\sigma_\Delta^-) + p(\sigma_0) \tag{3.20}$$

$$\text{cost of volga} = \frac{2[c_{\sigma\sigma}(\sigma_\Delta^+) - p_{\sigma\sigma}(\sigma_\Delta^-)]}{c_{\sigma\sigma}(\sigma_\Delta^+) + p_{\sigma\sigma}(\sigma_\Delta^-)}$$

$$\left[\frac{c(\sigma_\Delta^+) - c(\sigma_0) + p(\sigma_\Delta^-) - p(\sigma_0)}{2} \right], \tag{3.21}$$

and observe that the cost of vanna yields a perfect fit and the cost of volga is small, because in the first fraction we divide the difference of two quantities by the sum of the quantities, which are all of the same order.

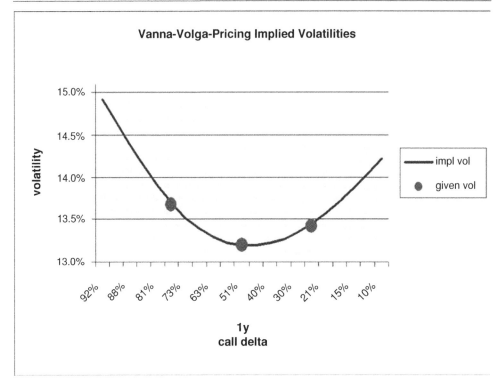

Figure 3.4 Consistency check of vanna-volga-pricing

Vanilla option smile for a one year maturity EUR/USD call, spot $= 0.9060$, $r_d = 5.07\,\%$, $r_f = 4.70\,\%$, $\sigma_0 = 13.20\,\%$, $\sigma_\Delta^+ = 13.425\,\%$, $\sigma_\Delta^- = 13.575\,\%$

For a target-Δ butterfly

$$\frac{c(\sigma_\Delta^+) + p(\sigma_\Delta^-)}{2} - \frac{c(\sigma_0) + p(\sigma_0)}{2} \tag{3.22}$$

we obtain analogously a perfect fit for the cost of volga and

$$\text{cost of vanna} = \frac{c_{\sigma x}(\sigma_\Delta^+) - p_{\sigma x}(\sigma_0) - [c_{\sigma x}(\sigma_0) - p_{\sigma x}(\sigma_\Delta^-)]}{c_{\sigma x}(\sigma_\Delta^+) - p_{\sigma x}(\sigma_0) + [c_{\sigma x}(\sigma_0) - p_{\sigma x}(\sigma_\Delta^-)]}$$
$$\left[c(\sigma_\Delta^+) - c(\sigma_0) - p(\sigma_\Delta^-) + p(\sigma_0) \right], \tag{3.23}$$

which is again small.

In the exercises we will point out that the consistency can actually fail for certain parameter scenarios. This is one of the reasons, why the traders' rule of thumb has been criticized repeatedly by a number of traders and researchers.

3.1.4 Abbreviations for first generation exotics

We introduce the abbreviations for first generation exotics listed in Table 3.1.

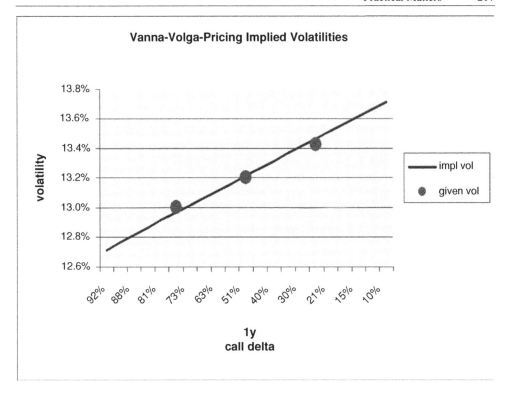

Figure 3.5   Consistency check of vanna-volga-pricing

Vanilla option smile for a one year maturity EUR/USD call, spot $= 0.9060$, $r_d = 5.07\,\%$, $r_f = 4.70\,\%$, $\sigma_0 = 13.20\,\%$, $\sigma_\Delta^+ = 13.425\,\%$, $\sigma_\Delta^- = 13.00\,\%$

3.1.5   Adjustment factor

The factor p has to be chosen in a suitable fashion. Since there is no mathematical justification or indication, there is a lot of dispute in the market about this choice. Moreover, the choices also may vary over time. An example for *one of many possible choices* of p is presented in Table 3.2.

Table 3.1   Abbreviations for first generation exotics

KO	knock-out
KI	knock-in
RKO	reverse knock-out
RKI	reverse knock-in
DKO	double knock-out
OT	one-touch
NT	no-touch
DOT	double one-touch
DNT	double no-touch

Table 3.2   Adjustment factors for the overhedge for first generation exotics

product	p
KO	no-touch probability
RKO	no-touch probability
DKO	no-touch probability
OT	0.9 * no-touch probability – 0.5 * bid-offer-spread *(TV – 33 %) / 66 %
DNT	0.5

For options with strike K, barrier B and type $\phi = 1$ for a call and $\phi = -1$ for a put, we use the following pricing rules which are based on no-arbitrage conditions.

KI is priced via $KI = \ vanilla \ - KO$.

RKI is priced via $RKI = \ vanilla \ - RKO$.

RKO is priced via

$$RKO(\phi, K, B) = KO(-\phi, K, B) - KO(-\phi, B, B) + \phi(B - K)NT(B).$$

DOT is priced via DNT.

NT is priced via OT.

3.1.6   Volatility for risk reversals, butterflies and theoretical value

To determine the volatility and the vanna and volga for the risk–reversal and butterfly the convention is the same as for the building of the smile curve, hence the 25 % delta risk–reversal retrieves the strike for 25 % delta call and put with the spot delta and premium included [left-hand-side in *Fenics*] and calculates the vanna and volga of these options using the corresponding volatilities from the smile.

The theoretical value (TV) of the exotics is calculated using the ATM–volatility retrieving it with the same convention that was used to build the smile, i.e. delta–parity with premium included [left-hand-side in *Fenics*].

3.1.7   Pricing barrier options

For regular knock-out options one can refine the method to incorporate more information about the global shape of the vega surface through time.

We chose M future points in time as $0 < a_1 \% < a_2 \% < \ldots < a_M \%$ of the time to expiration. Using the same cost of vanna and volga we calculate the overhedge for the regular knock-out with a reduced time to expiration. The factor for the cost is the no-touch probability to touch the barrier within the remaining times to expiration $1 > 1 - a_1 \% > 1 - a_2 \% > \ldots > 1 - a_M \%$ of the total time to expiration. Some desks believe that for at-the-money strikes the long time should be weighted higher and for low delta strikes the short time to maturity should be weighted higher. The weighting can be chosen (rather arbitrarily) as

$$w = \tanh[\gamma(|\delta - 50 \%| - 25 \%)] \tag{3.24}$$

with a suitable positive γ. For $M = 3$ the total overhedge is given by

$$\text{OH} = \frac{\text{OH}(1 - a_1\,\%) * w + \text{OH}(1 - a_2\,\%) + \text{OH}(1 - a_3\,\%) * (1 - w)}{3}. \qquad (3.25)$$

Which values to use for M, γ and the a_i, whether to apply a weighting and what kind varies for different trading desks.

An additional term can be used for single barrier options to account for glitches in the stop–loss of the barrier. The theoretical value of the barrier option is determined with a barrier that is moved by 4 basis points and, 50 % of that adjustment is added to the price if it is positive. If it is negative it is omitted altogether. The theoretical foundation for such a method is explained in [18].

3.1.8 Pricing double barrier options

Double barrier options behave similarly to vanilla options for a spot far away from the barrier and more like one-touch options for a spot close to the barrier. Therefore, it appears reasonable to use the traders' rule of thumb for the corresponding regular knock-out to determine the overhedge for a spot closer to the strike and for the corresponding one-touch for a spot closer to the barrier. This adjustment is the intrinsic value of the reverse knock-out times the overhedge of the corresponding one-touch. The border is the arithmetic mean between strike and the in-the-money barrier.

3.1.9 Pricing double-no-touch options

For double-no-touch options with lower barrier L and higher barrier H at spot S one can use the overhedge

$$\text{OH} = \max\{\text{Vanna-Volga-OH}; \delta(S - L) - \text{TV} - 0.5\,\%; \delta(H - S) - \text{TV} - 0.5\,\%\}, \quad (3.26)$$

where δ denotes the delta of the double-no-touch.

3.1.10 Pricing European style options

Digital options

Digital options are priced using the overhedge of the call– or put–spread with the corresponding volatilities, see Section 1.4.1.

European barrier options

European barrier options (EKO) are priced using the prices of European and digital options and the relationship

$$\text{EKO}(\phi, K, B) = \text{vanilla}(\phi, K) - \text{vanilla}(\phi, B) - \text{digital}(B)\phi(B - K). \qquad (3.27)$$

3.1.11 No-touch probability

The no-touch probability is linked to the values of no–touch options, see Equation (1.133), and similarly for no-touch probabilities in the case of two barriers. Note that the price of the

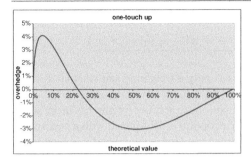
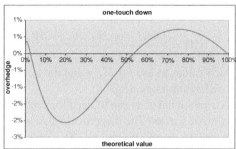

Figure 3.6 Overhedge of a one-touch in EUR-USD for both an upper touch level and a lower touch level, based on the traders' rule of thumb

one-touch is calculated using an iteration for the touch probability. This means that the price of the one-touch used to compute the no-touch probability is itself based on the the traders' rule of thumb. This is an iterative process which requires an abortion criterion. One can use a standard approach that ends either after 100 iterations or as soon as the difference of two successive iteration results is less than 10^{-6}. However, the method is so crude that it actually does not make much sense to use so much precision at just this point. So in order to speed up the computation we suggest omitting this procedure and take zero iterations, which is the TV of the no–touch.

3.1.12 The cost of trading and its implication on the market price of one-touch options

Now let us take a look at an example of the traders' rule of thumb in its simple version. We consider one-touch options, which hardly ever trade at TV. The tradable price is the sum of the TV and the overhedge. Typical examples are shown in Figure 3.6, one for an upper touch level in EUR-USD, one for a lower touch level.

Clearly there is no overhedge for one-touch options with a TV of 0 % or 100 %, but it is worth noting that low-TV one-touch options can be twice as expensive as their TV, sometimes even more. *SuperDerivatives*[1] has become one of the standard references of pricing exotic FX options up to the market. The overhedge arises from the cost of risk managing the one-touch. In the Black-Scholes model, the only source of risk is the underlying exchange rate, whereas the volatility and interest rates are assumed constant. However, volatility and rates are themselves changing, whence the trader of options is exposed to unstable vega and rho (change of the value with respect to volatility and rates). For short dated options, the interest rate risk is negligible compared to the volatility risk as shown in Figure 3.7. Hence the overhedge of a one-touch is a reflection of a trader's cost occurring due to the risk management of his vega exposure.

3.1.13 Example

We consider a one-year one-touch in USD/JPY with payoff in USD. As market parameters we assume a spot of 117.00 JPY per USD, JPY interest rate 0.10 %, USD interest rate 2.10 %,

[1] http://www.superderivatives.com.

Comparison of Vega and Rho

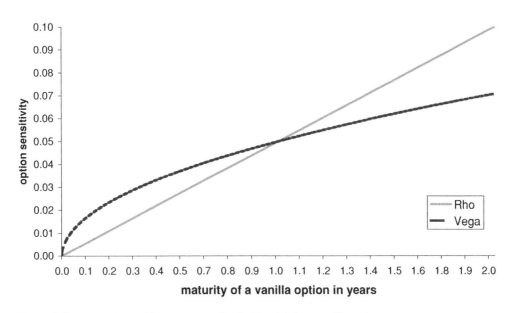

Figure 3.7 Comparison of interest rate and volatility risk for a vanilla option
The volatility risk behaves like a square root function (see Equation (1.18)), whereas the interest rate risk is close to linear (see Equation (1.21)). Therefore, short-dated FX options have higher volatility risk than interest rate risk

volatility 8.80 %, 25-delta risk reversal −0.45 %,[2] 25-delta butterfly 0.37 %.[3] The notion of risk reversals and butterflies is explained in Section 1.3.3.

The touch level is 127.00, and the TV is at 28.8 %. If we now only hedge the vega exposure, then we need to consider two main risk factors.

1. The change of vega as the spot changes, often called vanna
2. The change of vega as the volatility changes, often called volga or volgamma or vomma

To hedge this exposure we treat the two effects separately. The vanna of the one-touch is 0.16 %, the vanna of the risk reversal is 0.04 %. So we need to buy 4 (= 0.16/0.04) risk reversals, and for each of them we need to pay 0.14 % of the USD amount, which causes an overhedge of −0.6 %. The volga of the one-touch is −0.53 %, the volga of the butterfly is 0.03 %. So we need to sell 18 (= −0.53/0.03) butterflies, each of which pays us 0.23 % of the USD amount, which causes an overhedge of −4.1 %. Therefore, the overhedge is −4.7 %. However, we will get to the touch level with a risk-neutral probability of 28.8 %, in which case we would have to pay to unwind the hedge. Therefore the total overhedge is −71.2 %*4.7 % = −3.4 %. This leads to a mid market price of 25.4 %. Bid and offer could be 24.25 %–36.75 %. There are different beliefs among market participants about the unwinding cost. Other observed prices

---

[2] This means that a 25-delta USD call is 0.45 % cheaper than a 25-delta USD put in terms of implied volatility.
[3] This means that a 25-delta USD call and 25-delta USD put is on average 0.37 % more expensive than an at-the-money option in terms of volatility.

for one-touch options can be due to different existing vega profiles of the trader's portfolio, a marketing campaign, a hidden additional sales margin or even the overall condition of the trader in charge.

3.1.14 Further applications

The method illustrated above shows how important the current smile of the vanilla options market is for the pricing of simple exotics. Similar types of approaches are commonly used to price other exotic options. For long-dated options the interest rate risk will take over the lead in comparison to short dated options where the volatility risk is dominant.

3.1.15 Exercises

The following exercises are quite involved and can be research projects rather than simple tests of the material in this section.

1. Compute the vanna of a butterfly and the volga or a risk reversal and examine under what conditions they are close to zero and conversely, which parameter scenarios would cause problems in applying the traders' rule of thumb to the pricing of vanilla options. Along these lines, discuss the alternative of hedging vega, vanna and volga simply with three options, one at-the-money, one 25-delta call and one 25-delta put.
2. Implement the traders' rule of thumb for a selection of first generation exotics.
3. We have presented methods for double barrier options and the double-no-touch. Since a double-no-touch can be statically hedged with double barrier options, we can price a double-no-touch using the price of the hedging portfolio. Compare the two approaches. Which one do you think is better?
4. Double-barrier options can be replicated by a portfolio of single barrier options, as is described by Alessandro Sbuelz in [71]. This implies that one can find the tradable price of a double-barrier if we know all market prices of single barrier options. This would make the traders' rule of thumb redundant for double barrier options. Compare the method described here with the approach using [71]. Which one do you think is better?
5. Various authors have suggested methods how to statically hedge barrier options with a portfolio of vanilla options with known market prices, most prominently the work by Jan Maruhn, see [72] and [17]. Compare this approach to the traders' rule of thumb.
6. What do you think should be a consistent way to calculate Greeks in the traders' rule of thumb approach?

3.2 BID–ASK SPREADS

Bid-ask or bid-offer spreads are the price quotes for sellers and buyers of financial titles respectively. The spread indicates the sales margin a trading institution earns: the wider the spread, the higher the risk, and/or margin of the product. Wide spreads can also indicate a lack of liquidity. Different markets have different spreads. The inter bank market has the tightest spreads, because the banking community normally knows very well, how much financial products should cost. Spreads turn to be slightly wider for corporate and institutional clients and very wide for retail clients. There is no fixed rule, how bid-ask spreads should be set up.

Table 3.3   Spreads for one-touch options

EUR/USD	200
EUR/CHF	300
EUR/GBP	250
EUR/JPY	350
USD/JPY	250
GBP/USD	200

In an automated FX options trading environment it is important to set some rules how to compute spreads automatically. One starts with simple and liquid products like the vanilla and one-touch options and sets up some rules to derive spreads for other exotics from these basic spreads. For example, it can be done as follows.

3.2.1   One-touch spreads

The spreads for one-touch options are constant across time and barrier levels. Examples of one-touch spreads in basis points are exhibited in Table 3.3. Note that usually, 1 Bp = 0.01 % of the foreign currency. Especially, for one-touch spreads 1 Bp is 0.01 % of the foreign currency *or* of the domestic currency, according to the notional currency specified.

These spreads are subject to changes and have to be maintained by traders according to market conditions and the situation of the existing book of options. The spreads for one-touch options should be entered manually in the configuration area of the software and should be kept as variables. However, there may be phases of months of trading where these spreads do not have to be changed. One can also specify no-touch spreads. One must also keep in mind that the spreads can be set differently depending on the customer group.

3.2.2   Vanilla spreads

The spreads for vanilla options are constant across deltas, but vary over time and currency pair. The vanilla spreads are calculated for the maturity pillar $\{$1w, 2w, 1m, 2m, 3m, 6m, 9m, 1y, 18m, 2y$\}$ using the atm volatility and atm spread, the spot and the respective rates. A corresponding spread matrix expresses half the vanilla spread in terms of volatility for the maturity pillar. In order to calculate the vanilla spread for a maturity not corresponding to the maturity pillar, we have to interpolate linearly between the values of vanilla spread.

3.2.3   Spreads for first generation exotics

The spreads for First Generation Exotics are exhibited in Table 3.4. Vanilla spread means the equivalent vanilla spread for the same time to maturity, while the intrinsic value (IV) at the barrier for a call option is $IV = \max\left[\frac{B-K}{B}, 0\right]$ and for a put option is $IV = \max\left[\frac{K-B}{B}, 0\right]$. For a double barrier call we use the IV for the upper barrier, while for a double barrier put the IV for the lower barrier.

Regular barrier options are out-of-the-money at hitting time, whereas reverse barrier options are in-the-money at that time. Therefore, a barrier call is reverse when the barrier is larger than the strike, while a barrier put is reverse when the barrier is lower than the strike.

Table 3.4   Spreads for first generation exotics

OT/NT	OT Spread
DOT/DNT	$1.5 \cdot$ OT Spread
Regular Barrier	$1.5 \cdot$ Vanilla Spread and 7 bps $\leq$ Spread $\leq$ 11 bps
Reverse Barrier	$\max\{1.5 \cdot$ Vanilla Spread, OT Spread$\cdot$ IV Barrier $\}$
Double Barrier	$\max\{1.5 \cdot$ Vanilla Spread, OT Spread$\cdot$ IV Barrier $\}$

3.2.4   Minimal bid–ask spread

A minimum spread should be chosen to cover the cost of the ticket. We may assume this to be 400 EUR for vanilla options and 1200 EUR for exotic options. If the bid–ask spread is less than the minimal spread, then it is widened to ensure the minimum.

If the bid price is less than zero, then both bid and ask prices are adjusted to zero and the spread respectively.

3.2.5   Bid–ask prices

The bid and ask prices are calculated as a symmetric interval around the mid market price.

3.2.6   Exercises

1. Assuming a vanilla spread of 0.2 % in at-the-money volatility, and a one-touch spread as in Table 3.3, compute bid and ask prices for a 6-month reverse knock-out in EUR-GBP for various scenarios of strikes and barriers.
2. We have seen that a knock-out plus a knock-in is equivalent to a vanilla. Define how to compute bid-ask spreads for a knock-in to avoid arbitrage.
3. Table 5.1 shows how various exotics and structures can be built from basic products. Define rules for the computation of bid-ask spreads for all these products. This should simultaneously guarantee the absence of arbitrage.
4. When trading a portfolio of similar constituents like a risk reversal or a strip of vanillas a tight quote is generally attained by applying the spread only to the constituent with the highest vega and trading the others at market-mid-price. How would you justify this approach?

3.3   SETTLEMENT

Standard textbooks dealing with the valuation of options only deal with two times, one for the beginning and one for the end of the deal. In practice, the story is a bit more advanced and deals with the dates listed in Figure 3.8.

We are going to use the following notation.

T_h *horizon date*, represents the date on which the derivative is evaluated. In many cases it represents today.

T_{hs} *horizon spot date*, two business days after the horizon date.

T_e *expiry date*. For path independent options the payoff depends on the quoted spot or forward on this date.

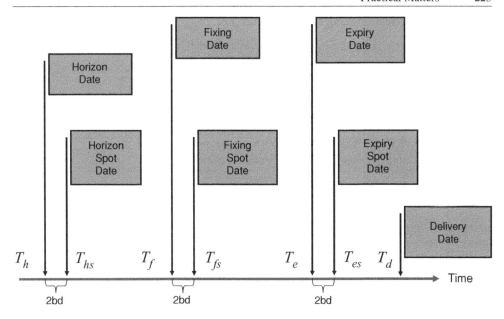

Figure 3.8 Relevant dates for trading options. The spot dates are usually two business days (2bd) after the horizon, fixing or expiry date

T_{es} *expiry spot date*, two business days after the expiry date.

T_d *delivery date*, represents the date on which cash-flows implied by the option payoff will be settled.

For corridors and faders an additional fixing date is introduced.

T_f *fixing date*, on this date it is decided if the underlying is inside a specified range.

T_{fs} *fixing spot date*, two business days after the fixing date.

In general we have

$$T_h \overset{2bd}{\leq} T_{hs} \leq T_f \overset{2bd}{\leq} T_{fs} \leq T_e \overset{2bd}{\leq} T_{es} \leq T_d. \tag{3.28}$$

The payoff of FX options depends either on the quoted (2bd) spot S_{T_e} at the expiry date T_e, or the forward F_{T_{es},T_d} from that date to a specific delivery date T_d. In many cases the delivery date T_d corresponds to the expiry spot date T_{es}, where we have $F_{T_{es},T_d} = S_{T_e}$.

The constant volatility used in the model (see Equation (1.1)) corresponds to the time period $T_h = 0$ to $T_e = T$.

All interest rates r_d and r_f are assumed to correspond to the respective period in their context, for example: the term $e^{-r_d(T_d-T_{hs})}$ represents the factor used for discounting the payoff, using the domestic (forward) interest rate from the spot date T_{hs} to the delivery date T_d.

Remark 3.3.1 *In rare cases the delivery date can be* before *the expiry spot date, that is* $T_{es} > T_d$. *However, it can never be before the expiry date* T_e.

3.3.1   The Black-Scholes model for the actual spot

The standard approach is to assume a Black-Scholes model as in Equation (1.1)

$$\frac{d\hat{S}_t}{\hat{S}_t} = (r_d - r_f)\,dt + \sigma\,dW_t \tag{3.29}$$

for the underlying, where $\hat{S}_0$ means the price of the underlying of today.

Instead of modeling this zero-day spot $\hat{S}$ we need to model the *2bd spot* S, which is usually quoted in FX markets.

Assuming no arbitrage opportunities leads to the relationships

$$\hat{S}_t = S_t e^{-(r_d - r_f)(T_{hs} - t)}, \tag{3.30}$$
$$\hat{S}_{T_e} = S_{T_e} e^{-(r_d - r_f)(T_{es} - T_e)}.$$

Assuming the exponents in (3.30) are deterministic, the quoted spot at some future time T_e satisfies

$$S_{T_e} = S_t \exp\left[(r_d - r_f)(T_{es} - T_{hs}) - \frac{1}{2}\sigma^2(T_e - t) + \sigma W_{T_e - t}\right], \tag{3.31}$$

which follows directly from (3.30) and (1.2).

3.3.2   Cash settlement

In case of *cash settlement* the seller of the option pays a cash amount depending on the payoff formula and the quoted spot S_{T_e} to the holder. By default, the cash arrives on the holder's account on the expiry spot date T_{es}, but in general on the delivery date T_d. For example, in case of a vanilla quoted in FOR-DOM, the DOM cash amount

$$\left(\phi\left(S_{T_e} - K\right)\right)^+ \tag{3.32}$$

is paid, where as usual $\phi = \pm 1$ for calls and puts respectively. The option will be exercised if $\phi S_{T_e} > \phi K$.

The value of the vanilla option at time $t = T_h$ is then given by

$$v_t^C = I\!E\left[e^{-r_d(T_d - T_{hs})}\left(\phi\left(S_{T_e} - K\right)\right)^+ \Big| S_t\right]$$
$$= I\!E\left[e^{-r_d(T_d - T_{es})} e^{-r_d(T_{es} - T_{hs})}\left(\phi\left(S_{T_e} - K\right)\right)^+ \Big| S_t\right]$$
$$= e^{-r_d(T_d - T_{es})} v_t^{PV}, \tag{3.33}$$

where v_t^{PV} denotes the value of a vanilla in the Black-Scholes model published in text books, compare Equation (1.7). In particular, we have

$$d_\pm^C = \frac{\ln\frac{S_t}{K} + (r_d - r_f)(T_{es} - T_{hs}) \pm \frac{1}{2}\sigma^2(T_e - t)}{\sigma\sqrt{T_e - t}}, \tag{3.34}$$

and

$$v_t^C = \phi e^{-r_d(T_d - T_{hs})}\left(e^{-(r_d - r_f)(T_{es} - T_{hs})} S_t \mathcal{N}(\phi d_+^C) - K\mathcal{N}(\phi d_-^C)\right)$$
$$= \phi e^{-r_d(T_d - T_{es})}\left(e^{-r_f(T_{es} - T_{hs})} S_t \mathcal{N}(\phi d_+^C) - e^{-r_d(T_{es} - T_{hs})} K\mathcal{N}(\phi d_-^C)\right). \tag{3.35}$$

For other options this works similarly.

3.3.3 Delivery settlement

In case of *delivery settlement* the cash amounts of the two involved currencies FOR and DOM are physically exchanged on the delivery date T_d. Therefore the intrinsic value is given by

$$\left(\phi\left(F_{T_{es},T_d} - K\right)\right)^+ \tag{3.36}$$

$$= \left(\phi\left(S_{T_e}e^{(r_d-r_f)\cdot(T_d-T_{es})} - K\right)\right)^+, \tag{3.37}$$

where the second equality is meant to hold at expiry date T_e, when the rates are known. The option will be exercised if

$$\phi F_{T_{es},T_d} > \phi K, \tag{3.38}$$

which is equivalent to

$$\phi S_{T_e} > \phi K e^{-(r_d-r_f)(T_d-T_{es})}. \tag{3.39}$$

The value of a vanilla option at time $t = T_h$ is then given by

$$v_t^D = \mathbb{E}\left[e^{-r_d(T_d-T_{hs})}\left(\phi\left(F_{T_{es},T_d} - K\right)\right)^+ \Big| S_t\right] \tag{3.40}$$

$$= \phi e^{-r_d(T_d-T_{hs})}\left(e^{-(r_d-r_f)(T_d-T_{hs})}S_t\mathcal{N}(\phi d_+^D) - K\mathcal{N}(\phi d_-^D)\right)$$

$$= \phi e^{-r_f(T_d-T_{hs})}S_t\mathcal{N}(\phi d_+^D) - \phi e^{-r_d(T_d-T_{hs})}K\mathcal{N}(\phi d_-^D),$$

$$d_\pm^D = \frac{\ln\frac{S_t}{K} + (r_d - r_f)(T_d - T_{hs}) \pm \frac{1}{2}\sigma^2(T_e - t)}{\sigma\sqrt{T_e - t}}.$$

3.3.4 Options with deferred delivery

Options in FX OTC markets are typically delivery-settled, as corporates do have cash to exchange. Options are bought for speculation as well, but this is not the default case.

In the case of an option with delivery settlement it becomes often important to the corporate client to have a settlement date significantly after the expiration date of the contract. The default is two business days, but corporates sometimes wish to delay the settlement up to one year or even further. The reason is that a decision of a cash-flow in the future is often taken much earlier than the actual payment, just like in the case of *compound* or *instalment* options. This means that the option under consideration is not an option on the FX *spot*, but rather an option on the FX *forward*, which is sometimes called *compound on forward*.

To be concrete, let us derive the formula for the deferred delivery settled vanilla call. We let the current time be T_h, the expiration time be T_e and the delivery time be T_d. The buyer of a deferred-delivery call with strike K has the right to enter into a forward contract with strike K at time T_e, which is then delivered at time T_d. In a Black-Scholes model framework with constant interest rates, the forward price at time t maturing at time T_d is given by the random variable

$$f_t(T_d) = S_t e^{(r_d-r_f)(T_d-t)}, \tag{3.41}$$

in particular, at time zero,

$$f_0(T_d) = S_0 e^{(r_d-r_f)T_d}, \tag{3.42}$$

is the current forward price. We let T_d be fixed and view t as the variable. Using Itô's formula,[4]

---

[4] $df(S_t) = f'(S_t)\,dS_t + \frac{1}{2}f''(S_t)(dS_t)^2.$

we see that the forward price satisfies

$$df_t(T_d) = \sigma f_t(T_d)dW_t, \tag{3.43}$$

whence it is a martingale. In a risk-neutral valuation approach, the value of a call on $f_t(T_d)$ is given by

$$v(0) = e^{-r_d T_d} I\!E[(f_t(T_d) - K)^+]. \tag{3.44}$$

In order to compute this, we notice that we can use the existing Black-Scholes Equation (1.7) for the special case $r_d = r_f$ (due to Equation (3.43)) and $S_0 = f_0(T_d)$, which is

$$v(0) = e^{-r_d T_d} [f_0(T_d)\mathcal{N}(d_+) - K\mathcal{N}(d_-)]$$
$$= S_0 e^{-r_f T_d}\mathcal{N}(d_+) - Ke^{-r_d T_d}\mathcal{N}(d_-), \tag{3.45}$$

$$d_\pm = \frac{\ln \frac{f_0(T_d)}{K} \pm \frac{1}{2}\sigma^2 T_e}{\sigma\sqrt{T_e}}$$

$$= \frac{\ln \frac{S_0}{K} + (r_d - r_f)T_d \pm \frac{1}{2}\sigma^2 T_e}{\sigma\sqrt{T_e}}. \tag{3.46}$$

This calculation works similarly for all European style options, even with barriers or as instalment options. The basic procedure is to reuse existing formulae for options of the spot for a zero drift $r_d = r_f$ and replace the spot variable by the forward.

3.3.5 Exercises

1. Discuss the implications of a deferred delivery on the value of a vanilla call with a fixed strike. What happens to the value if the forward curve is downward sloping? What are the main risk factors involved if the deferral period is very long? How about correlation between the spot and the interest rates?
2. Derive and implement a formula for barrier options with deferred delivery.
3. Derive and implement a formula for compound options with deferred delivery.
4. We have seen in Equation (3.35) how to find the value of a EUR call USD put that is *cash-settled* in USD. USD is the domestic currency in this case and Equation (3.35) just tells us that a USD cash-settled vanilla is worth a vanilla discounted by the domestic rate for the time left between expiry and delivery. What if the same option is cash-settled in EUR, the foreign currency? What if the currency in which the option is cash-settled is decided only at expiration? Does it matter whether the holder or the seller of the option is entitled to take this decision?
5. In principle it makes a difference to the value whether an option is cash-settled or delivery-settled. This difference is already present for standard delivery periods of two business days. Compare the impact on the value of the various versions of settlement in a scenario analysis.
6. Derive and implement a formula for a double-no-touch with deferred delivery. In this case deferred delivery means a deferred cash payment in the specified currency.

3.4 ON THE COST OF DELAYED FIXING ANNOUNCEMENTS

The results of this section are based on Becker and Wystup, see [73].

Markets' vanilla and barrier options are traded frequently. The market standard is a cutoff time of 10:00 a.m. in New York for the strike of vanillas and a knock-out event based on a continuously observed barrier in the inter bank market. However, many clients, particularly from Italy, prefer the cutoff and knock-out event to be based on the fixing published by the European Central Bank on the Reuters Page ECB37. These barrier options are called discretely monitored barrier options. While these options can be priced in several models by various techniques, the ECB source of the fixing causes two problems. First of all, it is not tradable, and secondly it is published with a delay of about 10–20 minutes. We examine here the effect of these problems on the hedge of those options and consequently suggest a cost based on the additional uncertainty encountered.

3.4.1   The currency fixing of the European Central Bank

The European Central Bank (ECB) sets currency fixings every working day in Frankfurt at 2:15 p.m. Frankfurt time. The actual procedure of this fixing is done by observing the spot rates in the inter bank market, in which the ECB also participates. Traders of the ECB in various locations get together to decide on how to set the fixing. The quantity quoted is not a bid price or an offer price the ECB or anybody else necessarily trades at, but is rather used for statistical and official means, for instance tax computation or economic research. An example of the ECB37 Reuters screen is presented in Figure 3.9.

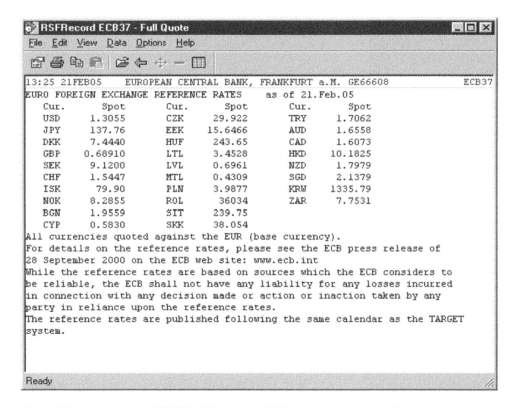

Figure 3.9   Reuters screen ECB37 of 21 February 2005 showing the fixings of all currencies against EUR

Corporate treasurers often prefer an independent source for currency exchange rates that provides a reference rate for their underlying under consideration. This way they are not bound to their own bank that might move the quoted cut-off rate in favor of their own position. The key features to stress are the following.

1. The ECB fixing is *not* tradable.
2. The ECB fixing is published with a delay of 10–20 minutes.

In this section we analyze the impact on the value for the short position of a discretely monitored reverse knock-out, as the problems mentioned above impose additional uncertainty when it comes to determining a proper hedge. Most of the hedging error is expected in the case of jumps in the payoff of the option, which is why we restrict ourselves to the liquidly traded up-and-out call option. The currency-pair under consideration is EUR-USD.

3.4.2 Model and payoff

To model the exchange rate we choose a geometric Brownian motion,

$$dS_t = S_t[(r_d - r_f)dt + \sigma dW_t], \tag{3.47}$$

under the risk-neutral measure. As usual, r_d denotes the domestic interest rate, r_f the foreign interest rate, σ the volatility. These parameters are assumed to be constant. For the contract parameters maturity in years T, strike K and knock-out barrier B, fixing schedule $0 = t_0 < t_1 < t_2 \ldots, t_n = T$, the payoffs for the vanilla and for a discretely monitored up-and-out barrier option under consideration are

$$V(F_T, T) = (\phi(F_T - K))^+, \tag{3.48}$$

$$V(F, T) = (\phi(F_T - K))^+ \, \mathbb{1}_{\{\max(F_{t_0}, \ldots, F_{t_n}) < B\}}, \tag{3.49}$$

where F_t denotes the fixing of the underlying exchange rate at time t, $\mathbb{1}$ the indicator function and ϕ a put-call indicator taking the value $+1$ for a call and -1 for a put. Of course, F_t is usually close to S_t, the spot at time t, but it may differ as well. We start with payoffs

$$V(S_T, T) = (\phi(S_T - K))^+, \tag{3.50}$$

$$V(S, T) = (\phi(S_T - K))^+ \, \mathbb{1}_{\{\max(S_{t_0}, \ldots, S_{t_n}) < B\}}, \tag{3.51}$$

whose values are explicitly known in the Black-Scholes model. Recall that in this model, the values are called *theoretical value (TV)*.

3.4.3 Analysis procedure

1. We simulate the spot process with a Monte Carlo simulation using an Euler-discretization. Furthermore, we use a *Mersenne Twister* pseudo random number generator by Takuji Nishimura and Makoto Matsumoto [74] and a library to compute the inverse of the normal cumulative distribution function written by Barry W. Brown et al. [27].
2. We model the ECB-fixing F_t by

$$F_t = S_t + \varphi, \quad \varphi \in \mathcal{N}(\mu, \sigma), \tag{3.52}$$

where μ and σ are estimated from historic data. Note that F_t denotes the ECB-fixing at time t, which is nonetheless only announced 10–20 minutes later. We denote this time delay by

Table 3.5 Estimated values for mean and standard-deviations of the quantity Spot-ECB-fixing from historic time series

Currency pair	Expected value	Standard deviation	Time horizon
EUR/USD	−3.125E-6	0.0001264	23.6–08.8.04

The time series were provided by Commerzbank AG.

$\Delta_{ECB}(T)$. This means that we model the error, i.e. the difference of fixing and traded spot, as a normally distributed random variable. The estimated values for the mean and the standard-deviation of the quantity Spot − ECB Fixing from historic time series are listed in Table 3.5.

3. We evaluate the payoffs for barrier options for each path and run the simulations with the appropriate delta hedge quantities to hold. Then we compute for each path the error encountered due to the fixing being different from the spot, and then average over all paths.

4. We do this for various currency pairs, parameter scenarios, varying the rates, volatilities, maturities, barriers and strikes. We expect a significant impact particularly for reverse knock-out barrier options due to the jump of the payoff and hence the large delta hedge quantity.

3.4.4   Error estimation

Note that since we expect the resulting errors to be fairly small, we introduce a bid/offer-spread δ for the spot, which is of the size of 2 basis points in the inter bank market. We consider the following options in detail.

European style up-and-out call

To determine the possible hedging error we propose the following to be appropriate. Note that the error is measured for a nominal of 1 unit of the underlying. We consider three cases.

1. Let $S_T \leq K$. In this case, the seller who is short the option decides not to hedge as the option is probably out of the money, i.e. delta $= 0$. If the option turns out to be in the money, i.e. $F_T > K$, the holder of the short position faces a P&L of $K - (S(T + \Delta_{ECB}(T)) + \delta)$ (units of the base currency).
2. Let $S_T > K$ and $S_T < B$. Hence, one assumes that the option is in the money and delta is 1. If now $F_T \leq K$ or $F_T \geq B$, there is a P&L of $S(T + \Delta_{ECB}(T)) - (S(T) + \delta)$.
3. Let $S_T \geq B$ and $F_T < B$. Here we have a P&L of $K - (S(T + \Delta_{ECB}(T)) + \delta)$. Note that other than in the first case, this P&L is of order $K - B$ due to the jump in the payoff.

Discretely monitored up-and-out call

We consider a time to maturity of one year with 250 knock-out-events, i.e., the possible knock out occurs every working day at 2:15 p.m. Frankfurt time, when the ECB fixes the reference rate of the underlying currency pair. We propose the following error determination to be appropriate. First of all, we adopt the procedure above for the maturity time. In addition, we consider every knock-out-event and examine the following cases.

1. Let $S_t < B$ and $F_t \geq B$ as in Figure 3.10.
   At time t the trader holds $\Delta(S_t)$ shares of stock in the delta hedge. He does not unwind the hedge at time t, as the spot is below the barrier. Only after the fixing announcement, it

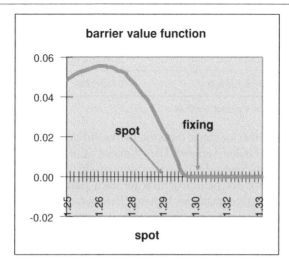

Figure 3.10   Value of a discretely monitored call. The traded spot is below the announced fixing

turns out that the hedge needs to be unwound, so he does this with delay and encounters a profit and loss (P&L) of

$$\Delta(S_t) \cdot (S_{t+\Delta_{ECB}(T)} - S_t), \tag{3.53}$$

where $\Delta(S_t)$ denotes the theoretical delta of the option under consideration, if the spot is at S_t. To see this, it is important to note, that the theoretical delta is negative if the underlying is near the barrier B. In this way, the seller of the option has been short the underlying at time t and must buy it in $t + \Delta_{ECB}(T)$ minutes to close out the hedge. Therefore, he makes profit if the underlying is cheaper in $t + \Delta_{ECB}(T)$, which is reflected in our formula. We shall elaborate later how to compute the theoretical delta, but we would like to point out that whenever we need a spot price at time t to calculate such a delta or to compute the value of a hedge, we refer to S as the tradable instrument instead of the contractually specified underlying F in order to account for the ECB fixing being non-tradable.

2. Let $S_t \geq B$ and $F_t < B$ as in Figure 3.11.

   Here the seller of the option closed out the hedge at time t, though she shouldn't have done so, and in $t + \Delta_{ECB}(T)$ she needs to build a new hedge. Note again that the theoretical delta is negative. This means that at time t the seller bought the underlying with the according theoretical delta-quantity, and in $t + \Delta_{ECB}(T)$ she goes short the underlying with the appropriate new delta-quantity. The P&L is calculated via

$$P\&L = \Delta(S_t) \cdot (S_t + \delta) - \Delta(S_{t+\Delta_{ECB}(T)}) \cdot S_{t+\Delta_{ECB}(T)}. \tag{3.54}$$

The other cases do not lead to errors due to an unexpected fixing announcement. Of course, delta hedging an option in the Black-Scholes model can lead to errors, because of hedge adjustments at discrete times and because of model risk in general, see, e.g. [75].

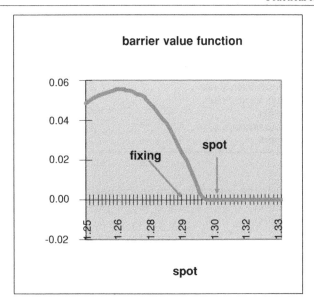

Figure 3.11   Value of a discretely monitored call. The traded spot is above the announced fixing

Calculating the delta-hedge quantity

The valuation of continuously monitored barrier options has been treated, e.g., in [76]. In order to compute the theoretical delta for the discretely monitored up-and-out call, for which no closed-form solution is known, in acceptable time and precision, we refer to an approximation proposed by Per Hörfelt in [77], which works in the following way. Assume the value of the spot is observed at times iT/n, $i = 0, \ldots, n$, and the payoff of the discretely monitored up-and-out call is given by Equation (3.51). We define the value and abbreviations

$$\theta_{\pm} \triangleq \frac{r_d - r_f \pm \sigma^2/2}{\sigma} \sqrt{T}, \tag{3.55}$$

$$c \triangleq \frac{\ln(K/S_0)}{\sigma\sqrt{T}}, \tag{3.56}$$

$$d \triangleq \frac{\ln(B/S_0)}{\sigma\sqrt{T}}, \tag{3.57}$$

$$\beta \triangleq -\zeta(1/2)/\sqrt{(2\pi)} \approx 0.5826, \tag{3.58}$$

where ζ denotes the Riemann zeta function. We define the function

$$F_+(a, b; \theta) \triangleq \mathcal{N}(a - \theta) - e^{2b\theta}\mathcal{N}(a - 2b - \theta) \tag{3.59}$$

and obtain for the value of the discretely monitored up-and-out call

$$V(S_0, 0) \approx S_0 e^{-r_f T} \left[F_+(d, d + \beta/\sqrt{n}; \theta_+) - F_+(c, d + \beta/\sqrt{n}; \theta_+) \right] \tag{3.60}$$
$$- K e^{-r_d T} \left[F_+(d, d + \beta/\sqrt{n}; \theta_-) - F_+(c, d + \beta/\sqrt{n}; \theta_-) \right].$$

Table 3.6   EUR-USD testing parameters

Spot	1.2100
Strike	1.1800
Trading days	250
Domestic interest rate	2.17 % (USD)
Foreign interest rate	2.27 % (EUR)
Volatility	10.4 %
Time to maturity	1 year
Notional	1,000,000 EUR

Using this approximation for the value, we take a finite difference approach for the computation of the theoretical delta,

$$\Delta = V_S(S, t) \approx \frac{V(S + \epsilon, t) - V(S - \epsilon, t)}{2\epsilon}. \tag{3.61}$$

3.4.5   Analysis of EUR-USD

Considering the simulations for a maturity T of one year, huge hedging errors can obviously only occur near the barrier. The influence of the strike is comparatively small, as we discussed in the error determination procedure above. In this way we choose the values listed in Table 3.6 to remain constant and only to vary the barrier.

Using Monte Carlo simulations with one million paths we show the *average* of the profit and loss with 99.9 % confidence bands and how the probability of a mishedge depends on the position of the barrier in Figure 3.12. It appears that the additional costs for the short position are negligible. We also learn that the mishedge is larger for a barrier in a typically traded distance from the spot, i.e. not too close and not too far.

In Figure 3.13 we plot the barrier against the ratio Hedging Error/TV of the up-and-out call and the ECB-fixing as underlying. This relationship is an important message for the risk-averse trader. For a one-year reverse knock-out call we see an average relative hedge error below 5 % of TV if the barrier is at least 4 big figures away from the spot. Traders usually ask for a risk premium of 10 basis points.

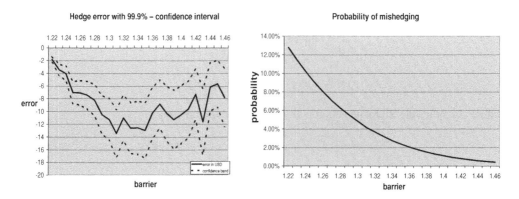

Figure 3.12   Additional average hedge costs and probability of a mishedge for the short position of a discretely monitored up-and-out call in EUR-USD

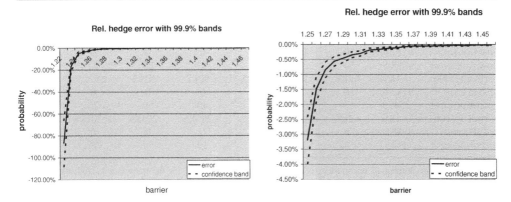

Figure 3.13   Hedging Error/TV for a discretely monitored up-and-out call in EUR-USD

Finally, we would like to point out that the *average* loss is not the full story as an average is very sensitive to outliers. Therefore, we present in Figure 3.14 the distribution of the maximal profits and losses, both in absolute as well as in relative numbers. The actual numbers are presented in Table 3.7. We have found that other parameter scenarios behave similarly. The crucial quantity is the intrinsic value at the knock-out barrier. The higher this value, the more dangerous the trade. In particular we do not exhibit the results for the vanilla as there is hardly anything to see. Varying rates and volatilities do not yield any noticeably different results.

As the analysis of the other currency pairs is of similar nature, we refer to the details in [73] and continue with the conclusion.

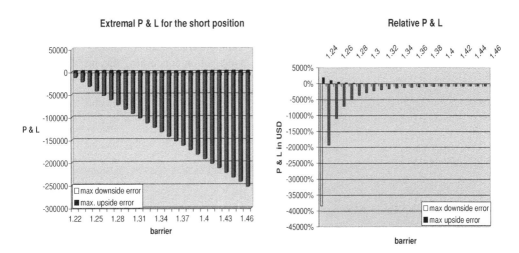

Figure 3.14   Absolute and relative maximum profit and loss distribution for a discretely monitored up-and-out call in EUR-USD

The upside error is the unexpected gain a trader will face. The downside error is his unexpected loss. On average the loss seems small, but the maximum loss can be extremely high. The effect is particularly dramatic for knock-out calls with a large intrinsic value at the barrier as shown in the left hand side. The right hand side shows the maximum gain and loss relative to the TV. Of course, the further the barrier is away from the spot, the smaller the chance of a hedging error occurring.

Table 3.7   EUR-USD distribution of absolute errors in USD

barrier 1.2500	<1k$	<2k$	<3k$	<39k$	<40k$	<41k$	<42k$	<43k$
upside error	951744	20	1	0	0	0	0	0
downside error	48008	54	2	5	59	85	21	1
barrier 1.3000	<1k$	<2k$	<3k$	<89k$	<90k$	<91k$	<92k$	
upside error	974340	20	1	0	0	0	0	
downside error	25475	43	0	2	40	59	20	
barrier 1.4100	<1k$	<2k$	<3k$	<199k$	<200k$	<201k$	<202k$	<203k$
upside error	994854	78	0	0	0	0	0	0
downside error	4825	194	3	1	19	17	8	1

The figures are the number of occurrences out of 1 million. For instance, for the barrier at 1.2500, there are 54 occurrences out of 1 million, where the trader faces a loss between 1000 and 2000 USD.

3.4.6   Conclusion

We have seen that even though a trader can be in a time interval where he does not know what delta hedge he should hold for an option due to the delay of the fixing announcement, the loss encountered is with probability 99.9 % within less than 5 % of the TV for usual choices of barriers and strikes and the liquid currency pairs, in which complex barrier options such as a discretely monitored up-and-out call are traded. However, the maximum loss quantity in case of a hedging error can be rather substantial. So in order to take this into account, it appears generally sufficient to charge a maximum of 10 % of the TV to cover the potential loss with probability 99.9 %. This work shows that the extra premium of 10 basis points per unit of the notional of the underlying, which traders argue is needed when the underlying is the ECB-fixing instead of the spot, is justified and well in line with our results. However, charging 10 basis points extra may be easy to implement, but is not really precise as we have seen, since the error depends heavily on the distance of the barrier from the spot.

Of course the level of complexity of the model can be elaborated further arbitrarily, but using a geometric Brownian motion and a Monte Carlo simulation appears sufficient. The relative errors are small enough not to pursue any further investigation concerning this problem.

4
Hedge Accounting under IAS 39

In this chapter we will provide an overview about Hedge Accounting under IAS 39 and then test the effectiveness of a Forward Plus in a case study. This is a joint project with Sebastian Krug based on [78].

4.1 INTRODUCTION

Globalization in business is progressing. Companies do not only deliver their products or services to many other parts of the world but investors also act on a global basis. For investors, it is absolutely necessary to obtain information about the companies they wish to invest in. The financial reporting of the target firms assists in reaching an investment decision. But national rules for the preparation of financial statements differ and investors would need to gain knowledge about the accounting guidelines of all countries they want to invest in. Obviously this is not possible. Accounting rules that are applicable for all companies, no matter what their home country is, would simplify the whole issue. International Accounting Standards aim to give exactly this sort of financial transparency to the users of the financial reporting.

IAS 39 provides accounting rules for financial instruments. This standard has to be applied for all companies reporting under IAS from 1 January 2005 onwards.

One section of IAS 39 deals with derivatives. Derivatives are used mainly for two purposes: speculation and hedging. In some national accounting rules, derivatives are not included in the balance sheet but only in the footnotes. This issue is critical, because derivatives may influence the income of the company considerably. The most famous example of this is the collapse of the Barings Bank. Nick Leeson speculated illegally with derivatives. He caused a loss of £619 million which caused the bankruptcy in February 1995 of Barings Bank. IAS 39 provides rules on how to include derivatives in the balance sheet and the profit and loss of the companies.

The objective of this standard is to establish principles for recognizing and measuring financial assets, financial liabilities and some contracts to buy or sell non-financial items. Requirements for presenting and disclosing information about financial instruments are set out in IAS 32 Financial Instruments: Disclosure and Presentation. (IAS 39.1)

Hedging risks is without any doubt economically meaningful. For accounting purposes, the treatment of a hedge relationship is not easy. IAS 39 provides rules for the treatment of hedge relationships. This is the most discussed accounting standard ever. The tight prerequisites that have to be fulfilled cumulatively often make companies face serious accounting problems.

Therefore, the topic of this chapter is to explain the most critical point in the context of hedge accounting under IAS 39 – the test for effectiveness.

Sections 4.2 and 4.3 provide relevant basic information about financial instruments, which assets and liabilities belong to this category and under which conditions they are recognized in the balance sheet and how they are initially and subsequently measured.

In Section 4.4 general topics of hedge accounting are discussed.

Section 4.5 deals with possible methods for testing hedge effectiveness.

Table 4.1   List of Abbreviations for Hedge Accounting relevant Material

AG	Application Guidance
BA	Basis Adjustment
BC	Basis for Conclusions
Δ	delta
ΔBC	change in fair value of the Basis Contract
ΔHI	change in fair value of the Hedging Instrument
DO	Dissenting Opinions
Ed.	Editor
HFV	Hedge Fair Value
HAC	Hedge Amortized Costs
IAS	International Accounting Standard
IE	Illustrative Example
IFRS	International Financial Accounting Standard
IG	Guidance on Implementing
IN	Introduction
OTC	Over The Counter
p.a.	per year
R^2	coefficient of determination
(S)FAS	(Statements of) Financial Accounting Standards
US-GAAP	United States Generally Accepted Accounting Principles
VRM	Variance Reduction Measure

A case study for effectiveness using a forecast transaction, which is hedged with a shark forward, is performed in Section 4.6. This is a very common situation, because most companies do business abroad and face foreign exchange risks. Within this framework, the question whether a structured foreign exchange derivative might satisfy the strict criteria of hedge accounting under IAS 39 will be answered.

4.2   FINANCIAL INSTRUMENTS

4.2.1   Overview

Hedge Accounting can be applied only for financial assets and financial liabilities. For this reason the following section gives the basic facts about financial instruments. In Section 4.3 the accounting rules, recognition and measurement of financial instruments will be explained. The appropriate standards which deal with these topics are IAS 32 and IAS 39.

IAS 32 deals with the presentation and disclosure of financial instruments. It does not give information about the recognition or measurement of financial instruments. IAS 39 gives the recognition and measurement rules for most of the financial instruments. Exceptions that are not covered by IAS 39 are named in IAS 39.2–7.

The aim of IAS 32 is to state the significance of financial instruments to the entity's financial position and financial performance to the users of the financial reporting, see IAS 32.1. Principally the application of IAS 39 is not limited to certain types of entities, see [79], p. 226. All entities no matter which size, industry or legal structure are within the scope of this standard. There are exceptions for the usage of IAS 39 to some financial items. These exceptions are listed in IAS 39.2 and IAS 32.4:

- *Interests in subsidiaries, associates and joint ventures that are accounted for under IAS 27, IAS 28 and IAS 31.* "Investments in subsidiaries, associates and joint ventures, that are consolidated, equity accounted or proportionately consolidated under IAS 27, IAS 28 and IAS 31 respectively [...] are excluded from the scope of IAS 32 and IAS 39." Nevertheless IAS 39 applies to derivatives on an interest in a subsidiary, associate or joint venture if the derivative does not meet the definition of an entity's equity instrument. IAS 39 also applies to derivatives that are held by the reporting entity on interests in subsidiaries, associates and joint ventures that are not owned by the reporting entity but by another party, see [80], p. 204.
- *Rights and obligation under leases that are recognized and measured under IAS 17 are not regulated by IAS 39.* However, lease receivables recognized by the lessor as well as finance lease payables recognized by the lessee are subject to the derecognition under IAS 39. For the lease receivables the impairment under IAS 39 also has to be applied, see [80], p. 203. Derivatives that are embedded in leases are also subject to an application of IAS 39 (see IAS 39.2(b)(iii)). Financial leases are defined as financial instruments and fall therewith into the scope of IAS 32 (IAS 32.AG 9).
- *Employers' rights and obligations under employee benefit plans that apply to IAS 19.*
- *Rights and obligations arising under insurance contracts.* However, insurance contracts do not meet the regulation of IAS 32 and IAS 39, it does not mean that insurance companies do not have to apply those standards. These companies have to apply the standards to all their financial instruments that do not meet the definition of an insurance contract as it is described in IFRS 4. Derivatives that are embedded into an insurance contract that is not an insurance contract itself fall again into the scope of IAS 39 (IAS 32.4 (d)).
- *Financial instruments issued by the entity including options and warrants that meet the definition of an equity instrument in IAS 32.* However, the holder of these financial instruments has to apply IAS 39, if the instruments do not fulfill the classification as interest in a subsidiary, associate or joint venture.
- *Financial guarantees including letters of credit and other credit default contracts that provide insurance against the default of a specified debitor.* However, financial guarantees that compensate in reaction to changes in a specified interest rate, commodity price, credit rating, foreign exchange rate or other underlying variables fall into the scope of IAS 39 because they have the characteristics of a derivative, see IAS 39.3 or [81], p.164.
- *Acquirers' contracts for contingent consideration in a business combination.*
- *Contracts that require a payment based on climatic, geological or other physical variables (IAS 39.AG 1).* As those contracts have the characteristics of an insurance contract where the transfer of the financial risk is not automatically included, they are not in the scope of IAS 39.
- *Loan commitments that cannot be settled net in cash or another financial instrument.* These loan commitments are not within the scope of IAS 39 as a special rule in IAS 39.4.

In IAS 39.5 and IAS 32.8 it is mentioned that contracts to buy or sell a non-financial item that can be settled net in cash or another financial instrument, or by exchanging financial instruments shall be treated under the standards. But this is only the case if the contract does not have the purpose to cover the receipt or delivery of a non-financial item with the entity's expected purchase, sale or usage requirements, so called *regular way contracts*. Further details and requirements to this issue are mentioned in IAS 32.9 and IAS 39.6 as well as in IAS 39.BC 24.

4.2.2 General definition

A financial instrument is according to IAS 32.11: "[. . .] any contract that gives rise to a financial asset of one entity and a financial liability or equity instrument of another entity." (IAS 32.11) Within this context an entity can be an individual, a partnership as well as an incorporated body, a trust or a government agency (IAS 32.14).

Such a contract is an agreement between two or more parties that has clear economic consequences which can usually be enforceable by law (IAS 32.13).

The term financial instrument means primary instruments and derivative instruments. A financial instrument has to contain a contractual obligation. Other obligations that are not due to a contract can therefore not be a financial instrument, e.g. a tax asset or tax liability.

Physical assets, leased assets and intangible assets are not financial assets, because the control over one of these assets creates the possibility to generate cash out of this asset, but it does not give the enforceable right to receive a benefit in terms of cash or another financial asset.

Prepaid expenses are also not financial assets (IAS 32.AG 10, IAS 32.AG 11 and IAS 32.AG 12). The Guidance on Implementing IAS 39 also clarifies that physical precious metals do not belong to the financial instruments, because there is no enforceable right to receive cash or another financial asset in exchange for that metal (IAS 39.IG B1).

4.2.3 Financial assets

A financial asset is defined as any asset that is

- Cash;
- An equity instrument of another entity;
- A contractual right such as
  1. to receive cash or another financial asset from another entity; or
  2. to exchange financial assets or financial liabilities with another entity under conditions that are potentially favorable to the entity; or
- a contract that will or may be settled in the entity's own equity instruments and is
  1. a non-derivative for which the entity is or may be obliged to receive a variable number of the entity's own equity instruments; or
  2. a derivative that will or may be settled other than by the exchange of a fixed number of the entity's own equity instruments (IAS 32.11).

Common examples are trade accounts receivable, notes receivable, loans receivable, and bonds receivable. These examples are mentioned in the *Application Guidance* of IAS 32 (see IAS 32.AG 4).

4.2.4 Financial liabilities

A financial liability is any liability that is

- A contractual obligation:
  1. to deliver cash or another financial asset to another entity; or
  2. to exchange financial assets of financial liabilities with another entity under conditions that are potentially unfavorable to the entity; or

- a contract that will or may be settled in the entity's own equity instrument and is:
    1. a non-derivative for which the entity is or may be obliged to deliver a variable number of the entity's own equity instruments; or
    2. a derivative that will or may be settled other than by exchange of a fixed amount of cash or another financial asset for a fixed number of the entity's own equity instruments (IAS 32.11).

Common examples are trade accounts payable, notes payable, loans payable, and bonds payable. These examples are mentioned in the Application Guidance of IAS 32 (IAS 32.AG 4).

Liabilities like deferred revenue in advance, prepaid expenses, and most warranty obligations are not financial liabilities (see [80], p. 205). This is due to the fact that the outflow of economic benefits associated with these items is more the delivery of goods and services rather than a contractual obligation to pay cash or another financial asset (IAS 32.AG 11).

4.2.5   Offsetting of financial assets and financial liabilities

As stated in IAS 1.33, it is generally not allowed to set off assets and liabilities. Assets and liabilities should be presented separately from each other, unless another International Accounting Standard requires an offsetting (IAS 1.33). This requirement is given in IAS 32:

A financial asset and a financial liability shall be offset and the net amount presented in the balance sheet when, and only when, an entity:

(a) currently has a legally enforceable right to set off the recognized amounts;
(b) intends either to settle on a net basis, or to realize the asset and settle the liability simultaneously.
    (IAS 32.42)

This regulation does not restrict the number of financial instruments to offset. It speaks of *two or more separate financial instruments* (IAS 32.43). Further the right to offset has to be a legally enforceable right. The pure intention of one or both parties is not sufficient for offsetting. In the other case of a legally enforceable right to settle on a net basis but without the intention of doing so, the entity has to present the instruments separately and has to disclose the effect on the entity's credit risk exposure in its notes (IAS 32.46 and IAS 32.47).

IAS 32.49 gives conditions when offsetting is inappropriate and therefore forbidden:

- several different financial instruments are used to imitate the features of a single financial instrument (synthetic instrument);
- financial assets and financial liabilities have the same primary risk exposure, but involve different counterparties;
- (financial) assets are pledged as collateral;
- financial assets are set aside for the purpose of discharging an obligation (for example a sinking fund arrangement);
- obligations are expected to be recovered from a third party under an insurance contract (IAS 32.49).

If settlement is done simultaneously by a clearing house, the cash flows may be seen as a single net amount and are therefore allowed to be set off (IAS 32.48). A master netting agreement does not provide the right to offset unless the general criteria mentioned under IAS 32.42 are met (IAS 32.50).

4.2.6   Equity instruments

An equity instrument is any contract that evidences a residual interest in the assets of an entity after deducting all of its liabilities. (IAS 32.11)

Equity instruments include shares, warrants and other items that do not bear a contractual obligation for the issuing entity to deliver cash or another financial asset or to exchange financial assets under potentially unfavorable conditions. These items are excluded from the scope of IAS 39 for the issuing entity. This is not the case for the holder of such items, and IAS 39 applies (see IAS 39.2 (e)).

A financial instrument that was issued by an entity is only allowed to classify this instrument as an equity instrument rather than a financial liability if, and only if, the following two conditions are simultaneously met.

(a) The instrument includes no contractual obligation:
    (a) to deliver cash or another financial asset to another entity; or
    (b) to exchange financial assets or financial liabilities with another entity under conditions that are potentially unfavorable to the issuer.
(b) If the instrument will or may be settled in the issuer's own equity instruments, it is:
    (a) a non-derivative that includes no contractual obligation for the issuer to deliver a variable number of its own equity instruments; or
    (b) a derivative that will be settled only by the issuer exchanging a fixed amount of cash or another financial asset for a fixed number of its own equity instruments. (IAS 32.16)

The issuer of a financial instrument has to take care to classify the instrument in accordance with the substance of the contractual arrangement and the appropriate definitions when distinguishing between financial asset, financial liability or equity instrument for first time recognition ([81], p. 170 and IAS 32.15). It is important to note that the substance of the financial instrument rather than its legal form governs its classification on the entity's balance sheet. Substance and legal form are not always consistent (IAS 32.18). Sometimes a financial instrument has the legal character of an equity instrument and the economic character of a financial liability or vice versa. An example for this inconsistency of legal form and substance is a preferred share, see IAS 32.18 (a) for further explanation.

In the case that an entity is able to settle its contractual obligation by delivering its own equity shares, it depends on the arrangement of the delivery of the shares whether this contract has to be recognized as equity or liability. If the payment is a fixed amount of equity shares the contractual obligation is treated as equity. In the case that the amount of equity shares that are required to fulfill the obligation vary with the changes in the fair value of the shares, the contractual obligation is treated as a liability (IAS 32.21).

4.2.7   Compound financial instruments

The issuer of a non-derivative financial instrument has to evaluate whether it contains an equity instrument component and a financial liability component. If this is the case the components shall be classified separately as financial liability, financial asset or equity instrument in accordance with IAS 32.15 (see IAS 323.28).

An example for such an instrument is a convertible bond, that entitles the holder to receive a fixed amount of equity instruments of the issuer in exchange for the bond. In this case the first component is a financial liability to pay cash or other financial assets to the holder of the instrument. The second component is a call option on equity shares of the issuing entity (see

IAS 32.29). The classification into the two components also has to be maintained in case the probability of an exercise of this call option has changed. The contractual obligation to fulfill the payments remains until it is sunk through conversion, maturity or some other transaction (IAS 32.30).

In order to allocate the initial carrying amount of the instrument to the components, the issuer has to determine first the value of the liability and then in a second step subtract this value from the overall value of the combined instrument. The residual is the initial carrying amount of the equity instrument component (IAS 32.31). No gain or loss should arise from the process of splitting the initial value of the combined instrument into its components.

4.2.8 Derivatives

In general a derivative is an instrument whose value is determined by changes of the underlying asset or variable. Derivatives are mainly used to give protection against changes in commodity prices, interest rates or exchange rates. They are of great importance to modern risk management. Derivatives can also be used for speculation purposes. The key characteristic of a derivative is the leverage effect it can offer which can result in extraordinary gain or losses combined with the characteristic of only an small initial investment.

The recognition of derivatives on the balance sheet has been a major issue for the standard setters. Specifically they should be displayed in a way that gives a fair view of the economic situation. Historically, derivatives are often treated as off-balance sheet transactions in many national accounting standards. The fact that derivatives often have an initial value of near to zero as well as the fact that many accounting policies display unrealized losses but not unrealized gains do not simplify the situation.

Derivative instruments can occur as conditional or absolute derivatives. Futures, forwards, and swaps are examples for absolute derivative instruments, because the obligations out of the derivative have to be fulfilled by both parties at the negotiated conditions. Options are conditional derivative instruments. The option holder has the right but not the obligation to demand for fulfillment of the contract (see [82], p. 42).

Definition 4.2.1   *In IAS 39.9 a derivative is defined as following:*

A derivative is a financial instrument or other contract within the scope of this standard [. . .] with all three of the following characteristics:

(a) *Its value changes in response to the change in a specified interest rate, financial instrument price, commodity price, foreign exchange rate, index of prices or rates, credit rating or credit index, or other variable, provided in the case of a non-financial variable that the variable is not specific to a party to the contract (sometimes called the* underlying*);*

(b) *It requires no initial net investment or an initial net investment that is smaller than would be required for other types of contracts that would be expected to have a similar response to changes in market factors; and*

(c) *It is settled at a future date.*

Typical examples of derivative contracts are presented in Figure 4.1.

For the definition of a derivative there is no difference whether the contract is settled on gross basis or on net basis. For the example of an interest rate swap this means that there is no

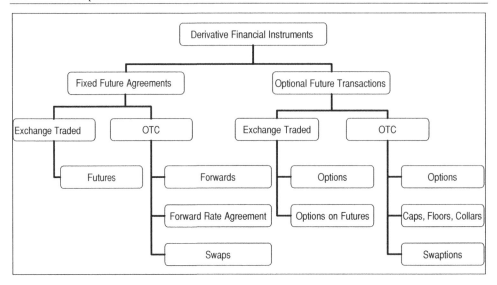

Figure 4.1   Typical derivative contracts, see e.g. [83], p. 137

difference between whether the parties pay the interest payment to each other or if settlement takes place on the net basis (IAS 39.IG B3).

For clarification it is important to mention that the term *underlying* as mentioned in Definition 4.2.1 of a derivative in the respective standard does not refer to an asset or liability in the balance sheet. It is a variable that creates changes in the value of a contract (see [80], p. 205).

Another aspect that is mentioned in IAS 39.9 is the 'smaller' initial net investment. There is no further quantification of the term 'smaller'. It can be interpreted as an amount relative to the investment that would be required to do a direct investment in a primary instrument that has the same or similar characteristics as the derivative (see [80], p. 205). The margin requirements that have to be met for derivatives like futures do not count to the net initial investment amount as they have the characteristic of a collateral (IAS 39.IG B10). If the net initial investment for a derivative is almost equal to the direct investment, it could be problematic to meet the requirements of a derivative according to IAS 39. IAS 39.IG B9 states an example for not meeting the requirement. KPMG also state their interpretation of this specific topic in [80], p. 208:

In the case that a call option may have a very low exercise price so that the option premium paid is nearly equivalent to the amount that would be paid to acquire the underlying asset outright instead of the option, the derivative does not meet the requirements according IAS 39 to have a small net initial investment. Such options should be treated as a purchase of the underlying asset and not as derivative.

Another example for the possible failure of the "smaller net investment test" is stated in the *Guidance on Implementing of IAS 39*. This example refers to a partial prepayment within a swap contract (see IAS 39.IG B4 and B5).

Concerning the third requirement of IAS 39.9 'settled at a future date' the settlement can take different forms. Even if an option is likely not to be exercised, e.g. because it is deep out of the money, it meets the requirement of future settlement. Expiration at maturity is also a form of settlement.

An exemption of the derivative treatment can occur if there is a commitment to buy or sell non-financial items. Usually these contracts are treated as derivatives unless the contract was entered into for the entity's purchase, sale or usage requirements. This was already discussed earlier in Section 4.2 referring to IAS 39.5.

Regular way contracts are contracts that will be settled within a time frame that is regulated or established by market conventions. These contracts are not treated as derivatives in the time between trade day and settlement date. In the case that there is a delay in the settlement procedure IAS/IFRS do not give any guidance whether to treat the contract as derivative or not.

KPMG states in [80], p. 207 that

In our view, a delay would not preclude the use of the regular way exemption if the contract requires delivery within the time frame established by the convention in the market, and the delay is caused by a factor that is outside the control of the entity.

Following this argument, the treatment as derivative has to be applied between trade day and settlement date if the delay is either caused by the entity or if the time period between trade and settlement negotiated between the entities deviates form the normal settlement period.

4.2.9   Embedded derivatives

An embedded derivative is a part of a hybrid instrument which also contains a non-derivative host contract. Typical for these hybrid instruments is the fact that a part of the cash flows of the combined instrument vary in a way that is similar to a stand-alone derivative (IAS 39.10). A derivative that is attached to another financial instrument and that is independent on a contractual basis or has another counterpart, is not an embedded derivative, but an independent derivative, see [81], p. 177. In order to ensure that the principle of measuring derivatives at fair value is not avoided, the embedded derivative has to be detached from the host contract and has to be treated on a stand-alone basis if certain conditions are fulfilled.

An embedded derivative shall be separated from the host contract and accounted for as a derivative under this standard if, and only if

(a) the economic characteristic and risks of the embedded derivative are not closely related to the host contract;
(b) a separate instrument with the same terms as the embedded derivative would meet the definition of a derivative; and
(c) the hybrid instrument is not measured at fair value with changes in fair value reported in income. (IAS 39.11)

If an entity is required to separate an embedded derivative from its host contract, but is not able to measure the fair value of the derivative separately at acquisition or at subsequent reporting dates, it shall treat the whole hybrid instrument as a financial asset or financial liability that is held for trading, see IAS 39.12. The classification of financial instruments will follow in Section 4.2.10.

In the case that the entity is unable to determine reliably the carrying amount of the embedded derivative on the basis of its term of conditions, then the carrying amount of the embedded derivative is the difference between the carrying amounts of the combined instrument and the host contract (IAS 39.13).

An embedded derivative that does not have the character of an option and that has to be detached from the host contract is to detach in a way that the fair value of the derivative is zero at first recognition. If the embedded derivative has *ceteris paribus* the character of an option, the fair value of the host instrument is the residual amount after separating the embedded derivative (IAS 39.AG 28). In the case that a hybrid instrument contains more than one embedded derivatives they shall be treated like a single compound derivative. This is not the case if the derivatives are independent, refer to different risk exposure and can be separated from each other. In that case the derivatives shall be recognized not only separated from the host instrument but also separated from each other (IAS 39.AG 29). In the *Application Guidance of IAS 39* several examples are given for not closely related economic characteristics and risks and closely related respectively.

Those not closely related are:

- an investment in a note or bond that is convertible into shares of the issuer, or another entity;
- an option to extend the remaining term of a debt instrument at an interest rate that is unequal to the market rate at the time of extension;
- a call, put or prepayment option in a debt instrument that is exercisable at an amount other than the amortized cost of the instrument;
- equity- or commodity-indexed principal or interest payments;
- an instrument that the holder has an option to put back to the issuer for an amount based on an equity or commodity price or index;
- an equity instrument that the issuer has an option to call;
- an embedded credit derivative that allows the holder to transfer the credit risk of an asset to another party, see [80], p. 233 and IAS 39.AG 30;
- an embedded foreign currency derivative is not closely related if:
  1. the currency is the functional currency of one of the parties to the contract;
  2. the currency is routinely used in international commerce for that good or service; or
  3. the currency is commonly used in business transactions in the economic environment in which the transaction takes place (IAS 39.AG 33(d)).

Those closely related are:

- an interest rate derivative that changes the interest payable on a debt instrument, if it could not increase the holder's initial return by more than twice what it would have been without the derivative and does not result in a rate of return that is double or more the market return for an instrument with the same terms as the host contract;
- a fixed rate note with an embedded fixed or floating swap;
- an option to extend the maturity of debt at market rates at the time of extension;
- a call, put or prepayment option at amortized cost in a debt instrument;
- an embedded cap (floor) on an interest rate or the purchase price of an asset, provided that the cap (floor) is out of the money when it is issued and not leveraged;
- a prepayment option in an interest-only or principal-only strip, as long as the original financial instrument did not contain any embedded derivative and the strip does not contain any terms not originally present in the host contract;
- certain inflation-linked lease payments;
- a foreign currency derivative that provides interest or principal payments denominated in a foreign currency;

- a foreign currency derivative that provides finance lease payments in a foreign currency provided that the embedded foreign currency derivative is not leveraged and does not contain an option feature;
- a natural gas supply contract that is indexed to another energy source, if there is no spot price for natural gas in the environment in which the entity operates, see [80], p. 233 and IAS 39.AG 33.

Entities may have a problem to identify embedded derivatives, especially those that are not included in financial instruments. The requirements related to the recognition of embedded derivatives will cause problems for entities adopting IFRS for the first time. Often the entity will not be aware of the identification of embedded derivatives and will not have knowledge of complex hybrid instruments (see [84]).

4.2.10 Classification of financial instruments

All financial instruments are classified into one of the following categories on initial recognition. IAS 39 distinguishes between four categories of financial assets and two categories for financial liabilities.

Financial Assets:

- Financial assets or financial liabilities at fair value through profit and loss
- Held-to-maturity investments
- Loans and receivables
- Available-for-sale assets

Financial Liabilities:

- Financial assets or financial liabilities at fair value through profit and loss
- Other liabilities

Financial assets or liabilities at fair value through profit and loss

The category 'financial asset or financial liability at fair value through profit and loss' contains two sub-categories. The first one is any financial asset or financial liability that was designated to this category when it was initially recognized. The second sub-category includes all financial instruments that are held for trading purposes.

A financial asset or financial liability is classified as held-for-trading if it is:

1. 'acquired or incurred principally for the purpose of selling or repurchasing it in near term;
2. part of a portfolio of identified financial instruments that are managed together and for which there is evidence of a recent actual pattern of short-term profit-taking; or
3. a derivative (except for a derivative that is designated and effective hedging instrument).' (IAS 39.9)

The term trading is explained in the *Application Guidance of IAS 39*:

It is generally reflected by active and frequent buying and selling under the objective to generate profits from short-term price fluctuations or the dealer's margin (see IAS 39.AG 14). In other words, the turnover and the average holding period of financial assets in a portfolio indicates the trading intention (see [80], p. 209).

According to KPMG an investment in an actively managed fund that is managed by an independent third party would not fall into the classification of held-for trading automatically, although the fund is traded actively (see [80], p. 209).

Financial instruments that are held for a longer time period, but that are part of a portfolio, which has the intention to realize short-term profits, are still held-for-trading instruments (see IAS 39.IG B11).

IAS 39.AG 15 specifies further financial liabilities that have to be classified as held-for-trading:

- 'derivative liabilities that are not accounted for as hedging instruments;
- obligations to deliver financial assets borrowed by a short seller [. . .];
- financial liabilities that are incurred with the intention to repurchase them in the near term [. . .]; and
- financial liabilities that are part of a portfolio of identified financial instruments that are managed together and for which there is evidence of a recent pattern of short-term profit-taking.'

A liability should not be considered as held-for-trading due to the fact that it funds trading activities.

For the sub-category of financial assets or financial liabilities that were designated to the category 'financial asset or financial liability at fair value through profit and loss', there are almost no restrictions concerning the designation of different financial assets or financial liabilities to that category. One constraint is that this designation is solely possible at first recognition of an asset or liability. The designation is irrevocable afterwards, i.e. the asset or liability cannot be re-designated to another category during its life. Another limitation regarding the assets and liabilities that are able to be designated to the mentioned category exists for equity instruments that do not have a quoted market price in an active market, and whose fair value cannot be measured reliably (see IAS 39.9, IAS 39.46(c), IAS 39.AG 80 and IAS 39.AG 81). This regulation gives the companies the opportunity to measure most financial assets and financial liabilities at its fair value and to recognize profits and losses directly.

Held-to-maturity

Investments that qualify for the category 'held-to-maturity' have to be non-derivative financial assets with fixed or determinable payments and fixed maturity. Further, the entity must have the positive intention and ability to hold the assets until maturity (see IAS 39.9).

As demanded by IAS 39.AG 25 the entity has to assess its intention and ability not only at first recognition but at each balance sheet date (see IAS 39.AG 25). An asset with variable interest payments like a floating rate note may also qualify for this classification (IAS 39.AG 17). Consistent with the criteria mentioned above, the following instruments cannot be qualified as held-to-maturity.

- Equity securities;
- An investment that the investor intends to hold for an undefined period or that does not have fixed or determinable payments;

- An investment that the investor stands ready to sell in response to changes in market conditions;
- A perpetual debt instrument that will pay interest in perpetuity;
- An instrument that is redeemable at the option of the issuer at an amount significantly below amortized cost;
- An instrument that is putable by the holder, because the put feature is inconsistent with the intention to hold the investment to maturity;
- An asset that an entity does not have adequate resources to hold to maturity;
- An asset that is subject to legal constraints that enable the entity to hold the asset to maturity. ([80], p. 210 based on IAS 39.9 and IAS 39.AG 17–25)

Further assets that are allocated to any other classification cannot be classified as 'held-to-maturity' at the same time (IAS 39.9).

Consequently the following instruments may meet the definition.

- A fixed maturity debt security that bears interest at a fixed or variable rate;
- A fixed maturity debt security even if there is a high risk of non-payment, provided that the security's contractual payments are fixed or determinable and the other criteria for classification are met;
- A perpetual debt instrument that will pay interest for a specified period only;
- A debt instrument that is callable by the issuer, as long as substantially all of the carrying amount would be recovered if the call were exercised;
- Shares with a fixed maturity (or callable by the issuer) that are classified as liabilities by the issuer. ([80], p. 210)

The entity is not allowed to classify any financial asset to the 'held-to-maturity' group if it has reclassified or sold more than an insignificant amount of 'held-to-maturity' investments before maturity. This restriction applies for the current financial year as well as the two preceding years. This means if the entity has reclassified more than an insignificant amount in the year zero, it is allowed to classify assets again in the year three to the 'held-to-maturity' group. But there are exceptions that do not fall into this 'tainting rule', as follows.

- When the asset was sufficiently close to maturity or the asset's call date that changes in market interest rates no longer had a significant effect on the asset's value;
- Sales after collecting substantially all of the principal;
- Sales due to an isolated non-recurring event that is beyond the entity's control and which it could not reasonably have anticipated ([80], p. 211).

If a sale or reclassification result in tainting, all assets that are currently in the 'held-to-maturity' group must be reclassified as available for sale until the classification is possible again within the third year after tainting (see IAS 39.52).

IAS 39 does not give further definition of what is 'more than insignificant'. An appropriate range could be 10–15 % of all 'held-to-maturity' assets, see [85], p. 411.

Loans and receivables

Loans and receivables are non-derivative financial assets with fixed or determinable payments that are not quoted in an active market (IAS 39.9).

Excluded from this category are

- 'Loans and receivables' that are quoted in an active market;
- 'Loans and receivables' that are actively and frequently purchased or originated and sold with the intention of generating profit from short-term fluctuation in price or dealer's margin;
- 'Loans and receivables' for which the entity may not recover substantially all its initial investment for reasons other than credit deterioration;
- 'Loans and receivables' that are designated as 'fair value through profit and loss' or 'available-for-sale'. ([80], p. 212)

Common examples for 'loans and receivables' are trade receivables, loan assets, deposits held in banks and non-listed debt instruments (IAS 39.AG 26).

Available-for-sale

This category includes all financial assets that are not assigned to any of the previous mentioned categories. Financial assets that the entity intends to hold to maturity or a loan or a receivable are also allowed to be classified in this category on initial recognition ([80], p. 212).

Other liabilities

All liabilities that are not 'held-for-trading' nor categorized 'at fair value through profit and loss' fall into the category 'other liabilities or non-trading liabilities'.

4.3   EVALUATION OF FINANCIAL INSTRUMENTS

In this section we deal with the question how financial assets and financial liabilities are recognized. Further, if recognition has taken place, we will illustrate which value has to be applied on the balance sheet at initial recognition and for the subsequent balance sheet dates.

4.3.1   Initial recognition

An entity shall recognize a financial asset or financial liability on its balance sheet when, and only when the entity becomes a party to the contractual provisions of the instrument. (IAS 39.14)

The connection between recognition and the contractual rights or obligations has the effect that all rights or obligations arising from derivatives have to be recognized on the balance sheet. An exception from this rule are derivatives that prevent a transfer of financial assets from being accounted for as a sale (IAS 39.AG 34).

As the transfer does not qualify for derecognition for the transferring party, the other party is not allowed to recognize the financial item (IAS 39.AG 50).

The transfer of cash from one party to another party as collateral for another transaction between these parties leads to a derecognition of the transferring party and a recognition of the receiving party of the collateral as asset (IAS 39.IG D1).

A non-derivative financial instrument that meets the definition of a 'regular way purchase or sale' shall be recognized and derecognized either on the trade day or on the settlement date (see IAS 39.38). Trade day specifies the day on which an entity commits itself to buy or sell an asset. Settlement day is the date the asset is delivered to or by an entity (see IAS 39.AG 53, IAS 39.AG 55–56).

The chosen method has to be applied consistently to all assets and liabilities that belong to this category. It is important to note that for this purpose the sub-categories 'held-for-trading' and assets or liabilities designated 'at fair value through profit and loss' form a separate category (IAS 39.AG 53).

A contractual right or obligation that permits net settlement of a change in the value of the contract does not belong to the 'regular way contracts'. Such contracts are accounted for as a derivative in the time period between trade day and settlement day (IAS 39.AG 54).

IAS 39 distinguishes further between unconditional rights and obligations and firm commitments that are conditional on other obligations. Unconditional receivables and payables are recognized as an asset or a liability directly at the time an entity becomes party to a contract. In the case of a firm commitment to purchase or sell goods for instance, these goods are not recognized until at least one of the parties has performed its part of the agreement, i.e. one party has paid for the goods or the other has shipped or delivered (IAS 39.AG 35 (a) and (b)).

As mentioned in the beginning of this section, derivatives are recognized at the moment an entity becomes a party to a contract. This means for derivatives with option character that they are recognized with their value. However, forward contracts are often negotiated in a way, that the net fair value of the rights and obligations of this contract is zero. If the net fair value is unequal to zero the forward contract is recognized as asset or liability. Consequently, as the value of the underlying may change during the time of the forward contract the contract may be recognized as asset at some point in its life and as liability at another point in its life, see IAS 39.AG 35 (c) and (d) and IAS 39.AG 66.

Planned future transactions, independent of the likelihood to take place are not recognized as an asset or a liability since there is no actual right or obligation (IAS 39.AG 35 (e)).

4.3.2   Initial measurement

At initial recognition of a financial asset or financial liability an entity shall measure it at fair value. Additionally, if the financial asset or liability is not at fair value through profit or loss, transaction cost that are directly attributable to the transaction shall be added to the fair value for financial assets or subtracted from the fair value for financial liabilities (IAS 39.43). Transaction costs within the framework of IAS 39 include incremental costs directly attributable to acquiring or issuing a financial instrument such as fees and commissions paid to agents, advisers, brokers or dealers, levies by regulatory agencies and securities exchanges as well as transfer taxes and duties. Not included in the transaction costs are debt premiums or discounts, financing costs or internal administrative or holding costs (IAS 39.AG 13).

For the financial instruments that are measured at fair value through profit and loss and that do not belong to the category of 'held-for-trading', transaction costs are shown directly in that reporting period (IAS 39.IG E1.1).

Transaction costs that might arise at disposal of financial assets or repayment of financial liabilities are subject for consideration neither at initial measurement nor at subsequent measurement (IAS 39.48).

The fair value is generally the transaction price that corresponds to the given or received item. For a financial asset or financial liability this is mostly a quoted price in an active market. If part of the consideration given or received is for something other than the financial instrument, the fair value of the financial instrument has to be estimated using valuation techniques (see IAS 39.AG 64). If the entity has immediate access to different markets it has to invoke the most advantageous quoted price (IAS 39.AG 71). IAS 39.AG 72 extends the specification of appropriate prices to bid prices for long positions and to ask prices for short positions. If the market is not active for the entity, it has to use a valuation technique to determine the fair value. This could include recent arm's length transactions as well as discounted cash flow analysis or option pricing models. The valuation technique has to incorporate all factors market participants would consider for pricing and should be consistent with generally accepted pricing methodologies for pricing financial instruments (IAS 39.AG 74–75).

Generally, it is not appropriate to recognize any gain or loss on the initial recognition of a financial instrument since the best evidence of the fair value is presumed to be the transaction price.

For equity instruments that do not have a quoted market price and for which other reasonable estimations for the fair value cannot be applied to get a reasonable fair value, the equity instrument is measured at cost less impairment. Similar procedures are used for the measurement of derivative financial liabilities that can only be settled by physical delivery of such unquoted equity instruments (see IAS 39.46, IAS 39.AG 80).

4.3.3   Subsequent measurement

For subsequent measurement IAS 39 proposes a so called 'mixed model' approach, where depending on the classification into a category the method of subsequent measurement varies. For hedged items there are special regulations which will be examined later. As financial assets and financial liabilities are treated differently under IAS 39, their subsequent measurements will be discussed separately in the following.

Subsequent measurement of financial assets

For subsequent measurement of financial assets, these items are classified according to the categories defined in IAS 39.9. Particularly, these are

- Financial assets at fair value through profit and loss;
- Held-to-maturity investments;
- Loans and receivables; and
- Available-for-sale financial assets (IAS 39.45).

Financial assets that are measured at fair value through profit and loss are measured subsequently at fair value (IAS 39.46). As the name of the category leads to suppose, all changes in the fair value, i.e. the realized as well as the unrealized, are recognized in the income statement at once (IAS 39.55 (a)). This category is composed of assets 'held-for trading', derivative assets and those assets that were designated to this category at initial recognition.

Subsequent to initial measurement 'held-to-maturity' investments are measured at amortized cost using the effective interest method. The carrying amount reported as amortized cost is the initially measured amount at initial recognition minus principal repayments, cumulative amortization and any reduction for impairment. The effective interest rate is the rate that allocates the interest income over the relevant period so that it exactly discounts the estimated future cash payments through the expected life of the financial instrument (IAS 39.9).

Table 4.2   Subsequent measurement of financial assets

Financial Assets	Measurement	Change in Carrying Amount	Impairment test
At Fair Value through Profit & Loss	Fair Value	Income Statement	No
Loans & Receivables	Amortized Costs	Income Statement	Yes
Held-to-Maturity Investments	Amortized Costs	Income Statement	Yes
Available-for-Sale Assets	Fair Value	Equity	Yes

Gains and losses of 'held-to maturity' investments are recognized in profit or loss when the item is derecognized or impaired and through the amortization process.

'Loans and receivables' are treated the same way as the 'held-to-maturity' investments at amortized cost using the effective interest method (IAS 39.46).

'Available-for-sale' assets are measured at fair value. Differently to the 'at fair value through profit or loss' category, gains and losses arising of remeasurements are shown directly in equity. This is not the case for impairment losses and foreign exchange gains or losses. At derecognition the cumulative gain or loss that was previously recognized in equity shall then be recognized in profit or loss (IAS 39.55 (b)).

Investments in equity instruments that do not have a quoted price in an active market and whose value cannot be measured reliably, shall be measured at cost. The same measurement rule applies for derivatives that are linked to the mentioned equity instruments and must be settled by delivery of the same (IAS 39.46).

For further clarification the subsequent measurement of financial assets are summarized in Table 4.2.

Another important aspect is the treatment of value changes resulting from reclassification of financial assets.

Transfers to or from the fair value through profit or loss category from or to any other category are prohibited. (see [80], p. 216)

In the case of a tainting of the 'held-to-maturity' portfolio, all items of this class have to be reclassified to 'available-to-sale'. Adjustments arising from remeasurement from amortized cost to fair value have to be recognized in equity at the date of transfer. The category of equity is the same as that used for revaluations of 'available-for-sale' items (see IAS 39.51 and IAS 39.55(b)).

A transfer from the category 'available-for-sale' to 'held-to-maturity' is possible in the case that a previously tainting period is over or if there is a change in the intention or ability to hold the financial asset to maturity. A reclassification of measurement at fair value to cost is only permitted in the case that the fair value is no longer being able to be determined reliably. The fair value that was measured directly prior to the transfer becomes the new 'cost' in the new category. The difference between the new 'cost' and the maturity amount is amortized for instruments that are carried at amortized cost. Therefore, the effective interest method has to be applied. Cumulative gains or losses that were recognized previously in equity, are transferred to income divided over the period to maturity of the asset (see [80], p. 216).

Impairment of financial assets

If there is an objective that the carrying amount of a financial asset exceeds its recoverable amount, the asset is impaired and an impairment loss has to be recognized. The objective evidence of an impairment has to be the result of an event that occurred after the asset's initial recognition and has to have an impact on the asset's estimated future cash flows. Losses that are expected as a result of future events are not recognized. At each balance sheet date it is necessary to assess whether there is objective evidence that any financial asset not measured at fair value through profit or loss is impaired or uncollectible (see IAS 39.58 and IAS 39.59).

Evidence that a financial asset may be impaired include

- Significant financial difficulty of the issuer;
- Payment defaults;
- Renegotiation of the terms of an asset due to financial difficulty of the borrower;
- Significant restructuring due to financial difficulty or expected bankruptcy;
- Disappearance of an active market for an asset due to financial difficulties; or
- Observable data indicating that there is a measurable decrease in the estimated future cash flows from a group of financial assets since their initial recognition, although the decrease cannot yet be identified with the individual asset in the group. ([80], p. 222)

It is important to note that a recognition of an impairment loss is not restricted to situations that are considered to be permanent.

For a debt security impairment takes place if there is an indication that the originally anticipated cash flows from the instrument are not recoverable. Therefore a change in the market interest rate that would result in a change of the fair value of the instrument is not an indication for impairment as long as the cash flows of the instrument are recoverable ([80], p. 222). For investments in equity instruments a significant or prolonged decline in the fair value below its cost is objective evidence of impairment (IAS 39.61). As IAS 39 does not give detailed guidance of the terms 'significant' and 'prolonged', one can believe that a decline in excess of 20 % below cost should be regarded as significant and a time period of three quarters of a year should be regarded as prolonged ([80], p. 223).

If there is not sufficient data available in order to measure the appropriate impairment loss reliably, the entity should use its past experience to estimate the amount (IAS 39.62).

For financial assets carried at amortized cost, that are 'loans and receivables' and 'held-to-maturity' investment, the impairment loss is recognized in the income statement. The impairment loss is the difference between the carrying amount and the recoverable amount. The recoverable amount is calculated by discounting the estimated future cash flows at the original effective interest rate. The carrying amount can be reduced either directly or through an allowance account (IAS 39.63). A reversal of an impairment loss for assets that are carried at amortized cost is recognized in the income statement with a corresponding increase in the carrying amount either directly or by the allowance account. The reversal is limited to the amount that does not state more than what the assets amortized cost would have been in the absence of an impairment (IAS 39.65).

For financial assets that are measured at cost the impairment loss is calculated as the difference between the carrying amount and the present value of estimated future cash flows discounted at the current market rate for similar financial assets. A reversal of impairment is not allowed (IAS 39.66).

For 'available-for-sale' investments changes in fair value are recognized directly in equity. If there is objective evidence for an impairment, the cumulative loss that had been recognized directly in equity shall be removed from equity and recognized in profit or loss. The impairment amount is the difference between acquisition cost and the current fair value less any impairment loss that was recognized in profit or loss previously. Impairment losses of investments in equity instruments shall not be reversed through profit or loss but is a revaluation and is recognized again directly in equity ([80], p. 225).

For investments in debt instruments, the reversal of impairment is recognized in profit or loss if there is evidence that the increase is attributable to an event that occurred after the impairment loss was recognized (IAS 39.67–70).

Subsequent measurement of financial liabilities

All financial liabilities shall be measured subsequently at amortized cost using the efficient interest method. Gains and losses are recognized in profit or loss via the amortization process. Excluded from the amortized cost measurement are those financial liabilities that are measured at fair value through profit and loss. These items including derivatives that are liabilities, are measured at fair value. Realized and unrealized gains and losses are recognized in income in the period they take place. Another exception are financial liabilities that arise when a transfer of a financial asset does not qualify for derecognition and that are accounted for using the continuing involvement approach (see IAS 39.47).

4.3.4 Derecognition

To achieve derecognition of a financial asset either the contractual rights to the cash flows from the financial asset expire or the entity transfers the financial asset and certain criteria must be met with respect to the transfer (IAS 39.17). In that context, a transfer is characterized as the transfer of the contractual rights to receive the cash flows out of the financial asset or retaining the contractual rights to receive the cash flows but assumes a contractual obligation to pay to other recipients (IAS 39.18). The latter named sort of transfer is also called a *pass-through arrangement*. It has to fulfill certain criteria in order to meet the character of a transfer in the sense of IAS 39.17, namely:

- There is no obligation to pay amounts to the transferee unless the entity collects equivalent amounts from the original asset;
- The entity is prohibited from selling or pledging the original asset under the term of the pass-through arrangement; and
- The entity is obliged to remit all cash flows it collects without material delay, see [80], p. 227 based on IAS 39.19.

The next appropriate step after ensuring that a transfer has taken place is to examine whether the transfer qualifies to meet the criteria for derecognition:

- If an entity transfers substantially all risks and rewards, the financial asset is derecognized. If substantially all of the asset's risks and rewards are retained, the asset is not derecognized.
- If some, but not substantially all of the asset's risks and rewards are transferred and the control of the asset is transferred as well, the asset is derecognized.

- If some, but not substantially all of the asset's risks and rewards are transferred and the control of the asset is not transferred, the asset is not derecognized. The entity continues to recognize the transferred asset to the extent of its continuing involvement in the asset (IAS 39.20).

The term 'substantially' is not explained in a quantitative way in IAS 39. Another question to be answered is whether the entity has control over the asset. Having control is described as the transferee having the practical ability to sell the asset unilaterally without the need to impose additional restrictions on the transfer (IAS 39.23). That means that if the transferee (that is the party that has received the asset by transfer) has the ability to sell the asset it has the control and, therefore, the control is not retained by the transferring entity. As a consequence, the transferring entity has to derecognize the asset if substantially all the risks and rewards of the asset were transferred and the entity does not have the control anymore.

If an entity transfers an asset entirely in a way that qualifies for derecognition and retains the right to service the financial asset for a fee, it shall recognize the servicing contract either as servicing asset for the case that the received fee is expected to compensate for the servicing or as servicing liability in the case the fee is not expected to compensate for the servicing (IAS 39.24).

On derecognition of a financial asset the difference of the carrying amount and the sum of the consideration received and any cumulative gains or losses that had been recognized directly in equity shall be recognized in profit or loss (IAS 39.26).

If only parts of a larger asset are transferred, the derecognition rules according to IAS 39.27 have to be applied. In this case the carrying amount of the entire asset before the transfer is allocated between the sold and retained portions based on their relative fair values on the date of the transfer ([80], p. 229).

If a transfer does not result in derecognition because the entity has retained substantially all the risks and rewards of ownership of the transferred asset, the entity shall continue to recognize the entire asset and shall additionally recognize a financial liability for the consideration received (IAS 39.29). The treatment of value changes in the financial liability should be consistent with those of the asset it refers to, i.e. the gains and losses are taken both into income or equity.

The extent of a continuing involvement and therefore the new carrying amount of a transferred asset that did not qualify for derecognition depends on the extent the entity is exposed to risk, reward and control the transferring entity has retained in the asset on the one hand and on the way the asset was measured previous to the transfer. IAS 39 provides a wide range of guidelines depending on different situations that are out of scope for detailed explanation, see IAS 39.30–37 for further explanation.

An entity shall derecognize a financial liability when it is extinguished, i.e. the obligation is discharged, cancelled or expired (IAS 39.39). The difference between the carrying amount of the financial liability and the total consideration received shall be recorded in income (IAS 39.41). If only parts of the financial liability are sold, the entity has to allocate the carrying amount prior to the transfer of the basis on relative fair values as with the method explained earlier for financial assets (IAS 39.42).

When a liability is restructured or refinanced by substantial modification of the terms, the transaction is accounted as extinguishment of the existing debt (with gain or loss) and the recognition of a new financial liability (new debt) at fair value. Terms are substantially different if the discounted present value of the cash flows under the new terms using the effective interest rate of the original instrument and including all fees, differs at least ten per cent from the old instrument (see IAS 39.AG 62 and IAS 39.40).

4.4 HEDGE ACCOUNTING

4.4.1 Overview

In various business areas, e.g. financial institutions, industrial businesses, or service providers it is normal business practice to enter into credit transactions with fixed or variable interest rates. Sometimes these or other transactions are also denominated in foreign currency. As a result the companies are exposed to various market risks. In order to steer these market risks, companies enter into derivative contracts. The process that compensates for the risks a company is involved in due to a contract, an obligation, or by even not yet accounted future transactions by entering into an opposite behaving transaction is called hedging, see [86], p. 3. Hedging can therefore be seen as a risk management strategy against certain market risks. With hedging, companies try to compensate market value movements or changes in cash flows of the hedged item by taking a position in a hedging instrument whose value or change in cash flows changes as far as possible in the opposite direction so that an offsetting of gains and losses is reached. Therefore hedging is a structure to eliminate risk but also limits the chance to participate in favorable value or cash flow movements of the hedged item, see [87], p. 4.

While hedging describes a risk management strategy, hedge accounting describes a method of accounting. It is a method that matches the applicable accounting methods of both, the hedged item and the hedging instrument that would normally be unequal, see [88], p. 14.

Hedge accounting recognizes the offsetting effects on profit or loss of changes in the fair values of the hedging instrument and the hedged item (IAS 39.85).

Entities are free to use hedge accounting, but it is permitted only when strict documentation and effectiveness testing requirements are met ([80], p. 235).

The regulations concerning hedge accounting are the most discussed regulations of IAS 39. The first time adoption of this standard does not only require an examination of all existing hedging relations and their accounting treatment, but also has consequences for risk management, see [82], p. 96.

The necessity of the regulations for hedge accounting results in the dissimilar treatment of the different categories of financial instruments within IAS 39. Hedging instruments always belong to the category 'trading', which is a sub-category of 'financial instruments at fair value through profit and loss'. Therefore these financial instruments are always measured at fair value; changes in the fair value are shown in income. The categories 'held-to-maturity' and 'loans and receivables' are measured at amortized cost, the category 'available-for-sale' is measured at fair value but without showing the changes in fair value in income. Regulations to hedge accounting make an exception to usual accounting treatment for financial instruments. The special regulations for hedge accounting are needed to match the timing of offsetting gains and losses of the hedged item and the hedging instrument. It is important to note that within hedge accounting following IAS 39 the accounting method of the hedged item follows the accounting method of the hedging instrument and not vice versa.

The following example will clarify the purpose of hedge accounting. Suppose that an entity has a loan and a swap that hedges the risk exposure of that loan perfectly. If hedge accounting is not applied, the measurement for the loan would be at amortized cost but the measurement of the swap would be at fair value through profit and loss. In the income statement a gain in fair value of the loan would not appear, but the corresponding loss of the swap would be measured in income. Applying hedge accounting, both items would be measured at fair value through profit and loss, so that the gain resulting from the loan as well as the loss resulting from the swap would be displayed in income and offset, see [87], p. 5.

4.4.2   Types of hedges

IAS 39 distinguishes between three types of (micro-) hedge relationships. These are the *fair value hedge*, the *cash flow hedge* and the *hedge of a net investment* in a foreign operation. The regulations for hedging of a portfolio of financial assets or financial liabilities (macro-hedge) will not be discussed in this book.

Fair value hedge

A fair value hedge is a hedge of changes in the fair value of a recognized asset or liability, an unrecognized firm commitment, or an identified portion of such an asset, liability or firm commitment that is attributable to a particular risk (IAS 39.86 (a)).

IAS 39 gives some examples for fair value hedges:

• A hedge of interest rate risk associated with a fixed rate interest bearing asset or liability;
• A hedge of a firm commitment to purchase an asset or incur a liability (see IAS 39.AG 102);
• A forward currency contract hedging a foreign currency receivable or payable, including debt.

A hedge of a foreign currency risk on a firm commitment may be accounted for as fair value hedge or as cash flow hedge (IAS 39.87).

In the case of a fair value hedge, hedge accounting accelerates income recognition of value changes of the hedged item in order to match the gain or loss with the income of the hedging instrument. The hedging instrument is measured at fair value whereas the changes in fair value are recognized in income. The hedged item is also measured at fair value with respect to the hedged risk. This is also true if the hedged item is usually measured in another way. Adjustments to the carrying amount of the hedged item related to the hedged risk are recognized in income although the usual treatment would recognize the change directly in equity (IAS 39.89). Summing up the regular valuation treatment of the hedged item is overruled and adjusted so that it is in accordance with the measurement rules of the hedging instrument.

It is important to note that only the changes in fair value attributable to the hedged risk are recognized in income.

For a fair value hedge of a firm commitment, with hedge accounting, a change in fair value of the firm commitment results in an asset or a liability during the time period of the hedge relationship. When the hedged transaction is finally recognized, the previous recognized amount with respect to the fair value of the commitment is transferred to adjust the initial measurement of the underlying transaction (see IAS 39.93 and IAS 39.94).

The adjustment to the carrying amount of the hedged item within a fair value hedge often results in a measurement that is neither at cost nor at fair value. It is more a mixture of both approaches. This phenomenon occurs due to the fact that the adjustment is only made for changes that are attributable to the hedged risk and not all changes in value. It only occurs during the time the item is hedged and is also limited to the extent that the item is hedged (IAS

39.90). This type of adjustment makes the identification and separate measurement of all risks factors that may influence the value of the hedge item necessary.

Within fair value hedges, any ineffectiveness is reported automatically in income, as the gain or loss of the hedged item, as well as the corresponding gain or loss of the hedging instrument, are recognized immediately in income. An ineffectiveness of the hedge results in a net position that is unequal to zero.

Cash flow hedge

A cash flow hedge is a hedge of the exposure to variability in cash flows that is attributable to a particular risk associated with recognized asset or liability or a highly probable forecast transaction and that could affect profit or loss, see [80], p. 246.

Examples of common cash flow hedges are given in the following list:

- Hedges of floating rate interest-bearing instruments;
- Hedges of currency exposure on foreign-currency denominated future operating lease payments;
- Hedges in highly probable forecast transactions.

The probability of forecast transactions is not defined in IAS 39; however a likelihood of 80 to 90 % gives a common interpretation.

Abstractly forecasted transactions fit better to the fair value hedges. However, they are treated as cash flow hedges since the treatment as fair value hedge would lead to the recognition of an asset or liability before the entity becomes party of a contract, which would actually not meet the definition of the IFRS framework.

Within a cash flow hedge, the hedging instrument is measured at fair value where the effective portion of changes in its fair value is recognized directly in a separate component of equity. This is called the hedging reserve. Any ineffectiveness of the hedging instrument is recognized in profit or loss (IAS 39.95). In the case that the hedged risk is a foreign currency risk and the hedging instrument is a non-derivative, the gains or losses of the foreign currency are recognized directly in equity.

The amount that is recorded in equity has to be adjusted to the lesser of absolute amounts of either

- the cumulative gain or loss on the hedging instrument from inception of the hedge;
- the cumulative gain or loss in fair value of the expected future cash flows on the hedged item from inception of the hedge (IAS 39.96 (a)).

In order to reduce complexity for accounting of forecasted transactions, IAS 39 allows basis-adjustments. The carrying amount of a non-financial asset or liability can be adjusted by the prior accumulated amount in equity when the forecasted transaction is realized. Therefore, the associated gains or losses from the hedging relationship are removed from equity and included in the initial recognition of the asset or liability, resulting out of the forecasted transaction. The same rule is applicable when forecast transactions become firm commitments for which fair value hedge accounting is the appropriate hedge accounting method (IAS 39.98). The other choice is to leave the cumulated gains or losses in equity and transfer it to the income statement at the time the asset or liability affects income e.g. through sale or depreciation. The chosen policy must be applied consistently to all cash flow hedges (IAS 39.99).

This choice is only relevant to transactions involving non-financial items. For financial assets or financial liabilities the amount deferred in equity remains there and is recognized in the period when the financial asset or financial liability affects profit or loss (IAS 39.97).

Hedges of a net investment

A hedge of a net investment is a hedge of the currency exposure on a net investment in a foreign operation using a derivative or a monetary item, see [80], p. 247. All criteria concerning hedge accounting stated in IAS 39.88 equally apply for this kind of hedge. The hedged risk is the foreign currency exposure on the carrying amount of the net investment.

For accounting, the hedge of a net investment shall be treated similarly to the cash flow hedge. This means in detail, that the hedging instrument is measured at fair value. The effective portion of the gains or losses on the hedging instrument is recognized in equity. Here it is called a currency translation reserve. Ineffectiveness is recognized instantly in income. When the net investment is sold, the cumulative amount recognized in the currency translation reserve is transferred to income and adjusts the result of disposal (IAS 39.102).

4.4.3   Basic requirements

Hedge accounting is tightly linked to a couple of requirements that all have to be fulfilled. These requirements are:

- There is a written documentation at the inception of the hedge that identifies the hedging instrument, the hedged item and the risk being hedged; the risk management objective and strategy for undertaking the hedge; and how effectiveness will be measured.
- The effectiveness of the hedge can be measured reliably.
- The hedge is expected to be highly effective.
- The hedge is assessed and determined to be highly effective on an ongoing basis throughout the hedge relationship.
- For a hedge of a forecast transaction, the transaction is highly probable and creates an exposure that ultimately could affect profit or loss, see [80], p. 236.

In the following subsections the most crucial facts will be discussed in more detail.

Hedging instruments

Generally only derivatives qualify as hedging instruments. But there are limitations and exceptions to consider. An exception is the hedging of foreign currency risks. Here also non-derivative financial assets or financial liabilities may qualify (see IAS 39.72). Limitations exists with regard to written options. Written options incur a potential loss that is by far greater than the potential gain in value of the hedged item. Therefore, a written option is not limiting the profit or loss potential of the hedged item. Written options can only qualify as hedging instruments in the case that they are designated to offset a purchased option. This purchased option may be part of a structured product (IAS 39.AG 94).

A derivative does not have to be designated as hedging instrument at the time of first recognition. A designation might occur at a later point in the derivative's life (IAS 39.IG F 3.9). But a designation can only occur on a prospective basis. A retrospective designation is not possible. Once designated as hedging instrument to a certain hedged item the hedging instrument remains in this relationship as long as the derivative is outstanding. In other words, once designated as hedging instrument a derivative has to stay designated for the remaining time to maturity (IAS 39.75). On the other hand, it is possible to hedge only a portion of the hedged item's life (IAS 39.IG F 2.17).

It is possible to designate only a portion of a derivative as hedging instrument or the other way around it is also possible to designate more than one derivative (or even parts of them) to hedge one item. This is also true if some of the derivatives' effects offset as long as none of them is a written option (see IAS 39.75 and IAS 39.77).

A designation as hedging instrument has the prerequisite that the fair value of the derivative is measurable reliably.

One hedging instrument may be designated to hedge against more than one different risk under the presumption that the risks can be identified clearly, the effectiveness of the hedge can be demonstrated and it must be possible to designate the derivative to the different risk positions (IAS 39.76).

Generally, a hedging instrument can only be measured at fair value as a whole. Therefore only entire derivatives or percentage portions can be designated as hedging instruments. It is assumed that the factors that cause changes in the fair value of the derivate are interdependent. Exceptions exist for options and forwards. For options it is possible to separate the intrinsic value from the time value. It is possible to exclude the time value from the hedging relationship and to consider only the intrinsic value.

Dynamic hedging strategies may qualify for hedge accounting as well, incorporating the intrinsic value and the time value. As a result of this, a delta-neutral hedging strategy may qualify for hedge accounting under the assumption that all other requirements especially the documentation of the strategy are fulfilled (IAS 39.IG F 1.9).

For forwards it is possible to separate the fair value in the interest element and the spot price. It is possible to designate only the interest element of a forward as hedging instrument (IAS 39.74).

If some terms of the hedging instrument and the hedged item differ from each other, a hedge relationship still may qualify for hedge accounting. The entity has to demonstrate that this hedge relationship is highly effective in terms of that there is a strong correlation between the hedged item and the hedging instrument. Additionally, all other requirements stated in IAS 39.88 have to be fulfilled (IAS 39.AG 100).

Intra-company derivative transactions can only be part of a hedge accounting relationship if the risk associated was transferred one-to-one to an external party, so that the external transaction can be designated as hedge transaction. The intra-company transaction has the purpose to clarify the relationship between the hedged item and the external hedging transaction. This issue is critical for banks that mainly use a centralized treasury department to allocate the risk exposure, see [89], p. 419.

Hedged item

A hedged item creates a risk exposure that will effect the income of the entity. A hedged item can be a single recognized financial asset or financial liability, an unrecognized firm commitment, a highly probable forecast transaction or a net investment in a foreign operation. Additionally, a hedged item can be a group of above mentioned possible items with the same risk characteristics or in a portfolio hedge of interest rate risk only, a portion of the portfolio of financial assets or financial liabilities that share the risk being hedged (IAS 39.78).

It is not possible to designate a derivative as hedged item. 'Held-to-maturity' investments may never be a hedged item in a hedge relationship against interest rate risk or prepayment risk. This is because the entity has the intention to hold this item until maturity and changes in the fair value arising from those risks do not have to bother the entity. But 'held-to-maturity' investments may be designated as hedged items for foreign exchange risk or credit rating risk (IAS 39.AG 95).

It is not possible to hedge against general business risk (IAS 39.AG 110). Further, the entity's own equity instruments, associated entities and subsidiaries cannot be the hedged item (see IAS 39.AG 99 and IAS 39.IG F 2.7).

For intra-company transactions the same rules as for the hedging instruments apply. An external hedged item that corresponds with the internal item must exist (IAS 39.80).

Generally, the hedged item's fair value or change in cash flow has to be measurable reliably with respect to the hedged risk.

Macro-hedges that hedge an overall net position instead of a specified hedged item do not qualify for hedge accounting under IAS 39 (see IAS 39.AG 101). If the portfolio to be hedged involves exclusively interest rate risk and is not a net position of assets and liabilities, the portion hedge may be designated in terms of an amount of a currency instead of the individual items (IAS 39.81A).

It is possible to designate only a portion of the cash flows or fair value as a hedged item . . . once the partial designation is made, hedge effectiveness is measured on the basis of the hedged exposure. (See [80], p. 236 for further explanation and IAS 39.AG 99A and B)

There are no restrictions on the timing of designation or dedesignation of a hedged item. Consequently it is possible to hedge an item after initial recognition and also merely for a portion of its period to maturity (IAS 39.IG F 2.17).

Coming back to portfolios as hedged items, this form of hedging relationship is solely possible if all items in the portfolio vary proportionally in response to changes in the hedged risk (IAS 39.78). Therefore it is important to take care of the items grouped in a portfolio. For loan portfolios for example it is necessary to group items in terms of time to maturity because long-term instruments are more volatile to changes in the yield curve than short-term instruments due to a longer duration, see [90], p. 84. Equity portfolios cannot qualify for portfolio hedging as the different equity shares do not react in the same way to the portfolio value movements (IAS 39.IG F 2.20).

Formal designation and documentation

In order to qualify for hedge accounting, each hedging relationship consisting of hedged item and hedging instrument has to be formally designated and documented at inception of the hedge. Further, the nature of the hedged risk, the entity's risk management objective and strategy as well as the assessment method used to prove hedge effectiveness have to be documented (IAS 39.88(a)). The documentation cannot be applied retrospectively. As a result, hedging relationships already existing that are not documented in the demanded extent do not qualify for hedge accounting.

It is important to clearly define interest rate exposure for the hedge item and the hedging instrument since changes in interest rates may result in a series of reactions, see [91], p. 271.

Hedge effectiveness

In a first step the entity has to decide against which risk it is willing to hedge the hedged item. The hedged risk must be able to affect the income statement (IAS 39.AG 110). Financial items can be hedged against exposure to a single or a combination of the single risks that are measurable. These risks include market prices, interest rates or a component of interest rates, foreign currency rates or credit rates. A non-financial item can only be hedged against either all of its risks or currency risk only (see IAS 39.82). As stated above, the hedged risk must be specific and measurable. However, hedging against general business risk does not qualify for hedge accounting (IAS 39.AG 110).

If a hedge is not perfect, the gain or loss on the hedging instrument will differ from the gain or loss on the hedged item. This difference is called *hedge ineffectiveness* ([80], p. 241). In order to qualify for hedge accounting, a hedge must be highly effective. The entity has to prove that this high effectiveness is expected to be met (prospectively) and that it is actually given (retrospectively). Only in the case when both, the **prospective** and the **retrospective** high effectiveness are given, the hedge can qualify for hedge accounting. The hedge has to be effective at inception and throughout the life of the hedge. The offsetting has to be in a range of 80 %–125 % for the retrospective effectiveness. For prospective effectiveness there is no exact range required, but the adoption of the same range is in line with the audit companies. For the hedged item only changes in fair value or cash flows that are attributable to the hedged risk are considered for the assessment of the hedge effectiveness. This is important as the change in the full fair value may incorporate changes attributable to other than the hedged risk. Therefore the determination of the so called hedge fair value, that is the change in fair value only due to the hedged risk has to be performed in order to get the appropriate basis for assessment. IAS does not give further guidance for the determination of the hedge fair value. For the hedging instrument the full fair value has to be adopted. A separation of parts of the instrument is only possible for options and forwards as mentioned in IAS 39.74 and discussed earlier in Section 4.4.3.

In IAS 39.88(c) the standard demands that the effectiveness of the hedge must be measurable reliably. Further, the effectiveness has to be proven on an ongoing basis. The minimum frequency to test for effectiveness is at each balance sheet date including interim reports (IAS 39.AG 106). However, it is advisable that the test is performed more often so that ineffectiveness is identified early enough and the entity can adjust or rebalance the hedge to minimize the impact of the ineffectiveness. Generally, if an entity does not meet the criteria concerning effectiveness anymore, hedge accounting is discontinued from the last date the hedge still met the criteria of being effective (IAS 39.AG 113). This is a clear incentive to perform the test for effectiveness more often than minimally required by the standard for hedges where passing the test is assumed to be critical. Most of the hedges that fulfill the requirement regarding the effectiveness to be in the demanded range will not offset perfectly. The actual ineffectiveness must be recognized in income in the period of time in which it occurs although it is in the range of 80 %–125 %, see IAS 39.95(b) and IAS 39.102(b).

Testing for hedge effectiveness can be performed on a period-by-period or a cumulative basis (IAS 39.107, IAS 39.IG F 4.2 and IAS 39.IG F 4.4). Further, the entity can choose whether to assess the effectiveness on a pre-tax or after-tax basis. Testing on a cumulative basis may have the advantage that hedge accounting may be continued even if one period does not fulfill the requirement as long as previous periods compensate this ineffectiveness and the effectiveness is expected to remain over the life of the hedge relationship.

IAS 39 does not specify methods to use for measuring hedge effectiveness. The methods should be in line with the risk management strategy of the entity. The method that is applied has to be specified in the hedge documentation.

An entity may use different methods for different types of hedges.

Different approaches may be used to measure prospective and retrospective effectiveness for a single hedge relationship. ([80], p. 242)

If an entity hedges less than 100 % of the exposure of an item, it must designate this percentage amount as hedged item and measure ineffectiveness based on the change in the designated exposure only (IAS 39.AG 107A).

Whichever method is used to determine hedge effectiveness, it should be consistent for similar transactions and over time.

IAS 39 does not specify methods to use for assessing hedge effectiveness. However, there are some methods that are commonly used. For the prospective effectiveness test these are the comparisons on a historical basis or the calculation based on sensitivities. For the retrospective effectiveness test the *Dollar-Offset Method*, the *Variance Reduction Measure* or the *Regression Analysis* are commonly used methods.

In practice the strict limits of effectiveness will limit the number of hedges that can qualify for hedge accounting significantly since most of the hedges will not be set up as perfect hedges. Even perfect hedges in the economic view will not always meet the definition of a highly effective hedge.

4.4.4 Stopping hedge accounting

Hedge accounting must be stopped prospectively if the hedged transaction is no longer highly probable, the hedging instrument expires, is sold, terminated or exercised. Further, if the hedged item is sold, settled or disposed in another way or the hedge is no longer highly effective, hedge accounting must be stopped as well, see [80], p. 246.

At the date the hedge accounting is stopped, the entity has to assess hedge effectiveness and report ineffectiveness in the income statement.

The hedging instrument and the hedged item are subsequently accounted for according to their usual treatment in IFRS. In the case that the hedging relationship is terminated due to ineffectiveness, hedge accounting will be stopped at the date at which effectiveness was proven the last time (IAS 39.AG 113). Therefore it could make sense to test for effectiveness more often than at each balance sheet date. If an entity identifies the event or change in circumstances that caused insufficient effectiveness for the hedging relationship and if the entity could demonstrate that the hedging relationship was effective prior to this event, the entity discontinues hedge accounting from the date of the event on (IAS 39.AG 113).

IAS 39 does not give guidance on the question whether hedge accounting is discontinued only for ending of the retrospective effectiveness or for ending of the prospective effectiveness as well.

In practice, the circumstance of failing the effectiveness test only slightly may not automatically lead to discontinuation of hedge accounting. If the ineffectiveness is merely temporary and prospective effectiveness is proven the overall effectiveness can be assumed. In this case the ineffectiveness is ignored due to insignificance, see [86], p. 11.

At the end of a fair value hedge, any adjustments to the carrying amount of the hedged item will be reversed at the time the item is sold or depreciated. If the item is normally measured at amortized cost, the adjustment is amortized to profit or loss by adjusting the hedged item's effective interest rate when amortization begins ([80], p. 248). Cumulative gain or loss recognized in equity arising from a cash flow hedge remain in equity until the transaction occurs, if the transaction is still expected to take place. If the transaction is not expected to occur anymore, the cumulative gain or loss is transferred to equity at once (IAS 39.101). For cumulative gain or loss previously recognized in equity of a hedge of a net investment in a foreign operation the amount is kept in equity until the investment is sold (IAS 39.102).

4.5   METHODS FOR TESTING HEDGE EFFECTIVENESS

IAS 39 does not give guidance on specific methods to apply for testing hedge effectiveness. It only states that the method should be in line with the risk management strategy. This may have the consequence that the method applied should be in line with the risk management strategy for a specific transaction. However the chosen method should be applied consistently for similar transactions. The choice of the method is of great importance because the implementation may influence the result whether a hedging relationship is effective or not.

4.5.1   Fair value hedge

According to IAS 39.AG 105 the entity has to perform a prospective test for effectiveness. Here the entity has to prove that the changes in fair value or cash flows of the hedged item and the hedging instrument will compensate in the future. In this section, we discuss three possible methods to prove the prospective effectiveness.

The first method is the historical review. Within this method the fair value of the hedging instrument and the hedge fair value of the hedged item are determined based on historical data sets. For the hedged item, the hedge fair value is determined. This means that only the changes in fair value due to the hedged risk are incorporated into the item's value. If the changes in (hedge) fair value of the hedging instrument and the hedged item have compensated each other in the past, the prospective effectiveness is considered guaranteed. The availability of the required market data is critical for this method.

Another method is the calculation of sensitivities. The hedge fair value of the hedged item and the fair value of the hedging instrument are examined for the case that the hedged risk factor changes by a predefined amount. A typical example is the calculation of the basis point value for interest rate related items. If the changes in value offset to a great extent, the hedge relationship is considered to be prospectively effective, see [87], p. 13.

A third method is the *critical term match* (IAS 39.AG 108). This is not equal to the *short-cut method* that is allowed under the regulation of **US-GAAP**. Following US-GAAP in a hedge relationship where the term, the notional amount, the dates of interest payment etc. match perfectly, a 100 % effectiveness is assumed. This is not allowed under IAS. However, for the test of prospective effectiveness, a similar alleviation is allowed in IAS. If the critical terms of the hedged item and the hedging instrument are the same, it is likely that the changes in fair value or cash flows offset entirely. This is valid for the evaluation of the prospective effectiveness at the beginning of the hedging relationship as well as during the hedging relationship. The critical term match is not permitted for the retrospective testing of effectiveness, see [86], p. 8.

For the retrospective testing of effectiveness, we now explain the *Dollar-Offset Method* and common statistical methods.

The *Dollar-Offset Method* sets the change in hedge fair value of the hedged item in relation to the change in fair value of the hedging instrument. The *Dollar-Offset Method* can be applied either on a period-by-period basis or on a cumulative basis, see [92], pp. 43–44. The cumulative method may have the advantage of compensating ineffectiveness of single periods. The continuity in application of a method is of relevance.

The relevant hedge effectiveness is given if the relation

$$\text{effectiveness} = \frac{\text{change in hedge fair value of hedged item}}{\text{change in fair value of hedging instrument}} \qquad (4.1)$$

is between -1.25 and -0.8. The result must be negative, because the changes shall offset each other. The advantage of this method is that it is easy and comprehensive. This is of special importance as the entities have to prove effectiveness on their own. The auditor is not allowed to perform the effectiveness test for the entity. A disadvantage of the *Dollar-Offset Method* is the fact that even for economically effective hedging relationships, the effectiveness requirements are not always met due to problems with small numbers. The problem occurs, if the change in value is small. Hailer and Rump discuss possible solutions for that problem in [93], pp. 599–603. Figure 4.2 illustrates the problem. We consider a system of coordinates with the change in hedge fair value of the hedged item (ΔBC) on the x-axis and the change in fair value of the hedging instrument (ΔHI) on the y-axis. For a perfect offsetting the hedging relationship is a straight line with a slope of -1. ($\Delta BC = -\Delta HI$, Figure 4.2a).

However, to be effective according to IAS 39 it is not necessary to offset 100 %. The tolerance level of the effectiveness is between 80 % and 125 %. This means that the coordinates must be within the cones between the lines $\Delta BC = -\frac{4}{5}\Delta HI$ and $\Delta BC = -\frac{5}{4}\Delta HI$. (Figure 4.2b)

The tolerance level is very small near the intersection of these lines. One method presented by Hailer and Rump to solve this problem is an approximation of the boundary function so that the interval is unchanged for large numbers and so that the cones overlap for small numbers. This is done with the formula

$$\Delta HI = \pm 0.225 \cdot \sqrt{(\Delta BC)^2 + c} - 1.025 \cdot \Delta BC. \qquad (4.2)$$

For the diagram in Figure 4.2c, the value of c is set equal to 10. The resulting diagram shows the positive effect of the approximation and gives a possible solution to the problem of small numbers. Figure 4.2d combines Figure 4.2b and Figure 4.2c to show the overlapping for small numbers where the area further apart from the origin stays almost unchanged.

A second common method to measure hedge effectiveness is the *Variability Reduction Method*. The scope of this method is to examine whether a reduction in variability of the fair value is obtained through the hedging relation. For this purpose, the variability of the hedged item's fair value on a sole basis is compared with the variability of the fair value of the combined hedge position (consisting of the hedge fair value of the hedged item and the fair value of the hedging instrument), see [94], p. 103. The measure used for this comparison is the variance. The smaller the variance of the hedging relationship relative to the unhedged item, the more effective the hedge. The formula for the variance reduction is given by

$$\text{effectiveness} = 1 - \frac{\textbf{var}(\text{hedging relationship})}{\textbf{var}(\text{hedge fair value hedged item})}. \qquad (4.3)$$

Effectiveness according IAS 39 holds if the result of the *Variance Reduction Measure* is above 0.96, see [95], p. 96.

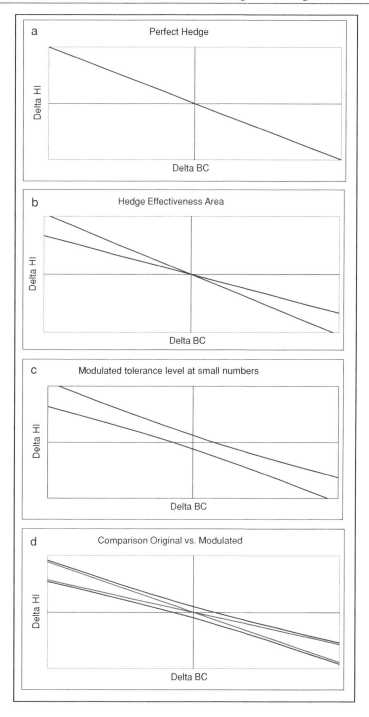

Figure 4.2 Dollar-offset and solution for small numbers

The question whether to prefer changes solely of the period since the last measurement or the total change on a cumulative basis does not arise, since the method does not use changes but the fair value itself.

In practice, this method is not used very often, because it is more complicated and less illustrative than the *Dollar-Offset Method*, see [96], pp. 54–55.

A variation of this method uses the variability of the changes ([94], p. 103) or the standard deviation ([95], pp. 93–99) instead of the variance of the fair values.

A third very common method to determine hedge effectiveness is the *Regression Analysis*. It is a statistical method to test for hedge effectiveness. Within the context of a *Regression Analysis* the relation between a depended variable and one or more independent variables is examined. The basis for this effectiveness test is the change in value of the hedged item and the hedging instrument in the past. For testing hedge effectiveness, a linear regression is sufficient in most cases. Therefore the regression model

$$y = \alpha + \beta x \qquad (4.4)$$

is used, where y denotes the change in fair value of the hedging instrument and x denotes the change in hedge fair value of the hedged item. The interception of the regression line with the y-axis is α. The coefficient β is the slope of the regression line. It is calculated using the correlation between y and x and the standard deviations of these two variables,

$$\beta = \mathbf{corr}(y, x)\frac{\mathbf{stdev}(y)}{\mathbf{stdev}(x)}. \qquad (4.5)$$

In this context the interception term α is the average amount per period, by which the change in value differs between the hedged item and the hedging instrument.

The slope of the regression line should be -1 for a perfect hedge relation. As IAS does not ask for perfect offsetting, the slope may be in the interval $[-1.25; -0.8]$. Fulfilling the slope argument is not enough to prove effectiveness. Even if the scattering of values is very wide, the slope can be within the desired interval. Therefore the coefficient of determination, R^2, also plays a role in determination whether the hedge is effective. In this simple linear regression model, R^2 is the squared correlation of the underlying variables and gives an indication about the quality of how the dots fit the regression line. Generally, a coefficient of determination of at least 0.8 is considered to interpret a hedge as highly effective, see [97], p. 63.[1]

In order to achieve reliable results it is necessary to have a sufficient number of observations available as historic data. Therefore, a decision regarding the frequency of observations has to be done, i.e. daily, weekly or monthly. For statistically reliable results, a minimum of 25–30 observations should be considered ([97], p. 63). If this is not the case, for example at the beginning of a hedging relationship, the entity has to search for alternative methods. One alternative might be to generate synthetic observations of a point in time prior to hedge designation. Another alternative is the use of the *Dollar-Offset Method* until the minimum required data set is available. For the later alternative this change in testing has to be documented prior to application to avoid failure of hedge effectiveness due to a forbidden change in methods, see [87], p. 16.

An advantage of the *Regression Analysis* is the better results compared to the *Dollar-Offset Method*. Disadvantages arise through complexity and the treatment of outliers.

---

[1] note that R^2 takes values in the interval [0, 1].

Balance sheet treatment of the fair value hedge

As far as the requirements for hedge accounting are fulfilled, the changes in fair value of the hedging instruments as well as the changes in fair value attributable to the hedged risk have to be reported in income in the period they occur. Changes in fair value of the hedged item lead to an adjustment in the carrying amount.

Changes in fair value of the hedged item and the changes in fair value of the hedging instrument are reported directly in income. Preferably, the entity has a line called hedging result where the result of the hedge is reported. Ineffectiveness is shown automatically as a net position as the changes in fair value of the hedge relationship are both shown in income. The portion that is not compensated, remains as net position or ineffectiveness respectively.

The *hedge fair value (HFV)* is the fair value of the hedged item that is determined on the basis of the hedged risk. Other risk factors that are not hedged do not contribute to determining the HFV. IAS 39 does not give guidance for the calculation of the HFV. The adjustment of the hedged item's carrying amount to the hedge fair value has to be amortized recognizing the amortization in income. The amortization may begin at the earliest at designation of the hedge but not later than at the end of the hedge (see IAS 39.92).

For interest bearing instruments one common possibility is to keep the actual credit spread at designation of the hedge constant. Therefore, the HFV at designation is the full fair value or cost. The HFV has to be determined for all hedges that have an interest rate risk as defined hedge risk. The HFV should be a clean price. Therefore it has to be adjusted eventually for accrued interest payments. For subsequent calculation of the HFV the current interest term structure is applied adjusted by the credit spread which is kept constant from designation of the hedge.

For the hedging instrument the HFV has to be calculated likewise. Applying IAS 39.AG 107, it is possible to assign only the intrinsic value of an option or the spot price component of a forward contract as HFV ([86], pp. 13–14).

In the case where equity prices or foreign exchange risks are being hedged with options or forward contracts using the possibility of omitting the time value according IAS 39.AG 107 a distinctive feature has to be borne in mind. If the option is out of the money and the time component is not included in the hedge, the option does not have a hedge fair value and can therefore not have an offsetting effect. If the option is in the money, it is possible to determine the hedge fair value which will offset fluctuations in the stock price.

For financial assets that are measured at amortized cost, the *hedge amortized costs (HAC)* have to be calculated. Therefore it is important to distinguish whether the hedge relationship was designated at first recognition of the hedged item or if the designation took place at a later point in time. For the first case, the HAC are equal to the amortized costs. For the other case, the HAC are calculated as the difference between the full fair value at designation and the repayment amount, distributed to the remaining time to maturity using the effective interest rate method. The amortization of this difference amount is not shown in income ([86], p. 15).

The *basis adjustment (BA)* is the amount by which the carrying amount of the hedged item has to be adjusted in order to reflect the gain or loss recognized in income that incurred due to the hedged risk in the framework of a fair value hedge.

The BA for the hedging of interest rate risk is calculated as the difference between the HFV and the HAC at a specific point in time.

For loans and receivables, as well as for all other liabilities that are measured at amortized cost, the carrying amount is calculated by adding the BA to the amortized cost. For securities of the category 'available for sale', the carrying amount is the full fair value. The BA is added or subtracted from the amortized cost and recognized in income. For the hedging of stock prices and foreign exchange risks the calculation is much simpler. The BA is the difference between the current HFV and the HFV at the last date of evaluation.

4.5.2 Cash flow hedge

As stated above, IAS 39 does not give guidance on the methods to use for testing for effectiveness. Although the *cash flow hedge* transforms variable cash flows into fixed cash flows, the way to measure effectiveness uses the fair value as in the fair value hedge. Therefore the changes in fair value of the hedging instrument and the hedged item will be examined. The methods to do this are the same as for the *fair value hedge*, namely the *Dollar-Offset Method* or statistical methods such as the *Variability Reduction Method* and *Regression Analysis*.

The American counterpart to IAS 39, FAS 133 allows a short-cut method similar to the critical term match for testing effectiveness. This method is not allowed under IAS. However, this short-cut method is not always allowed under US-GAAP either, but gives information about alternative methods to use. These methods belong to the family of *Dollar-Offset Methods* and might be allowed under IAS for cash flow hedges as well ([86], p. 17).

The first method is the *change in fair value method*. Here the cumulative absolute change in fair value of the future cash flows of the hedged asset or liability is compared with the cumulative absolute change in full fair value of the hedging instrument. For testing effectiveness, the values are set in relation to each other. If the result is within the interval [0.8; 1.25], a retrospective effectiveness holds. An inefficient amount arises if the cumulative absolute change in full fair value of the hedging instrument is greater than the cumulative absolute change in fair value of the future cash flows. This difference amount has to be recognized in income. This difference amount may have a significant size, although the hedge relationship is perfect from an economic perspective ([86], p. 20).

Example
Assume an entity has a variable interest rate liability with a notional amount of 1,000,000 (3M EURIBOR). This liability is hedged with an interest rate swap with the same notional amount so that the entity receives 3M EURIBOR and pays 5 % fixed interest rate. From an economic point of view, this hedge is perfect. However, there may arise an inefficiency from an accounting perspective. The fair value of the variable interest rate liability is calculated via the actual fixed EURIBOR and the forward rates. These cash flows are discounted with the appropriate zero rates. The value of the swap is calculated as the net position of the present value of the variable leg and the fixed leg. The variable leg uses the same calculation as for the variable interest rate liability. The fixed leg present value is the fixed rate multiplied with the notional amount and discounted with the appropriate zero rates.

The change in full fair value of the swap can be greater than the change in fair value of the cash flows. This would result in an ineffectiveness according to IAS 39 and would be recognized in income.

The second method is the *change in variable cash flow method*. This method is also described in the context of a variable interest rate bearing instrument and an interest rate swap. As the method's name already hints, only the variable side is of importance. For effectiveness testing, the method assumes that only the variable leg of the swap substantiates the cash flow hedge.

Therefore, changes in fair value of the swap that are attributable to the fixed leg do not play a role for the hedge of the variable interest rate cash flows arising from the hedged item. In other words, changes in the swap's fair value attributable to the fixed leg are not included in testing effectiveness of the cash flow hedge. This is in line with the definition in IAS 39, to measure effectiveness of a cash flow hedge. A limitation for the *change in variable cash flow method* is the prerequisite that the fair value of the hedging instrument must be zero or at least almost zero at designation to the hedge.

Effectiveness is tested in the way that the cumulated changes in fair value of the variable leg of the hedging instrument (swap) is compared to the change in fair value of the expected cash flows of the hedged financial instrument in future. Ineffectiveness has to be recognized in income for the case that the change in fair value of the hedging instrument relating to the variable leg is greater than the change in fair value of the future expected cash flows. If the change in fair value of the hedging instrument is smaller than the corresponding change of the cash flows, ineffectiveness is not recognized in income.

Independent from the measurement of the effectiveness, the hedging instrument is recognized with full fair value in the balance sheet. The financial instrument that generates the expected cash flows in future is accounted for following the appropriate rules normally applying to this sort of instrument, see [86], pp. 20–21.

A third method is called the *hypothetical derivative method*. Within this method the effectiveness is measured by comparing the change in fair value of a fictitious perfect hedging instrument with the change in fair value of the real hedging instrument. This fictitious hedging instrument replicates the relevant terms of the hedged cash flows with its variable leg, see [87], p. 38. Therefore the change in fair value of this instrument is the 'deputy' for the cumulative changes in fair value of the expected future cash flows of the hedged transaction. The measurement of the hypothetical derivative is based on the appropriate market conditions. At inception, the fair value of the hypothetical derivative must be zero. Further, the hypothetical derivative should compensate completely the hedged cash flows.

The fair value of the real hedging instrument does not necessarily have to be zero at inception to the hedge.

Ineffectiveness has to be recognized in income in the case that the cumulative absolute change in fair value of the real hedging derivative is greater than the cumulative absolute change in fair value of the hypothetical hedging instrument.

In order to fulfill effectiveness retrospectively the relation of the cumulative change in fair value of the two hedging derivatives must be in the range between 0.8 and 1.25, see [86], p. 22.

Balance sheet treatment of the cash flow hedge

If a cash flow hedge fulfills the general requirements according to IAS 39.88 the recognition takes place as described below.

The transaction on which the variable cash flows are based is recognized following the general rules. There is no difference in accounting for that instrument whether it is part of a hedging relationship or not.

The hedging instrument is measured at full fair value where the change in fair value is separated into an effective and an ineffective portion. The portion of the gain or loss on the hedging instrument that is determined to be effective is recognized directly in equity. The ineffective portion is recognized in income (IAS 39.95).

The portion of the gain or loss that is recognized in equity has to be adjusted at each balance sheet date to the smaller of the following two amounts (measured in absolute terms):

• "The cumulative gain or loss on the hedging instrument from inception of the hedge; or
• The cumulative change in fair value (present value) of the expected future cash flows on the hedged item from inception of the hedge." (IAS 39.96 (a))

As long as the hedge is effective in terms of having an effectiveness of 80 % to 125 %, the ineffectiveness is treated as follows. If the cumulative gain or loss of the hedging instrument is smaller than the cumulative change in fair value of the expected future cash flows, the difference amount is recognized in equity. If the cumulative gain or loss of the hedging instrument is greater, the difference amount is recognized in income, see [87], p. 38.

The amounts that were recognized previously in equity as ineffectiveness, are derecognized and shown in income at the time the hedged transaction is recognized on the balance sheet or in income.

4.6 TESTING FOR EFFECTIVENESS – A CASE STUDY OF THE FORWARD PLUS

Having illustrated the theoretical concept of hedge accounting under IAS 39, including its requirements and possible methods, the following case study will demonstrate the practical implementation of testing for effectiveness for a *Forward Plus* introduced in Section 2.1.5.

It is assumed that a EUR-zone based exporter (= USD seller) will have a forecast transaction in USD that has a worth of EUR 100,000,000. He will receive the USD amount in six months. Knowing about the variability in exchange rates, the exporter is willing to fix the exchange rate now. He is aware that he needs protection against a rising EUR-USD exchange rate. At the same time he knows that a falling exchange rate improves his position. The exporter believes that the exchange rate is going to decline moderately, i.e. move in a favorable direction. However, he is not willing to spend money for a possible better position. Therefore he enters into a Forward Plus contract. The included forward is not fair, i.e. the exchange rate fixed representing his *worst case*, is worse than the one he would receive by entering into an outright forward contract. On the other hand, he has the chance to participate in moderate favorable exchange rate movements. If the exchange rate drops sharply and hits the knock-out barrier, the exporter will again receive the *worst case* rate specified in the unfair forward contract.

The key data used for the case study are shown in Table 4.3.

All calculations, on which the data shown here are based upon, are performed in the Microsoft Excel 2003 spread sheet named **hedgeaccounting.xls** on the CD-ROM enclosed with this book.

Table 4.3 Specifications for the case study of the forward plus

Spot exchange rate in time t_0	1.3000 EUR/USD
USD interest rate r_d	2.00 % p.a.
EUR interest rate r_f	2.20 % p.a.
Volatility σ	10.00 % p.a.
Time to maturity	180 days
Day count	365 days
Notional amount	EUR 100,000,000.00

4.6.1   Simulation of exchange rates

At inception of a hedge relationship, the entity has to prove that the hedge is going to be effective in the future. For a structured product like the *American style Forward Plus*, not only the exchange rate at the end of the hedge decides whether the hedge relationship is effective or not. Instead, the path itself is crucial, due to the barrier option included in the product. For this purpose a Monte Carlo Simulation is performed to show possible exchange rate paths.

Therefore, the current spot exchange rate is the starting point of the simulation. The spot rate of the next observation point, that is one day later, is modeled by a geometric Brownian motion,

$$S_{t_{i+1}} = S_{t_i} \cdot \exp\left[\sigma\sqrt{\Delta t}Z + \left(r_d - r_f - \frac{1}{2}\sigma^2\right)\Delta t\right],\qquad(4.6)$$

where $S_{t_{i+1}}$ represents the next simulated spot exchange rate, S_{t_i} the current spot rate, r_d and r_f denote the two local interest rates for the USD and the EUR respectively as specified in Table 4.3 and σ denotes the volatility of the exchange rate. The time interval is denoted by $\Delta t = t_{i+1} - t_i$ and Z is a standard-normal random variable (see [3], p. 3). Following this model the exchange rate is simulated on a daily basis in which the next exchange rate depends only on the preceding exchange rate, see [98], p. 48. Therefore, Δt is one day. The model assumes that exchange prices are determined every day and every day of the year is a business day.

Figure 4.3 shows a part of the Monte Carlo Simulation as it is used to test for effectiveness in the example. The simulation has the dimension of 180 time steps as the hedge relationship is determined for 6 months and 1000 simulated paths. All calculations are performed for every single path. At the end, the average over the final calculation value is determined in order to obtain a representative result.

In Figure 4.4, 150 of the 1000 simulated exchange rate paths are displayed.

As is clearly visible, there is a certain concentration in the range of 1.2000 to 1.4000. However, outliers are also included in this selection of simulated paths.

4.6.2   Calculation of the forward plus value

The data gathered from the Monte Carlo Simulation is used to calculate the value of the Forward Plus. In this case the (bank's) client is an exporter and the participation takes place in the case of a falling EUR-USD rate. The client's components of the Forward Plus are a long EUR forward position (long EUR call and short EUR put) and a long EUR put with a reverse knock-out barrier (American style). The valuation of these options is performed according to the formulas for the theoretical value given in [3].

In the second step, the specifications of the barrier option and the notional amount of the hedge transaction have to be determined. For the hedge transaction, it is important that the initial expenditure for the Forward Plus is at zero cost, see Section 2.1.5. In the example, it is assumed that the strike of all options is equal to the spot price at initiation of the hedge relationship S_0. Therefore, the adjustable variable to obtain zero cost is the knock-out barrier. In order to find out the zero-cost generating barrier without calculating all prices, a *Zero Cost Calculator* is included in the worksheet. It is important to note that the *Solver* in Microsoft Excel 2003 does not deliver reasonable results if the starting value for the zero-search is out

	A	B	C	D	E
1	Volatility [%]	0.10		Time in Days	180
2	rf [%]	0.022		Daycount	365
3	rd [%]	0.02			
4	Spot [EUR/USD]	1.3000			
5			N		180
6	Time	0.493150685	Delta T		0.002740
7	Trials	1000			
8	Current trial	1000		blue input variables	
9	Trial	Timestep			

Monte Carlo

Trial	1	2	3	4	5	6	7	8	9	10
Average	1.3000	1.3001	1.3001	1.3002	1.3004	1.3006	1.3006	1.3006	1.3005	1.3008	1.3009
1	1.3000	1.2911	1.2935	1.2925	1.2861	1.2809	1.2779	1.2767	1.2724	1.2604	1.2683
2	1.3000	1.3047	1.3107	1.3148	1.3073	1.2990	1.2996	1.2978	1.3046	1.2975	1.2923
3	1.3000	1.3018	1.3017	1.2959	1.2947	1.2926	1.2932	1.2891	1.2965	1.2940	1.2811
4	1.3000	1.3106	1.3089	1.2931	1.2955	1.2866	1.2892	1.2869	1.2866	1.2734	1.2770
5	1.3000	1.3041	1.2974	1.2990	1.2995	1.3038	1.2904	1.2819	1.2805	1.2893	1.2910
6	1.3000	1.3054	1.3140	1.3233	1.3194	1.3207	1.3193	1.3305	1.3320	1.3362	1.3266
7	1.3000	1.2933	1.2809	1.2934	1.3051	1.3013	1.2981	1.2950	1.2949	1.2864	1.2943
8	1.3000	1.3048	1.3032	1.3047	1.2971	1.3066	1.3014	1.3015	1.3015	1.3046	1.3068
9	1.3000	1.2955	1.2967	1.2952	1.3052	1.3152	1.3109	1.3096	1.3170	1.3169	1.3210
10	1.3000	1.2945	1.2924	1.2868	1.2804	1.2830	1.2675	1.2709	1.2766	1.2796	1.2781
11	1.3000	1.2998	1.3060	1.3025	1.3096	1.3190	1.3198	1.3173	1.3127	1.3083	1.2986
12	1.3000	1.3079	1.2987	1.2978	1.3045	1.3145	1.3205	1.3302	1.3352	1.3336	1.3410
13	1.3000	1.3161	1.3253	1.3302	1.3369	1.3355	1.3287	1.3304	1.3347	1.3391	1.3381
14	1.3000	1.2982	1.2905	1.2764	1.2772	1.2657	1.2609	1.2679	1.2746	1.2891	1.2832
15	1.3000	1.2870	1.2875	1.2813	1.2755	1.2944	1.3062	1.2991	1.3047	1.3132	1.3118
16	1.3000	1.3056	1.3158	1.3080	1.3010	1.3113	1.3234	1.3348	1.3295	1.3271	1.3470
17	1.3000	1.3000	1.2997	1.3036	1.3148	1.3057	1.2964	1.2823	1.2917	1.2982	1.2919
18	1.3000	1.3143	1.3098	1.2943	1.2934	1.2967	1.2923	1.3013	1.2972	1.3068	1.3097
19	1.3000	1.2995	1.2907	1.2966	1.2934	1.2941	1.2949	1.2991	1.2836	1.2804	1.2921
20	1.3000	1.2957	1.2989	1.2974	1.3011	1.2851	1.2847	1.2790	1.2700	1.2790	1.2884
21	1.3000	1.3019	1.3084	1.3109	1.3059	1.2960	1.2985	1.3054	1.3165	1.3111	1.3128
22	1.3000	1.3067	1.2998	1.2899	1.2828	1.2877	1.2880	1.2892	1.2997	1.3147	1.3114
23	1.3000	1.3047	1.3081	1.3112	1.3173	1.3232	1.3238	1.3221	1.3105	1.3012	1.3202
24	1.3000	1.2963	1.2930	1.2902	1.2887	1.2881	1.2865	1.2868	1.2929	1.2960	1.3003
25	1.3000	1.2979	1.3028	1.2951	1.3035	1.3079	1.3115	1.3113	1.3127	1.3142	1.3166
26	1.3000	1.2913	1.2885	1.2873	1.2802	1.2845	1.2879	1.2940	1.3032	1.3133	1.3217
27	1.3000	1.2905	1.2947	1.2946	1.2946	1.2908	1.2896	1.2930	1.2893	1.2770	1.2677
28	1.3000	1.2923	1.2832	1.2772	1.2756	1.2831	1.2721	1.2942	1.2861	1.2870	1.2929
29	1.3000	1.2920	1.2891	1.2760	1.2740	1.2781	1.2758	1.2776	1.2847	1.2926	1.2920
30	1.3000	1.2927	1.2979	1.2967	1.2916	1.2877	1.2912	1.2988	1.2990	1.3041	1.3017

Figure 4.3   Screenshot Monte Carlo Simulation

The variables on which the simulation is based are shown in the shaded area in the upper left corner. The bold numbers can be varied. Generally, for a prospective test for effectiveness, all simulated exchange rate paths are used, except the path with the title 'Average'.

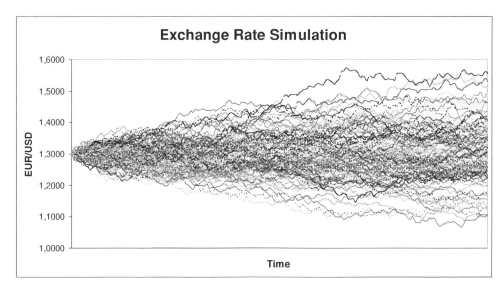

Figure 4.4   150 simulated paths of the exchange rate

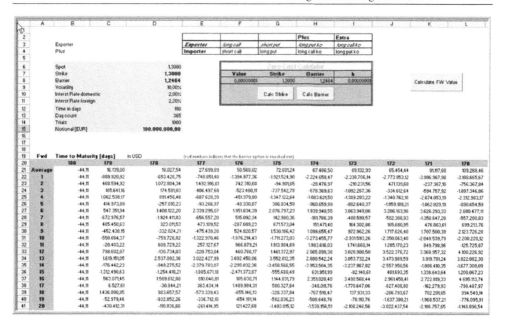

Figure 4.5 Screenshot: calculation of Forward Plus values
Inside the box, the knock-out barrier for the given specification can be calculated so that the initial value is near zero without calculating all paths and time steps.

of an acceptable range.[2] Generally, it is virtually impossible to determine the barrier in a way that the costs for the Forward Plus is exactly zero. The fact that an exchange rate is quoted as a four-digit number further limits the chance to obtain a zero cost. Therefore, the definition of a small range of acceptable costs seems to be sensible. In fact, costs of USD 50 for hedging a transaction worth EUR 100,000,000 is virtually zero in this context. In practice, the value is actually not zero, but the sales margin of the bank. This is set as a target quantity of say 2,000 EUR, but due to rounding it will end up being 1,973.90 EUR. The appropriate knock-out barrier B can be entered into the cell for the calculation of payoffs based on all exchange rate paths. If the barrier is hit or passed, the barrier option becomes worthless from this point onwards for the remaining time to maturity of the Forward Plus. If this occurs, the value of the Forward Plus is shown in red. Moreover, the option pricing formulae do not work at maturity. The options have their intrinsic value as payoff. For the Forward Plus the payoff is given by

$$(S_T - K) + (K - S_T)^+ \, II_{\{S(u) > B, 0 \leq u \leq T\}}, \tag{4.7}$$

where K denotes the strike and worst case. Within this payoff formula, it is apparent that a problem might occur at a later point of the test for effectiveness: in the case that the barrier option is not knocked out and the spot exchange rate is within the participation interval at maturity, the payoff of the Forward Plus is zero.

Figure 4.5 shows the calculation sheet for the Forward Plus values.

Recalling Figure 4.4, which shows a selection of simulated exchange rate paths, Figure 4.6 now includes the specifications of the Forward Plus contract. The bold black line indicates

---

[2] Putting the initial barrier value 0.02–0.04 EUR/USD below the strike might lead to a reasonable result.

Exchange Rate Simulation

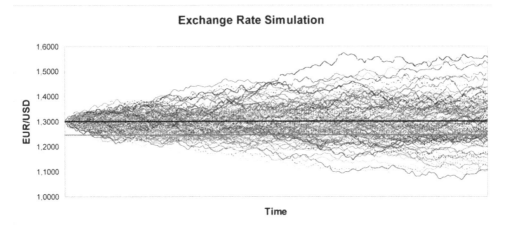

Figure 4.6   150 simulated paths of the exchange rate including strike and barrier of Forward Plus

the strike exchange rate representing also the client's worst case and the bold grey line shows the knock-out barrier of the long reverse knock-out put option. As clearly visible, several of the simulated paths hit or cross the barrier so that the Forward Plus loses its possibility to participate in favorable exchange rate movements. This issue is shown in Figure 4.7. It shows

10	9	8	7	6	5	4	3	2	1	0
1.083.403,44	1.049.149,36	1.008.918,89	967.617,64	903.250,19	829.222,84	772.873,41	709.125,27	605.789,46	506.095,72	342.325,20
-22.063.101,26	-21.037.117,62	-21.159.889,34	-21.061.976,75	-21.030.837,33	-20.877.558,46	-19.884.229,07	-19.434.251,71	-19.270.097,83	-19.420.210,86	-19.197.930,17
4.164.223,05	3.696.962,33	4.182.929,14	3.493.992,77	2.538.497,38	1.996.025,77	2.189.685,16	2.316.187,20	3.532.911,82	3.236.600,29	2.498.527,35
8.488.751,96	7.299.892,36	7.430.228,33	7.188.700,61	7.851.699,91	7.022.217,89	7.335.672,47	7.084.997,65	6.555.659,23	7.886.329,90	7.235.559,88
6.287.453,46	5.727.053,03	5.448.896,69	5.395.457,55	5.356.070,37	5.380.466,19	5.686.621,20	4.834.655,72	6.574.674,73	7.450.114,08	6.237.746,78
3.607.195,33	4.490.047,63	4.877.493,17	4.751.701,16	5.173.654,40	5.454.262,81	6.211.639,77	7.536.993,66	7.389.971,82	8.308.048,62	8.116.329,29
17.197.886,31	16.800.797,35	15.738.399,63	16.323.548,96	16.372.970,55	17.767.232,90	16.419.103,24	16.078.658,67	16.903.460,54	16.420.622,72	16.405.438,34
-11.104.431,11	-10.729.097,00	-10.478.278,71	-10.035.501,72	-9.691.000,26	-10.073.386,04	-3.552.069,39	-3.945.731,47	-9.681.299,92	-10.122.543,05	-9.907.524,27
-4.042.897,62	-3.475.812,77	-3.329.979,39	-2.934.322,75	-2.385.769,76	-2.685.628,61	-1.638.821,47	-2.312.223,47	-2.722.459,88	-2.072.254,52	-1.312.095,02
9.275.421,87	7.938.985,46	7.846.306,86	8.358.530,93	7.326.121,83	7.448.417,12	6.890.882,95	7.023.208,15	7.065.862,66	7.711.965,44	8.900.743,27
-6.026.463,28	-5.976.941,64	-4.978.311,36	-4.825.427,87	-3.795.125,72	-4.515.188,00	-4.928.310,13	-5.056.363,62	-5.471.735,05	-3.998.161,90	-3.965.340,27
-3.016.905,79	-4.016.111,28	-3.404.073,35	-3.018.832,19	-3.090.382,13	-3.784.278,54	-3.217.343,73	-3.487.237,37	-4.202.076,15	-3.853.954,88	-3.701.054,40
1.485.332,16	1.212.453,54	759.826,60	1.065.102,20	676.793,91	364.583,45	93.017,75	33.430,03	37.402,03	14.934,93	0,00
7.204.565,07	6.920.923,75	7.335.179,31	6.993.803,21	6.645.898,68	5.852.203,44	6.202.797,93	6.511.181,57	6.944.262,25	7.425.064,21	7.457.894,45
-16.277.642,88	-16.324.785,05	-15.970.957,08	-16.088.148,35	-15.405.550,23	-16.279.979,34	-16.650.703,67	-14.699.713,91	-14.221.332,85	-13.965.835,67	-13.559.921,29
1.235.634,94	790.686,79	1.066.652,78	587.137,57	491.501,26	570.060,54	1.292.501,21	1.717.931,35	853.547,68	154.631,92	547.813,62
9.812.644,85	9.585.280,54	8.532.459,65	8.815.187,49	9.602.373,25	9.778.222,05	10.266.561,29	11.228.488,65	11.288.216,19	11.364.401,17	10.912.213,10
-7.503.383,21	-8.488.842,84	-7.832.011,27	-8.638.208,81	-8.756.555,51	-8.344.463,70	-9.568.037,33	-9.465.214,31	-10.344.005,35	-10.274.634,12	-10.181.250,99
-6.735.719,71	-5.895.062,11	-6.766.557,59	-7.042.251,00	-7.784.939,77	-8.005.812,75	-8.429.288,74	-8.535.130,17	-8.882.252,64	-8.541.988,71	-7.510.526,59
-5.466.264,17	-5.695.715,40	-5.730.441,72	-6.545.483,50	-6.994.604,20	-5.757.325,07	-5.240.235,74	-6.455.525,08	-7.067.812,62	-7.371.477,20	-7.206.597,99
-14.736.538,56	-13.835.073,98	-13.668.523,47	-13.735.128,99	-14.226.367,68	-14.643.049,54	-14.337.157,31	-14.547.467,60	-14.966.614,77	-15.668.434,30	-15.849.291,30
14.755.646,70	15.045.483,41	14.896.904,80	14.648.255,70	14.947.333,58	15.154.166,40	15.748.587,88	16.492.234,02	17.415.952,06	17.017.103,49	17.615.786,42
-1.763.705,13	-1.015.586,91	-40.532,40	211.239,53	654.046,52	1.414.916,65	1.739.166,71	1.490.239,86	2.354.075,75	2.868.274,91	2.099.263,99
3.293.640,09	2.878.449,55	2.173.912,62	1.191.043,41	1.496.251,70	1.441.162,52	619.300,88	874.167,69	590.002,25	721.389,40	0,00
-13.916.238,20	-14.607.298,44	-14.957.293,12	-14.705.369,34	-13.845.825,71	-14.553.754,60	-15.683.253,37	-15.725.489,06	-15.610.104,25	-16.230.117,82	-16.707.342,83
7.308.389,51	8.002.690,67	7.563.267,32	7.795.782,74	7.762.899,99	7.460.678,54	8.614.924,25	8.214.447,87	8.573.271,82	8.329.177,34	7.545.403,18
-5.778.803,78	-5.535.645,51	-5.741.101,86	-4.828.658,86	-6.052.981,57	-5.764.545,71	-6.187.915,41	-5.936.216,60	-4.822.295,16	-4.335.845,58	-4.205.252,91
-5.295.154,67	-4.909.252,46	-5.465.422,72	-5.378.818,56	-6.269.299,24	-5.511.993,77	-5.026.006,63	-3.882.842,72	-3.474.599,58	-3.307.148,34	-2.561.402,66
4.572.804,83	4.345.827,42	5.100.443,51	6.343.058,21	7.364.681,83	7.263.706,08	6.286.195,67	5.764.292,20	5.800.138,06	6.096.872,37	6.377.301,65
-17.432.822,33	-17.308.859,79	-17.344.198,32	-17.161.040,60	-16.933.685,42	-17.147.564,76	-17.470.039,09	-18.504.906,19	-19.814.041,90	-20.052.362,93	-19.480.097,81
4.853.430,93	5.383.175,11	6.084.323,21	7.478.662,72	7.546.060,40	6.738.911,82	7.851.122,80	7.742.909,53	6.780.365,97	7.576.165,90	8.191.246,14
-484.755,60	155.341,96	-55.963,97	-4.050,96	152.552,70	-1.001.523,42	-1.519.817,86	-1.016.160,78	-432.270,64	210.853,81	876.746,78
3.884.997,23	3.585.723,65	3.348.196,69	2.967.370,82	2.764.593,01	3.079.324,50	2.975.359,86	3.846.000,72	3.501.055,44	4.608.722,70	5.345.341,68
701.814,73	282.905,05	183.671,97	94.422,39	-156.969,35	18.501,63	103.488,22	28.086,28	42.339,42	54,86	0,00
-2.335.816,34	-3.481.107,87	-2.339.566,16	-1.565.082,50	-2.571.412,83	-1.911.329,73	-904.284,73	-1.747.654,81	-2.414.340,37	-2.472.229,78	-2.347.968,98
-6.720.836,94	-5.777.600,40	-5.556.617,83	-6.392.949,29	-5.600.556,47	-6.278.415,64	-5.378.090,07	-5.111.761,86	-5.600.443,31	-5.892.359,70	-6.959.309,37
1.551.432,19	2.498.860,21	1.480.750,12	2.176.556,38	2.627.792,79	2.754.226,69	3.824.932,73	5.133.765,18	5.023.737,39	5.070.817,77	4.478.996,61

Figure 4.7   Screenshot: calculation of Forward Plus values at maturity
Light grey numbers indicate that the barrier was hit along the path.

the first simulated exchange rate paths as shown in Figure 4.5 for the last ten days of the simulation period.

4.6.3 Calculation of the forward rates

The next worksheet displayed in Figure 4.8 calculates the forward exchange rates for the current point in time until the specified time to maturity. The time period of the forward rates is reduced from column to column by one day. The forward rate is not required for the calculation of the Forward Plus. But it is necessary to evaluate the forecast transaction the Forward Plus will hedge. The calculation is performed according to the usual formula

$$f = S_0 e^{(r_d - r_f)T},\qquad(4.8)$$

where f and S_0 denote the current forward rate and the current spot exchange rate respectively. The remaining time period until the forecast transaction takes place is denoted by T.

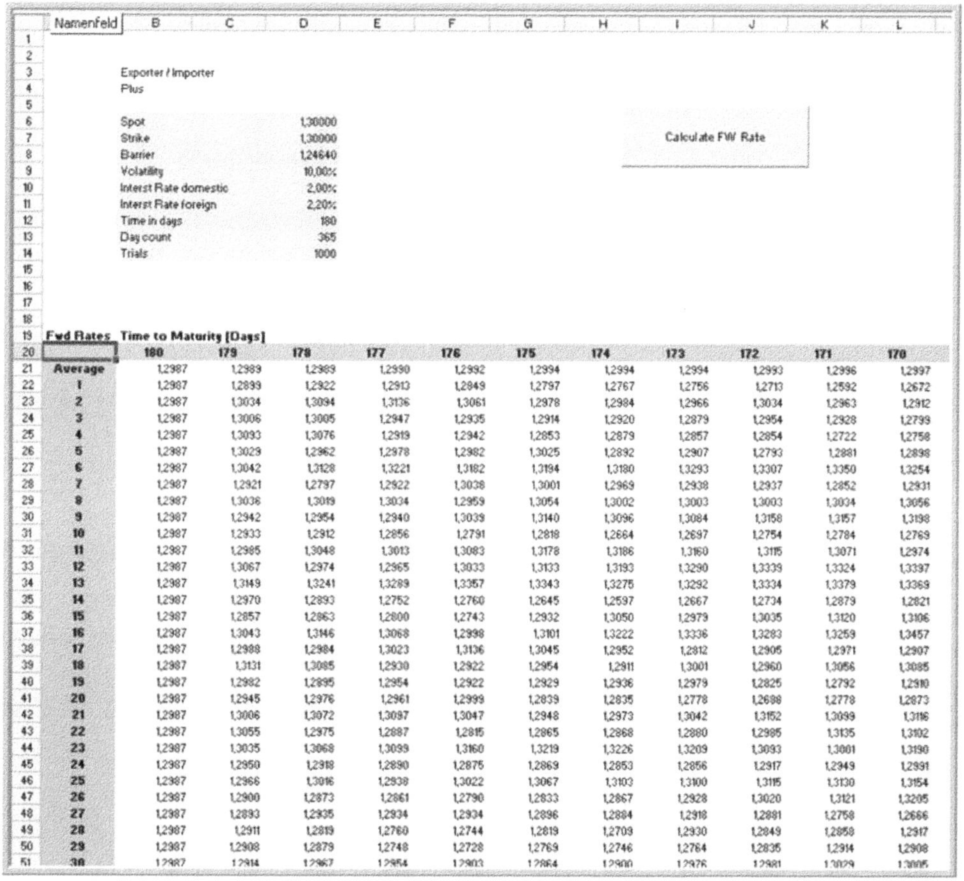

Namenfeld	B	C	D	E	F	G	H	I	J	K	L
Exporter / Importer											
Plus											
Spot			1,30000								
Strike			1,30000				Calculate FW Rate				
Barrier			1,24640								
Volatility			10,00%								
Interst Rate domestic			2,00%								
Interst Rate foreign			2,20%								
Time in days			180								
Day count			365								
Trials			1000								

Fwd Rates Time to Maturity [Days]

	180	179	178	177	176	175	174	173	172	171	170
Average	1,2987	1,2989	1,2989	1,2990	1,2992	1,2994	1,2994	1,2994	1,2993	1,2996	1,2997
1	1,2987	1,2899	1,2922	1,2913	1,2849	1,2797	1,2767	1,2756	1,2713	1,2592	1,2672
2	1,2987	1,3034	1,3094	1,3136	1,3061	1,2978	1,2984	1,2966	1,3034	1,2963	1,2912
3	1,2987	1,3006	1,3005	1,2947	1,2935	1,2914	1,2920	1,2879	1,2954	1,2928	1,2799
4	1,2987	1,3093	1,3076	1,2919	1,2942	1,2853	1,2879	1,2857	1,2854	1,2722	1,2758
5	1,2987	1,3029	1,2962	1,2978	1,2982	1,3025	1,2892	1,2907	1,2793	1,2881	1,2898
6	1,2987	1,3042	1,3128	1,3221	1,3182	1,3194	1,3180	1,3293	1,3307	1,3350	1,3254
7	1,2987	1,2921	1,2797	1,2922	1,3038	1,3001	1,2969	1,2938	1,2937	1,2852	1,2931
8	1,2987	1,3038	1,3019	1,3034	1,2959	1,3054	1,3002	1,3003	1,3003	1,3004	1,3056
9	1,2987	1,2942	1,2954	1,2940	1,3039	1,3140	1,3096	1,3084	1,3158	1,3157	1,3198
10	1,2987	1,2933	1,2912	1,2856	1,2791	1,2818	1,2664	1,2697	1,2754	1,2784	1,2769
11	1,2987	1,2985	1,3048	1,3013	1,3083	1,3178	1,3186	1,3160	1,3115	1,3071	1,2974
12	1,2987	1,3067	1,2974	1,2965	1,3033	1,3133	1,3193	1,3290	1,3339	1,3324	1,3397
13	1,2987	1,3149	1,3241	1,3289	1,3357	1,3343	1,3275	1,3292	1,3334	1,3379	1,3369
14	1,2987	1,2970	1,2893	1,2752	1,2760	1,2645	1,2597	1,2667	1,2734	1,2879	1,2821
15	1,2987	1,2857	1,2863	1,2800	1,2743	1,2932	1,3050	1,2979	1,3035	1,3120	1,3106
16	1,2987	1,3043	1,3146	1,3068	1,2998	1,3101	1,3222	1,3336	1,3283	1,3259	1,3457
17	1,2987	1,2988	1,2984	1,3023	1,3136	1,3045	1,2952	1,2812	1,2905	1,2971	1,2907
18	1,2987	1,3131	1,3085	1,2930	1,2922	1,2954	1,2911	1,3001	1,2960	1,3056	1,3085
19	1,2987	1,2982	1,2895	1,2954	1,2922	1,2929	1,2936	1,2979	1,2825	1,2792	1,2910
20	1,2987	1,2945	1,2976	1,2961	1,2999	1,2839	1,2835	1,2778	1,2698	1,2778	1,2873
21	1,2987	1,3006	1,3072	1,3097	1,3047	1,2948	1,2973	1,3042	1,3152	1,3099	1,3116
22	1,2987	1,3055	1,2975	1,2887	1,2815	1,2865	1,2868	1,2880	1,2995	1,3135	1,3102
23	1,2987	1,3035	1,3068	1,3099	1,3160	1,3219	1,3226	1,3209	1,3093	1,3001	1,3190
24	1,2987	1,2950	1,2918	1,2890	1,2875	1,2869	1,2853	1,2856	1,2917	1,2949	1,2931
25	1,2987	1,2966	1,3016	1,2938	1,3022	1,3067	1,3103	1,3100	1,3115	1,3130	1,3154
26	1,2987	1,2900	1,2873	1,2861	1,2790	1,2833	1,2867	1,2928	1,3020	1,3121	1,3205
27	1,2987	1,2893	1,2935	1,2934	1,2934	1,2896	1,2884	1,2918	1,2881	1,2758	1,2666
28	1,2987	1,2911	1,2819	1,2760	1,2744	1,2819	1,2709	1,2930	1,2849	1,2858	1,2917
29	1,2987	1,2908	1,2879	1,2748	1,2728	1,2769	1,2746	1,2764	1,2835	1,2914	1,2908
30	1,2987	1,2914	1,2967	1,2954	1,2903	1,2864	1,2900	1,2976	1,2981	1,3029	1,3005

Figure 4.8 Screenshot: calculation of forward rates

As the time to maturity shortens, the forward rate converges towards the current spot rate. As visible in Figure 4.8, there are no more specifications needed for the calculations in this worksheet.

4.6.4 Calculation of the forecast transaction's value

The calculation of the forecast transaction's value uses the information given in the preceding calculations. At initiation of the hedge relationship, the value is set to zero as the standard value. For the remaining points in time, the value is calculated as the difference between the strike of the Forward Plus and the current forward exchange rate. This difference multiplied with the notional amount represents the time value of the forecast transaction during the hedge relationship, see [99], p. 34. This calculation makes sense considering the following explanations. The transaction is hedged at initiation of the hedge relationship. The *worst case* exchange rate the entity obtains, is the strike of the options the Forward Plus consists of. If the entity hedges the forecast transaction at a later point in time with an outright forward, it would of course fix the exchange rate at the current forward rate. So the difference between the two rates multiplied with the notional amount represents the value gained or lost through not hedging at a later point in time. The resulting figure displays the value of the forecast transaction. Figure 4.9 shows an excerpt of the exemplary calculation results.

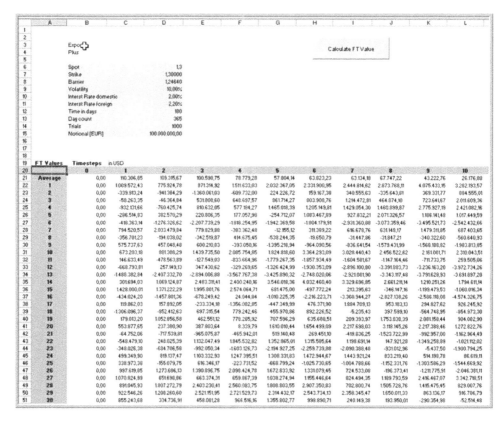

Figure 4.9   Screenshot: calculation of the forecast transaction's value

4.6.5 Dollar-Offset Ratio – prospective test for effectiveness

As described in Section 4.5.1, the *Dollar-Offset Ratio* is an easy way to measure hedge effectiveness. On the other hand this method also involves weaknesses. One weakness is that for small changes in value, a resulting ratio that is out of the range accepted as effective might occur. In this case, the ineffectiveness is high relative to the change in value from an accounting perspective, although the hedge is economically highly effective. Recall that the *Dollar-Offset Ratio* is calculated using Equation (4.1). Therefore, in a first step the changes in values for both the Forward Plus and the forecast transaction have to be calculated. The change in value is determined by subtracting the previous value from the current value. This is done for every time step and all simulated exchange rate paths. In the second step, the appropriate changes of the specified point in time are set in a ratio according to Equation (4.1). The result of this represents the one-day period *Dollar-Offset Ratio*.

An exception from this method is the value at initiation of the hedge. At the first date of observation, a previous value does not exist. Therefore, the ratio is set to zero. For the second point in time the ratio should be very near to minus one. This is due to the fact that the hedged item has a value of zero at the previous point in time and the value of the Forward Plus should also be near zero in the previous point in time as it has zero cost. As one can see in Figure 4.10, the second column is headed by 'Cumulative'. In this column the cumulative *Dollar-Offset Ratio* is shown. It is calculated using the ratio of the final value of the forecast transaction and the final payoff of the Forward Plus.

	A	B	C	D	E	F	G	H	I	J	K	L	M
1													
2													
3									Calculate				
4	trials	1000											
5	Timesteps	180											
6													
7	Path	Cumulative	180	179	178	177	176	175	174	173	172	171	170
8	1	-1,00	0,00	-0,99	-1,00	-0,99	-0,99	-0,99	-0,99	-0,99	-0,98	-0,98	-0,98
9	2	-1,00	0,00	-1,00	-1,00	-1,00	-1,00	-0,98	-1,00	-0,99	-1,00	-0,99	-0,99
10	3	-1,00	0,00	-1,08	-0,99	-1,00	-1,00	-0,98	-0,99	-0,99	-0,99	-0,99	-0,99
11	4	-1,00	0,00	-1,00	-0,99	-0,99	-0,99	-0,99	-0,99	-1,01	-0,99	-0,98	-0,99
12	5	-1,00	0,00	-1,00	-0,99	-0,97	-0,99	-0,99	-0,98	-0,99	-0,99	-0,98	-0,99
13	6	-1,00	0,00	-1,00	-1,00	-1,01	-0,99	-1,01	-1,00	-1,00	-1,00	-1,01	-1,00
14	7	-1,00	0,00	-0,99	-0,99	-0,99	-1,00	-1,00	-0,99	-1,06	-0,99	-0,99	-0,99
15	8	-1,00	0,00	-1,00	-0,99	-1,00	-0,99	-1,00	-0,92	-0,29	-0,99	-0,99	-0,98
16	9	-1,00	0,00	-0,99	-1,00	-0,99	-1,00	-1,00	-1,01	-1,00	-1,11	-1,00	-1,00
17	10	-1,00	0,00	-1,00	-0,99	-0,99	-0,98	-0,99	-0,98	-0,98	-0,98	-0,99	-0,99
18	11	-1,00	0,00	-0,99	-1,00	-0,99	-1,00	-0,99	-1,01	-1,00	-1,00	-1,00	-0,99
19	12	0,00	0,00	-1,00	-1,00	-0,99	-1,00	-1,00	-1,00	-1,00	-1,01	-1,01	-0,99
20	13	-1,00	0,00	-1,00	-1,00	-1,01	-1,02	-1,01	-1,00	-1,00	-1,01	-1,02	-1,01
21	14	-1,00	0,00	-0,99	-0,99	-0,98	-0,98	-0,98	-0,98	-0,98	-0,99	-0,99	-0,99
22	15	-1,00	0,00	-0,98	-0,99	-0,99	-0,99	-0,99	-1,00	-0,99	-1,00	-1,01	-0,99
23	16	-1,00	0,00	-1,00	-1,00	-1,00	-1,00	-1,00	-1,00	-1,01	-1,01	-1,01	-1,01
24	17	-1,00	0,00	-1,02	-0,99	-1,00	-1,00	-1,00	-0,99	-0,99	-0,99	-0,99	-0,99
25	18	-1,00	0,00	-1,00	-1,00	-1,00	-0,99	-0,99	-0,99	-1,00	-0,99	-0,99	-0,99
26	19	-1,00	0,00	-0,99	-0,99	-0,99	-0,98	-0,98	-0,99	-0,99	-0,99	-0,99	-0,98
27	20	-1,00	0,00	-0,99	-1,00	-0,99	-0,99	-1,00	-0,99	-0,98	-0,98	-0,99	-0,99
997	990	0,00	0,00	-1,00	-1,00	-1,00	-1,01	-1,01	-1,01	-1,01	-1,01	-1,01	-1,02
998	991	-1,00	0,00	-1,00	-0,99	-1,00	-1,00	-0,99	-0,99	-1,00	-1,00	-1,00	-1,00
999	992	-1,00	0,00	-1,00	-1,00	-1,00	-1,00	-0,99	-1,00	-1,00	-1,00	-1,00	-1,00
1000	993	-1,00	0,00	-1,00	-0,98	-1,00	-1,00	-1,00	-0,99	-1,00	-1,00	-1,00	-1,00
1001	994	-1,00	0,00	-0,99	-0,99	-0,99	-0,99	-0,99	-0,99	-0,99	-0,98	-0,99	-0,99
1002	995	0,00	0,00	-1,00	-1,00	-0,98	-1,00	-1,00	-1,01	-1,00	-1,00	-1,00	-0,99
1003	996	-1,00	0,00	-0,99	-0,99	-0,99	-0,99	-0,99	-0,99	-0,99	-1,00	-0,99	-0,99
1004	997	-1,00	0,00	-0,99	-0,99	-0,99	-0,99	-0,99	-0,99	-0,99	-0,99	-0,99	-1,00
1005	998	-1,00	0,00	-1,00	-0,99	-1,00	-1,00	-0,99	-0,99	-0,99	-0,98	-0,98	-0,99
1006	999	0,00	0,00	-1,00	-1,00	-0,99	-0,99	-0,99	-0,98	-0,98	-0,98	-0,98	-0,98
1007	1000	-1,00	0,00	-1,00	-0,99	-1,01	-1,00	-1,03	-0,99	-1,00	-0,99	-1,00	-1,00
1008													
1009	Average	-0,92	0,00	-0,99	-0,99	-0,99	-0,99	-0,99	-0,99	-1,00	-0,99	-0,98	-1,00

Figure 4.10 Screenshot: prospective Dollar-Offset Ratio

As described above, a problem may arise at this stage, if the barrier option was not hit and the spot exchange rate is within the participation range. In this case the final payoff would be zero and the cumulative *Dollar-Offset Ratio* is not defined due to a division by zero. In this case, the value of the *Dollar-Offset Ratio* is set to zero in the spread sheet. This problem only arises for the Forward Plus, but not for a Forward Extra. This is because of the offsetting option position within the participation range. For the Forward Extra, the barrier option enforces the option positions that replicate the forward contract, see Section 2.1.5.

For the calculation of the prospective hedge effectiveness per time period, the *Dollar-Offset Ratios* of the single paths are averaged for every point in time. For the expected cumulative *Dollar-Offset Ratio* the cumulative *Dollar-Offset Ratios* of each path are averaged. As one can see the expected cumulative *Dollar-Offset Ratio* is −0.92. This is within the acceptable range of [−1.25; −0.8] and would prove the prospective hedge effectiveness for the given example according to this method.

Averaging over the average *Dollar-Offset Ratios* per time step would come to another result. The ratio is −1.50, and the hedge would fail according to this criterion. So the cumulative ratio leads to a better result in terms of effectiveness due to an offsetting effect of outliers from the accepted range. The day-by-day average *Dollar-Offset Ratio* is not calculated automatically in the spread sheet.

4.6.6 Variance Reduction Measure – prospective test for effectiveness

The calculation according to the *Variance Reduction Measure* (VRM) involves multiple steps. In the first step, the changes in value of the hedged item, that is the forecast transaction, are observed. Now the variance of the change in value is calculated per exchange rate path over the observed time period. In the next step, the changes in value of the combined hedge relationship, i.e. the changes in value of the hedging instrument and the changes in value of the forecast transaction are added up for each day. The variance is calculated also from the joint change in value (hedging relationship). This variance should be much smaller because the aim of the hedge is that the changes in value are offset for the most part. The *Variance Reduction Measure* is calculated by Equation (4.3). This procedure is repeated for every exchange rate path from the Monte Carlo Simulation. Finally, the average of the calculated VRM-Ratios gives an indication of the prospective hedge effectiveness. This is shown in the last line of Figure 4.11. We notice that the ratio is always near one, indicating that the variance is reduced to a large extent. The literature does not give any information as to which threshold value should be reached. A value of 0.96 would be equal to an offset of 80 % of the changes in value, see [95], p. 96. Other authors merely mention that the reduction must be specified in order to be useful, see [94], p. 44 and [94], p. 103.

The average reduction in variance amounts to 99.51 % in this example. This means that the hedge fulfills the prospective test for effectiveness.

4.6.7 Regression Analysis – prospective test for effectiveness

The third method that can be used to test the hedge relationship for effectiveness is the *Regression Analysis*. For this method, the changes in value of the forecast transaction (hedged item) and the Forward Plus (hedging instrument) are employed. For the linear regression model we use

$$y = \alpha x + \beta + \epsilon, \qquad (4.9)$$

	A	B	C	D	E	F
1						
2						
3						Calculate
4	**Trials**	**1000**				
5	**Timesteps**	**180**				
6						
7	**Path**	**Variance Combined**	**Variance FT Value**	**Ratio**		
8	**1**	514.820.862	40.228.429.099.030	0,999987		
9	**2**	6.115.629.465	20.007.647.521.951	0,999694		
10	**3**	11.447.395.892	18.698.297.374.851	0,999388		
11	**4**	7.063.004.783	8.847.301.865.045	0,999202		
12	**5**	1.311.001.192	15.935.920.716.922	0,999918		
13	**6**	4.139.317.579	20.017.322.736.582	0,999793		
14	**7**	1.341.860.594	13.331.324.741.414	0,999899		
15	**8**	11.406.496.541	9.322.250.540.988	0,998776		
16	**9**	11.168.315.329	9.458.501.012.721	0,998819		
17	**10**	1.928.270.354	8.022.912.513.834	0,999760		
18	**11**	3.415.704.591	6.340.165.969.192	0,999461		
19	**12**	116.075.995.302	17.907.321.846.962	0,993518		
20	**13**	13.856.658.240	6.726.612.196.436	0,997940		
21	**14**	1.147.960.781	14.056.416.067.052	0,999918		
22	**15**	42.672.430.927	5.337.737.154.385	0,992006		
23	**16**	9.453.643.714	21.215.742.224.047	0,999554		
24	**17**	1.063.123.828	5.145.942.243.086	0,999793		
25	**18**	2.514.562.920	9.689.352.029.492	0,999740		
26	**19**	3.266.143.396	5.029.457.255.012	0,999351		
27	**20**	1.124.284.903	18.923.082.720.628	0,999941		
28	**21**	8.033.179.713	26.944.242.269.150	0,999702		
29	**22**	2.199.820.610	4.249.376.927.048	0,999482		
30	**23**	15.780.011.015	1.968.580.271.170	0,991984		
31	**24**	1.959.119.613	30.161.542.828.057	0,999935		
32	**25**	7.553.752.158	12.819.366.301.902	0,999411		
33	**26**	2.106.001.646	6.095.152.700.988	0,999654		
34	**27**	1.180.458.653	5.311.546.512.163	0,999778		
35	**28**	6.599.570.763	18.774.628.705.371	0,999648		
36	**29**	1.247.081.404	25.484.382.876.885	0,999951		
37	**30**	11.554.455.312	10.375.110.570.721	0,998886		
997	**990**	343.806.459.894	6.737.693.906.789	0,948973		
998	**991**	16.423.371.030	3.469.295.568.807	0,995266		
999	**992**	8.248.142.385	13.329.626.883.078	0,999381		
1000	**993**	6.037.264.515	17.255.479.753.948	0,999650		
1001	**994**	1.118.942.255	8.086.663.155.793	0,999862		
1002	**995**	239.725.606.536	4.886.525.611.621	0,950942		
1003	**996**	6.993.352.530	7.040.273.895.607	0,999007		
1004	**997**	19.717.427.411	7.939.244.632.204	0,997516		
1005	**998**	4.533.332.743	23.110.419.078.790	0,999804		
1006	**999**	272.621.403.749	2.135.113.771.336	0,872315		
1007	**1000**	30.363.704.087	2.573.359.402.514	0,988201		
1008						
1009	**Average**			0,995123		

Figure 4.11 Screenshot: prospective Variance Reduction Measure

where y denotes the change in fair value of the hedging instrument and x denotes the change in hedge fair value of the hedged item. The interception of the regression line with the y-axis is α. The term β is the slope of the regression line and ϵ represents the error term. With the regression the change in value of the hedging instrument is explained by the change in value of the forecast transaction.

The slope of the regression line should be close to minus one. In order to deem the hedge as effective in accordance with IAS 39, R^2, which is a measure of how good the regression line explains the data points, should be at least 80 %.

For the prospective test for hedge effectiveness, the regression parameters α, β and R^2 are calculated for each exchange rate path. The next appropriate step is to average the regression parameters over the different paths. The averages are the expected values for the parameters and give an indication for the anticipated hedge effectiveness. As mentioned in Section 4.5.1, it is important to have a sufficient number of data points per path in order to obtain reasonable results. Figure 4.12 shows a selection of results for the *Regression Analysis* from the given example.

The **Average** line shows the expected values. The prospective hedge effectiveness holds according to the *Regression Analysis*. The slope of the regression line is -0.9911 which is sufficiently close to minus one. The measure of determination is $R^2 = 99.55\,\%$ and thereby

	A	B	C	D	E	F
1						
2						
3						
4	Trials	1000			Calculate	
5	Timesteps	180				
6						
7		Slope	Intercept	R-Squared		
8	1	-0,9962	-406,38	0,9997		
9	2	-0,9899	139,50	0,9994		
10	3	-1,0147	-587,90	0,9988		
11	4	-0,9826	598,37	0,9994		
12	5	-0,9992	37,04	0,9998		
13	6	-0,9902	886,12	0,9997		
14	7	-0,9980	-107,76	0,9997		
15	8	-1,0127	92,44	0,9992		
16	9	-0,9758	1.191,97	0,9992		
17	10	-1,0018	40,13	0,9997		
18	11	-1,0002	4,43	0,9997		
19	12	-0,9527	8.390,75	0,9827		
20	13	-0,9948	214,80	0,9984		
21	14	-1,0032	239,87	0,9997		
22	15	-0,9364	192,79	0,9877		
23	16	-0,9913	526,18	0,9997		
24	17	-0,9976	-136,08	0,9998		
25	18	-1,0061	251,55	0,9997		
26	19	-1,0043	169,46	0,9996		
27	20	-0,9981	-168,80	0,9997		
997	990	-0,9765	20.749,31	0,9817		
998	991	-0,9791	335,58	0,9971		
999	992	-1,0045	-123,62	0,9996		
1000	993	-0,9887	784,03	0,9996		
1001	994	-0,9994	-26,48	0,9997		
1002	995	-0,9680	11.446,98	0,9666		
1003	996	-0,9695	878,76	0,9984		
1004	997	-0,9584	458,57	0,9984		
1005	998	-0,9876	944,24	0,9995		
1006	999	-0,9896	17.460,68	0,9611		
1007	1000	-0,9624	397,44	0,9881		
1008						
1009	Average	-0,9911	1.251,28	0,995501		
1010						

Figure 4.12   Screenshot: prospective Regression Analysis

clearly above the necessary threshold to qualify as highly effective hedge in combination with the slope-coefficient.

4.6.8   Result

According to the *Dollar-Offset Method*, which seems to be the method most likely to fail, we have calculated a *cumulative Dollar-Offset ratio* of −0.92. This is clearly in the range of [−1.25; −0.8] which is categorized as highly effective. Taking a closer look at the calculated results, one can see that the ratios nearly always have values of −1.00. In some cases the values of the cumulative ratios are zero. This is the case if the barrier of the Forward Plus has not been reached and the spot exchange rate is within the participation range at maturity, i.e. the barrier option has an intrinsic value at maturity. In this case the ratio cannot be calculated, because this would be a division by zero. As such the ratio is defined as zero. In practice, this means that the exporter receives a gain from the forecast transaction, but on the other side does not suffer a loss from the Forward Plus. For the exporter, this is an ideal scenario, but from an accounting perspective the hedge is at risk of overcompensation and being ineffective.

Looking at the *day-by-day Dollar-Offset ratio* the hedge fails the test for effectiveness. The average over the paths and the time result in a Dollar-Offset ratio of -1.50. This is clearly out of the range regarded as being highly effective. So the *Dollar-Offset Ratio* can testify the effectiveness requirements only on a cumulative basis.

Using the *Variance Reduction Measure*, high effectiveness is achieved. The hedge reduces the variance for the combined position compared with the unhedged position by more than 99.50 % on average. The worst result of variance reduction is 76.31 %. This is below the threshold of 96 %, but there are only 36 paths out of 1000 that fail to reduce the variance by at least 96 %. For the third method, the *Regression Analysis*, the crucial figures are R^2 and the slope. For R^2, the regression results lie between 85.51 % and 99.99 %. For the slope of the regression line the results are in a range between -1.1022 and -0.8918. This is slightly more than 10 % from the perfect value, but is overall a satisfactory result. The average values are -0.9911 for the slope coefficient and 0.995501 for R^2. This average result gives a clear indication that the hedge is highly effective on a prospective basis.

Summing up, three of the observed four methods result in the hedge fulfilling the test for high prospective effectiveness. Only the *Dollar-Offset Method* on a *day-by-day basis* fails to meet the required effectiveness. Considering this circumstance, it is questionable whether a *Dollar-Offset ratio on a day-by-day basis* makes sense at all. But this result is not surprising. As mentioned in Section 4.5.1 and in the literature, the *Dollar-Offset Method* in general and especially in the period-by-period Dollar-Offset Method is likely to fail.

As entities have to choose one method for testing for effectiveness, it is advisable to choose either the *Variance Reduction Measure* or the *Regression Analysis*, as these methods appear to give more reasonable and stable results.

4.6.9 Retrospective test for effectiveness

For the retrospective test for hedge effectiveness, the methods can be applied in the same manner. The only difference is that the exchange rate path does not have to be simulated but is given. Therefore, there is only one path which has to be examined. The results obtained can not be averaged. For this reason the effectiveness results may be different.

As the real exchange rate path is not known in this example, one of the simulated paths is selected randomly as the path that really happened during the time period of the hedge. In the following, four paths are examined, see Figure 4.13. They represent four basic scenarios which might happen at maturity. The first scenario is that the barrier option is knocked out during the hedge and the end value of the Forward Plus is negative. The second scenario is that the barrier is knocked out, as in the first scenario, but the Forward Plus has a positive value at maturity. The third scenario is that the barrier is not knocked out and the Forward Plus has a value of zero at maturity. The last scenario is that the barrier was not knocked out and the Forward Plus value is positive at the end of the hedge.

This selection is just an example of possible scenarios. However, their effectiveness is dependent on the exchange rate path, not only on the value of the derivative at maturity. The criteria whether the barrier option is knocked out or not and the value at maturity, are possibilities for categorization.

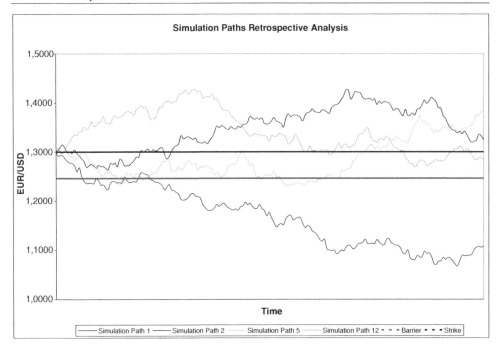

Figure 4.13   Selected paths for the retrospective test for effectiveness

Scenario 1, Simulation path 1

In the first scenario the barrier option is knocked out. The value of the Forward Plus is negative at maturity of the derivative. Testing the effectiveness using the *Dollar-Offset Method*, the hedge can be classified as highly effective. As visible in Figure 4.14 the cumulative Dollar-Offset ratio is −1.00.

Even the *day-by-day Dollar-Offset ratio* would qualify for a highly effective hedge relationship as all values are within the range [−1.25; −0.8], except the ratio for the first day. There, the ratio is set to zero as the value of the forecast transaction is zero per definition.

5	Timesteps	180					
6	Selected Path:	1					
			Delta FV		Delta FT		
7	Nr.	FV Value	Value	FT Value	Value	Ratio	
178	170	-22.063.101,26	1.208.090,59	22.075.074,57	-1.210.009,47	-1,00	
179	171	-21.037.117,62	1.025.983,64	21.047.392,22	-1.027.682,35	-1,00	
180	172	-21.159.889,34	-122.771,71	21.169.075,36	121.683,14	-0,99	
181	173	-21.061.976,75	97.912,58	21.069.977,11	-99.098,25	-1,01	
182	174	-21.030.837,33	31.139,42	21.037.684,46	-32.292,65	-1,04	
183	175	-20.877.558,46	153.278,88	20.883.222,66	-154.461,80	-1,01	
184	176	-19.884.229,07	993.329,39	19.888.544,71	-994.677,94	-1,00	
185	177	-19.434.251,71	449.977,36	19.437.415,11	-451.129,60	-1,00	
186	178	-19.270.097,83	164.153,88	19.272.188,90	-165.226,22	-1,01	
187	179	-19.420.210,86	-150.113,02	19.421.264,50	149.075,61	-0,99	
188	180	-19.197.930,17	222.280,69	19.197.930,17	-223.334,34	-1,00	-1,00
100							

Figure 4.14   Screenshot: cumulative Dollar-Offset Ratio Path 1

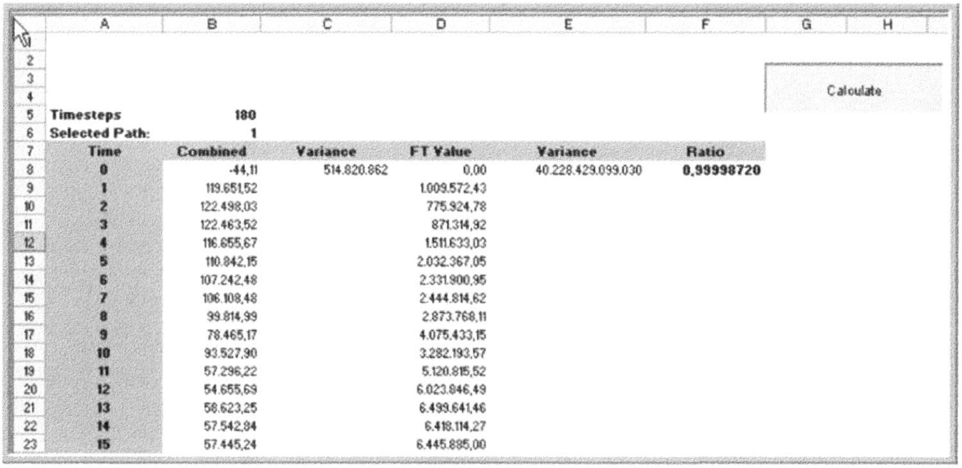

Timesteps	180
Selected Path:	1

Calculate

Time	Combined	Variance	FT Value	Variance	Ratio
0	-44,11	514.820.862	0,00	40.228.429.099.030	0,99998720
1	119.651,52		1.009.572,43		
2	122.498,03		775.924,78		
3	122.463,52		871.314,92		
4	116.655,67		1.511.633,03		
5	110.842,15		2.032.367,05		
6	107.242,48		2.331.900,95		
7	106.108,48		2.444.814,62		
8	99.814,99		2.873.768,11		
9	78.465,17		4.075.433,15		
10	93.527,90		3.282.193,57		
11	57.296,22		5.120.815,52		
12	54.655,69		6.023.846,49		
13	58.623,25		6.499.641,46		
14	57.542,84		6.418.114,27		
15	57.445,24		6.445.885,00		

Figure 4.15 Screenshot: Variance Reduction Measure Path 1

For the *Variance Reduction Measure*, the result definitely proves high effectiveness. The hedge reduced the variance nearly 100 %. This is demonstrated in the Figure 4.15.

The third method introduced for testing the hedge effectiveness, the *Regression Analysis*, leads to the same result. For the first path, the slope is −0.9962 and thereby close to minus one. The crucial measure R^2 explains 99.97 % of the data points. The full *Regression Analysis* result can be seen in Figure 4.16.

Summing up, all methods to test for effectiveness come up with a positive assessment result for simulation path one.

Scenario 2, simulation path 5

In the second scenario, path five is selected. Within this path the barrier option is knocked out during the hedge. The value of the derivative is positive at the end of the derivative's life.

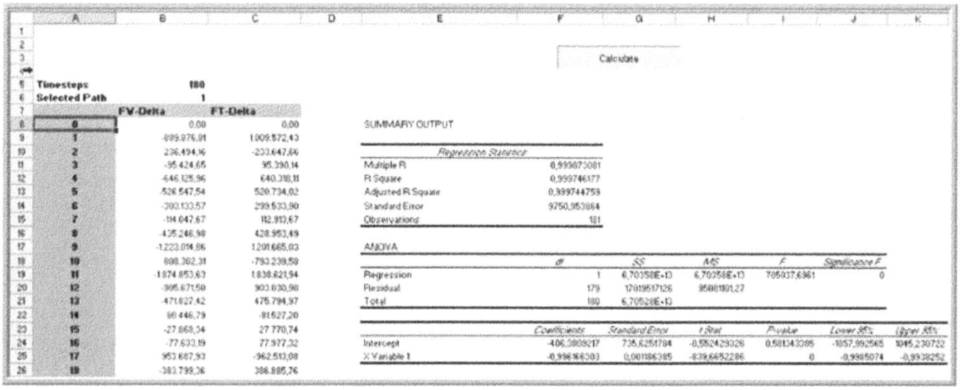

Calculate

Timesteps	180
Selected Path	1

	FV-Delta	FT-Delta
0	0,00	0,00
1	-889.876,91	1.009.572,43
2	236.494,16	-233.647,66
3	-95.424,65	95.390,14
4	-646.125,96	640.318,11
5	-526.547,54	520.734,02
6	-303.133,57	299.533,90
7	-114.047,67	112.913,67
8	-435.246,98	428.953,49
9	-1.223.014,86	1.201.665,03
10	808.302,31	-793.239,59
11	-1.874.853,63	1.838.821,94
12	-905.671,50	903.030,98
13	-471.827,42	476.794,97
14	90.446,79	-91.527,20
15	-27.868,34	27.770,74
16	-77.633,19	77.977,32
17	953.687,93	-962.513,08
18	-383.799,36	386.885,76

SUMMARY OUTPUT

Regression Statistics	
Multiple R	0,999873081
R Square	0,999746177
Adjusted R Square	0,999744759
Standard Error	9750,953884
Observations	181

ANOVA

	df	*SS*	*MS*	*F*	*Significance F*
Regression	1	6,70358E+13	6,70358E+13	705037,6961	0
Residual	179	17019517126	95081101,27		
Total	180	6,70528E+13			

	Coefficients	*Standard Error*	*t Stat*	*P-value*	*Lower 95%*	*Upper 95%*
Intercept	-406,3808217	735,6251784	-0,552429326	0,581343386	-1857,992565	1045,230722
X Variable 1	-0,996166303	0,001186385	-839,6652286	0	-0,9985074	-0,9938252

Figure 4.16 Screenshot: Regression Analysis Path 1

	A	B	C	D	E	F	G	H	I	J
1										
2										
3									Calculate	
4										
5	Timesteps	180								
6	Selected Path:	5								
7	Nr.	FV Value	Delta FV Value	FT Value	Delta FT Value	Ratio				
8	0	-44,11	0,00	0,00	0,00	0,00				
9	1	414.973,89	415.018,00	-286.514,83	-286.514,83	-0,69				
10	2	-257.010,23	-671.984,12	382.570,29	669.085,11	-1,00				
11	3	-93.266,97	163.743,26	220.806,35	-161.763,94	-0,99				
12	4	-48.330,87	44.936,10	177.057,98	-43.748,37	-0,97				
13	5	386.834,59	435.165,46	-254.712,07	-431.770,04	-0,99				
14	6	-960.659,99	-1.347.494,58	1.083.467,89	1.338.179,95	-0,99				
15	7	-802.640,37	158.019,63	927.832,21	-155.635,68	-0,98				
16	8	-1.959.189,21	-1.156.548,84	2.071.326,57	1.143.494,36	-0,99				
17	9	-1.062.029,19	897.160,01	1.186.141,48	-885.185,09	-0,99				
18	10	-890.654,59	171.374,61	1.017.449,59	-168.691,89	-0,98				
19	11	-114.356,34	776.298,25	249.191,19	-768.258,40	-0,99				
20	12	-225.098,47	-110.742,14	360.022,51	110.831,32	-1,00				
21	13	-609.684,90	-384.586,43	742.036,05	382.013,54	-0,99				
22	14	-1.783.966,06	-1.174.281,16	1.902.572,45	1.160.536,40	-0,99				
23	15	-2.990.775,91	-1.206.809,84	3.089.769,98	1.187.197,52	-0,98				

Figure 4.17   Screenshot: Dollar-Offset Ratio Path 5

Following the *period-by-period Dollar-Offset Method*, the hedge would not qualify for hedge accounting. Not only the first ratio, which is zero for the above mentioned reason, but also the second ratio is out of the accepted range. All other ratios would fulfill the demands. The crucial value that would have terminated the hedge accounting treatment in the very beginning of the hedge relationship is shown in Figure 4.17.

Applying the *cumulative Dollar-Offset Method*, the hedge is highly effective. The cumulative Dollar-Offset ratio is −1.00. This is shown is Figure 4.18.

Using the *Variance Reduction Measure* for testing the hedge effectiveness, the calculated ratio of 0.9999 is a clear sign towards high effectiveness. This is illustrated in Figure 4.19.

The *Regression Analysis* also confirms the high effectiveness that is necessary to qualify for hedge accounting. The slope is calculated with a value of −0.9991 and $R^2 = 99.98\%$. The full regression is displayed as screen shot in Figure 4.20.

			Delta FV		Delta FT		
5	Timesteps	0					
6	Selected Path:	5					
7	Nr.	FV Value	Value	FT Value	Value	Ratio	
178	170	3.607.195,33	-542.556,41	-3.609.152,90	543.076,11	-1,00	
179	171	4.490.047,63	882.852,31	-4.492.240,59	-883.087,69	-1,00	
180	172	4.877.493,17	387.445,54	-4.879.610,61	-387.370,03	-1,00	
181	173	4.751.701,16	-125.792,01	-4.753.506,09	126.104,52	-1,00	
182	174	5.173.654,40	421.953,24	-5.175.338,81	-421.832,73	-1,00	
183	175	5.454.262,81	280.608,41	-5.455.742,58	-280.403,77	-1,00	
184	176	6.211.639,77	757.376,96	-6.212.987,94	-757.245,36	-1,00	
185	177	7.536.993,66	1.325.353,89	-7.538.220,49	-1.325.232,55	-1,00	
186	178	7.389.971,82	-147.021,85	-7.390.773,73	147.446,76	-1,00	
187	179	8.308.048,62	918.076,81	-8.308.499,38	-917.725,65	-1,00	
188	180	8.116.329,29	-191.719,33	-8.116.329,29	192.170,08	-1,00	-1,00

Figure 4.18   Screenshot: cumulative Dollar-Offset Ratio Path 5

	A	B	C	D	E	F	G	H
5	Timesteps	180						
6	Selected Path:	5						
7	Time	Combined	Variance	FT Value	Variance	Ratio		
8	0	-44,11	1.311.001.192	0,00	15.935.920.716.922	0,99991773		
9	1	128.459,07		-286.514,83				
10	2	125.560,05		392.570,29				
11	3	127.539,38		220.806,35				
12	4	128.727,11		177.057,98				
13	5	132.122,52		-254.712,07				
14	6	122.807,89		1.083.467,89				
15	7	125.191,84		927.832,21				
16	8	112.137,36		2.071.326,57				
17	9	124.112,29		1.186.141,48				
18	10	126.795,01		1.017.449,59				
19	11	134.834,86		249.191,19				
20	12	134.924,04		360.022,51				
21	13	132.351,15		742.036,05				
22	14	118.606,39		1.902.572,45				
23	15	98.994,07		3.089.769,98				

Figure 4.19   Screenshot: Variance Reduction Measure Path 5

Scenario 3, simulation path 12

In scenario three, the barrier option is not knocked out. At the end of the hedge relationship the spot exchange rate is below the strike, so that the value of the Forward Plus is zero.

Testing the effectiveness with the *day-by-day Dollar-Offset ratio*, hedge accounting treatment has to be denied. There are multiple cases in which the ratio is not within the demanded range. Using the cumulative ratio as the method to test for hedge effectiveness, the accepted range is missed as well. This is shown in Figure 4.21.

If the *Variance Reduction Measure* is used to prove hedge effectiveness, the result is different. Following this method the reduction of the variance is 99.35 %. This is sufficiently high to qualify for hedge effectiveness and very close to the previously examined paths which have proven effectiveness.

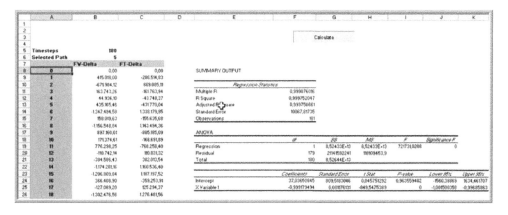

Figure 4.20   Screenshot: Regression Analysis Path 5

5	Timesteps	180				
6	Selected Path:	12				
			Delta FV		Delta FT	
7	Nr.	FV Value	Value	FT Value	Value	Ratio
178	170	1.485.332,16	297.377,73	-1.068.078,51	-477.486,64	-1,61
179	171	1.212.453,54	-272.878,62	-719.537,99	348.540,52	-1,28
180	172	759.826,60	-452.626,94	-30.689,05	688.848,94	-1,52
181	173	1.065.102.20	305.275,60	-616.004,76	-585.315,71	-1,92
182	174	676.793,91	-388.308,29	-34.113,78	581.890,97	-1,50
183	175	364.583,45	-312.210,46	546.572,73	580.686,52	-1,86
184	176	93.017,75	-271.565,70	1.385.549,55	838.976,82	-3,09
185	177	33.430,03	-59.587,72	1.670.749,07	285.199,52	-4,79
186	178	37.402,03	3.972,00	1.311.698,07	-359.051,00	-90,40
187	179	14.934,93	-22.467,10	1.099.277,47	-212.420,60	9,45
188	180	0,00	-14.934,93	1.594.112,52	494.835,05	-33,13 **0,00**

Figure 4.21   Screenshot: cumulative Dollar-Offset Ratio Path 12

The *Regression Analysis* also comes to the result that hedge effectiveness holds. The slope of the regression line is -0.9527 and R^2 is 98.27 %. Compared to the previously examined paths and the one in the last scenario, these are the worst results for the regression parameters as well as for the Variance Reduction ratio. However, they are still good enough to qualify for hedge accounting treatment of the examined path. The results of the *Variance Reduction Measure* and the *Regression Analysis* are shown in Figures 4.22 and 4.23.

Scenario 4, simulation path 2

The last scenario examines simulation path two. Within this path, the barrier option is not knocked out. The value of the Forward Plus is positive at maturity.

Assessing the hedge effectiveness with the *day-by-day Dollar-Offset Method*, the preferred accounting treatment cannot be employed. There are several ratios that are out of the accepted range. It is important to note that these ratios depend on the simulation path and are not necessarily characteristic for this scenario. The *cumulative Dollar-Offset Method* results in

	A	B	C	D	E	F	G	H
1								
2								
3								Calculate
4								
5	Timesteps	180						
6	Selected Path:	12						
7	Time	Combined	Variance	FT Value	Variance	Ratio		
8	0	-44,11	116.075.995.302	0,00	17.907.321.846.962	**0,99351796**		
9	1	129.809,06		-668.793,81				
10	2	126.415,10		257.149,13				
11	3	126.676,78		347.430,62				
12	4	131.496,52		-329.269,65				
13	5	134.947,97		-1.326.424,99				
14	6	135.545,30		-1.930.353,09				
15	7	132.799,69		-2.896.100,80				
16	8	130.492,99		-3.391.883,73				
17	9	132.794,12		-3.236.163,20				
18	10	127.492,66		-3.972.734,26				
19	11	127.924,51		-4.038.541,83				
20	12	118.418,16		-4.924.892,89				
21	13	124.773,06		-4.512.512,11				
22	14	121.331,25		-4.865.616,99				
23	15	104.453,95		-6.042.542,63				

Figure 4.22   Screenshot: Variance Reduction Measure Path 12

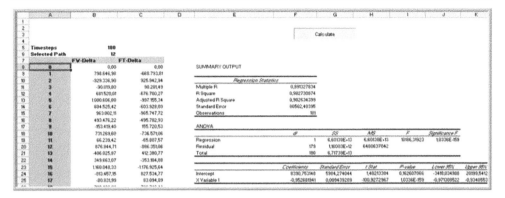

Figure 4.23 Screenshot: Regression Analysis Path 12

a ratio of -1.00, which would qualify for hedge accounting in contrast to the previously mentioned method. The result is displayed in Figure 4.24.

Using the *Variance Reduction Measure* to test for hedge effectiveness, the result is, as in all previously examined simulation paths clearly above the threshold to testify to high effectiveness. The value of the calculated ratio is 0.9997. This is displayed in Figure 4.25.

Following the *Regression Analysis*, the necessary hedge effectiveness to qualify for hedge accounting holds as well.

The regression parameters slope and R^2 take the values -0.9899 and 99.94 %, respectively. The complete *Regression Analysis* result is displayed in Figure 4.26.

4.7 CONCLUSION

IAS 39 formulates broad regulations for the treatment of financial instruments. These include the recognition as well as the initial and subsequent measurement of financial assets and financial liabilities. In Sections 4.2 and 4.3 the most important regulations concerning financial instruments under IAS were introduced and made comprehensible. These regulations form the basis of the main topic of this chapter: hedge accounting. This is an important topic for most companies. Hedge accounting means that the hedged item, which is a financial asset or a

5	Timesteps	180				
6	Selected Path:	2				
7			**Delta FV**		**Delta FT**	
	Nr.	FV Value	Value	FT Value	Value	Ratio
178	170	4.164.223,05	291.568,41	-4.142.049,98	-311.586,71	-1,07
179	171	3.696.962,33	-467.260,72	-3.667.080,39	474.969,58	-1,02
180	172	4.182.929,14	485.966,81	-4.173.250,02	-506.169,63	-1,04
181	173	3.499.992,77	-682.936,38	-3.481.598,94	691.651,08	-1,01
182	174	2.538.497,38	-961.495,38	-2.487.535,92	994.063,02	-1,03
183	175	1.996.025,77	-542.471,61	-1.919.406,48	568.129,43	-1,05
184	176	2.189.685,16	193.659,38	-2.156.046,18	-236.639,70	-1,22
185	177	2.316.187,20	126.502,04	-2.304.673,89	-148.627,71	-1,17
186	178	3.532.911,82	1.216.724,62	-3.533.260,47	-1228.586,58	-1,01
187	179	3.236.600,29	-296.311,52	-3.236.775,72	296.484,74	-1,00
188	180	2.498.527,35	-738.072,95	-2.498.527,35	738.248,37	-1,00	**-1,00**

Figure 4.24 Screenshot: cumulative Dollar-Offset Ratio Path 2

Calculate

Timesteps	180
Selected Path:	2

Time	Combined	Variance	FT Value	Variance	Ratio
0	-44,11	6.115.629.465	0,00	20.007.647.521.951	0,99969434
1	128.681,68		-339.913,24		
2	131.420,05		-941.384,29		
3	132.855,58		-1.360.061,03		
4	132.578,69		-609.732,00		
5	129.325,08		224.226,72		
6	130.690,41		159.167,38		
7	130.324,07		340.555,63		
8	135.495,87		-335.643,81		
9	131.964,67		369.331,77		
10	128.187,18		884.555,01		
11	121.853,24		1.506.210,21		
12	115.586,36		2.011.868,66		
13	95.871,68		3.212.865,04		
14	102.277,67		2.888.104,82		
15	108.148,63		2.587.463,57		

Figure 4.25 Screenshot: Variance Reduction Measure Path 2

financial liability, is treated in another way under certain circumstances. The relation of the hedged item and the hedging instrument is in the scope. The regulations concerning hedge accounting partly overrule the general regulations for financial instruments accounting and are again very extensive. In Sections 4.4 and 4.5, these regulations were reviewed in more depth. The crucial part of the substantial prerequisites for hedge accounting treatment is the high effectiveness, which has to be proven to exist on a prospective as well as on a retrospective basis.

This issue and possible methods for measurement of the effectiveness were discussed in theory and in examples. In the case study, the question as to whether the prospective and retrospective hedge effectiveness exists is tested in the framework of a cash flow hedge for a foreign exchange forecast transaction that is hedged with a Forward Plus.

As an overall result, the hedge effectiveness for the example could be confirmed for both, the prospective and the retrospective hedge effectiveness. One critical issue is the choice of an

Calculate

Timesteps	180
Selected Path	2

	FV-Delta	FT-Delta
0	0,00	0,00
1	468.639,03	-339.913,24
2	604.209,42	-601.471,04
3	420.112,27	-418.676,74
4	-750.605,93	750.329,03
5	-837.212,33	833.958,72
6	66.424,68	-65.059,34
7	-181.754,59	181.388,25
8	681.371,23	-676.199,44
9	-708.506,78	704.975,58
10	-519.000,74	515.223,24
11	-627.989,13	621.655,19
12	-511.925,34	505.658,46
13	-1.220.711,05	1.200.996,37
14	331.166,20	-324.760,22
15	306.512,22	-300.641,25
16	-316.051,50	310.956,67
17	-454.177,77	445.939,66

SUMMARY OUTPUT

Regression Statistics	
Multiple R	0,999692397
R Square	0,999384889
Adjusted R Square	0,999381453
Standard Error	16274,48464
Observations	181

ANOVA

	df	*SS*	*MS*	*F*	*Significance F*
Regression	1	7,70277E+13	7,70277E+13	290825,344	2,4343E-289
Residual	179	47409734212	264858850,3		
Total	180	7,70751E+13			

	Coefficients	*Standard Error*	*t Stat*	*P-value*	*Lower 95%*	*Upper 95%*
Intercept	139,4994737	1209,938271	0,115294703	0,908340771	-2248,075794	2527,074741
X Variable 1	-0,989911939	0,00183561	-539,2822489	2,4343E-289	-0,993534155	-0,98628972

Figure 4.26 Screenshot: Regression Analysis Path 2

appropriate method to test for the effectiveness. The *Variance Reduction Measure* as well as the *Regression Analysis* deliver stable results for both tests. The *Dollar-Offset Method* is likely to fail the test, especially when using the period-by-period method instead of the cumulative method.

Summing up, hedge accounting is possible for the Forward Plus. However, the choice of the method to test for effectiveness is crucial for the result. For the entity it is also a question of the effort that is required to set up the more complicated methods like the *Variance Reduction Measure* or *Regression Analysis*, compared to the simpler *Dollar-Offset Method*. Within this context the effort is often rewarded with a better result for the desired hedge effectiveness.

4.8   RELEVANT ORIGINAL SOURCES FOR ACCOUNTING STANDARDS

1. International Accounting Standards Board,
   International Accounting Standard 1, Financial Instruments:
   Disclosure and Presentation, (1997), as at July 1997
2. International Accounting Standards Board,
   International Accounting Standard 32, Financial Instruments:
   Disclosure and Presentation, (2004), as at 31 March 2004
3. International Accounting Standards Board,
   International Accounting Standard 39, Financial Instruments:
   Recognition and Measurement, (2004), as at 31 March 2004
4. International Accounting Standards Board,
   Guidance of Implementing International Accounting Standard 39,
   Financial Instruments: Recognition and Measurement, (2004), as of 31 March 2004

4.9   EXERCISES

1. What happens to the calculation of the forecast transaction value if the notional of the Forward Plus is specified in USD rather than EUR? This is normally the case if a EUR-zone based corporate exports to the US and expects incoming USD cash.
2. Redo the case study for other structured forward contracts, in particular the forward extra, the butterfly forward, the range forward and the boosted forward.
3. What effect does the choice of the strike and the barrier have on hedge effectiveness of the Forward Plus? Are there scenarios that would disqualify the Forward Plus from hedge accounting?

5

Foreign Exchange Markets

5.1 A TOUR THROUGH THE MARKET

We would like to conclude with a round of interviews with and statements by some of the leading players in the FX options industry. This should give us a flavor of the market, the products, the language and the spirit of FX Options.

5.1.1 Statement by GFI Group (Fenics), 25 October 2005

Fenics has provided pioneering work in standardizing the pricing of FX options in the 1990s and has established itself as a reference for many traders, structurers and sales in FX. Here is a statement from GFI Group about what makes Fenics so successful.

Fenics has been successful and continues to be successful by continually meeting changing market requirements. For example

GFI launched **FENICS dealFX** *in May 2005, providing the technology for banks to build FX option pricing, risk management and trading solutions for their clients. One major US bank is already live with its GFI-enabled solution.*

GFI's STP (see Section 5.2.4) **initiative with UBS** *is an extension of electronic trading of options. GFI connected FENICS FX to UBS's electronic currency derivative trading screen, FX Option Trader, feeding FX option trades conducted through FX Option Trader into FENICS FX. This has meant a simpler workflow, reduced ticket entry time and fewer errors because of the elimination of manual intervention.*

With **Zurich Cantonal Bank (ZKB)**, *the largest cantonal bank in Switzerland, GFI created a white-label solution. This has made FX option pricing technology available to ZKB clients as part of its currency option trading services.*

To facilitate online trading of options, **GFI Linked FENICS FX to live Bank of America volatility surfaces data**. *This has enhanced the sales relationship Bank of America has with its clients as well as opened up the 8,000 FENICS users to Bank of America. This demonstrates FENICS FX's open architecture and GFI's commitment to enabling FX Option e-commerce.*

The latest version of **FENICS FX, version 9.1**, *adds exotic option types, enhances calculation methodologies such as volatility interpolations, and includes new sales and risk functions as well as improved reporting.*

GFI also provided completely **new option pricing methodologies** *in partnership with third party vendors CSIRO. The Reditus maths library relies on a finite-element and Monte-Carlo engines to facilitate quicker, more accurate and flexible price discovery.*

Also very important is access to live GFI inter-dealer broker market data for accurate option pricing.

Contact Information

GFI Group
One Snowden Street
London EC2A 2DQ
United Kingdom
http://www.gfigroup.com

5.1.2   Interview with ICY Software, 14 October 2005

Uwe Wystup: Nicolas, your software is well-known for one of the leading FX structuring tools. Can you please explain what it does?

N. de Breteuil: ICY FX is an FX option pricing, marketing and position management tool. The concept behind the product is to help any FX actor to take a decision, the structurer and sales people to develop their business flow. With ICY FX sales and structurer can, very easily price any kind of option package including their markups, prepare a term-sheet for a customer in one click displaying payoff or conversion rate profile to help corporate or institutional customers to take a comprehensive decision. The user can analyze and stress test through matrix the package behavior according to market change and measure impact due to accounting standard like IAS39 or FASB133. When they have traded with their counterparts they can save to monitor their customers positions and help them to restructure or roll positions by creating some aggregate position. A structurer can build complex or innovative option packages with very specific features, which will be retailed by sales people in any kind of currencies pair without having to remember how to build them.

Uwe Wystup: Seems like an excellent idea to help sales to simplify their complex working environment ⌣. How did you get the idea of developing such a software?

N. de Breteuil: Charles Monot, who was head of the research group at Smith Barney, noticed that in the mid nineties you could only find FX option pricers developed for traders. No tools were available for sales and structurers. As you know, traders' pricing tool and analytics are run from a different perspective than the marketing one. When Smith Barney closed its Paris offices in 1997, he set up ICY software. ICY FX took a year of development and the first release was available in September 1998. The first reference was the difficult part, but when one has signed the others follow. When I joined in 2000, we were two, Charles on the IT side and myself being on the commercial side. I would say that our strength lies in the fact that being both from the financial markets, we very easily surrounded our customers' needs. Having a global coverage it brings different approaches, and new features are included. We like to think that we are very reactive and prone to make ICY FX evolve faster than others.

Uwe Wystup: Where do you see the FX Options market develop over the next years?

N. de Breteuil: Ten years ago, if you had a talk with a treasurer FX options were seen as very complex and dangerous products. Due to the very good work done by the banks on their customers' education as well as the clearer presentation to the buy side of the higher return offered by such a vehicle, the "darkside" seems to have vanished. Every actor in this market has understood that if you don't have a clear view of what you buy or sell on the derivatives side you better avoid the trade. On the other side options are high margin product for bankers. Their interest is to develop those products. The introduction of the Euro was supposed to drag down volume, but if you stick to figures like the BIS report it is not the case. I think that more and more countries and players are entering in the FX option world. We felt it with Eastern Europe banks signing for ICY FX in the past two years. Therefore, I suppose that FX options could gain new players with new emerging countries currencies. It depends mainly on their economical stability, which is supported by globalization. Product-wise, the simpler we keep them the better it is.

Uwe Wystup: Who needs FX structured products?

N. de Breteuil: I would like to say that anyone who wants to play on the FX market needs them. After all, you can find them on the hedging side, as investment vehicle with a capital protection level and a given return or with a boosted yield. It is up to the imagination of the structurer. The offer is very wide mainly in Asia where people are fond of them. You can very easily invest a small nominal amount, whereas in Europe you have to be rated as a high net worth individual.

Uwe Wystup: Why do you think corporates buy structuring tools?

N. de Breteuil: Corporates as any FX player need to evaluate and monitor their FX exposure and therefore they are looking for the most suitable tool according to their requirements. Moreover depending on their size and organization the treasury department is a proposal force and sometimes viewed as a profit center so they need a tool.

Uwe Wystup: In fact, several traditional industry sectors make more money with treasury management than with their ships and cars ⌣. Do you also propose new ideas for structured products to your clients?

N. de Breteuil: Being a software company, we are not proposing trade ideas ourselves, even though we enclose in ICY FX a *structure wizard* offering a large number of the most commonly traded ones. We leave this aspect to our bank customers, who have very skilled and imaginative people.

Uwe Wystup: Who are your target clients for the strategy pricer and your plans for the future?

N. de Breteuil: I would like to say that we would like anyone having a role on the FX and FX option to get ICY FX. We are aiming at the Bank's sales and structuring desks as well as corporates and fund managers. I can tell you it's enough work.

Uwe Wystup: Can the user include his/her own pricing library into your software?

N. de Breteuil: Pricing has always been a key aspect for decision makers.

Uwe Wystup: Thank you very much for taking the time, Nicolas.

Contact Information

ICY Software
41, rue de Richelieu
75001 Paris, France
http://www.icysoftware.com

Example
We take a look at an example of the pricing screen in *Fenics view* in Figure 5.1

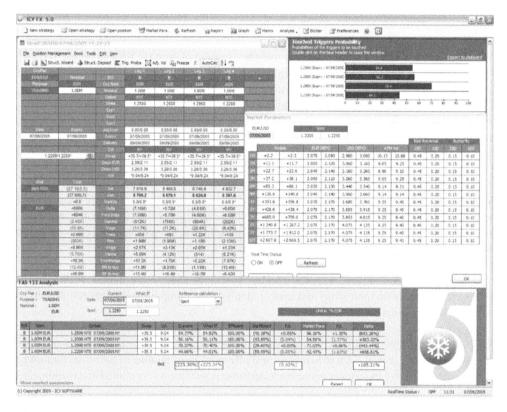

Figure 5.1   Screen shot of ICY FX 5.0

5.1.3   Interview with Bloomberg, 12 October 2005

Uwe Wystup: Phil and Peter, Bloomberg is well-known as one of the leading financial data sources and as a widely used communication tool in equity and bond markets. Can you please explain what services it provides in FX Options?

Phil Brittan: Compared with equity and fixed income, foreign exchange has been underdeveloped in the past, but now we can offer a comprehensive suite of tools including FX options, with both historic and current market quotes. For example, our **OVDV** (Option Valuation

Default Volatility) page contains implied volatilities from brokers and dealers for a wide range of maturities and moneyness such as at-the-money, 25-delta, 10-delta, butterflies and risk reversals. As a bank you can also contribute your own quotes with customized spreads, so it serves as a communication tool. Our **OVML** page serves as a calculator, just like a pricing screen in *Fenics*, which is going to become a leading system in the market.

Uwe Wystup: Peter, you are in charge of feeding this screen with the pricing libraries. Can you give me an example of a special feature?

Peter Carr: Sure, besides a lot of visualization we offer comparing historic volatility with the implied, historic skewness implied from risk reversals with the current market and many other back-testing tools, and provide implied volatilities for illiquid crosses.

Uwe Wystup: Like?

Peter Carr: Like MEX/PLN, where we use the liquid implied vols of USD/MEX and USD/PLN.

Uwe Wystup: So, how does this work?

Peter Carr: We use the Heston model.

Uwe Wystup: But the ratio of two Heston processes is not a Heston process, how does this work?

Peter Carr: Obviously, we need to use the same mean reversion speed and vol of vol, we only allow the initial instantaneous volatility, the long-term volatility and correlation to differ in the two liquid markets.

Uwe Wystup: I see, so is Heston's model your favorite pricing model for FX Options and is it implemented in Bloomberg?

Peter Carr: The Heston model is only one of several models we are currently testing. It is not available for exotics in Bloomberg at this time, but we are testing it in particular for all first generation exotics at the moment. I think there should be a final decision on how to price the barriers and touches, as the market is using these as standard products. We would like to give our clients a variety of models and provide a solid guidance of which one to use.

Uwe Wystup: Excellent, so *Bloomberg sorts out the barriers*, if I may summarize?

Peter Carr: Yes, like 15 years ago Fenics has standardized vanillas. For barriers, still nobody knows the *right price*.

Uwe Wystup: Which are the models you are testing?

Peter Carr: We consider the following models. They are all being run through a back testing procedure. Eventually, we want to nominate the model with the best hedging performance as the leader.

1. Black-Scholes with the spot as the only risk and the corresponding delta hedge.
2. Heston with spot and vol as the two sources of risk and the corresponding hedge in the spot and vanilla market.
3. A stochastic skew model we have developed, which takes care of the fact that risk reversals are stochastic over time.
4. Static hedging.
5. A local-volatility model with the usual delta hedge.
6. A vanna-volga model, determining the cost of setting all Greeks to zero at inception of the trade, but neglecting the costs of rebalancing.

You wrote a paper about the last one, have you ever thought about how to determine the Greeks in such a model?

Uwe Wystup: Well, I am not really an advocate of the vanna-volga model. The Greeks are in fact a problem. If you run a front office system without smile, then taking the Black-Scholes delta probably makes most sense. But I think I will make this an exercise of the book or if need be a master's thesis. However, I am bit surprised, knowing you, that Lévy models do not appear in your list. How is that?

Peter Carr: Even though I like Lévy models a lot, they tend to be quite complicated and the numerics very time consuming, whence we have decided to first work though our six model list and then take it from there. Have you actually seen any work on back testing of such models?

Uwe Wystup: There is a lot of work on back testing hedging performance carried out by Stewart Hodges in the Financial Options Research Centre at Warwick University. Also Jurgen Tistaert of ING SWE in Brussels has compiled a lot of work comparing models. I understand your hesitation to put Lévy models into an FX front office system. What is the speed you intend to offer in Bloomberg?

Phil Brittan: Actually, we shoot for a maximum of six seconds for any price calculation.

Uwe Wystup: Coming back to your models, Peter, can you tell me a bit more about the stochastic skew model?

Peter Carr: We actually have two, one for liquid currency pairs such as EUR/USD, where pretty much as a successor of Heston we also take the skew as a stochastic input variable to capture reality, i.e. the uncertainty of the risk reversal. For illiquid currency pairs we take a model from *credit default swap* valuation to account for possible jumps.

Uwe Wystup: So finally, credit and FX are merging. Congratulations! Where do you see the FX Options market develop over the next years?

Phil Brittan: Very standardized, with a lot more activity in emerging markets.

Uwe Wystup: This would be for the vanillas. Do you have all the exotic options covered that are needed for the coming years?

Peter Carr: One of the developments are third generation exotics, in particular multi-currency options.

Phil Brittan: We are not and do not intend to be extremely sophisticated on the exotics side. Our primary goal in Bloomberg is to reach the mass transaction markets and make Bloomberg a universal platform.

Uwe Wystup: Does this mean that you are not competing with SuperDerivatives?

Phil Brittan: Not really, SuperDerivatives is highly sophisticated in the exotics, whereas we are shooting for the bread and butter business. We like to be seen as *the one shop* for financial data and analysis. As all our platforms are growing, other systems could eventually become redundant.

Uwe Wystup: I am impressed. However, this seems like a long way to go. Does Bloomberg plan to offer also a structuring tool for FX Options?

Phil Brittan: Yes, this is under construction including all standard services like solving for certain parameters such as strikes for a given value of the structure.

Uwe Wystup: Does Bloomberg prepare term sheets automatically?

Phil Brittan: This is not really our core business.

Uwe Wystup: And how about interfaces to other systems like Murex, or are you going to offer portfolio analytics, position keeping and back-office functionalities?

Phil Brittan: We have a very easy link to Excel, and then there is a general API, a COM-interface. What is already possible at this stage is saving and reloading saved trades. Links to other systems are not in place by default.

Uwe Wystup: When are the prices you show going to be tradable?

Phil Brittan: We are very close to that, starting with two banks and more thereafter in the future, so that for example, if ABN AMRO feeds a quote into Bloomberg, then users can trade.

Uwe Wystup: Phil, may I ask you a personal question? You are one of the founding directors of *Fenics*, why did you leave Fenics?

Phil Brittan: The Fenics System was sold in 1995 to Inventure, which is when I left it. Later it was again sold to GFI.

Uwe Wystup: Now that you are at Bloomberg, do you want to extend Bloomberg to a better FX system than Fenics?

Phil Brittan: We will do our very best.

Uwe Wystup: Thank you for taking the time, gentlemen.

Peter Carr: It's been a pleasure talking to you again, Uwe.

Contact Information

Bloomberg L.P.
http://www.bloomberg.com

5.1.4   Interview with Murex, 8 November 2005

Uwe Wystup: Murex is well-known for providing one of the first full front-office systems for FX options. When did you release the first version, what has changed since then, and what is the name of your currently released FX system?

Murex: Murex first started releasing software in 1986. The earliest foreign exchange option system was called Murex Currency+, since then we have been through a couple of generations of software, with the majority of our customers currently on Murex MXG2000.2.10. We have several customers now operational on our newest generation, MX.3, which will probably start rolling out as the core FX option platform late in 2006.

Uwe Wystup: Can you please explain what services it provides in FX Options and structured products?

Murex: Our software provides full end-to-end functionality, much more than classical *straight-through-processing* which typically starts at pricing/trade capture, but encompassing pre-trade as well as post-trade workflows. Credit and market risk limit checking and compliance controls can be effected even before automatically marked up data are used to price products. Trade capture, including relevant hedges and back-to-back, injects deals to a full processing workflow and into a powerful risk management and simulation engine, obviously immediately impacting, for example, credit risk utilization. Because Murex is a multi asset platform FX options can be not only structured in isolation, but combined with other asset classes, such as interest rate, equity, commodities, etc., whether simple or complex products, to deliver the same full STP to multi asset and hybrid transactions. All of our products are web-deployable through a configurable distribution framework meaning that our services truly extend from customer price discovery through trade capture and risk management to eventual confirmation and settlement.

Uwe Wystup: How did you get the idea of building your product and how long did it take?

Murex: The management team of Murex comes from varied backgrounds, including option trading, engineering, mathematics. Working closely within the finance and software arenas in the early days of options markets in Europe we identified that there was a need for truly practitioner led software design, coupled with world class architecture. Markets develop and migrate, sometimes very rapidly, and for Murex the journey is never ending, we seek to identify new areas where specialized software can really make a difference, and continuously improve our offering to keep abreast of changing market trends. As we approach our 20th anniversary, and implement our third true generation of software, we are aware that our job is never finished.

Uwe Wystup: What are your favorite pricing models for FX Options and are they implemented in your software? What do you think of the *vanna-volga pricing approach*? What do you think is better?

Murex: Rather than having a "favorite" or dictating the modeling approach we prefer to provide a growing suite of pricing models including simple and fast analytical models, such as vega-vanna-volga replication models to rapidly price barriers, alongside more complex stochastic models. Dedicated teams develop newer and more specifically adapted models within Murex, so that clients can acquire software that is usable without addition, but we also have APIs that allow customers to integrate their own "favorite" models.

Uwe Wystup: Where do you see the FX Options market develop over the next years?

Murex: Any specific answer to that question is probably disclosing views that our clients share with us, and vice-versa, in confidence. In generic terms one can assume that volume and product sophistication increases, there is a need for growing automation and broad spread product distribution, both internal and external. One can assume that FX Option providers will tend towards greater industrialization standards in the way they present products toward customers. We can also expect to continue to focus on pushing the sophisticated approach taken to handling core market products towards rapidly emerging markets, in an appropriately tailored manner.

Uwe Wystup: Do you have all the exotic options covered that are needed for the coming years?

Murex: We have covered the majority of market standard exotics, plus a range of newer generation exotics. Customers often choose to integrate further new products that they develop themselves directly through the flex APIs. The reality is that whilst we believe we currently have a comprehensive offering, the coming years will unquestionably see new products being brought to market, and we will necessarily continue working to integrate these. As such, we can look to the coming years as the continuation of a *work in progress*.

Uwe Wystup: How many of your clients use Flex Deals?

Murex: Whilst many customers now use Murex analytics, probably 90% of those who develop their own analytic tools use the flex module, and many others use flex products developed by Murex as a "rapid reaction" means of meeting customer demands.

Uwe Wystup: How far did you progress in developing and selling the structuring tool? Which structures do you think are most widely used?

Murex: We have a structuring tool that we believe sets the industry standard for comprehensiveness and flexibility. Being a multi-asset platform has been a considerable advantage in this respect, but we never lose sight of the fact that different asset classes have very different utilizations and conventions, and our specialist teams enable our structured trade builder to handle very specific requirements for individual asset classes alongside the broader range of functions useful for all asset classes, or indeed for cross asset hybridization. Client take up of the structured trade builder has been good, and accelerates, and we anticipate that this will become the standard method of pricing, structuring and capturing trades to the system. Other than standard products, such as straddles, risk reversals, butterflies etc., which are perhaps no longer even regarded as structures, probably the most commonly sold FX Option structures are **Dual Currency Deposits**, which are a volume product in the retail sector.

Uwe Wystup: Do you have any intentions in offering tradable prices of options with some banks as a backbone?

Murex: Our anticipation is not to enter the financial transacting arena either as a principal or agent. There are always questions in such instances of whether you are supporting customers, or competing with them to capture trades from their clients or route trades to their competitors. We prefer to maintain a neutral position and support our customers in their businesses by focusing on our business which is software development, deployment and support.

Uwe Wystup: What interfaces with other applications like SuperDerivatives, Fenics, Excel do you offer?

Murex: Murex is by its nature an "open" system, and can be interfaced using standardized protocol to many other applications. We do not generally offer "out of the box" solutions but a range of interfaces that customers can utilize.

Uwe Wystup: Who are your target clients and your plans for the future?

Murex: Our clients are broadspread, including banks, asset managers, corporate treasuries, energy manufacturers and distributors, etc. Our target client is really any practitioner with a need for sophisticated financial market software, and we plan to keep addressing their needs by expanding the scalability and extensibility of our platform, growing the list of asset classes handled, and continually enhancing the sophistication of the systems functionality whilst never losing sight of the end-user, and the simplicity and ergonomic ease they require.

Uwe Wystup: How do you compare yourself with SuperDerivatives, Bloomberg, ICY, Fenics and LPA or others?

Murex: Well, we have already commented on our cross asset platform and our end to end functionality, so let's focus on the nature of our company. Approaching 600 employees globally, and present in several offices in every major time zone, we are no longer the "smallest fish in the pond". We remain, however, small or "close" enough that we can retain a very high level of flexibility and reactivity to customer needs. Whilst our "out of the box" offering is very comprehensive, it's configurability means that it can be tailored much more rapidly than monolithic systems. Conversely, whilst used to providing a "rapid reaction", as a company owned by practitioners and not external shareholders we can take a longer term view, and invest over several years, without being constrained to continually focus on quarterly results, although these do present an impressively continuous growth record. Again, due to our size and hands on approach, the most senior management can have an oversight of every client and every project.

Uwe Wystup: Who are your main competitors if any?

Murex: In every asset class we face respectably strong competition, (and for FXO you have mentioned a few), which keeps us honed and focused. Everyone has their strengths and weaknesses, but we don't believe that we are materially outclassed on any individual asset, are reasonably confident that no particular competitor features as consistently strongly across the whole range of assets that we support.

Uwe Wystup: What makes the murex software in FX special?

Murex: Many things! As mentioned we believe our multi-asset capability is a great advantage, whether to FXO traders hedging interest rate risk with a system that truly handles interest rate derivatives, or to structurers combining other assets with FX derivatives. At the same time we believe our specialization, led by partnership with many of the major players in the FX options market adds great depth to our breadth of coverage. The business of FX options is complex, and our great flexibility and configurability let us handle very varied requirements in a rapidly tailored manner. We never stop focusing on our business, and our continuing re-investment rate is much higher than industry norms. Of course the real answer to what makes Murex software special is "our people". We are as good as the aggregated strength of our colleagues, and we are very proud of our staff, and the collegiate atmosphere that means we have one of the lowest turnover rates in any industry.

Uwe Wystup: After 20 years and a good success record, why haven't we tired, why do we keep going?

Murex: The answer is *passion*. It's one of the common denominators of Murex' staff. The markets haven't stopped, they keep accelerating, and we have to keep pace, something we do with a passion.

Contact Information

Murex
8 rue Bellini
75782 Paris cedex 16
France
Phone +33 1 4405 3200
`http://www.murex.com`

5.1.5   Interview with SuperDerivatives, 17 October 2005

This interview was conducted with David Gershon, the CEO of SuperDerivatives.

Uwe Wystup: David, SuperDerivatives has become a standard reference for FX options prices over the last few years. Can you tell me something about how it came up?

David Gershon: When I was working for Deutsche Bank and later Barclays, market prices for FX options were not accessible. The only people that could see them were a few FX options traders that constantly spoke with their inter bank broker. Only the top traders from the top ten banks in the world could really make accurate prices of exotic options on a consistent basis. There were many other market makers that were not comfortable in making prices and occasionally mis-priced options. So there was a huge need to be able to price options accurately but no decent tool available.

Uwe Wystup: Did you then learn at Barclays how to price FX options?

David Gershon: No, just the opposite: in those years, there was just no model in place and banks didn't like their traders to develop models but to trade and make money. Models were left for quants. As a trader, I learned and improved my capability to price options by observing the prices that traded in the inter-bank broker market. When I left Barclays to found SuperDerivatives I formulated the model that would produce bid and ask prices consistent with the inter-bank prices for options. The new pricing system was launched in 2001.

Uwe Wystup: That was quick. And what happened to Barclays?

David Gershon: SuperDerivatives has a wonderful relationship with Barclays. We had a beta-site for our system at Barclays and they became a precious customer. They are still using SuperDerivatives.

Uwe Wystup: According to your view, what is a *good price*?

David Gershon: When you need a price of an option and you call the top ten banks, you will typically get very similar prices from all of them, up to a few basis points. For example 20/28; 21/29; 20/29; 19/28 and so on. These prices are made by traders with lots of experience who just know where the price is. The right price is the price that can be defined as the *consensus price*. In the above example you will agree that 20/28 is a good price.

Uwe Wystup: Yes, but how do you quantify and automate this?

David Gershon: Our pricing approach is very different than methods that were used before. It is based on quantifying risk which is more consistent with traders' intuition. We do not use modifications of the distribution function of the spot like Heston, simply because everybody tried these methods and they clearly don't produce the right prices. So I had to look for something else, creating new principles to avoid any kind of real and pseudo-arbitrage, develop guidelines for upper and lower bounds, higher order Greeks, and blend our *gut feeling*. For all our options there exist formulae replacing Black-Scholes.

Uwe Wystup: Where can these be found?

David Gershon: Unfortunately, at the moment we cannot publicize our formulas but I think that in a later stage we will certainly consider it. We believe that the typical options user/hedger doesn't worry about the mathematical detail of the price if the outcome is reliable. We drive safely with our cars but never bother to learn how their engine works. We use electric machines and don't know the mechanism behind them.

Uwe Wystup: I understand it is proprietary and among your biggest assets. What input variables do you use?

David Gershon: The biggest revelation of SuperDerivatives to options pricing is the fact that three points on the volatility smile are enough to price any option. For FX we use the at-the-money volatility and the 25-delta risk reversal and butterfly. For other markets like equity, we use the most liquid exchange strikes. The key is that we use the same model in FX, equity, commodity and interest rates.

Uwe Wystup: I would fully agree to using only three volatility sources of the smile, the rest usually tends to be interpolated anyway. Do you take the term structure and forward volatility risk into account, when you price for example a regular knock-out?

David Gershon: Yes, we do, we have three volatility quotes for each bucket. We also invented very quick ways to take into account term structure effects in the price of exotic options.

Uwe Wystup: What other markets do you work in?

David Gershon: We have pricing platforms also in interest rates, equity and commodity. We recently launched a pricing system for shipping- or freight. But certainly the biggest growth lately is in the interest rates product. We believe that the transparency we are bringing to interest rates options is going to have dramatic effects, even more than that we did in FX options.

Uwe Wystup: SuperDerivatives can be proud to cover all the first generation exotics and several of later generations. Are there still products and issues you are working on?

David Gershon: For the second generation exotics, there is still an open issue how to obtain a market price when you need to take into account term structure of correlation, simply since there are no hedging tools. Consider for example a simple compound option – there could be an effect of the correlation of the term structure of volatility and skew, like the volatility at expiration of the compound option and the volatility at the expiration time of the underlying option. Since there is no liquid market for such products, for such options classes, nobody can be absolutely sure what is the correct price. Therefore, we have to work with historic data and no-arbitrage bounds.

Uwe Wystup: Do you also invent new exotics? Or which new ones do you see coming up in the market?

David Gershon: We do not invent new exotics. Our role in the financial industry it to create transparency and provide tools for the existing markets. We are a *focal mirror* of the market. But we do see many new exotic options coming to the market. For example, we are observing some increasing interest for compounds with several decision dates and accumulators with additional knock-out features. Besides that, ideas from the fixed income market are beginning to merge with FX.

Uwe Wystup: Like callable and cancelable structures. Are you prepared?

David Gershon: Yes, since we have built a fixed income part of SuperDerivatives, we are very familiar with these.

Uwe Wystup: How about structured products?

David Gershon: Of course we offer many structure products. Especially we offer Forward structures – which are options embedded structure that internally can be viewed as forward transaction, like rest forwards. These structures are designed for those corporations that are still restricted to hedge with forwards.

Uwe Wystup: LPA offers a structuring tool for FX that also allows their clients to trade the prices they see. When will SuperDerivatives offer trading?

David Gershon: This is going to come very soon. We want to provide any kind of tools that can help our clients. But we do not intend to make trading a core business but an additional service. We provide real time pricing, risk management and analysis systems and are happy to link up users to other trading platforms.

Uwe Wystup: As a mathematician I am curious to find out how many quants are working at SuperDerivatives?

David Gershon: Our maths group comprises currently ten people but it will certainly have to continue to grow.

Uwe Wystup: That's substantial. Why do you need so many?

David Gershon: We need to support both the pricing systems and the risk management systems. We keep adding structures and options all the time and in order to respond to requests from clients we always find that we are short staffed.

Uwe Wystup: Where do you see the most exciting FX Options business?

David Gershon: It is very interesting how differently FX business is done all over the world. If we can generalize, I would say that the most sophisticated users are in France. French clients are not *afraid* of options and are open to new structures and strategies. Typically the client side drives the sell side and when it is open to new ideas in options it becomes the engine for new structures.

Uwe Wystup: I can confirm that, indeed. Finally, what makes SuperDerivatives special?

David Gershon: First of all, it is the only company that provides accurate prices for options and this by itself is extremely important for our clients. Obviously SuperDerivatives wouldn't be so successful if our prices were not very accurate. But equally important, it is the first time that a vendor lets the market design a product. Even the most absurd requests from a client get our attention. By constantly staying in touch with our clients we are always tuned with the trends in the different parts of the world, learn what could be useful for our clients, what happens to bid offer spreads of options when the market becomes more liquid, and so on.

Contact Information

SuperDerivatives Inc
25 Old Broad Street
London, EC2N 1HN
United Kingdom
http://www.superderivatives.com

5.1.6   Interview with Lucht Probst Associates, 27 February 2006

This interview was conducted with Wolfram Boenkost of LPA.

Uwe Wystup: Wolfram, LPA is well-known for providing one of the leading structuring tools in Germany. What is the name of your structuring tool?

Wolfram Boenkost: The software is called **LPA Toolbox**.

Uwe Wystup: Can you please explain what services it provides in FX Options and structured products?

Wolfram Boenkost: LPA helps our customer banks to increase their structured product sales to corporate clients. Part of our service is the **LPA Toolbox**, which we give to our clients. We help our clients on all aspects of the process of the integration of new products into their bank. We understand ourselves as a consultancy for structured products and see the **LPA Toolbox** as a part of our consultancy business.

The **LPA Toolbox** provides simple access to a wide range of structured Products for FX, Money Market and Capital market products. It allows the user to price structures and create documents like term sheets and confirmations with a few mouse clicks. It targets sales persons within a bank, allowing them to price a structure and create a term sheet while talking to a customer on the phone.

Uwe Wystup: How did you get the idea of building your product and how long did it take?

Wolfram Boenkost: The idea was a result of the experiences we had on our previous jobs within a bank. We tried to build a tool we would have loved inside the bank to support structured product sales. The current version of our software has been developed during the last four years. The development continues as we continuously improve and extend our software.

Uwe Wystup: What are your favorite pricing models for FX Options and are they implemented in your software? What do you think of the vanna-volga pricing approach? What do you think is better?

Wolfram Boenkost: We mainly use Black-Scholes based models augmented with vega-vanna-volga related adjustments, because of the speed and stability of the model. However, we do research with stochastic volatility models and also with hybrid models, where we jointly model the interest and FX rates. We take a rather pragmatic view on the model selection quest and believe in a product driven choice. There are many models around, which all have their strengths and weaknesses.

Uwe Wystup: Where do you see the FX Options market develop over the next years?

Wolfram Boenkost: The market moves to hybrid products, combining different asset classes. Today it is quite common to have an FX link in an exotic interest derivative structure. We expect this trend to continue and to include other asset classes, like credit and inflation links.

Uwe Wystup: Do you have all the exotic options covered that are needed for the coming years?

Wolfram Boenkost: Our product focus is sales and client driven. It is solution based. The types of options which are an answer to clients' problems are or will be implemented.

Uwe Wystup: Does LPA (plan to) offer also a structuring tool for products other than FX?

Wolfram Boenkost: Our tool covers FX, Money Market and interest rate products for the liability side. We always consider the inclusion of new product areas, currently we are focusing on inflation derivatives and equity derivatives as a potential area to include in our software.

Uwe Wystup: LPA offers tradable products, so you work with a backbone of banks. Which are these banks and are you looking for more?

Wolfram Boenkost: LPA is independent from any bank. If our customer is not able to trade our structure in their trading book we try to support back to back trading.

Uwe Wystup: What interfaces with front-office applications like Murex do you offer?

Wolfram Boenkost: Our next version will include an FpML Interface to export and import position data. Other client specific interfaces have been developed for special purposes.

Uwe Wystup: Where else other than Germany is your tool available?

Wolfram Boenkost: We currently have Customers in Germany, Austria and Norway. We currently support documents in German, English and Norwegian language.

Uwe Wystup: Who are your target clients and your plans for the future?

Wolfram Boenkost: We are focusing on public and cooperative banks in Germany and smaller banks with a significant corporate client business. Outside Germany, we are open to talk to any bank interested in our product and service.

Uwe Wystup: How do you compare yourself with SuperDerivatives, Bloomberg, ICY, Fenics and Murex?

Wolfram Boenkost: Our company focuses on the requirements of a multi product sales staff and tries to give them the best possible support including the **LPA Toolbox**. This focus makes it different to any of the above software providers.

Uwe Wystup: What makes the LPA software in FX special?

Wolfram Boenkost: Its focus is on structured products, their marketing and processing. While single legged instruments can be priced in the **LPA Toolbox** as well, its strength is the speed in which a sales person can market structures to their customer from a range of more than 80 structures.

Contact Information

Lucht Probst Associates GmbH
Große Gallusstraße 9
60311 Frankfurt am Main
Germany
http://www.l-p-a.com

5.2   SOFTWARE AND SYSTEM REQUIREMENTS

5.2.1   Fenics

Besides the software companies in the interviews *Fenics* is certainly a market standard in FX Options. Getting an option price different from Fenics is likely to cause excitement among traders and sales. Fenics was among the first to offer a fully working pricing screen for vanilla options and first generation exotics later on. It was also among the first to offer a structuring tool by allowing several contracts to be placed in columns and priced as a whole. This column by column setup one for each option is what is called the *Fenics view* in the FX options community.

5.2.2   Position keeping

For running an FX Options book, many banks use their in-house systems. Particularly, larger banks tend to build front-office systems themselves. The software company Murex, headquartered in Paris, offers a fully working front-office application including pricing, structuring, portfolio analysis, back-office functionalities. Besides in-house systems, Murex does not really have competition in FX Options. The big plus point is really the back-office part, where all deals can be watched, exercised, early terminated, expired, confirmed, etc. One of the problems is of course the pricing of contracts, particularly of exotics. As this is mostly proprietary bank information, Murex does not even attempt to cover exotic options in a full range but rather offers what they call *flexible deals*, which is a shell of an option, whose details and interfaces have to be programmed by the bank staff.

5.2.3   Pricing

There is an enormous amount of pricing software for options available, some of the more serious ones are SuperDerivatives, LPA, ICY FX, Bloomberg, next to numerous other vendors and web sites. To date, what is missing is a certified price of exotics, i.e. a source that would guarantee any type of correct price. Pricing remains after all the job of the traders, where nowadays many software packages help, but the final decision remains with the trader.

5.2.4   Straight Through Processing

Straight Through Processing (STP) means that when a trade is done, the entire booking and back-office machinery is fully automated. After trading in the *front-office*, a trade has to be booked, i.e. stored in the database of all live trades, the details have to be checked by the *middle-office*, the trade confirmation has to be written up, signed and sent to the counterpart by the *back-office*. A complete treatment of FX back office procedures can be found in the thesis by Hervas-Zurita in [100]. The issues concerning counterparty credit and limits have to be added to the respective counterpart, so it is clear how much of the credit limit is still available for a potential future trade. *Risk controlling* has to be informed about the market risk and credit risk of the trade, double check it and determine if extra cash needs to be set aside. Legal issues have to be checked, like compliance and counterparty origin. Furthermore the trade has to appear correctly in the balance sheets of the bank. The sales margins of respective sales people, structurers, traders and branches have to be booked in the respective profit centers to keep track of the success of staff and departments. Necessary hedges of the deals should be automatically executed and also booked and confirmed. Only if all these things happen automatically rather than manual, a bank can make a product into a mass or retail business, lower the spreads or prices and attract new deals. Any kind of manual interference with deals management slows down the process, increases labor costs. It has become a job called *derivatives trading process engineering* to ensure all these processes run smoothly and clarify with all the parties involved if a new product can find its way through all the applications and necessities running in a bank. Overall, the need for STP shows how dominantly important a working software structure is for a bank.

5.2.5   Disclaimers

Usually issuers and banks insert a disclaimer at the bottom of their term sheets to avoid legal problems if an investor buys a structure and gets hit by the market. It could look like this:

There are significant risks associated with the product described above including, but not limited to, interest rate risk, price risk, liquidity risk, redemption risk, and credit risk. Investors should consult their own financial, legal, accounting, and tax advisors about the risk associated with an investment in these products, the appropriate tools to analyze that investment, and the suitability of that investment in each investor's particular circumstances. No investor should purchase the product described above unless that investor understands and has sufficient financial resources to bear the price, market, liquidity, structure, redemption, and other risks associated with an investment in these products.

The market value can be expected to fluctuate significantly and investors should be prepared to assume the market risks associated with the product under consideration.

5.3   TRADING AND SALES

Option traders trade options and are supposed to risk manage their option portfolios and generate profit for their desk. Sales sell options (among other things) and are supposed to generate sales margin for their desk. If these desks are separate profit centers, then conflicts are immediately programmed into the system. When an option is traded, there is always a discussion of how much of the mark up is the sales margin, and how much is the trading margin. It is a job for the management of the bank to set up clear rules how these profits should be split among desks. For structures there are often structurers in the middle who also claim their share, which makes it even more challenging.

In the following we briefly describe the different areas of trading and sales.

5.3.1 Proprietary trading

Proprietary trading primarily means actively taking risky positions, i.e. designing a portfolio of financial products aiming for prosperous growth. The management sets the degree of risk appetite. Since always one counterpart is long and another one short, this will tend to work well on average in 50 % of all cases. Successful desks will continue, loss-generating desks will disappear, the causers often being promoted to higher positions.

5.3.2 Sales-driven trading

Another approach of trading is taking in the positions originating from sales activities and risk managing these. This approach is often preferred by smaller enterprises or by very risk averse institutions. Of course, one can mix sales-driven and proprietary trading.

5.3.3 Inter bank sales

As the name suggests, an inter bank sales desk trades with other banks. As one can imagine, the counterparts being experts in financial products will quote each other *very tight* bid-offer spreads. This market is very fast and is profitable mainly due to the mass of traded products.

5.3.4 Branch sales

Banks entertaining a branch network usually have sales desk responsible for the branch clients. The products are often standardized and profits are generated by the turnover on the one hand and the sales skills of the branch employees on the other. As branch clients are not always able to verify market prices of structured products, a noticeable sales margin can often be hidden. The strategy is to sell clients zero-cost structures that look attractive, but actually bear a certain amount of risk. Products with a known worst case are particularly popular.

5.3.5 Institutional sales

Institutional sales means selling big institutions such as funds or insurance companies or government sectors foreign exchange protection. It lies in the nature of these clients that they are inclined to trade only with very highly rated banks. For the government and the insurance sector, structured products are difficult to sell as there are often regulatory restrictions. Hedge funds, on the other hand, are keen on trading complex structures.

5.3.6 Corporate sales

Multi-national companies (MNCs) are often served from a bank's head office rather than a branch. They often need foreign exchange rate protection, whence they prefer trading spot, forward and vanilla options. Structured products trade sometimes depending on many factors, such as country, risk appetite, knowledge of the corporate treasurer, credit lines. Several corporates know the FX market very well and are able to buy the components of structured products and structure the desired position themselves. That way, they can save on the sales margin for the bank, as they buy only liquid ingredients that are quoted with tight bid-offer spreads.

5.3.7 Private banking

Serving a private client is often subject to numerous legal restrictions. Moreover, FX exposure is not very common for the private investor. For these reasons, private banking and FX Options have very little overlap.

The Danish *Saxo Bank* offers trading of OTC vanilla options in 24 currency pairs online and for retail clients. First generation exotics are planned for the end of 2006. Clients have to maintain a margin account.

5.3.8 Listed FX options

The private investor who wants to participate in FX markets and bet on certain events certainly has numerous opportunities to buy listed FX derivatives offered by many banks. Besides vanilla options, we find many exotic derivative securities, mostly barrier options, touch options, range notes, participation notes and power options. Since the investor pays and receives domestic currency, listed FX options are often quantoed.

5.3.9 Trading floor joke

We conclude this section with a story describing very accurately the difference between a trader and a sales representative.

A guy in a balloon had fallen asleep and when he woke up wanted to find out where he was. So he approached the earth and asked the nearest person on the ground that he found, "Excuse me, sir, do you know where I am?". The man on the ground replied, "Yes, you are 45° and 17 north, 14° and 03 west and 2.55 meters above ground zero." The man in the balloon was stunned and answered, "You must be an FX trader." – "Indeed, yes I am, but how do you know?" – "You appear very busy, you speak loud and fast, you tell me a lot of detailed but useless information, and I still don't know where I am." – "And you must be in FX sales, right?" – "I am, but now how did you know?" – "Very obvious: you fall asleep in the middle of the day, you have risen to your current position due to a lot of hot air, you don't know where you are, you don't understand what I am telling you, have no clue what's going and as the cherry on the cake, you make me feel like it's my fault."

Bibliography

[1] Shamah, S. (2003), *A Foreign Exchange Primer*. John Wiley & Sons, Ltd, Chichester.

[2] Shreve, S.E. (2004), *Stochastic Calculus for Finance I+II*. Springer.

[3] Hakala, J. and U. Wystup (2002), *Foreign Exchange Risk*. Risk Publications, London.

[4] Lipton, A. (2001), *Mathematical Methods for Foreign Exchange*. World Scientific, Singapore.

[5] Black, F. and M. Scholes (1973), The Pricing of Options and Corporate Liabilities. *J. Political Economy*, **81**, 637–659.

[6] Reiss, O. and U. Wystup (2001), Efficient Computation of Option Price Sensitivities Using Homogeneity and other Tricks. *The Journal of Derivatives*, **9(2)**, pp. 41–53.

[7] Bates, D. (1988), *Crashes, Options and International Asset Substitutability*. Ph. D. Dissertation, Economics Department, Princeton University.

[8] Bates, D. (1991), The Crash of '87 – Was It Expected? The Evidence from Options Markets. *The Journal of Finance*. **46(3)** July 1991, 1009–1044.

[9] Bowie, J. and P. Carr (1994), Static Simplicity. *Risk*, **(8)**.

[10] Carr, P. (1994), *European Put Call Symmetry*. Cornell University Working Paper.

[11] Borowski, B. (2005), *Hedgingverfahren für Foreign Exchange Barrieroptionen*. Diplom Thesis, Technical University of Munich.

[12] Frahm, G. and U. Jaekel (2005), Robust Covariance Matrix Estimation with Incomplete Data: The Spectral Density Approach. Working paper.

[13] Čížek, P., W. Härdle and R. Weron (2005), *Statistical Tools for Finance and Insurance*. Springer. Also available as ebook at http://www.quantlet.com/mdstat/scripts/stf/html/stfhtml.html.

[14] Spies G. (1995), *Währungsoptionen*. Gabler, Wiesbaden.

[15] Hakala, J. and U. Wystup (2001), Foreign Exchange Derivatives. *The Euromoney Foreign Exchange and Treasury Management Handbook 2001*. Adrian Hornbrook.

[16] Giese, A. (2002), *On the Pricing of Discrete Barrier Options in Models Beyond Black-Scholes*. TU Berlin.

[17] Maruhn, J.H. and E.W. Sachs (2005), *Robust Static Super-Replication of Barrier Options in the Black-Scholes Model*. To Appear in *Proceedings of the Conference on Robust Optimization-Directed Design (RODD), Shalimar, Florida*.

[18] Schmock, U., S.E. Shreve and U. Wystup (2002), Dealing with Dangerous Digitals. In *Foreign Exchange Risk*. Risk Publications. London.

[19] Shreve, S.E. (1996), *Stochastic Calculus and Finance*. Lecture notes, Carnegie Mellon University.

[20] Revuz, D. and M. Yor (1995), *Continuous Martingales and Brownian Motion*, Second Edition. Springer.

[21] Schilling, H. (2002), Compound Options. In *Foreign Exchange Risk*. Risk Publications. London.

[22] Griebsch, S., C. Kühn and U. Wystup (2006), *Instalment Options: Closed Form Solution, Implementation and the Limiting Case*. Research Report, HfB–Business School of Finance and Management, Center for Practical Quantitative Finance.

[23] Geske R. (1979), The Valuation of Compound Options. *Journal of Financial Economics*, **7**, 63–81.

[24] Curnow, R.N. and C.W. Dunnett (1962), The Numerical Evaluation of Certain Multivariate Normal Integrals. *Ann. Math. Statist*, **33**, 571–579.

[25] Thomassen, L. and M. van Wouve (2002), *A Sensitivity Analysis for the N-fold Compound Option*. Research Paper, Faculty of Applied Economics, University of Antwerpen.

[26] Ben-Hameur, H., M. Breton and P. François (2002), *Pricing Installment Options with an Application to ASX Installment Warrants*. Working Paper, HEC Montréal.

[27] Brown, B., J. Lovato and K. Russell (2004), CDFLIB – C++ – library, http://www.csit.fsu.edu/~burkardt/cpp_src/dcdflib/dcdflib.html

[28] El Karoui, N., J.P. Lepeltier and A. Millet (1992), A Probabilistic Approach of the Reduite. *Probability and Mathematical Statistics*, **13**, 97–121.

[29] Hansen, A.T. and P. Jorgensen (2000), Analytical Valuation of American-Style Asian Options. *Management Science*, August, Vol. 46, Issue 8.

[30] Henderson, V. and R. Wojakowski (2002), On the Equivalence of Floating and Fixed-Strike Asian Options. *Journal of Applied Probability*, **39**, 391–394.

[31] Kemna, A.G.Z. and A.C.F. Vorst (1990), A Pricing Method for Options Based on Average Asset Values. *Journal of Banking and Finance*, March 1990, Vol. 14, Issue 1, 113–129.

[32] Wystup, U. (2006), *Formula Catalogue*, taken from http://www.mathfinance.com

[33] Večeř, J. (2001), A new PDE Approach for Pricing Arithmetic Average Asian Options. *Journal of Computational Finance*, **4(4)**, 105–113.

[34] Lévy, E. (1992), Pricing European average rate currency options. *Journal of International Money and Finance*, October, Vol. 11, Issue 5, 474–491.

[35] Turnbull, S.M. and L.M. Wakeman (1991), A Quick Algorithm for Pricing European Average Options. *Journal of Financial and Quantitative Analysis*, September, **26(3)**, 377–389.

[36] Glasserman, P. (2004), *Monte Carlo Methods in Financial Engineering*. Springer.

[37] Clewlow, L. and C. Strickland (1998), *Implementing Derivatives Models*, John Wiley & Sons, Ltd, Chichester.

[38] Perilla, A. and D. Oancea (2003), *Pricing and Hedging Exotic Options with Monte Carlo Simulations*, Master Thesis, University of Lausanne.

[39] Tompkins, R.G. (1998), *Static versus Dynamic Hedging of Exotic Options: An Evaluation of Hedge Performance via Simulation*, Working Paper.

[40] Lévy, E. (1996), Exotic Options I, in Carol Alexander, ed., *The Handbook of Risk Management and Analysis*, John Wiley & Sons, Ltd, 83–109.

[41] Conze, A. and Viswanathan (1991), Path dependent Options: The Case of Lookback Options, *The Journal of Finance*, Vol. XLVI, No 5.

[42] Choi, S. and M. Jameson (2003), Lookback Option Valuation: A simplified Approach, *The Journal of Derivatives*, Winter 2003.

[43] Garman, M. (1989), Recollection in Tranquillity, re-edited version in *From Black Scholes to Black Holes*, 171–175. Originally in *Risk*, London.

[44] Heynen, R. and H. Kat (1994), Selective Memory: Reducing the Expense of Lookback Options by Limiting their Memory, re-edited version in *Over the Rainbow: Developments in Exotic Options and Complex Swaps*, *Risk*, London.

[45] Heynen, R. and H. Kat (1994), Crossing Barriers, *Risk*, **7(6)**, 46–51.

[46] Goldman, B.M., H.B. Soson and M.A. Gatto (1979), Path-Dependent Options: Buy at the low, sell at the high. *Journal of Finance* **34(5)**, 1111–1127.

[47] Haug, E.G. (1997), *Option Pricing Formulas.* McGraw Hill.

[48] Nahum, E. (1998), *The Pricing of Options Depending on a Discrete Maximum.* Working Paper, Department of Statistics, University of California, Berkeley.

[49] Broadie, M., P. Glasserman and S.G. Kou (1998), Connecting Discrete and Continuous Path-dependent Options. *Finance and Stochastics*, **2**.

[50] Taleb, N. (1997), *Dynamic Hedging: Managing Vanilla and Exotic Options*, John Wiley & Sons, Inc.

[51] Cunningham, J. and P. Karumanchi (2004), Hedging Strategies for Exotic Options, taken from `http://deepthought.ecn.purdue.edu/ie690d/projects/HED-R.pdf`, accessed 1 September 2004.

[52] Tompkins, R.G. (1999), Power Options: Hedging Nonlinear Risks. *The Journal of Risk*, **2(2)**, 31.

[53] Reed, N. (1994), Square Deal. *Risk*, **7(12)**, 6.

[54] Hart, I. and M. Ross (1994), Striking Continuity, *Risk*, **7(6)**, 51–56.

[55] Zhang, P.G. (1998), *Exotic Options,* Second edition. World Scientific, London.

[56] Carr, P. (2006), *Vanilla – One-Touch Duality.* Conference Paper presented at the Frankfurt MathFinance Workshop, `http://workshop.mathfinance.com`

[57] Poulsen, R. (2006), Barrier Options and Their Static Hedges: Simple Derivations and Extensions. *Quantitative Finance*, to appear.

[58] Frishling, V. (1997), Barrier Rife, *Risk*, **10(8)**, 23–24.

[59] Ravindran, A. (1993), Low-fat Spreads, *Risk*, October 1993.

[60] Hakala, J. and U. Wystup (2002), Making the Best out of Multiple Currency Exposure: Protection with Basket Options. *The Euromoney Foreign Exchange and Treasury Management Handbook 2002.* Adrian Hornbrook.

[61] Avellaneda, M., R. Buff, C. Friedman, N. Grandechamp, L. Kruk and J. Newman (2001), Weighted Monte Carlo: A new Technique for Calibrating Asset-Pricing Models. *International Journal of Theoretical and Applied Finance*, **4(1)**, 91–119.

[62] Stulz, R. (1982), Options on the Minimum or Maximum of Two Assets, *Journal of Financial Economics*, **10**, 161–185.

[63] Mahomed, O. (2004), *Pricing of Himalaya Options.* Honours Project, School of Computational and Applied Mathematics, University of Witwatersrand, Johannesburg, `http://www.cam.witz.ac.za/mfinance/projects/obeidmahommed.pdf`.

[64] Carr, P. and R. Lee (2004), *Robust Replication of Volatility Derivatives.* Presentation at the *Columbia Financial Engineering Seminar.*

[65] Bernard, C., O. Le Courtois and F. Quittard-Pinon (2005), A New Procedure for Pricing Parisian Options. *The Journal of Derivatives*, Summer 2005.

[66] Baker, G., R. Beneder and A. Zilber (2004), *FX Barriers with Smile Dynamics*. Working Paper.

[67] Boenkost, W. and W.M. Schmidt (2005), *Cross Currency Swap Valuation*. Research Report, HfB–Business School of Finance and Management, Center for Practical Quantitative Finance.

[68] Baum, S. (2005), *Power Reverse Dual Structures*. Master Thesis, HfB–Business School of Finance and Management.

[69] Lipton, A. and W. McGhee (2002), Universal Barriers. *Risk*, May 2002.

[70] Wystup, U. (2003), The Market Price of One-touch Options in Foreign Exchange Markets. *Derivatives Week* Vol. XII, No. 13, London.

[71] Sbuelz, A. (2005), Hedging Double Barriers with Singles. *International Journal of Theoretical and Applied Finance*, **8(3)**, 393–406.

[72] Giese, A.M. and J.H. Maruhn (2005), *Cost-Optimal Static Super-Replication of Barrier Options – An Optimization Approach*. Preprint, University of Trier.

[73] Becker, C. and U. Wystup (2005), *On The Cost of Delayed Fixing Announcements in FX Options Markets*. Research Report, HfB–Business School of Finance and Management, Center for Practical Quantitative Finance.

[74] Matsumoto, M. (2004), Homepage of Makoto Matsumoto on the server of the University of Hiroshima: http://www.math.sci.hiroshima-u.ac.jp/~m-mat/eindex.html

[75] Anagnou-Basioudis, I. and S. Hodges (2004), *Derivatives Hedging and Volatility Errors*. Warwick University Working Paper.

[76] Fusai G. and C. Recchioni (2003), *Numerical Valuation of Discrete Barrier Options* Warwick University Working Paper.

[77] Hörfelt, P. (2003), Extension of the corrected barrier approximation by Broadie, Glasserman, and Kou. *Finance and Stochastics*, **7**, 231–243.

[78] Krug, S. (2005), *Hedge Accounting under IAS 39: An Overview and Testing for Effectiveness using the Example of a Foreign Exchange Forward Plus*. Master Thesis at HfB – Business School of Finance and Management, Frankfurt am Main, Germany.

[79] Förschle, G., B. Holland and M. Kroner (2000), *Internationale Rechnungslegung: US-GAAP, HGB und IAS*, Fifth revised Edition. Economics-Verlag, Bonn.

[80] KPMG (Ed.) (2004), *Insights into IFRS, A practical guide to International Financial Reporting Standards*.

[81] Raschke, R. (2005), Rechnungslegung von Finanzinstrumenten nach International Accounting Standards, Revidierte Versionen von IAS 32 und IAS 39. In *Kahlert, H. and Seeger, N., (Hrsg.) Aktuelle Schwerpunkte der Konzernbilanzierung nach IAS/IFRS*, 153–282. Bankakademie-Verlag, Frankfurt am Main.

[82] Ernst & Young A.G. Wirtschaftsprüfungsgesellschaft (Ed). (2004), *Rechnungslegung von Financial Instruments nach IAS 39, Eine Darstellung der Bilanzierung auf der Basis von IAS 32 und IAS 39 (revised 2003)*, 3. überarbeitete Auflage.

[83] Achleitner, A. and G. Behr (2000), *International Accounting Standards, Ein Lehrbuch zur Internationalen Rechnungslegung*, Second completely revised Edition. Vahlen, München.

[84] Dombeck, M. (2002), Die Bilanzierung von strukturierten Produkten nach deutschem Recht und nach den Vorschriften des IASB. In *Die Wirtschaftsprüfung*, Jahrgang 55, Heft 20, 1065–1075.

[85] Baily, G. and K. Wild (2000), *International Accounting Standard, A Guide to Preparing Accounts*, Second Edition.

[86] Scharpf, P. (2004), Hedge Accounting nach IAS 39: Ermittlung und bilanzielle Behandlung der Hedge (In-) Effektivität. *Zeitschrift für Kapitalmarktorientierte Rechnungslegung*, Beilage 1/2004.

[87] PricewaterhouseCoopers. (2004), *Die Vorschriften zum Hedge Accounting nach IAS 39, Anforderungen und Umsetzung bei Kreditinstituten*.

[88] KPMG (Ed.) (2001), *Rechnungslegung von Finanzinstrumenten nach IAS 39, Die wichtigsten Bestimmungen*.

[89] Eckes, B., K. Barz, M. Bäthe-Guski and W. Weigel (2004), Die aktuellen Vorschriften zum Hedge Accounting. In *Die Bank* (2004, A), Heft 6–7, 416–420.

[90] Mishkin, F. (2001), *The Economics of Money, Banking and Financial Markets*, Sixth Edition. Addison-Wesley Publications, Reading, Mass.

[91] Tanski, J. (2002), *Internationale Rechnungslegungsstandards*, IAS/IFRS Schritt für Schritt. Beck Juristischer Verlag.

[92] Finnerty, J. and D. Grant (2003), Testing Hedge Effectiveness under SFAS 133. In *The CPA Journal*, Volume 73, Issue 4, 40–47.

[93] Hailer, A. and S. Rump (2003), Hedge-Effektivität: Lösung des Problems der kleinen Zahlen. In *Zeitschrift für das gesamte Kreditwesen*, Jahrgang 56, Heft 11, 599–603.

[94] Finnerty, J. and D. Grant (2002), Alternative Approaches to Testing Hedge Effectiveness under SFAS No. 133. In *Accounting Horizons*, Volume 16, Issue 2, 95–108.

[95] Kalotay, A. and L. Abreo (2001), Testing Hedge Effectiveness for SFAS 133: The Volatility Reduction Measure. In *Journal of Applied Corporate Finance*, Volume 13, Winter Issue, 93–99.

[96] Eckes, B., K. Barz, M. Bäthe-Guski and W. Weigel (2004), Die aktuellen Vorschriften zum Hedge Accounting II. In *Die Bank* (2004, B), Heft 8, 54–59.

[97] Kawaller, I. (2002), Hedge Effectiveness Testing using Regression Analysis. In *AFP Exchange*, September/October, 62–68.

[98] Baxter, M. and A. Rennie (1996), *Financial Calculus, an Introduction to Derivative Pricing*. Cambridge University Press.

[99] Ohayon, E. (2004), *Testing Hedge Effectiveness for Innovative Solutions*, Bank of America, Presentation of RISK EUROPE 2004.

[100] Hervas-Zurita, M. (2005), *Der interne Informationsprozess, Durchführung und Kontrolle von Devisengeschäften. Analyse des Devisenhandels einer deutschen Universalbank*. Dissertation, Universidad San Pablo-CEU, Madrid.

Index

Table 5.1   Common Replication Strategies and Structures

digital(ϕ, K)	$\lim_{n\to\infty} n[\text{vanilla}(K) - \text{vanilla}(K + \phi/n)]$
knock-in	vanilla $-$ knock-out
EKO(ϕ, K, B)	vanilla(ϕ, K) $-$ vanilla(ϕ, B) $-$ digital(ϕ, B)ϕ($B - K$)
EDKOCall(K, L, H)	call(L) $-$ call(H) $+ (L - K)$digital(L) $- (H - K)$digital(H)
$\quad$($K < L < H$)	
vanilla(K)	digital$_{for}$ $- K \cdot$ digital$_{dom}$
RKO(ϕ, K, B)	KO($-\phi$, K, B) $-$ KO($-\phi$, B, B) $+ \phi(B - K)$NT(B)
(D)OT	e^{-rT} $-$ (D)NT
DOT$_{for}$(L, H, S_0, r_d, r_f, σ)	S_0DOT$_{dom}$($\frac{1}{H}$, $\frac{1}{L}$, $\frac{1}{S_0}$, r_f, r_d, σ)
DNT$_{dom}$(L, H)	[DKOCall($K = L$, L, H) $+$ DKOPut($K = H$, L, H)]/[$H - L$]
DNT$_{for}$(L, H)	[$H \cdot$ DKOCall($K = L$, L, H) $+ L \cdot$ DKOPut($K = H$, L, H)]/
	$\quad$[($H - L$)S_0]
EDNT(L, H)	digital(L) $-$ digital(H)
two-touch(L, H)	OT(L) $+$ OT(H) $-$ DOT(L, H)
second DNT($A < B < C < D$)	DNT(A, C) $+$ DNT(B, D) $-$ DNT(B, C)
KIKO($L = ko$, $H = ki$)	KO(L) $-$ DKO(L, H)
forward(K)	call(K) $-$ put(K)
paylater premium	vanilla/digital
spread(ϕ)	vanilla(K, ϕ) $-$ vanilla($K + \phi \cdot$ spread, ϕ)
risk reversal	call(K_+) $-$ put(K_-)
straddle(K)	call(K) $+$ put(K)
strangle	call(K_+) $+$ put(K_-)
butterfly	call(K_+) $+$ put(K_-) $-$ call$_{ATM}$ $-$ put$_{ATM}$
shark forward	forward $+$ RKO
bonus forward	forward $+$ DNT
butterfly forward	forward $+$ DKO straddle
accrued forward	forward $+$ corridor
participating forward	call $- P\%$put
fade-in forward	forward $+$ fade-in vanilla
dcd($r >$ market)	deposit($r =$ market) $-$ vanilla
range deposit($r >$ market)	deposit($r <$ market) $+$ DNT
performance note($r_{max} >$	deposit($r <$ market) $+$ call
$\quad$market)	

Printed and bound by CPI Group (UK) Ltd, Croydon, CR0 4YY